# A·N·N·U·A·L E·D·I·T·I·O·N·S

# Human Development 00/01

*Twenty-Eighth Edition*

W9-CHK-856

## EDITOR

## Karen L. Freiberg
*University of Maryland, Baltimore County*

Dr. Karen Freiberg has an interdisciplinary educational and employment background in nursing, education, and developmental psychology. She received her B.S. from the State University of New York at Plattsburgh, her M.S. from Cornell University, and her Ph.D. from Syracuse University. Freiberg has worked as a school nurse, a pediatric nurse, a public health nurse for the Navajo Indians, an associate project director for a child development clinic, a researcher in several areas of child development, and a university professor. She is the author of an award-winning textbook, *Human Development: A Life-Span Approach,* which is now in its fourth edition. Dr. Freiberg is currently on the faculty at the University of Maryland, Baltimore County.

*Dushkin/McGraw-Hill*
Sluice Dock, Guilford, Connecticut 06437

**Visit us on the Internet**
*http://www.dushkin.com/annualeditions/*

# Credits

**1. Genetic and Prenatal Influences on Development**
Unit photo—courtesy of World Health Organization.
**2. Development during Infancy and Early Childhood**
Unit photo—© 1999 by Cleo Freelance Photography.
**3. Development during Childhood: Cognition and Schooling**
Unit photo—© 1999 by Cleo Freelance Photography.
**4. Development during Childhood: Family and Culture**
Unit photo—courtesy of Louis P. Raucci.
**5. Development during Adolescence and Young Adulthood**
Unit photo—© 1999 by Cleo Freelance Photography.
**6. Development during Middle and Late Adulthood**
Unit photo—© 1999 by Cleo Freelance Photography.

# Copyright

Cataloging in Publication Data
Main entry under title: Annual Editions: Human Development. 2000/2001.
   1. Child study—Periodicals. 2. Socialization—Periodicals. 3. Old age—
Periodicals. I. Freiberg, Karen L., *comp.* II. Title: Human development.
ISBN 0-07-236416-5      155'.05      72-91973      HQ768.A44      ISSN 0278-4661

Twenty-Eighth Edition

Cover image © 2000 PhotoDisc, Inc.

Printed in the United States of America      1234567890BAHBAH543210      Printed on Recycled Paper

# To the Reader

In publishing ANNUAL EDITIONS we recognize the enormous role played by the magazines, newspapers, and journals of the public press in providing current, first-rate educational information in a broad spectrum of interest areas. Many of these articles are appropriate for students, researchers, and professionals seeking accurate, current material to help bridge the gap between principles and theories and the real world. These articles, however, become more useful for study when those of lasting value are carefully collected, organized, indexed, and reproduced in a low-cost format, which provides easy and permanent access when the material is needed. That is the role played by ANNUAL EDITIONS.

New to ANNUAL EDITIONS is the inclusion of related World Wide Web sites. These sites have been selected by our editorial staff to represent some of the best resources found on the World Wide Web today. Through our carefully developed topic guide, we have linked these Web resources to the articles covered in this ANNUAL EDITIONS reader. We think that you will find this volume useful, and we hope that you will take a moment to visit us on the Web at *http://www.dushkin.com* to tell us what you think.

It is difficult to reflect on the last decade of the twentieth century without sensing the tension. Regional wars. A special prosecutor looking into misdeeds of the U.S. president. Senate ethics jokes. Violence: school shootings, road rage, sports, videos, games, movies, television, the news. Why do some people resist behaving badly while others act out? The world's economies: why do some cultures prosper while others go bankrupt? What agencies lead human development, for better or worse? Selecting a few representative articles of good quality is difficult due to the magnitude of the subject. I am grateful to all the members of my advisory board for helping me cull through the collection and select some of the best articles available for 2000/2001 to shed light on the above questions and many others.

*Annual Editions: Human Development 00/01* is organized according to the absolute time concept of chronos, chronological time, from conception to death. However, the reader should be aware of other relative time concepts: kairos (God's time); preterition (retrospective time) and futurity (prospective time); transientness (short duration) and diuturnity (long duration); and recurrent time. Human development is more akin to a continuous circle of life than to a line with a distinct beginning and end. Like stars whose light reaches us thousands of years after they expire, our ancestors influence our behaviors long after their deaths. Our hopes for our own futures and for our children's futures also predestine our development. With an eye to the circle of life, articles have been selected that bridge the gap left by clocked time and indiscrete ages and stages. Thus, prenatal articles may discuss adult development and late adulthood articles may focus on children.

As you explore this anthology, you will discover that many articles ask questions that have no answers. As a student, I felt frustrated by such writing. I wanted answers, right answers, right away. Part of the lessons in tolerance that are necessary to achieve maturity are lessons in accepting relativity and in acknowledging extenuating circumstances. Life frequently has no right or wrong answers, but rather various alternatives with multiple consequences. Instead of right versus wrong, a more helpful consideration is "What will bring about the greater good for the greater number?" Controversies promote healthy discussion. Different viewpoints should be weighed against societal standards. Different cultural communities should be celebrated for what they offer in creativity and adaptability to changing circumstances. Many selections in this anthology reflect the cultural diversity and the cultural assimilations with which we live today.

The selections for *Annual Editions: Human Development 00/01* have attempted to reflect an ecological view of growth and change. Some articles deal with microsystems such as family, school, and employment. Some deal with exosystems such as television and community. Some writers discuss macrosystems, such as economics and government. Most of the articles deal with mesosystems, those that link systems such as economics, health and nutrition, schools and culture, or heredity and environment. The unique individual's contribution to every system and every system linkage is always paramount.

We hope you will be energized and enriched by the readings in this compendium. Please complete and return the postage-paid article rating form on the last page to express your opinions. We value your input and will heed it in future revisions of *Annual Editions: Human Development.*

*Karen Freiberg*

Karen Freiberg, Ph.D.
*Editor*

# Contents

## A. GENETIC INFLUENCES

## B. PRENATAL INFLUENCES

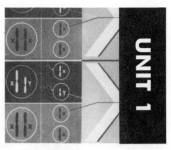

**UNIT 1**

# Genetic and Prenatal Influences on Development

Seven selections discuss genetic influences on development, cloning, and the role of lifestyle, including the effects of substance abuse, on prenatal development.

UNIT 2

# Development during Infancy and Early Childhood

Six selections profile the impressive
abilities of infants and young children,
examine the ways in which children
learn, and discuss the development
of empathy in early childhood.

The concepts in bold italics are developed in the article. For further expansion please refer to the Topic Guide and the Index.

Overview **82**

A. *COGNITION*

B. *SCHOOLING*

UNIT 3

# Development during Childhood: Cognition and Schooling

Seven selections examine human development during childhood, paying specific attention to social and emotional development, cognitive and language development, and development problems.

## Overview    122

### A. FAMILY

**UNIT 4**

# Development during Childhood: Family and Culture

Six selections discuss the impact of home and culture on child rearing and child development. The topics include parenting styles, family structure, and cultural influences.

The concepts in bold italics are developed in the article. For further expansion please refer to the Topic Guide and the Index.

**UNIT 5**

# Development during Adolescence and Young Adulthood

Seven selections explore a wide range of issues and topics concerning adolescence and early adulthood.

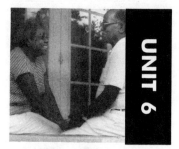

**UNIT 6**

# Development during Middle and Late Adulthood

Eight selections review a variety of biological and psychological aspects of aging, questioning the concept of set life stages.

The concepts in bold italics are developed in the article. For further expansion please refer to the Topic Guide and the Index.

The concepts in bold italics are developed in the article. For further expansion please refer to the Topic Guide and the Index.

This topic guide suggests how the selections and World Wide Web sites found in the next section of this book relate to topics of traditional concern to human development students and professionals. It is useful for locating interrelated articles and Web sites for reading and research. The guide is arranged alphabetically according to topic.

The relevant Web sites, which are numbered and annotated on pages 4 and 5, are easily identified by the Web icon ( ◎ ) under the topic articles. By linking the articles and the Web sites by topic, this ANNUAL EDITIONS reader becomes a powerful learning and research tool.

| TOPIC AREA | TREATED IN | TOPIC AREA | TREATED IN |
|---|---|---|---|
| **Adolescence** | 27. Growing Up Goes On and On<br>28. Why the Young Kill<br>29. Secret Life of Teens<br>◎ *3, 11, 26, 27, 28, 29* | **Drug Abuse** | 3. Role of Lifestyle<br>5. Fetal Psychology<br>6. Drug-Exposed Infants<br>7. Sperm under Siege<br>21. Father Love<br>29. Secret Life of Teens<br>35. Age of Anxiety<br>◎ *3, 26, 27, 28* |
| **Aggression/<br>Violence** | 21. Father Love<br>24. Effects of Poverty<br>25. Effects of Maltreatment<br>28. Why the Young Kill<br>29. Secret Life of Teens<br>35. Age of Anxiety<br>◎ *2, 10, 21, 23, 28* | **Early Childhood** | 11. Language Explosion<br>12. Defining the Trait<br>13. Highlights of the Quality 2000 Initiative<br>◎ *12, 13, 14* |
| **Cognition** | 5. Fetal Psychology<br>6. Drug-Exposed Infants<br>9. Baby Talk<br>10. Cultural Context of Infant Caregiving<br>13. Highlights of the Quality 2000 Initiative<br>14. Genetics of Cognitive Abilities<br>15. Basing Teaching on Piaget's Constructivism<br>16. First Seven . . . and the Eighth<br>19. In Search of . . . Brain-Based Education<br>21. Father Love<br>24. Effects of Poverty<br>25. Effects of Maltreatment<br>34. Memory<br>◎ *2, 6, 9, 15, 16, 17, 18, 24, 25* | **Education/<br>School** | 12. Defining the Trait<br>15. Basic Teaching on Piaget's Contructivism<br>16. First Seven . . . and the Eighth<br>17. Bell, Book, and Scandal<br>18. Death of Child Nature<br>19. In Search of . . . Brain-Based Education<br>20. Caution–Praise Can Be Dangerous<br>23. Kids Who Don't Fit In<br>24. Effects of Poverty<br>39. Age Boom<br>◎ *9, 15, 16, 17, 18, 19, 20* |
| **Creativity** | 13. Highlights of the Quality 2000 Initiative<br>16. First Seven . . . and the Eighth<br>18. Death of Child Nature<br>33. Nature and Uses of Dreaming<br>◎ *12, 14, 17, 19, 20, 24* | **Emotions/<br>Personality** | 5. Fetal Psychology<br>6. Drug-Exposed Infants<br>8. Temperament and the Reactions to Unfamiliarity<br>10. Cultural Context of Infant Caregiving<br>12. Defining the Trait<br>13. Highlights of the Quality 2000 Initiative<br>21. Father Love<br>22. Parent Trap<br>23. Kids Who Don't Fit In<br>24. Effects of Poverty<br>25. Effects of Maltreatment<br>27. Growing Up Goes On and On<br>28. Why the Young Kill<br>32. Science of a Good Marriage<br>33. Nature and Uses of Dreaming<br>40. Emotion in the Second Half of Life<br>◎ *2, 4, 5, 8, 9, 10, 15, 16, 18, 20, 21, 23, 27, 28, 30, 32* |
| **Culture** | 10. Cultural Context of Infant Caregiving<br>11. Language Explosion<br>17. Bell, Book, and Scandal<br>18. Death of Child Nature<br>21. Father Love<br>24. Effects of Poverty<br>25. Effects of Maltreatment<br>26. Tomorrow's Child<br>39. Age Boom<br>◎ *2, 4, 12, 14, 16, 17, 19, 20, 24* | | |
| **Depression** | 21. Father Love<br>25. Effects of Maltreatment<br>27. Growing Up Goes On and On<br>35. Age of Anxiety<br>36. Understanding Perimenopause<br>◎ *3, 21, 23, 24, 25* | **Ethics/Morality** | 1. Designer Babies<br>28. Why the Young Kill<br>29. Secret Life of Teens<br>◎ *1, 6, 27, 28, 29* |
| **Divorce** | 30. Brain Sex<br>32. Science of a Good Marriage<br>◎ *24, 25* | **Family/<br>Parenting** | 10. Cultural Context of Infant Caregiving<br>12. Defining the Trait<br>21. Father Love<br>22. Parent Trap<br>23. Kids Who Don't Fit In<br>26. Tomorrow's Child |

# ● AE: Human Development

The following World Wide Web sites have been carefully researched and selected to support the articles found in this reader. If you are interested in learning more about specific topics found in this book, these Web sites are a good place to start. The sites are cross-referenced by number and appear in the topic guide on the previous two pages. Also, you can link to these Web sites through our DUSHKIN ONLINE support site at *http://www.dushkin.com/online/.*

**The following sites were available at the time of publication. Visit our Web site—we update DUSHKIN ONLINE regularly to reflect any changes.**

## General Human Development Issues

### 1. Association for Moral Education
*http://www.wittenberg.edu/ame/index.html*
This association is dedicated to fostering communication, co-operation, training, curriculum development, and research that links moral theory to educational practices.

### 2. Behavior Analysis Resources
*http://www.coedu.usf.edu/behavior/bares.htm*
Dedicated to promoting the experimental, theoretical, and applied analysis of behavior, this site encompasses contemporary scientific and social issues, theoretical advances, and the dissemination of professional and public information.

### 3. Healthfinder
*http://www.healthfinder.org/default.htm*
Healthfinder is a consumer health site that contains the latest health news, prevention and care choices, and information about every phase of human development.

### 4. Social Influence
*http://www.influenceatwork.com/intro.html*
Persuasion, compliance, and propaganda are the main focus of this site. It includes practical examples and applications.

## Genetic and Prenatal Influences on Development

### 5. American Academy of Pediatrics (AAP)
*http://www.aap.org*
AAP provides data for optimal physical, mental, and social health for all children. The site links to professional educational sources and current research.

### 6. Basic Neural Processes
*http://psych.hanover.edu/Krantz/neurotut.html*
An extensive tutorial on brain structures is provided here.

### 7. Evolutionary Psychology: A Primer
*http://www.psych.ucsb.edu/research/cep/*
A link to an evolutionary psychology primer is available on this site. Extensive background information is included.

### 8. Human Genetics and Human Genome Project
*http://www.kumc.edu/gec/*
The University of Kansas Medical Center provides information on human genetics and the human genome project at this site. Included are a number of links to research areas.

### 9. Serendip
*http://serendip.brynmawr.edu/serendip/*
Organized into five subject areas (brain and behavior, complex systems, genes and behavior, science and culture, and science education), this site contains interactive exhibits, articles, links to other resources, and a forum.

## Development during Infancy and Early Childhood

### 10. Aggression and Cooperation: Helping Young Children Develop Constructive Strategies
*http://ericps.crc.uiuc.edu/eece/pubs/digests/1992/jewett92.html*
This ERIC Digest report is on helping children deal effectively with aggression. Developing prosocial attitudes and behaviors is its goal.

### 11. Children's Nutrition Research Center (CNRC)
*http://www.bcm.tmc.edu/cnrc/*
CNRC is dedicated to defining the nutrient needs of healthy children, from conception through adolescence, and of pregnant and nursing mothers.

### 12. Early Childhood Care and Development
*http://www.ecdgroup.com*
Child development theory, programming and parenting data, and research can be found on this site of the Consultative Group. It is dedicated to the improvement of conditions of young children at risk.

### 13. Society of Pediatric Psychology (SPP)
*http://macserv.psy.miami.edu/SPP/*
The home page for SPP provides a forum for scientists and professionals who are interested in the health care of children, adolescents, and their families, with links to publications and other sites.

### 14. Zero to Three: National Center for Infants, Toddlers, and Families
*http://www.zerotothree.org*
Zero to Three is dedicated solely to infants, toddlers, and their families. Organized by recognized experts in the field, it provides technical assistance to communities, states, and the federal government.

## Development during Childhood: Cognition and Schooling

### 15. Children Now
*http://www.childrennow.org*
Children Now focuses on improving conditions for children who are poor or at risk. Articles include information on education, the influence of media, health, and security.

### 16. Council for Exceptional Children
*http://www.cec.sped.org*
This is the home page of the Council for Exceptional Children, which is dedicated to improving education for exceptional children and the gifted child.

### 17. Educational Resources Information Center (ERIC)
*http://www.ed.gov/pubs/pubdb.html*
Sponsored by the U.S. Department of Education, this site will lead to numerous documents related to elementary and early childhood education.

### 18. Federation of Behavioral, Psychological, and Cognitive Science
*http://www.am.org/federation/*

The Federation's mission is fulfilled through legislative and regulatory advocacy, education, and information dissemination to the scientific community. Hotlink to the National Institutes of Health's Project on the Decade of the Brain.

### 19. The National Association for the Education of Young Children (NAEYC)
*http://www.naeyc.org*
The NAEYC is the nation's largest organization of early childhood professionals. It is devoted to improving the quality of early childhood education programs for children from birth through the age of eight.

### 20. Project Zero
*http://pzweb.harvard.edu*
Following 30 years of research on the development of learning processes in children and adults, Project Zero is now helping to create communities of reflective, independent learners; to enhance deep understanding within disciplines; and to promote critical and creative thinking.

## Development during Childhood: Family and Culture

### 21. Childhood Injury Prevention Interventions
*http://depts.washington.edu/hiprc/*
Systematic reviews of childhood injury prevention interventions on such diverse subjects as adolescent suicide, child abuse, accidental injuries, and youth violence are offered on this site.

### 22. Families and Work Institute
*http://www.familiesandworkinst.org*
The Families and Work Institute conducts policy research on issues related to the changing workforce, and it operates a national clearinghouse on work and family life.

### 23. National Committee to Prevent Child Abuse (NCPCA)
*http://www.childabuse.org*
Dedicated to the NCPCA's child abuse prevention efforts, this site provides statistics, parenting tips, chapter data, and other resources.

### 24. The National Parent Information Network (NPIN)
*http://ericps.crc.uiuc.edu/npin/*
NPIN's site contains resources related to many of the controversial issues faced by parents raising children in contemporary society. Discussion groups are also available.

### 25. Parentsplace.com: Single Parenting
*http://www.parentsplace.com/family/singleparent/*
This resource focuses on issues concerning single parents and their children. The articles range from parenting children from infancy through adolescence.

## Development during Adolescence and Young Adulthood

### 26. AMA—Adolescent Health On Line
*http://www.ama-assn.org/adolhlth/adolhlth.htm*
This AMA adolescent health initiative describes clinical preventive services that primary care physicians and other health professionals can provide to young people.

### 27. American Academy of Child and Adolescent Psychiatry
*http://www.aacap.org/web/aacap/*

Up-to-date data on a host of topics that include facts for families, public health, and clinical practice may be found here.

### 28. Ask NOAH About: Mental Health
*http://www.noah.cuny.edu/illness/mentalhealth/mental.html*
NOAH's Web site contains information about child and adolescent family problems, mental conditions and disorders, suicide prevention, and much more.

### 29. Biological Changes in Adolescence
*http://www.personal.psu.edu/faculty/n/x/nxd10/biologic2.htm*
This site offers a discussion of puberty, sexuality, biological changes, cross-cultural differences, and nutrition for adolescents, including a look at obesity.

## Development during Middle and Late Adulthood

### 30. The Alzheimer Page
*http://www.biostat.wustl.edu/ALZHEIMER/*
Links to a wide range of sites devoted to Alzheimer's disease and dementia can be found here.

### 31. American Psychological Association's Division 20, Adult Development and Aging
*http://www.iog.wayne.edu/APADIV20/lowdiv20.htm*
Dedicated to studying the psychology of adult development and aging, this division provides links to research guides, laboratories, instructional resources, and other related areas.

### 32. Gero Web
*http://www.iog.wayne.edu/GeroWebd/GeroWeb.html*
This virtual library on aging contains information on gerontology, geriatrics, and the process of aging.

### 33. Grief Net
*http://rivendell.org*
Produced by a nonprofit group, Rivendell Resources, this site provides many links to the Web on the bereavement process, resources for grievers, and support groups.

### 34. Huffington Center on Aging
*http://www.hcoa.org*
The Huffington Center on Aging home page offers links to sites on aging and Alzheimer's disease.

### 35. National Aging Information Center (NAIC)
*http://www.aoa.dhhs.gov/naic/*
This service by the Administration on Aging is a central source of data on demographic, health, economic, and social status of older Americans.

### 36. Rose.Net "For Seniors Only"
*http://www.rose.net/seniors.htm*
Several sites are listed here that could be of interest to members of the senior community.

**We highly recommend that you review our Web site for expanded information and our other product lines. We are continually updating and adding links to our Web site in order to offer you the most usable and useful information that will support and expand the value of your Annual Editions. You can reach us at:**
**http://www.dushkin.com/annualeditions/.**

www.dushkin.com/online/

# Unit 1

## Key Points to Consider

❖ Will a complete genetic blueprint of humans allow molecular biologists to alter germ cells (eggs, sperm)? Should this type of gene therapy be ethically acceptable in the twenty-first century? Defend your answer.

❖ Do studies of identical twins give answers to the age-old nature-nurture questions? What strategies can reduce the numbers of babies born with low birth weight and at risk of developmental disabilities?

❖ How will technology change the course of pregnancy in the future? Will state-of-the-art gestation include medical care of the fetus? Explain.

❖ What kind of prenatal nurture produces the most psychologically healthy fetuses?

❖ What is the status of drug abuse prevention and treatment programs for pregnant women?

❖ How do sperm contribute to prenatal development?

 **Links**

### www.dushkin.com/online/

5. **American Academy of Pediatrics (AAP)**
   *http://www.aap.org*
6. **Basic Neural Processes**
   *http://psych.hanover.edu/Krantz/neurotut.html*
7. **Evolutionary Psychology: A Primer**
   *http://www.psych.ucsb.edu/research/cep/*
8. **Human Genetics and Human Genome Project**
   *http://www.kumc.edu/gec/*
9. **Serendip**
   *http://serendip.brynmawr.edu/serendip/*

These sites are annotated on pages 4 and 5.

September 1998, a controversial book, *The Nurture Assumption* (Judith Rich Harris, Free Press), was published. Readers were told that genes shape human development much more than other humans do. Personality, temperament, character, intelligence: these are the products of genes. Are they? For years people have assumed that parenting, education, nutrition, health care, peers, culture, and other nurturing human variables were more important than genes. Are they? The question may be hypothetical, but that does not mean it is not a heated topic for debate. Research in behavioral genetics, the field that studies the extent to which heredity shapes personality, has excited scientists with documentation of DNA programming for some human conduct. However, the unfolding of genetic potential still depends on prenatal nurture, and on all of the learning that takes place in the years of a person's life. Both nature and nurture are important. How they interact is yet to be resolved.

The human genome (23 pairs of chromosomes with their associated genes) is being mapped. As the arrangement of gene sites on chromosomes is uncovered, so too are are genetic markers (DNA sequences associated with particular traits). This is of vast significance to students of human development. No longer are genes just thought of as important because some carry certain physical traits. Genes can be compared to an incredibly complicated computer program. They dictate every aspect of human development, including personality.

Human embryology (the study of the first through seventh weeks after conception) and human fetology (the study of the eighth week of pregnancy through birth) have given verification to the idea that behavior precedes birth. The developing embryo/fetus reacts to the internal and external environments provided by the mother and to substances that diffuse through the placental barrier from the mother's body. The embryo reacts to toxins (viruses, antigens) that pass through the umbilical cord. The fetus reacts to an enormous number of other stimuli, such as the sounds from the mother's body (digestive rumblings, heartbeat) and the mother's movements, moods, and medicines. How the embryo/fetus reacts (e.g., weakly to strongly, positively to negatively) depends, in large part, on his or her genetic preprogramming. Genes and environment are so inextricably intertwined that the effect of each cannot be studied separately. Prenatal development always has strong genetic influences and vice versa.

The National Human Genome Research Institute (NHGRI) hopes to have the sequence of human genes mapped by 2005. Working in collaboration with geneticists worldwide, the U.S. team is snipping and cloning and mapping strands of DNA. Computers are now interpreting these findings through bioinformatics. Knowledge of the human genome will provide a giant leap forward in human development.

The first article included in the genetic section of this unit predicts a future in which parents will use the results of the Human Genome Project to design their own child, in a petri dish, before implantation into the mother's uterus. A fertilized egg will then be scanned for genes carrying familial diseases (for example, breast cancer, prostate cancer). Made-to-order genes will be injected with instructions for the unwanted disease cells to self-destruct. Not only can the future child be disease-free, but the genes that the person will pass on to his or her children will prevent descendants from having the diseases. Today, an overwhelming majority of scientists polled about this type of gene therapy oppose it. But the opposition may be paper-thin, especially if molecular biologists find ways to circumvent the ethical questions raised by this germline (eggs and sperm) procedure.

The second article contemplates the phenomenon of twinning. Are identical twins nature's handmade clones? What behaviors, if any, of monozygotic twins are predetermined by their identical genes? Research studies are reviewed that both support and refute the twin evidence of biological behavior propensities. The role of environmental limitations to biological propensities is also judiciously considered. The play of nature-nurture in twins is telling. It has implications for future developments in cloning. The exercise of reading the twin research data will stimulate many new questions.

The study of teratology (malformations of the embryo/fetus) and the study of normal prenatal development have historically focused on environmental factors. Until recently, genetic influences on how the embryo/fetus would react to teratogens or nutrients was ignored. Today we know that the same environmental factors may influence uniquely developing fetuses in different ways due to their genes. Keeping individual differences in mind, certain teratogens are dangerous to all fetuses and certain nutrients are necessary for all fetuses.

The first article in the prenatal-influence section of this unit explores the role of the mother's lifestyle in protecting her baby from, or subjecting her baby to, an at-risk birth status. At-risk infants are born with low birth weights and immature organ systems that put them in danger of dying or of experiencing delayed or disabled development. The article's authors discuss not only lifestyle choices but also demographic and stress risks, assessment of risk factors, barriers to change, and directions for prevention and intervention. It is an important paper that highlights the need for healthy mothers in order to have healthy babies.

The second article in this section discusses high-technology prenatal tests that can detect abnormal development during pregnancy. Skilled doctors may soon be able to treat many problems of fetuses in the uterus to change the birth outcome, and, potentially, alter the health of the future human being.

The third article reviews research on fetal psychological development. Human behaviors such as intelligence and personality may be profoundedly influenced by the environment of the mother's uterus. Nurture is important both before and after birth.

The fourth selection is an update on how pregnant women are being educated on the dangers that prenatal ingestion of drugs pose to unborn fetuses and on how known substance-abusing pregnant women are being treated. While some programs show some effectiveness, there is a continuing need for more rigorous evaluation and treatment.

The fifth article in the prenatal section has been retained once again, despite its age, because of rave reviews from readers. The contributions of fathers to prenatal growth and change have long been overlooked. This article discusses how important it is for prospective fathers to practice health maintenance and to protect themselves from toxins (chemicals, alcohol, tobacco, drugs) for their sperm's sake. It is an eye-opening article for both males and females.

# Designer Babies

**Scientists say that, with gene therapy, they may soon be able to cure a child's inherited disease before he is even born. But should they be allowed to create kids with made-to-order traits?** BY SHARON BEGLEY

IT IS ONLY A MATTER OF TIME. ONE day—a day probably no more distant than the first wedding anniversary of a couple who are now teenage sweethearts—a man and a woman will walk into an in vitro fertilization clinic and make scientific history. Their problem won't be infertility, the reason couples now choose IVF. Rather, they will be desperate for a very special child, a child who will elude a family curse. To create their dream child, doctors will fertilize a few of the woman's eggs with her husband's sperm, as IVF clinics do today. But then they will inject an artificial human chromosome, carrying made-to-order genes like pearls on a string, into the fertilized egg. One of the genes will carry instructions ordering cells to commit suicide (graphic). Then the doctors will place the embryo into the woman's uterus. If her baby is a boy, when he becomes an old man he, like his father and grandfather before him, will develop prostate cancer. But the cell-suicide gene will make his prostate cells self-destruct. The man, unlike his ancestors, will not die of the cancer. And since the gene that the doctors gave him copied itself into every cell of his body, including his sperm, his sons will beat prostate cancer, too.

Genetic engineers are preparing to cross what has long been an ethical Rubicon. Since 1990, gene therapy has meant slipping a healthy gene into the cells of one organ of a patient suffering from a genetic disease. Soon, it may mean something much more momentous: altering a fertilized egg so that genes in all of a person's cells, including eggs or sperm, also carry a gene that scientists, not

parents, bequeathed them. When the pioneers of gene therapy first requested government approval for their experiments in 1987, they vowed they would *never* alter patients' eggs or sperm. That was then. This is now. One of those pioneers, Dr. W. French Anderson of the University of Southern California, recently put the National Institutes of Health on notice. Within two or three years, he said, he would ask approval to use gene therapy on a fetus that has been diagnosed with a deadly inherited disease. The therapy would cure the fetus before it is born. But the introduced genes, though targeted at only blood or immune-system cells, might inadvertently slip into the child's egg (or sperm) cells, too. If that happens, the genetic change would affect that child's children unto the nth generation. "Life would enter a new phase," says biophysicist Gregory Stock of UCLA, "one in which we seize control of our own evolution."

Judging by the 70 pages of public comments NIH has received since Anderson submitted his proposal in September, the overwhelming majority of scientists and ethicists weighing in oppose gene therapy that changes the "germline" (eggs and sperm). But the opposition could be a boulevard wide and paper thin. "There is a great divide in the bioethics community over whether we should be opening up this Pandora's box," says science-policy scholar Sheldon Krimsky of Tufts University. Many bioethicists are sympathetic to using germline therapy to shield a child from a family disposition to cancer, or atherosclerosis or other illnesses with a strong genetic component. As James Watson, president of the Cold Spring Harbor Laboratory and codiscoverer of the double-helical structure of DNA, said at a recent UCLA conference, "We might as well do what we finally can to take the threat of Alzheimer's or breast cancer away from a family." But something else is suddenly making it OK to discuss the once forbidden possibility of germline engineering: molecular biologists now think they have clever ways to circumvent ethical concerns that engulf this sci-fi idea.

There may be ways, for instance, to design a baby's genes without violating the principle of informed consent. This is the belief that no one's genes—not even an embryo's—should be altered without his or her permission. Presumably few people would object to being spared a fatal disease. But what about genes for personality

## Pruning the Family Tree

Recent experiments suggest genetic engineering of human embryos could one day provide an early cure for inherited diseases.

An egg is fertilized. One gene that kills prostate cells, and one that triggers this gene, are added.

The engineered egg divides several times. This pre-embryo is implanted in the woman's uterus.

A baby boy is born. Several decades later, he is diagnosed with early prostate cancer.

An injection activates the cell-killing gene. All the prostate cells die; the man does not.

SOURCE: JOHN CAMPBELL, UCLA. DIAGRAM BY CHRISTOPH BLUMRICH — NEWSWEEK

traits, like risk-taking or being neurotic? If you like today's blame game—it's *Mom's fault* that you inherited her temper—you'll love tomorrow's: she intentionally stuck you with that personality quirk. But the child of tomorrow might have the final word about his genes, says UCLA geneticist John Campbell. The designer gene for, say, patience could be paired with an on-off switch, he says. The child would have to take a drug to activate the patience gene. Free to accept or reject the drug, he retains informed consent over his genetic endowment.

There may also be ways to make an end run around the worry that it is wrong to monkey with human evolution. Researchers are experimenting with tricks to make the introduced gene self-destruct in cells that become eggs or sperm. That would confine the tinkering to one generation. Then, if it became clear that eliminating genes for, say, mental illness also erased genes for creativity, that loss would not become a permanent part of man's genetic blueprint. (Of course, preventing the new gene's transmission to future generations would also defeat the hope of permanently lopping off a diseased branch from a family tree.) In experiments with animals, geneticist Mario Capecchi of the University of Utah has designed a string of genes flanked by the molecular version of scissors. The scissors are activated by an enzyme that would be made only in the cells

that become eggs or sperm. Once activated, the genetic scissors snip out the introduced gene and, presto, it is not passed along to future generations. "What I worry about," says Capecchi, "is that if we start messing around with [eggs and sperm], at some point—since this is a human enterprise—we're going to make a mistake. You want a way to undo that mistake. And since what may seem terrific now may seem naive in 20 years, you want a way to make the genetic change reversible."

There is no easy technological fix for another ethical worry, however: with germline engineering only society's "haves" will control their genetic traits. It isn't hard to foresee a day like that painted in last year's film "Gattaca," where only the wealthy can afford to genetically engineer their children with such "killer applications" as intelligence, beauty, long life or health. "If you are going to disadvantage even further those who are already disadvantaged," says bioethicist Ruth Macklin of Albert Einstein College of Medicine, "then that does raise serious concerns." But perhaps not enough to keep designer babies solely in Hollywood's imagination. For one thing, genetic therapy as done today (treating one organ of one child or adult) has been a bitter disappointment. "With the exception of a few anecdotal cases," says USC's Anderson, "there is no evidence of a gene-therapy protocol that

helps." But germline therapy might actually be easier. Doctors would not have to insinuate the new gene into millions of lung cells in, say, a cystic fibrosis patient. They could manipulate only a single cell—the fertilized egg—and still have the gene reach every cell of the person who develops from that egg.

How soon might we design our children? The necessary pieces are quickly falling into place. The first artificial human chromosome was created last year. By 2003 the Human Genome Project will have decoded all 3 billion chemical letters that spell out our 70,000 or so genes. Animal experiments designed to show that the process will not create horrible mutants are under way. No law prohibits germline engineering. Although NIH now refuses to even consider funding proposals for it, the rules are being updated. And where there is a way, there will almost surely be a will: none of us, says USC's Anderson, "wants to pass on to our children lethal genes if we can prevent it—that's what's going to drive this." At the UCLA symposium on germline engineering, two thirds of the audience supported it. Few would argue against using the technique to eradicate a disease that has plagued a family for generations. As Tuft's Krimsky says, "We know where to start." The harder question is this: do we know where to stop?

# Nature's Clones

Can genes explain our passions and prejudices, the mates we choose, that mystery we call the self? New research on twins upsets some of our most cherished notions about how we become who we are—and gives nature and nurture a whole new meaning. By JILL NEIMARK

**Last April I went down to West 27th Street** in Manhattan to sit in the audience of the *Maury Povich* show, and meet four sets of identical twins who had been separated at birth and adopted into different families. I wanted to see if the same soul stared out of those matched pairs of eyes, to contemplate the near miracle of DNA—double helix twisting around itself like twin umbilical cords—ticking out a perfect code for two copies of a human. One pair, a Polish nun and a Michigan housewife, had been filmed at the airport by CNN the week before, reunited for the first time in 51 years and weeping in each other's arms, marveling at their instinctive rapport. Yet how alike were they really, if one spent her days on rescue missions to places like Rwanda, while the other cleaned houses to supplement her husband's income?

Twins are nature's handmade clones, doppelgangers moving in synchrony through circumstances that are often eerily similar, as if they were unwitting dancers choreographed by genes or fate or God, thinking each other's thoughts, wearing each other's clothes, exhibiting the same quirks and odd habits. They leave us to wonder about our own uniqueness and loneliness, and whether it's possible to inhabit another person's being. Twins provoke questions about the moment our passions first ignite—for they have been seen on sonogram in the

womb, kissing, punching, stroking each other. They are living fault lines in the ever shifting geography of the nature/nurture debate, and their peculiar puzzle ultimately impacts politics, crime and its punishment, education, and social policy. It isn't such a short leap from studies of behavioral genetics to books like the infamous *The Bell Curve* (by Richard Herrnstein and Charles Murray) and a kind of sotto-voce eugenics. And so everything from homosexuality to IQ, religious affiliation, alcoholism, temperament, mania, depression, height, weight, mortality, and schizophrenia has been studied in identical and fraternal twins and their relatives.

Yet the answers—which these days seem to confirm biology's power—raise unsettling questions. Twin research is flawed, provocative, and fascinating, and it topples some of our most cherished notions—the legacies of Freud and Skinner included—such as our beliefs that parenting style makes an irrevocable difference, that we can mold our children, that we are free agents piecing together our destinies.

Today, we've gone twin-mad. Ninety thousand people gather yearly at the International Twins Day Festival in Twinsburg, Ohio. We're facing a near epidemic of twins. One in 50 babies born this year will have a fraternal or identical double; the number of such births

rose 33 percent in 1994 alone, peaking at over 97,000—largely due to women delaying childbirth (which skewers the odds in favor of twins) and to the fertility industry, which relies on drugs that superovulate would-be mothers. Recently, a stunning scientific feat enabled an ordinary sheep to give up a few cells and produce a delayed identical twin—a clone named Dolly, who was born with her donor's 6-year-old nucleus in every cell of her body. The international furor this Scottish lamb engendered has at its heart some of the same wonder and fear that every twin birth evokes. Twins are a break, a rift in the customary order, and they call into question our own sense of self. Just how special and unique are we?

The history of twins is rich with stories that seem to reveal them as two halves of the same self—twins adopted into different families falling down stairs at the same age, marrying and miscarrying in the same year, identical twins inventing secret languages, "telepathic" twins seemingly connected across thousands of miles, "evil" twins committing arson or murder together, conjoined twins sharing a single body, so that when one coughs the other reflexively raises a hand to cover the first one's mouth. And yet the lives of twins are full of just as many instances of discordance, differences, disaffection. Consider the 22-year-old Korean twins, Sunny and

Jeen Young Han of San Diego County; Jeen hired two teenagers to murder her sister, hoping to assume her identity.

So what is truly *other*, what is *self*? As the living embodiment of that question, twins are not just the mirrors of each other, they are a mirror for us all.

## Separated at Birth But Joined at the Hip

The woman seated alone onstage at the opening of the *Maury Povich* show was already famous in the twin literature: Barbara Herbert, a plump 58-year-old with a broad, pretty face and short, silver hair, found her lost twin, Daphne Goodship, 18 years ago. Both had been adopted as babies into separate British families after their Finnish single mother killed herself.

The concordances in their lives send a shiver up the spine: both women grew up in towns outside of London, left school at 14, fell down stairs at 15 and weakened their ankles, went to work in local government, met their future husbands at age 16 at the Town Hall dance, miscarried in the same month, then gave birth to two boys and a girl. Both tinted their hair auburn when young, were squeamish about blood and heights, and drank their coffee cold. When they met, both were wearing cream-colored dresses and brown velvet jackets. Both had the same crooked little fingers, a habit of pushing up their nose with the palm of their hand—which both had nicknamed "squidging"—and a way of bursting into laughter that soon had people referring to them as the Giggle Twins. The two have been studied for years now at the University of Minnesota's Center for Twin and Adoption Research, founded by Thomas J. Bouchard, Ph.D. It is the largest, ongoing study of separated twins in the world, with nearly 100 pairs registered, and they are poked, probed, and prodded by psychologists, psychiatrists, cardiologists, dentists, ophthalmologists, pathologists, and geneticists, testing everything from blood pressure to dental caries.

At the center, it was discovered that the two women had the same heart murmurs, thyroid problems, and allergies, as well as IQ's a point apart. The two showed remarkably similar personalities on psychological tests. So do the other sets of twins in the study—in fact, the genetic influence is pervasive across most domains tested. Another set of twins had been reunited in a hotel room when they were young adults, and as they unpacked found that they used the same brand of shaving lotion (Canoe), hair tonic (Vitalis), and toothpaste (Vademecum). They both smoked Lucky Strikes, and after they met they returned to their separate cities and mailed each other identical birthday presents. Other pairs have discovered they like to read magazines from back to front, store rubber bands on their wrists, or enter the ocean backwards and only up to their knees. Candid photos of every pair of twins in the study show virtually all the identicals posed the same way; while fraternal twins positioned hands and arms differently.

Bouchard—a big, balding, dynamic Midwesterner who can't help but convey his irrepressible passion about this research—recalls the time he reunited a pair of twins in their mid-30s at the Minneapolis airport. "I was following them down the ramp to baggage claim and they started talking to each other. One would stop and a nanosecond later the other would start, and when she stopped a nanosecond later the other would start. They never once interrupted each other. I said to myself, 'This is incredible, I can't carry on a conversation like that with my wife and we've been married for 36 years. No psychologist would believe this is happening.' When we finally got to baggage claim they turned around and said, 'It's like we've known each other all our lives.' "

## Just Puppets Dancing To Music of the Genes?

I asked Bouchard if the results of his research puncture our myth that we consciously shape who we are.

"You're not a believer in free will, are you?" he laughed, a little too heartily. "What's free will, some magical process in the brain?"

Yet I am a believer (a mystical bent and fierce independence actually run in my family, as if my genes have remote controlled a beguiling but misbegotten sense of freedom and transcendence). I was mesmerized and disturbed by the specificity of the twins' concordances. David Teplica, M.D., a Chicago plastic surgeon who for the last 10 years has been photographing more than 100 pairs of twins, has found the same number of crow's feet at the corners of twins' eyes, the same skin cancer developing behind twins' ears in the same year. Says Teplica, "It's almost beyond comprehension that one egg and one sperm could predict that."

I could imagine, I told Bouchard, that since genes regulate hormones and neurochemicals, and thus impact sexual attraction and behavior, DNA might influence the shaving lotion twins liked or the hue they tinted their hair. But the same esoteric brand of toothpaste? Walking into the sea backwards? This implies an influence so far-reaching it's unnerving.

"Nobody has the vaguest idea how that happens," he admitted, unfazed. "We're studying a set of triplets now, two identical females and a brother, and all three have Tourette's syndrome. How can the genes get so specific? I was talking yesterday in Houston to a bunch of neuroscientists and I said, 'This is the kind of thing you guys have to figure out.' There is tons of stuff to work on here, it's all open territory."

He paused to marvel over the tremendous shift in our understanding of human behavior. "When we began studying twins at the university in 1979, there was great debate on the power of genetics. I remember

# MY TWIN MARRIAGE

A few years ago, I was playing the messages back on my answering machine just as my husband, Jeff, was coming into the apartment. He heard a familiar voice and ran for the answering machine.

"It's Phil!" he yelled, shrugging out of his coat. "Pick up the phone. Phil's calling."

Only it wasn't Phil. It was Phil's identical twin brother, Jeff.

"Oh, it's me," my husband said sheepishly. Sheepish in the sense of Dolly, the cloned sheep.

When I was first dating Jeff, the prospect of marrying an identical twin seemed magical. Jeff spoke of his brother as if he were talking about himself, almost as if he could bi-locate and live two contrasting yet mutually enriching lives. Jeff worked at a literary agency in Manhattan and loved boy fiction, thrillers, and horror novels, while Phil was overtly spiritual, editing a journal dedicated to the study of myth and tradition. When they were together they seemed to merge into one complex yet cohesive personality. They talked like hyper-bright little boys, each of them bringing equal heat and erudition to Stephen King and esoteric teachings, baseball, and the possibility of spiritual transformation. They argued—and still argue—like Trotsky and Lenin, desperate to define themselves as individuals, yet they define themselves against each other. Jeff and Phil love their wives and children, but they obey the orders they get from the mothership of their identical DNA.

My husband and his twin brother live by E. M. Forster's admonition, "Only connect." The pair e-mail each other at their respective offices two, four, even more times a day. A few weeks ago, Phil wrote Jeff that he was trying to decide his favorite 10 films of all time. He listed *Journey to the Center of the Earth, Star Wars*, seven other boy classics, and asked for Jeff's help thinking up a 10th.

"Phil and I decided that *Jurassic Park* is our favorite movie of all time," announced Jeff the other evening at dinner. In the course of dozens of soothing little dispatches Phil's movie list and Jeff's movie list had become one.

My marriage to Jeff has locked me into a triangle. The bond between these twins amazes and amuses me, yet it fills me with an unappeasable longing. After all, unlike Phil's wife, Carol, who is an only child, I was conditioned even before I was born to be with a twin. I am a fraternal twin, a girl born 10 minutes after a boy.

"What do you get out of being a twin?" I asked my husband the first day we had lunch. "What insight does it give you that's harder for single people to understand?"

"Trust," said my husband. "That pure physical trust that comes when you know someone loves and accepts you completely because they are just like you are."

I knew the primordial closeness he was talking about. As tiny premature babies, my brother Steve and I used to cuddle in the same crib holding hands. My earliest memory is of being lifted up high and feeling incredible joy as I gazed into my mother's vast, radiant face. I was put back down on a big bed. I remember sensing another baby lying next to me, my twin. His presence felt deeply familiar, and I know I had sensed him before we were born. For me, in the beginning there was the light but there was also the son. In addition to the vertical relationship I had with Mommy, I also had a lateral relationship, a constant pre-verbal reassurance that I had a peer. I was in it with somebody else. This feeling of extending in two directions, horizontal and vertical, made up the cross of my emotional life.

At the age of 3, I remember standing in the grass on a hot, bright day in El Paso, Texas, aware as never before that my brother was different from me, not just because he was smaller then and a boy, but because

arguing in one graduate school class that the major psychoses were largely genetic in origin. Everyone in the classroom just clobbered me. It was the era of the domination of behaviorism, and although there's nothing wrong with Skinner's work, it had been generalized to explain everything under the sun. Nothing explains everything. Even genetics influences us, on the average, about 50 percent."

Yet that 50 percent seems omnipresent. It impacts everything from extroversion to IQ to religious and social attitudes—and drops only in the influence on homosexuality and death. Though some researchers have criticized Minnesota's twin sample for being too small and perhaps self-selected (how many separated twins out there don't participate or don't even know they're twins?), it generally confirms the results of larger studies of twins reared together—studies that have taken place around the world.

Twin studies allow us to double blind our nature/nurture research in a unique way. Identical twins share 100 percent of their genes, while fraternals share 50 percent. But usually they grow up together, sharing a similar environment in the womb and the world. When separated, they give us a clue about the strength of genetic influence in the face of sometimes radically different environments. Soon Bouchard and his colleagues will study siblings in families that have adopted a twin, thus testing environmental influences when no genes are shared. Like a prism yielding different bands of light, twin studies are rich and multifaceted. Here are some of the major findings on nature and nurture thus far:

• **Political and social attitudes**, ranging from divorce to the death penalty, were found to have a strong genetic influence in one Australian study. A Swedish study found genes significantly influenced two of the so-called "big five" personality traits—"openness to experience" and "conscientiousness"—while environment had little impact. In contrast, environment influenced "agreeableness" more than genes did. (The two other traits are "neuroticism" and "extroversion.") Another study, at the University of Texas at Austin, found that personality in identicals correlated 50 percent, in fraternals about 25 percent.

• **Body fat is under genetic influence.** Identical twins reared together will have the same amount of body fat 75 percent of the time; for those reared apart it's 61 percent, showing a heavy genetic and mild environmental influence, according to a 1991 study.

• **Both optimism and pessimism** are heavily influenced by genes, but shared environment influences only optimism, not pessimism, according to a study of 522 pairs of middle-aged identical and fraternal twins. Thus family life and genes can be equal contributors to an optimistic outlook, which influences both mental and physical health. But pessimism seems largely controlled by genes.

• **Religiosity is influenced by genes.** Identical and fraternal twins, raised together and apart, demonstrate that 50 percent of religiosity (demonstrated by religious conviction and church attendance) can be attributed to genes.

• **Sexual orientation** is under genetic influence, though not solely, according to studies by Michael Bailey, Ph.D., associate professor of psychology at Northwestern University. In one study he found that if one identical twin is gay, the other is also gay 50 percent of the time. However, when Bailey analyzed a sample of 5,000 twins from the Australian twin registry, the genetic impact was less. In identical male twins, if one was gay the likelihood of his twin being gay was 20 percent; in fraternal twins the likelihood was almost zero. In women, there was little evidence of heritability for homosexuality.

• **When substance abuse** was studied in 295 identical and fraternal twin pairs, year of birth was the most powerful predictor of drug

---

he was different inside. I loved him and felt protective towards him, as I would throughout my childhood, but I also felt the first stirrings of rebellion, of wanting to go vertical in my identity, to make it clear to my parents and everybody else that I was not the same as Steve.

I began to relish the idea of not being completely knowable. I developed a serious underground life. At 8, I twinned myself with an invisible black panther I called Striker. At 10, I became a spy. I made cryptic notes in a notebook. I had sinister passport photos taken. I had a plastic revolver I carried in a plastic attaché case. You may call me one of the twins, I thought to myself, but I come from a foreign country that has malevolent designs on your own.

No one ever calls me and Steve "the twins" anymore, except as an artifact of childhood. I tend to think of my birth twin, who is now a Porsche mechanic and a big, outdoorsy guy who lives with his wife and two kids in a small town outside of Boston, as the brother who was with me when I was born, who shared space with me in the womb. I feel close to him not because we are exactly the same, but because I still have bedrock sensation and empathy for his life.

Jeff claimed that his knowledge of trust from being an identical let him know that I was the person he wanted to marry. He felt twinship towards me right from the start he said, and I wasn't surprised. Accustomed to being twins, my husband and I fell right into acting like twins. We co-authored a book and both edit at *Publisher's Weekly*, yet we sometimes argue over who gets to use the little study in our apartment as if our identities were at stake. Lately, I've noticed that when I feel dominated by Jeff I tend to yearn for a "real" twin, a twin who mirrors me so lovingly and acceptingly that I can let go and be myself without fear or explanation. A single person might escape by daydreaming about a perfect lover, but my fantasies of romantic enmeshment have always incorporated the twin.

Years ago in Manhattan I was invited to attend a ceremony for the Santeria religion's god of thunder, Shango, because Shango loves twins. On the way, a revered old Cuban santera told me that twins were sacred in Santeria and in the African mother religion of Yoruba because they reflect the intersection of spirit and matter. Girl and boy twins were especially fascinating, according to the santera. Most girls were killed by the boy energy, they believed. A girl had to be very strong to survive.

The moment I heard that I realized that being a twin has heightened the drama of my life. Human beings are born double, pulled between the desire to merge with another yet emerge as an authentic self. Twins fascinate, I believe, because we are an externalized representation of an internal struggle everybody lives with all their lives. We cast the illusion of solving the unsolvable, though we're no closer than anyone else.—*Tracy Cochran*

---

use. Younger twins were most likely to have abused drugs, reflecting widespread drug use in the culture at large. Alcoholism, however, has a significant genetic component, according to Andrew Heath, Ph.D., at the Virginia Institute for Psychiatric and Behavioral Genetics at Virginia Commonwealth University School of Medicine.

• **Attention deficit disorder** may be influenced by genes 70 percent of the time, according to Lindon Eaves, M.D., director of the Virginia Insti-

tute for Psychiatric and Behavioral Genetics. Eaves and colleagues studied 1,400 families of twins and found genetic influence on "all the juvenile behavior disorders," usually in the range of 30 to 50 percent.

• **Twins tend to start dating,** to marry, and to start having children at about the same time. David Lykken, Ph.D., and Matthew McGue, Ph.D., at the University of Minnesota, found that if an identical twin had divorced, there was a 45 percent chance the other had also. For frater-

# BEYOND NATURE AND NURTURE: TWINS AND QUANTUM PHYSICS

I've been interested in identical twins ever since I was old enough to realize I am one. When my brother and I were young we were close but nonetheless epitomized the struggle of twins to achieve individual identities. Now in our 50s, we have both noticed a real convergence of our intellectual, spiritual and philosophical views.

Are the strikingly similar thoughts and behaviors of twins, even those reared apart, due to nature or nurture—or to a third factor? What if what I call the "nonlocal" nature of the mind is involved?

Nonlocal mind is a term I introduced in 1989 to account for some of the ways consciousness manifests, ways suggesting that it is not completely confined or localized to specific points in space or time. Nobel physicist Erwin Schrödinger believed that mind by its very nature is singular and one, that consciousness is not confined to separate, individual brains, that it is ultimately a unified field. David Chalmers, a mathematician and cognitive scientist from the University of California at Santa Cruz, has suggested that consciousness is fundamental in the universe, perhaps on a par with matter and energy, and that it is not derived from, nor reducible to, anything else. Nobel physicist Brian Josephson, of Cambridge University's Cavendish Laboratory, has proposed that nonlocal events at the subatomic level for example, the fact that there are correlations between the spin of subatomic particles, even after they are separated—can be amplified and may emerge in our everyday experience.

In other words, the macrocosm reflects the microcosm. Systems theorist Erwin Laszio has suggested that nonlocal mind may mediate events such as intercessory prayer, telepathy, precognition, and clairvoyance.

If consciousness is unbounded and unitary, strikingly similar thoughts and behaviors of identical twins, even separated twins, would not be surprising. Genes do determine how individual brains function, how we each process information, and nonlocal mind could be easier to access if two brains were almost identical in their functioning. Indeed, some people see analogies between the behavior of separated, identical twins and separated, identical subatomic particles.

According to the late Irish physicist John S. Bell, if two subatomic particles once in contact are separated to some arbitrary distance, a change in one is correlated with a change in the other—instantly and to the same degree. There is no travel time for any known form of energy to flow between them. Yet experiments have shown these changes do occur, instantaneously. Neither can these nonlocal effects be blocked or shielded—one of the hallmarks of nonlocality. Perhaps distant twins are mysteriously linked, like distant particles—or, to quote Ecclesiastes, "All things go in pairs, one the counterpart of the other."
—*Larry Dossey, M.D.*

identical twins are truly identical, or share all their genetic traits. In one tragic instance, one twin was healthy and a gymnast, while the other suffered from severe muscular dystrophy, a genetic disorder, and was dead by age 16. Yet the twins were identical.

> Some twins are bonded by a lifelong passion for each other that the rest of us experience only in the almost unbearably intense first flush of romantic love. England's notorious Gibbons twins were one such pair.

One way twins can differ is in the sex chromosomes that turn them into a male or female, and which contain other genes as well, such as those that code for muscular dystrophy or color blindness. All girls inherit two X chromosomes, one from each parent, while boys inherit an X and a Y. Girls automatically shut off one X in every cell—sometimes some of the mother's and some of the father's, in other cases all the mother's or all the father's. A girl may not shut off her extra set of X chromosomes in the same pattern as her identical twin does.

Identical twins may not be exposed to the same world in the womb, either. It depends on the time their mother's fertilized egg splits—and that timing may explain why some identical twins seem more eerily alike than others. At Lutheran University, researchers have looked at the placentas of some 10,000 twin births. They've found that an egg that separates in the first four days of pregnancy develops not only into separate twins, but results in separate placentas, chorionic casings, and amniotic sacs. These twins are

nals, the chance was 30 percent. The researchers think this is due to inherited personality traits.

- **Schizophrenia** occurs more often in identical twins, and if one twin suffers from the disorder, the children of the healthy identical sibling are also at greater risk, according to psychiatrist Irving Gottesman, M.D., of the University of Virginia. The risk is about twice as high for the children of a twin whose identi-

cal counterpart is ill, as it is for the children of a twin whose fraternal counterpart is ill.

## Hidden Differences Between Twins

A few fascinating kinks in the biology of twin research have recently turned up, weaving an even more complex pattern for us to study and learn from. It turns out that not all

like two singletons in the womb and have the best chance of survival. Twins who separate between the fifth and eighth days share a single placenta and chorion, but still have the benefit of two amniotic sacs. Here, one twin can have a distinct advantage over the other. The umbilical cord may be positioned centrally on one sac, while the other is on the margin, receiving fewer nutrients. Studies of these twins show that with a nurturing environment, the weaker twin will catch up in the first few years of life. However, it's possible that viruses may penetrate separate sacs at different rates or in different ways—perhaps increasing the risk for schizophrenia or other illnesses later in life.

Twins who split between the eighth and 12th days share their amniotic sac, and often their cords get entangled. One cord may be squeezed until no blood flows through it, and that twin dies. Finally, twins who split after the 12th day become conjoined—and even though they share organs and limbs, anecdotal evidence suggests that they often have distinctly different temperaments, habits, and food cravings.

In one hotly debated hypothesis, pediatrician and geneticist Judith Hall, of the University of British Columbia in Vancouver, speculates that twinning occurs because of genetic differences within an embryo. Perhaps mutations occur at a very early stage in some cells, which then are sensed as different, and expelled from the embryo. Those cells may survive and grow into a twin. Hall suggests this could account for the higher incidence of birth defects among twins.

While identical twins can be more distinct than we imagine, fraternal twins might come from the same egg, according to behavioral geneticist Charles Boklage, M.D., of the East Carolina University School of Medicine. Boklage proposes that occasionally an older egg may actually split before it is fertilized by two of the father's sperm. With advances in

gene mapping and blood testing, he says, we may find that one-egg fraternal twins occur as often as do two-egg fraternals. We may be mistaking some same sex fraternal twins for identical twins.

## Twins Who Vanish, Twins Who Merge

Whatever the cause of twinning, once it begins, mysterious and unsettling events can occur. Some twins disappear or even merge together into one person. Ultrasound equipment has revealed twin pregnancies that later turn into singletons. One of the twins is absorbed into the body, absorbed by the other twin, or shed and noticed by the mother only as some extra vaginal bleeding.

"Only one in 80 twin conceptions makes it to term as two living people," notes Boklage. "For every one that results in a twin birth, about 12 make it to term as a sole survivor. And those people never know they were twins." Because twins tend to be left-handed more often than singletons, Boklage speculates that many left-handers could be the survivors of a twin pregnancy. And a few of those twin pregnancies may lead to what Boklage terms a "chimera," based on the Greek monster with a tail of a serpent, body of a goat, and head of lion—a mosaic of separate beings. "We find people entirely by accident who have two different blood types or several different versions of a single gene. Those people look perfectly normal, but I believe they come from two different cell lines."

It's as if fantastical, primitive acts of love, death, merging, and emerging occur from the very moment life ignites, even as the first strands of DNA knit themselves into the human beings we will later become— carrying on those same acts in the world at large, acts that define us, and that we still are not certain we can call our own.

## When Twins Die, Kill, Hate, and Burn

Though it doesn't happen often, occasionally in history a set of mythic twins seem to burst into our awareness, more wedded and bonded than any couple, even darkly so. Some twins live with a passion the rest of us experience only in the almost unbearably intense first flush of romantic love. England's Gibbons twins are one such pair.

Jennifer and June Gibbons were born 35 years ago, the youngest children of Aubrey Gibbons, a West Indian technician for the British Royal Air Force. The girls communicated with each other in a self-made dialect and were elective mutes with the rest of the world. By the time they were 11, they refused to sit in the same room with their parents or siblings. Their mother delivered their meals on a tray and slipped mail under the door. They taught themselves to read, and eventually locked themselves in their bedroom, writing literally millions of words in diaries.

Later they lost their virginity to the same boy within a week of each other, triggering jealous rage. Jennifer tried to strangle June with a cord, and June tried to drown Jennifer in a river. When publishers rejected their work, they went on a spree of arson and theft, and were committed to Broadmoor, England's most notorious institution for the criminally insane.

"Nobody suffers the way I do," June wrote in her diary. "This sister of mine, a dark shadow robbing me of sunlight, is my one and only torment." In another passage, Jennifer described June lying in the bunk bed above her: "Her perception was sharper than steel, it sliced through to my own perception... I read her mind, I knew all about her mood... My perception. Her perception... clashing, knowing, cunning, sly."

After more than a decade of confinement, they were set free. That same afternoon, Jennifer was rushed to the hospital with viral myocarditis, an inflammation of the heart, and that night she died. The pathologist who saw her heart seemed to be speaking poetically of their lethal passion when he described Jennifer's illness as "a fulminating, roaring inflammation with the heart muscle completely destroyed." June, the survivor, has said that she was "born in captivity, trapped in twinship." Eventually, June claims, they began to accept that one must die so the other could be free. Today, June lives in Wales.

Another set of twins, 22-year-old Jeen Young Han (nicknamed Gina) and her sister Sunny, have been dubbed the "evil" and "good" twins by the media, after one tried to murder the other. Although the twins were both valedictorians at their small country high school in San Diego County and got along well, after they graduated they began to battle one another. Both sisters were involved in petty crime, but when Gina stole Sunny's BMW and credit cards, Sunny had her jailed. She escaped, but in November 1996 Sunny and her roommate were attacked and Gina was arrested for conspiracy to commit murder. She'd planned to have Sunny killed at her Irvine condominium, and then assume her identity.

For twin researcher and obstetrician Louis Keith, M.D., of Northwestern University Medical School, the idea of killing a twin is practically unthinkable. "I'm an identical twin, and yesterday I attended the funeral of another identical twin. I kept trying to imagine what my life would be like without my twin. My brother and I have had telepathic experiences. I was in East Germany, being driven on a secluded highway with evening snow falling, and suddenly felt intense heat over the entire front of my body and knew it could only mean one thing, that my brother was sending intense signals to me to call him. When one of the Communist telephone operators agreed to put the call through, I found out that my aunt had died and my twin wanted me to come to the

funeral. The twin bond is greater than the spousal bond, absolutely."

Raymond Brandt, publisher of *Twins World* magazine, agrees. "I'm 67, and my identical twin died when we were 20. I love my wife and sons in a very special way, but my twin was one half of me, he was my first love. Living without my twin for 47 years has been a hell of an existence."

These remarkable stories seem to indicate an extra dimension to the twin bond, as if they truly shared a common, noncorporeal soul. What little study has been done on paranormal phenomena and twins, however, indicates that—once again—genes may be responsible. A study by British parapsychologist Susan Blackmore found that when twins were separated in different rooms and asked to draw whatever came into their minds, they often drew the same things. When one was asked to draw an object and transmit that to the other twin, who then was asked to draw what she telepathically received, the results were disappointing. Blackmore concluded that when twins seem to be clairvoyant, it's simply because their thought patterns are so similar.

## Is There No Nurture?

Over a century ago, in 1875, British anthropologist Francis Galton first compared a small group of identical and fraternal twins and concluded that "nature prevails enormously over nurture." Time and research seem to have proved him right. "It's no accident that we are what we are," contends Nancy Segal, Ph.D., professor of developmental psychology at California State University at Fullerton and director of the Twin Studies Center there. "We are born with biological propensities that steer us in one direction or another."

Yet critics of twin studies scoff. Richard Rose, Ph.D., professor of psychology and medical genetics at Indiana University in Bloomington, has studied personality in more than 7,000 pairs of identical twins and

concluded that environment, both shared and unshared, has nearly twice the influence of genes.

However, both the nature and nurture camps may be looking at the same data and interpreting it differently. According to Lindon Eaves, unshared environment may actually be "chosen" by the genes, selected because of biological preferences. Scientists dub this the "nature of nurture." Genetically influenced personality traits in a child may cause parents to respond in specific ways. So how can we ever tease out the truth? Nature and nurture interact in a never-ending Mobius strip that can't be traced back to a single starting point.

Yet if genes are a powerful and a-priori given, they nonetheless have a range of activity that is calibrated in the womb by nutrition and later in life by the world. "Remember," says Eaves, "only 50 percent of who you are is influenced by genes. The other 50 percent includes the slings and arrows of outrageous fortune, accidents of development, sheer chaos, small and cumulative changes both within and without."

Environment, it turns out, may be most powerful when it limits—through trauma, deprivation, malnutrition. Studies by Sandra Scarr, Ph.D., professor of psychology at the University of Virginia, show that IQ scores for white twins at the bottom of the socioeconomic ladder, and for all black twins, are heavily influenced by environment. Social and economic deprivation keep scores artificially lower than twins' genetic potential.

Otherwise, Scarr postulates, genes bias you in a certain direction, causing you to select what you are already genetically programmed to enjoy. Children may be tiny gene powerhouses, shaping their parents' behavior as much as parents shape their children.

"Where does this leave us?" concludes Bouchard. "Your job as a parent is really to maximize the environment so that you and your children can manifest your full genetic potential."

Under the best of environmental circumstances, our genes might be free to play the entire symphony of self.

And yet what of Irina, the Michigan housewife, and her twin, Yanina, the Polish nun? I sat with them over lunch, newly united twins who couldn't stop smiling at each other, clasping each other's hands. Their luminous hazel eyes were virtual replicas, but the two women couldn't have appeared more different otherwise: Irina bejeweled and blonde, Yanina in a combat-green nun's habit, a few tufts of brown hair peeping out, skin weathered. She described rescuing bloodied children from the arms of mothers who'd been shot to death and rising at dawn in the convent to pray silently for hours; her American counterpart portrayed a life filled with errands, cleaning homes, and caring for family.

"Rushing, rushing, rushing to get everything done" was Irina's summary of her life. "Teaching love, the kind of love that will make you happy," was her sister's. Listening to them speak, one in slow, gentle Midwestern cadences, the other in the rolled drumbeat of a Slavic tongue enriched by laughter and hand gestures, it was hard to believe they carried the same genetic imprint.

To me, their differences are so striking they seem to defy the last 20 years of twin research. "Right now we understand a little bit about human behavior and its biological and cultural roots," says Eaves. "But our lived understanding is far richer than any of that. People are yielding the ground too easily to genetics."

As I mused over the intricate turnings of twin research, I could only conclude the findings were as complex as the self we hope to illuminate with these studies. Fascinating, tantalizing, yes, but twin research, like any great scientific endeavor, ultimately points us toward the ineffable, inexplicable.

As Charles Boklage notes: "The development of the self is chaotic, nonlinear, and dynamic. Very small variations in conditions can lead to huge changes. Different twin studies give different answers. And whenever the mind tries to understand something, it has to be bigger than the subject it compasses. You cannot bite your own teeth."

"In the end," says Eaves, "I don't give a damn whether you call it God or natural selection, we're trying to find words that instill reverence for the mysterious stuff from which we are made."

God, fate, genes, luck, a random event like a move to America or Poland, or perhaps something stubbornly individual and free about us all, something that can never be quantified but can only be lived . . . The play of self goes on, and whatever hand or eye has orchestrated us, who in the end, twin or not, can know the dancer from the dance?

# The Role of Lifestyle in Preventing Low Birth Weight

Virginia Rall Chomitz
Lilian W. Y. Cheung
Ellice Lieberman

## Abstract

Lifestyle behaviors such as cigarette smoking, weight gain during pregnancy, and use of other drugs play an important role in determining fetal growth. The relationship between lifestyle risk factors and low birth weight is complex and is affected by psychosocial, economic, and biological factors. Cigarette smoking is the largest known risk factor for low birth weight. Approximately 20% of all low birth weight could be avoided if women did not smoke during pregnancy. Reducing heavy use of alcohol and other drugs during pregnancy could also reduce the rate of low birth weight births. Pregnancy and the prospect of pregnancy provide an important window of opportunity to improve women's health and the health of children. The adoption before or during pregnancy of more healthful lifestyle behaviors, such as ceasing to smoke, eating an adequate diet and gaining enough weight during pregnancy, and ceasing heavy drug use, can positively affect the long-term health of women and the health of their infants. Detrimental lifestyles can be modified, but successful modification will require large-scale societal changes. In the United States, these societal changes should include a focus on preventive health, family-centered workplace policies, and changes in social norms.

*Virginia Rall Chomitz, Ph.D., is project manager of the Eat Well and Keep Moving Project, Department of Nutrition, Harvard School of Public Health.*

*Lilian W. Y. Cheung, D.Sc., R.D., is a lecturer in the Department of Nutrition and director of the Harvard Nutrition and Fitness Project, Harvard School of Public Health, Department of Nutrition and Center for Health Communication.*

*Ellice Lieberman, M.D., Dr.PH., is assistant professor in the Department of Obstetrics, Gynecology, and Reproductive Biology, Harvard Medical School and in the Department of Maternal and Child Health, Harvard School of Public Health.*

**M**any of the known risk factors associated with low birth weight, such as socioeconomic status, ethnicity, genetic makeup, and obstetric history, are not within a woman's immediate control. However, there are things that a woman can do to improve her chances of having a normal, healthy child. Lifestyle behaviors, such as cigarette smoking, use of other drugs, and nutrition, play an important role in determining fetal growth. Detrimental habits can be modified, but successful modification requires more than just a dose of individual "self control." Stopping lifelong addictive behaviors is very difficult, and a woman who suffers from them requires support and assistance not only from family members and individuals close to her, but also from the health care system and society.

The relationship between lifestyle risk factors and low birth weight is very complex and is affected by psychosocial, socioeconomic, and biological factors. While it is important to describe the independent effects of different behavioral and socioeconomic risk factors, we must bear in mind that these factors are not isolated events in women's lives, but are a part of many interrelated complex behaviors and environmental risks. Factors associated with the perinatal health of women and children include demographic factors, medical risks, and maternal behaviors. These risk factors may influence maternal and infant health directly (in terms of physiology) or indirectly (in terms of health behavior). In this article we focus primarily on lifestyle behavioral risk factors that are amenable to change and that, if modified before or during pregnancy, can improve the likelihood of the delivery of a full-term healthy infant of appropriate size.

*There are things that a woman can do to improve her chances of having a normal, healthy child.*

*This paper is based on* Healthy Mothers—Healthy Beginnings, *a paper written with a grant from the CIGNA Foundation and CIGNA Corporation, 1992.*

## Demographic Factors

Socioeconomic status and race/ethnicity are indicators of complex linkages among environmental events, psychological states, and physiologic factors which may lead to low birth weight or preterm delivery. While we do not fully understand the specific biological pathways responsible, we do know that a woman's social and economic status will influence her general health and access to resources. (See the article by Hughes and Simpson in this journal issue for a detailed analysis of the effects of social factors on low birth weight.) In this section, we review the effects of some demographic indicators.

## Socioeconomic Status

Low birth weight and infant mortality are closely related to socioeconomic disadvantage. Socioeconomic status, however, is difficult to measure accurately. Educational attainment, marital status, maternal age, and income are interrelated factors and are often used to approximate socioeconomic status, but no single factor truly measures its underlying influence.

Maternal education, maternal age, and marital status are all reflective of socioeconomic status and predictive of low birth weight. Twenty-four percent of the births in 1989 were to women with less than a high school education.[1] Low educational attainment is associated with higher rates of low birth weight.[2] For example, relative to college graduates, white women with less than a high school education were 50% more likely to have babies with very low birth weight (less than 1,500 grams, or 3 pounds, 5 ounces) and more than twice as likely to have babies with moderately low birth weight (between 1,500 grams and 2,500 grams, or 3 pounds, 5 ounces and 5 pounds, 8 ounces) than were women who graduated from college.[2] Teenage mothers are at greater risk of having a low birth weight baby than are mothers aged 25 to 34.[1] However, it is not clear if the risk of teenage childbearing is due to young maternal age or to the low socioeconomic status that often accompanies teenage pregnancy.

The marital status of the mother also appears to be independently associated with the rate of low birth weight,[2,3] although the relationship appears to vary by maternal age and race. The association of unmarried status with low birth weight is probably strongest for white women over 20 years of age.[2,4] Marital status may also serve as a marker for the "wantedness" of the child, the economic status of the mother, and the social support that the mother has—all of which are factors that may influence the health of the mother and infant.

It has been hypothesized that economic disadvantage may be a risk factor for low birth weight partly because of the high levels of stress and negative life events that are associated with being poor. Both physical stress and fatigue—particularly related to work during pregnancy—and psychological distress have been implicated.[5] In addition, stress and negative life events are associated with health behaviors such as smoking.[6] Social support may act as a moderator or as a buffer from the untoward effects of stressful life experiences and emotional dysfunction.[7]

## Race/Ethnicity

The prevalence of low birth weight among white infants is less than half of that for African-American infants (6% and 13%, respectively). This difference reflects a twofold increase of preterm and low birth weight births among African-American mothers.[1] African-American mothers are more likely to have less education, not to be married, and to be younger than white mothers.[1] However, at almost all educational levels and age categories, African-American women have about double the rates of low birth weight as white women.[8] This fact indicates that these demographic differences in education, marital status, and age do not account for the large disparity between African Americans and whites in the incidence of low birth weight.

Among infants of Hispanic origin, who represented approximately 15% of live births in 1989, the rate of low birth weight was relatively low (6.1% overall), particularly given that Hispanic women (except Cuban women) had limited educational attainment and were not as likely as non-Hispanic white women to receive prenatal care early in pregnancy.[1]

However, Hispanics are a very diverse group, and the low birth weight rates vary considerably by national origin. Low birth weight rates range from 9.4% among Puerto Rican mothers to 5.6% among Cuban mothers. Among Asian infants in 1989, the incidence of low birth weight ranged from 5.1% for Chinese births to 7.3% for Filipino births.[1]

It is not known why infants of African-American mothers are twice as likely as all other infants to be born with low birth weights. The etiology of racial disparities in infant mortality and low birth weight is probably multifactorial in nature and is not completely explained by differences in demographics, use of tobacco and other drugs, or medical illnesses.[9] During the primary childbearing years (ages 15 to 29), the general mortality of African-American women exceeds that of white women for virtually every cause of death.

African-American women have higher rates of hypertension, anemia, and low-level lead exposure than other groups,[10] suggesting that the general health status of African-American women may be suboptimal. Infants of African-American foreign-born mothers have lower risks of neonatal mortality than infants of African-American U.S.-born mothers, a relationship that is not seen between foreign- and U.S.-born white women.[11] In addition, racial or ethnic differences in familial structure and social networks may affect morbidity and mortality.[12] More research will be needed to clarify the reasons for these disparities.

## Nutrition and Weight Gain

Concerns about nutrition during pregnancy fall into two basic areas, maternal weight gain and nutrient intake, both of which can potentially affect the health of the mother and infant. As with other lifestyle factors, a woman's nutrition and weight gain are closely linked to her socioeconomic status, cigarette smoking, and other health-related behaviors.

## Maternal Weight Gain

Maternal weight gain during pregnancy results from a variety of factors, including maternal dietary intake, prepregnancy weight and height, length of gestation, and size of the fetus. The mother's prepregnancy weight and height are, in turn, a consequence of her genetic makeup, past nutritional status, and environmental factors. The relationship between a woman's caloric intake during pregnancy and her infant's birth weight is complex and is moderated through maternal weight gain and other mechanisms during pregnancy.[13,14]

Epidemiologic evidence has demonstrated a nearly linear association between maternal weight gain during pregnancy and birth weight,[15,16] and an inverse relationship to the rate of low birth weight.[16] It comes as no surprise that maternal weight gain during pregnancy is highly correlated with the birth weight of the infant because a large propor-

*It is not known why infants of African-American mothers are twice as likely as all other infants to be born with low birth weights.*

tion of the weight gain is due to the growth of the fetus itself. Women with total weight gains of 22 pounds (10 kilograms) or less were two to three times more likely to have growth-retarded full-term babies than were women with a gain of more than 22 pounds. Once corrected for the duration of pregnancy, the relationship between weight gain and preterm delivery is uncertain.[17,18]

On average, women gain about 30 pounds during pregnancy. Teenage mothers, older mothers, unmarried mothers, and mothers with less than a high school education are most likely to have low or inadequate weight gain during pregnancy. Even after accounting for gestational age and socioeconomic status, African-American mothers gain less weight than white mothers (28 versus 31 pounds).[19] It has been estimated that from 15% to 33% of women gain an inadequate amount of weight (less than 22 pounds) during pregnancy.[13,19] Low weight gain may in part be the result of outdated medical advice and personal beliefs. In one study, one-quarter of the pregnant women believed that they should not gain more than 20 pounds during pregnancy.[20] In addition, belief that a smaller baby is easier to deliver and thus that weight gain and fetal birth weight should be limited influences the amount of weight gained by some women.[21]

tionship between specific vitamins and minerals and low birth weight is unclear, and controversy exists over the association between maternal hematocrit levels (which is a marker for anemia) and preterm birth.[23–26]

A pregnant woman's current nutritional status is determined by her prepregnant nutritional status, her current intake of nutrients, and her individual physiological nutrient requirements. Members of the National Academy of Sciences recently reviewed the available literature on dietary intake of nutrients and minerals among pregnant women. They found that the energy intake (calories) for U.S. women was consistently below recommended levels and that the amount of important vitamins and minerals in their diet was also substantially lower than the recommended daily allowance. On average, intakes of protein, riboflavin, vitamin B-12, niacin, and vitamin C exceeded the recommended daily allowance.[27]

Women at particular risk of nutritional inadequacy during pregnancy may require nutritional counseling. Groups at risk include women voluntarily restricting caloric intake or dieting; pregnant adolescents; women with low income or limited food budgets; women with eating patterns or practices that require balancing food choices, such as strict

Approximately 20% to 25% of American women smoke cigarettes during pregnancy.[31,32] White, young, unmarried, and unemployed women, as well as women with fewer than 12 years of education and low socioeconomic status, are more likely to smoke during pregnancy, compared with nonwhite, older, married women with more than 12 years of education and higher socioeconomic status.[27,30,33,34] For example, 35% of mothers with less than a high school education smoke compared with 5% of college graduates.[35]

Smoking retards fetal growth. Birth weight is reduced by 150 to 320 grams (5.3 to 11.4 ounces) in infants born to smokers compared with those born to nonsmokers.[36] It has been consistently reported that, even after controlling other factors, women who smoke are about twice as likely to deliver a low birth weight baby as are women who do not smoke.[37] A dose-response relationship exists between the amount smoked and birth weight: the percent of low birth weight births increases with increasing number of cigarettes smoked during pregnancy. In addition, exposure to environmental cigarette smoke has also been associated with low birth weight.[38] Preterm birth is associated with smoking, but the association is weak compared with the association between low birth weight and smoking.[9,37] Cigarette smoking during pregnancy may account for up to 14% of preterm deliveries.[37]

Studies of women who quit cigarette smoking at almost any point during pregnancy show lower rates of low birth weight. Most fetal growth takes place in the last trimester, so that quitting early in pregnancy can decrease the negative effect of smoking on birth weight.[33] Quitting even as late as the seventh or eighth month has a positive impact on birth weight.[39]

Overall, about one-quarter of women who smoke prior to pregnancy quit upon learning of their pregnancies, and an additional one-third reduce the number of cigarettes they smoke.[33,40] Older women and more educated women are more likely to quit smoking during pregnancy.[41] Light smokers are more likely to quit smoking than heavier smokers. Heavier smokers are likely to reduce the amount they smoke, but are unlikely to quit.[42] Social support appears to be a critical factor in changing smoking behavior.[40]

Even among women who do quit smoking during pregnancy, about a third will relapse before childbirth.[43] In addition, nearly 80% of women who stop smoking during pregnancy relapse within one year after the delivery.[40] These high relapse rates reflect the physiological addictive nature of nicotine. While 57% of the pregnant smokers in one study were able to decrease their intake, 40% "tried and failed" to reduce.[44] Of women who both drank and smoked before pregnancy, fewer women were able to decrease

---

*Smoking during pregnancy has been linked to 20% to 30% of low birth weight births.*

---

While higher maternal weight gain is linked with healthier fetal weight gains, women and clinicians are concerned that women may retain weight after delivery and be at greater risk for obesity. Recent studies have shown that weight retention following delivery increased as weight gain increased, and African-American women retained more weight than white women with comparable weight gains during pregnancy (7.2 versus 1.6 pounds).[22] Thus, weight management programs would be appropriate for some women after delivery, but not during pregnancy.

### Diet and Nutrient Intake

During pregnancy, the need for calories and nutrients, such as protein, iron, folate, and the other B vitamins, is increased to meet the demands of the fetus as well as the expansion of maternal tissues that support the fetus. As noted by Nathanielsz in this journal issue, the nutritional needs of the fetus are second only to the needs of the mother's brain. Thus, it is important for a pregnant woman to have a well-balanced, nutritious diet to meet the changing needs of her body and her fetus. Unfortunately, the direct rela-

vegetarians; women with emotional illness; smokers; women with poor knowledge of nutrition due to lack of education of illiteracy; and women with special difficulties in food resource management because of limited physical abilities and poor cooking or budgeting skills.[28]

### Lifestyle Choices: Cigarette Smoking, Alcohol, Caffeine, and Illicit Drugs

#### Cigarette Smoking

Since the 1970s, the Surgeon General has reported that cigarette smoking during pregnancy is linked to fetal growth retardation and to infant mortality.[29] Smoking during pregnancy has been linked to 20% to 30% of low birth weight births and 10% of fetal and infant deaths.[30] Cigarette smoking is unequivocally the largest and most important known modifiable risk factor for low birth weight and infant death.

or quit smoking than drinking, despite feelings of social pressure to quit and feelings of guilt at continuing to smoke.[44] The high recidivism rate after childbirth also reflects diminished maternal contact with the health care system as health care provision shifts from obstetrics to pediatrics.[45]

The bulk of evidence shows a clear and consistent association between low birth weight (primarily due to growth retardation, not preterm birth) and infant mortality and smoking during pregnancy. Smoking also impacts on other aspects of the health status of women and infants. Smoking has been linked to long-term effects in infants such as physical, mental, and cognitive impairments.[46,47] The linkages between smoking and illnesses, such as cancer and cardiovascular and respiratory disease, are well known.[48] In addition, research on the effects of passive smoke indicates an increased frequency of respiratory and ear infections among infants and children exposed to this smoke.[33,49]

## Alcohol Use

Alcohol use during pregnancy has long been associated with both short- and long-term negative health effects for infants. Alcohol abuse during pregnancy is clearly related to

*Heavy alcohol consumption has been cited as the leading preventable cause of mental retardation worldwide.*

a series of congenital malformations described as fetal alcohol syndrome. However, the effects of moderate drinking on the fetus are not well established. Alcohol use among women of childbearing age and, specifically, among pregnant women has apparently declined significantly in the past decades.[44] This decreasing trend has generally been confined to more educated and older women. However, there has been little or no change in drinking during pregnancy among smokers, younger women, and women with less than a high school education.[50]

### Heavy Drinking During Pregnancy

Numerous studies report an association between chronic alcohol abuse and a series of fetal malformations. Fetal alcohol syndrome is characterized by a pattern of severe birth defects related to alcohol use during pregnancy, which include prenatal and postnatal growth retardation, central nervous system

disorders, and distinct abnormal craniofacial features.[51] Heavy alcohol consumption has been cited as the leading preventable cause of mental retardation worldwide.[52] It has been estimated that the prevalence of fetal alcohol syndrome is 1 to 3 per 1,000 live births with a significantly increased rate among alcoholics of 59 per 1,000 live births. Prenatally alcohol-exposed babies with birth defects who do not meet all required criteria for the syndrome are categorized as having fetal alcohol effects. The prevalence of fetal alcohol effects may be threefold that of fetal alcohol syndrome.[52]

The children of women who continued to drink an average of greater than one drink daily throughout their pregnancies are significantly smaller, shorter, and have smaller head circumferences than infants of control mothers who stop drinking.[53] The risk of low birth weight to women drinking three to five drinks per day was increased twofold over nondrinking mothers and almost threefold for those drinking six or more drinks daily when compared with women who did not drink.[54] A study of French women showed that those who consumed 35 drinks or more a week gave birth to infants that weighed 202 grams (about 7 ounces) less than the infants of women who consumed six or fewer drinks per week.[55]

### Moderate Drinking During Pregnancy

While the effects of heavy daily drinking are well documented, the impact of moderate drinking is not as well established. Approximately 40% to 60% of pregnant women consume one drink or less a day. Alcohol use exceeding one drink daily ranges from 3% to 13%. Abstinence levels in pregnant women have been reported to range from 16% to 53%.[50,54,56] Women who consumed less than one alcoholic drink per day had only an 11% increased chance of delivering a growth-retarded infant.[54] Decrements in birth weight from 32 to 225 grams (1.1 to 8 ounces) have been reported for children born to women who drank one to three drinks daily.[55,57] Some studies with long-term follow-up have reported deleterious short-term effects and long-term effects, such as growth, mental, and motor delays, for infants of mothers who drink alcohol during pregnancy.[58,59] However, a number of studies demonstrate insignificant or no effects of "low to moderate" intake on growth at birth[60] and at four and five years of age.[58,61] The role of binge drinking is unknown.

## Profile of the Pregnant Drinker

The profile of the pregnant drinker varies by the type of drinking. Any alcohol use during pregnancy is associated with older, white, professional, college-educated women with few previous children. Drinkers are also more likely to be unmarried and to smoke than are nondrinkers.[50] However, heavier alcohol use, in excess of two drinks daily, has been associated with African-American and Hispanic race/ethnicity, less than a high school education, and multiparity. Conversely, women who abstained during pregnancy were more likely to be younger, African-American, and/or of moderate income.[62]

During pregnancy, many women reduce their drinking[63] with decreases occurring in all types of drinkers.[64] In addition, as pregnancy advances, the proportion of women drinking decreases. In one study, 55% of women drank in the week prior to conception, 50% drank after 32 weeks, and only 20% drank in the last week of their pregnancies.[65]

Many of the studies investigating the relationship of maternal alcohol use to fetal effects suffer from methodologic problems common to substance use research. Most of the studies rely on self-reporting which, because of the stigma attached to alcohol use during pregnancy, may be inaccurate. Studies of drug use also often fail to consider other important factors, such as maternal nutrition, general health, or marijuana use. In addition, the usual dose, frequency of intake, and timing of drinking during pregnancy may result in different consequences, but this information is often lacking.

## Caffeine Consumption

Caffeine is one of the most commonly used drugs. At least 52% of people in the United States drink coffee, 29% drink tea, and 58% consume soft drinks.[66] Caffeine is most commonly consumed in beverages such as coffee, tea, and soft drinks; eaten in the form of chocolate; and also taken as part of various prescription and nonprescription drugs. No consistent associations between caffeine and low birth weight or preterm birth have been observed.[67] Most studies have found no association between caffeine use and low birth weight, but some studies report positive yet inconsistent associations.[67] Several studies have found an interaction between caffeine and cigarette smoking, where the adverse effects of caffeine were observed only among smokers. The existence of such an interaction may help to explain the conflicting results.

## Illicit Drug Use

In recent years, the rise in use of illegal drugs, particularly prenatal drug and cocaine, or "crack," use has received extensive coverage in the popular press and sparked many investigations. Prenatal cocaine and heroin abuse are clearly associated with adverse birth outcomes. Other factors in a drug addict's lifestyle, including malnutrition, sexually transmitted diseases, and polysubstance abuse, may contribute to an increased risk of adverse pregnancy outcome and often complicate the ability to examine the effects of individual drugs. The effect of marijuana use on the health of women and their infants is not as clear, nor are the effects of the occasional use of cocaine and other drugs.

Several methodologic problems hinder the interpretation and generalizability of much of the research on both the prevalence and effects of prenatal drug exposure. Studies are often based on small, nonrepresentative samples of mothers, and the bulk of the literature regarding illicit drug use relies on self-reporting. It is difficult to elicit valid information about illegal drug use, and a significant amount of underreporting probably takes place.[68] It is also unclear whether some of the effects of drug use are due to fetal drug exposure or to the generally poorer health and limited prenatal care of many addicted women. Finally, most research has been conducted with low-income urban women who are often in poorer health and under greater stress than their middle-class counterparts. The timing of drug use during the course of pregnancy and the dosage undoubtedly influences the consequences of the actions. However, most studies have been unable to characterize accurately the use of drugs in pregnancy. In addition, interactive effects of illicit drugs with alcohol, tobacco, or other drugs have not as yet been adequately examined.

Despite the limitations of the research, a number of studies have shown significant effects of individual illicit substances on women and infants. Elevated rates of fetal growth retardation, perinatal death, and pregnancy and delivery complications—such as abruptio placentae, high blood pressure, and preeclampsia—have been observed among drug-abusing women and their infants.[69–73]

## Cocaine Use

Maternal cocaine use has been associated with low birth weight, preterm labor, abruptio placentae, and fetal distress.[68,74,75] Brain damage and genitourinary malformations of the neonate have been reported, as well as fetal hyperthermia, thyroid abnormalities, stroke, and acute cardiac events.[76] Neurobehavioral effects found in neonates born to cocaine-abusing mothers have also been reported. These effects include decreased interactive behavior and poor organizational response to environmental stimuli.[72,74]

## Marijuana Use

The effects of prenatal marijuana use on pregnancy and infant outcomes are inconclusive. Children exposed to marijuana *in utero* may be smaller than nonexposed infants.[68] Other reports suggest that pregnant women who smoke marijuana are at higher risk of preterm labor, miscarriage, and stillbirth.[76] However, other studies find no difference between users of marijuana and nonusers in terms of rate of miscarriage, type of presentation at birth, Apgar status, and frequency of complications or major physical anomalies at birth.[77]

Very little is known about the number of women who use drugs while pregnant, their pattern of drug usage during pregnancy, or the intensity of use. The prevalence of illicit drug use among pregnant women has been estimated using state level and hospital-based studies. Based on anonymous urine toxicology analysis combined with self-reporting, the prevalence of drug use among pregnant women has been estimated at 7.5% to 15%.[78,79]

Cocaine use among pregnant women has been estimated at 2.3% to 3.4%.[79,80] Regional and hospital-based data report marijuana use during pregnancy in the range of 3% to 12%

---

*Prenatal cocaine and heroin abuse are clearly associated with adverse birth outcomes.*

---

and opiate (heroin) use in the range of 2% to 4%.[78,79] Regional data, such as New York City birth certificate data,[81] documented the dramatic increase in cocaine use relative to other drugs during the 1980s.

Figure 1 presents a profile of substance use among one sample of pregnant women.[62] Extrapolation of the data suggests that about half of all pregnant women may completely abstain from cigarette, alcohol, or drug use. However, approximately 14% of pregnant women engage in two or more high-risk behaviors during pregnancy, with about 2.5% of pregnant women, possibly about 100,000 nationwide, combining smoking, drinking, and recreational drug use.

Recent evidence suggests that, for pregnant women who receive treatment for drug abuse before their third trimester, the risks of low birth weight and preterm birth due to cocaine use may be minimized.[82] Little is known about which women quit or reduce drug use and why. In one study, college-educated, employed women were more likely to quit recreational drug use during pregnancy

*Stress is widely cited in the popular literature as a serious risk to mothers and infants, but current research has not characterized its effects.*

than were teenagers. The cessation rates were similar by racial/ethnic background and household income.[62] In another study, 14% of white women who used marijuana stopped using it upon starting prenatal care, as compared with 6% of African-American women.[83]

## Stress, Physical Activity, Employment, Social Support, Violence, and Sexually Transmitted Diseases

As discussed in the previous section on demographic risk factors, physical and psychosocial stress may be associated with low birth weight. Stress is widely cited in the popular literature as a serious risk to mothers and infants, but current research has not characterized its effects. The scientific literature linking stress and anxiety to obstetric outcome has been equivocal, but there is some basis for the notion that maternal emotional distress may be linked to poor reproductive outcome.[84]

## Stress

Stress is believed to influence maternal and infant health via changes in neuroendocrine functioning, immune system responses, and health behaviors. Thus, stress may influence pregnancy outcome directly (in terms of physiology) or indirectly (in terms of health behavior). Physiologically, stress has been associated with anxiety and depression.[85] It has been suggested that anxiety may increase metabolic expenditure and may lead to a lower gestational weight gain or to an anxiety-mediated change in catecholamine or hormonal balance which could provoke preterm labor.[37] Maternal psychological stress or emotional distress may interfere with the utilization of prenatal care or co-occur with particular health behaviors such as smoking and alcohol consumption.

However, the many methodological problems in much of the literature on stress and social support limit the extent to which studies can inform and guide policy and research. The studies are often based on small and ungeneralizable samples, and suffer from possible recall biases, poor reliability, and validity of study instruments and confounding. These difficulties arise from the multifactorial nature of stress and social support and from the problems inherent in trying to characterize these poorly understood elements of people's lives.

## Physical Activity

Concerns about weight gain and health have resulted in a high level of consciousness about weight control. More than one-third of American women participate in some form of regular physical activity.[86] Moderate aerobic exercise during pregnancy appears to have little adverse effect on pregnancy outcomes, and the potential benefits of exercise appear to be considerable.[87] Moderate exercise may be particularly beneficial for women at risk of developing diabetes during pregnancy. Lower levels of blood sugar were observed among diabetic women who were randomly assigned to moderate exercise regimens.[88] Decreases in the discomforts of pregnancy, improved self-esteem, and reduced tensions were reported among women who had participated in moderate physical conditioning programs during pregnancy.[89]

## Employment

The majority of American women are employed during pregnancy.[90] Women are employed in a wide range of occupations, which have varying degrees of physical and emotional demands, and varying levels of exposure to employment-related chemicals, radiation, or other toxic substances. Thus, defining a particular "exposure" that characterizes the potential risks of employment has been difficult. In addition, the interrelationship between employment and socioeconomic status is unavoidable. Employed mothers also may accrue positive effects of employment through increased socioeconomic status, better access to medical care, and improved overall lifestyle.[91]

In general, the results of studies evaluating the relationship between employment and low birth weight have been inconclusive.[92] Studies conducted outside the United States have found increased rates of low birth weight and preterm birth among employed women whose jobs required heavy physical labor. However, results of studies conducted in the United States are more mixed and have even demonstrated positive effects of employment. Further advances in this area will be hampered until we are able to better understand the complex relationship among socioeconomic status, employment, stress, and lifestyle.

## Domestic Violence

Depending on the population surveyed and the questions asked, the prevalence of battering of pregnant women has been estimated to be 8% to 17%.[93,94] There is some evidence of low birth weight among women

## Figure 1

## Profile of Substance Use Among Pregnant Women

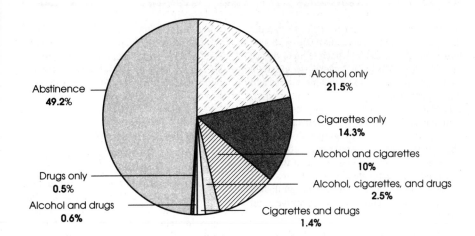

Abstinence
49.2%

Alcohol only
21.5%

Cigarettes only
14.3%

Alcohol and cigarettes
10%

Alcohol, cigarettes, and drugs
2.5%

Cigarettes and drugs
1.4%

Alcohol and drugs
0.6%

Drugs only
0.5%

Source: Adapted from Johnson, S. F., McCarter, R. J., and Ferencz, C. Changes in alcohol, cigarette, and recreational drug use during pregnancy: Implications for intervention. *American Journal of Epidemiology* (1987) 126,4:701. Reprinted with permission of the *American Journal of Epidemiology*.

who have been abused during pregnancy,[95] possibly due to a physical trauma that initiates abruption, infections, or uterine contractions leading to early onset of labor. In addition, victimization of women may lead to a neglect of chronic medical conditions or to later initiation of prenatal care.[94]

## Sexually Transmitted Diseases

Whether or not a woman gets infected with a sexually transmitted disease is highly associated with her sexual behavior and the sexual behavior of her partners. The chance of being infected increases with the number of sexual partners. There is increasing evidence to indicate that various genital infections are associated with low birth weight and preterm delivery.[96] However, the large number of implicated organisms combined with the numerous genital tract sites that they might infect has made the investigation of sexually transmitted diseases and low birth weight very challenging. Aside from the devastating effects on the fetus of untreated syphilis or gonorrhea, few specific organisms or defined genital tract infections have conclusively been shown to be highly correlated with preterm birth or low birth weight.[96] Most of the evidence linking genital organisms or infections to birth outcomes has been inconsistent and has shown only a low to moderate association. Clinical trials of antibiotics aimed at removing the organisms or infections have not consistently improved pregnancy outcomes.[96]

Other maternal infections during pregnancy, such as cytomegalovirus, genitourinary infections, pyelonephritis, and HIV, as well as food- or environmentally-borne infections such as toxoplasmosis and listeriosis, may endanger the health of the mother and fetus.[5,97-99]

## Assessing the Impact of Lifestyle Risk Factors on Maternal and Infant Health

In this section, we try to estimate the number of excess low birth weight or small-for-gestational-age babies born due to maternal lifestyle risk factors. As noted earlier, the risk factors for low birth weight described above do not occur as isolated events; rather, they are part of a complex web of social, environmental, and individual factors. To understand the importance of these individual risk factors, we must try to fit them into a framework that represents a realistic picture of what is occurring in women's lives. This task is made more difficult because of our limited knowledge of the many common risk factors and the many potential interactions between factors which would result in a compounding of adverse effects—such as alcohol abuse and heavy cigarette smoking—as well as the role of protective factors.

### Figure 2

## Prevalence of Low Weight Gain and Substance Use Among Pregnant Women

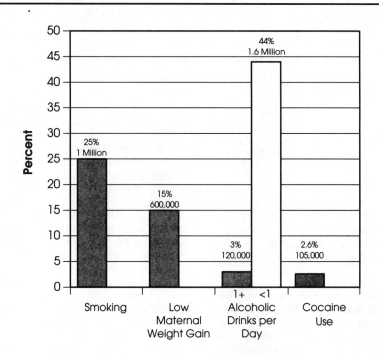

**Maternal Risk Factors**

Source: Chomitz, V. R., Cheung, L., and Lieberman, E. *Healthy mothers—Healthy beginnings.* A white paper prepared by the Center for Health Communication, Harvard School of Public Health, Boston: President and Fellows of Harvard College, 1992.

*The prevalence of battering of pregnant women has been estimated to be 8% to 17%.*

We started by selecting the risk factors that have a consistent relationship with low birth weight and have been shown to be modifiable. These risk factors are cigarette smoking, alcohol abuse, cocaine abuse, and inadequate weight gain during pregnancy. The data on the prevalence of these factors and the risk incurred were derived from a variety of national and regional studies, and thus the estimates presented reflect the demographic and regional profile of the sample used. The estimates are not the result of a meta-analysis, but are based on published analyses that represent conservative and plausible risk.

We estimated the extra adverse birth outcomes attributed to high-risk lifestyle factors by applying the rate of low birth weight deliveries among cigarette smokers, women with inadequate weight gain, alcohol drinkers, and cocaine users, minus a baseline rate

of low birth weight among low-risk women. The effects of reducing stress and exposure to infectious agents cannot be quantified at this time. The numbers we derived are very rough estimates and should be regarded only as order of magnitude estimates.

### Prevalence of Lifestyle Risk Factors

From the literature, we extrapolated estimates of the prevalence of high-risk behaviors among pregnant women to the number of live births in the United States in 1989. Some 20% to 25% of pregnant women, or approximately one million, smoked during pregnancy.[32,33] (See Figure 2.) Approximately 15%, or about 600,000 nonobese women, may have an inadequate total weight gain of less than 22 pounds during their pregnancy. More than 40% of women may not completely abstain from alcohol but consume less than one drink per day during pregnancy; about 3%, or 120,000 women, may have one or more drinks per day.[54] Approximately 105,000, or 2.6% of women, may use cocaine around the time of delivery.[79]

## Excess Adverse Birth Outcomes

In 1990, there were 4,158,212 births in the United States, and 6.97% (approximately 290,000) of these infants were born low birth weight.[100] It comes as no surprise that reducing cigarette smoking has the largest potential to reduce the incidence of low birth weight. Approximately 48,000 low birth weight births could have been prevented if women had not smoked during pregnancy.

Women who failed to gain adequate weight (less than 22 pounds) by term gave birth to approximately 22,000 extra low birth weight babies who were born at full term. Approximately 14,000 infants a year may be born small for their gestational age due to

maternal alcohol consumption, and 10,000 excess low birth weight births could be attributed to prenatal cocaine abuse.

The low birth weight births that are potentially preventable due to smoking, inadequate weight gain, and alcohol use would generally reduce the number of infants who were born too small due to growth retardation but would have little effect on the number of infants born preterm. The lack of a relationship between these risk factors and preterm birth indicates that little improvement in preterm birth rates could be expected with the elimination of these risk factors.

Our estimates of the number of low birth weight births are very rough and may be inaccurate, as these numbers are only as good as our current knowledge of the true relationships between these risk factors and birth outcomes. The number of low birth weight births estimated to be due to each of these factors cannot simply be added together to

derive the total number of births that might be prevented by lifestyle changes because these estimates do not take into consideration the interrelationships among the risk factors. For example, a woman who is a heavy smoker and drinker would be counted twice in these calculations.

## Directions for Future Research: Identifying Barriers to Change

Women face systemic, psychosocial, biological, or knowledge and attitudinal barriers to lifestyle changes. Further research must identify successful strategies for influencing behaviors. Figure 3 illustrates the complexity and interrelationship of common barriers to improving prenatal care and nutritional status, and for modifying smoking, drinking, and drug use.

## Figure 3

## Barriers to Behavioral Change

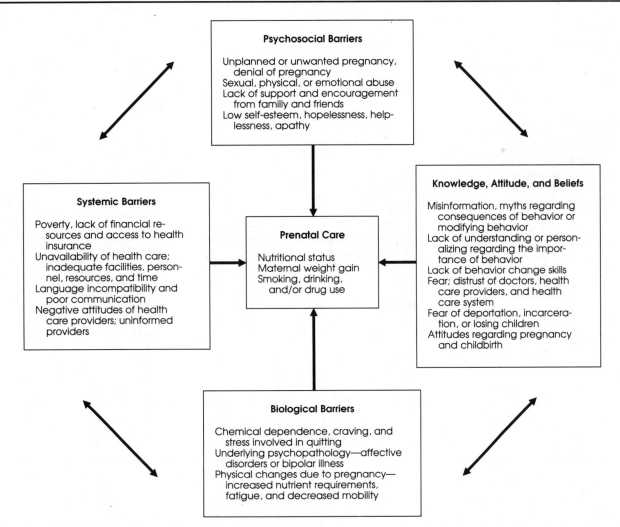

Source: Center for Health Communication, Harvard School of Public Health.

Although some individuals within an economically depressed or stressful situation may be involved in adverse lifestyle behaviors, most women are not. It is therefore important not only to conduct research with those individuals who have less healthy lifestyles, but also to profile and learn from those who, given similar environmental pressures, do not engage in high-risk behaviors or who have been able to change; that is, we

must overcome. Expecting women simply to change or modify their behavior without support and attention from the health care system, society, and influential people in their lives is unrealistic and may help to foster the belief that women are solely to blame for undesirable behaviors.

Barriers to successful intervention will not be overcome in the short term and will require both system-level reform and indi-

Strategies that can reduce the burden of low birth weight do exist. The public and private sectors must work together to define, develop, and implement these strategies.

---

*Pregnancy and the prospect of pregnancy provide a window of opportunity to improve a woman's health before pregnancy, during pregnancy, and after the birth of her child.*

---

must discover the protective strategies or resilience among individuals who are not engaged in adverse lifestyle behaviors, and apply the lessons learned to intervention programs.

## Directions for Prevention/Intervention

Pregnancy and the prospect of pregnancy provide a window of opportunity to improve a woman's health before pregnancy, during pregnancy, and after the birth of her child. Pregnancy provides an opportunity for increased contact with the health care system and is associated with a heightened concern regarding health. Moreover, healthier mothers are more likely to provide more healthful beginnings for their children.

The adoption of healthful lifestyle behaviors before or during pregnancy, such as ceasing to smoke cigarettes, eating foods that supply adequate nutrition and produce an appropriate pregnancy weight gain, ceasing or reducing alcohol consumption, and ceasing illicit drug use, can also positively affect the long-term health of women, future pregnancy outcomes, and the health of children.

The health of the family, in general, may also be improved through household dietary changes and the reduction of environmental risks such as secondhand smoke. However, it must be reiterated that behaviors should not be isolated from the environment (society, community, and family) that fosters and supports them, and thus a change in the elements within the environment will facilitate an individual's ability to change his or her behavior. Despite the importance of maternal behavior modification to the health of mothers, infants, and families, it is important to recognize that there are systemic, biological, psychosocial, and belief and attitudinal barriers to behavioral change which women also

vidual efforts. Many women who smoke, engage in high-risk behaviors, eat poorly, or lack access to health care also live surrounded by poverty and violence, and go without adequate housing or employment. Under such circumstances, living a healthful lifestyle may not be a priority compared with day-to-day survival.

Overcoming these social circumstances will require increased access and availability to quality health care, as well as other affiliated resources and facilities such as child care, social services, law enforcement services, affordable and quality food, transportation, and maternity provisions during employment.

Finding ways to improve maternal and infant health and decrease the low birth weight rate is difficult, at least in part because the known causes of low birth weight are multifactorial, and much of the etiology remains unknown. The independent effects of economic disadvantage and inadequate health care coverage on maternal and infant health are difficult to isolate. In addition, medical risk factors that are identified and managed either before or during pregnancy can positively influence the health of women and their infants. Thus, linking women to continuous health care early in pregnancy or, ideally, before conception is a high priority for intervention.

Health promotion efforts aimed at improving infant health must do so by improving women's health. Improving women's health before, during, and after pregnancy is the key to reducing the human and economic costs associated with infant mortality and morbidity. To improve both women's and infants' health, efforts must target long-term, societal elements that involve policy or legislative changes.

These efforts should include an emphasis on preventive health care services, family-oriented work site options, changes in social norms, and individual behavior modification.

## Notes

1. National Center for Health Statistics. *Advance report of final natality statistics, 1991.* Monthly Vital Statistics Report, Vol. 42, No. 3, Suppl. Hyattsville, MD: Public Health Service, September 9, 1993.
2. Kleinman, J., and Kessel, S. Racial differences in low birthweight: Trends and risk factors. *New England Journal of Medicine* (1987) 317,12:749–53.
3. Ahmed, F. Unmarried mothers as a high-risk group for adverse pregnancy outcomes. *Journal of Community Health* (1990) 15,1:35–44.
4. Bennett, T. Marital status and infant health outcomes. *Social Science Medicine* (1992) 35,9:1179–87.
5. Institute of Medicine, Committee to Study the Prevention of Low Birthweight. *Preventing low birthweight.* Washington, DC: National Academy Press, 1985.
6. McCormick, M. C., Brooks-Gunn, J., Shorter, T., et al. Factors associated with smoking in low income pregnant women: Relationship to birthweight, stressful life events, social support, health behaviors, and mental distress. *Journal of Clinical Epidemiology* (1990) 43:441–48.
7. Brooks-Gunn, J. Support and stress during pregnancy: What do they tell us about low birthweight? In *Advances in the prevention of low birthweight: An international symposium.* H. Berendes, S. Kessel, and S. Yaffe, eds. Washington, DC: National Center for Education in Maternal and Child Health, 1991, pp. 39–60.
8. Collins, Jr., J. W., and David, R. J. The differential effect of traditional risk factors on infant birthweight among blacks and whites in Chicago. *American Journal of Public Health* (1990) 80,6:679.
9. Shiono, P., Klebanoff, M., and Rhoads, G. Smoking and drinking during pregnancy. *Journal of the American Medical Association* (1986) 255:82–84.
10. Geronimus, A. T., and Bound, J. Black/white differences in women's reproductive-related health status: Evidence from vital statistics. *Demography* (1990) 27,3:457–66.
11. Kleinman, J., Fingerhut, L. A., and Prager K. Differences in infant mortality by race, nativity status, and other maternal characteristics. *American Journal of Diseases of Children* (1991) 145:194–99.
12. Moss, N. Demographic and behavioral sciences five year research plan. Draft. Bethesda, MD: National Institute of Child Health and Human Development, 1991.
13. Scholl, T., Hediger, J., Khoo, C., et al. Maternal weight gain, diet and infant birth weight: Correlations during adolescent pregnancy. *Journal of Clinical Epidemiology* (1991) 44:423–28.
14. Susser, M. Maternal weight gain, infant birth weight, and diet: Causal sequences. *American Journal of Clinical Nutrition* (1991) 53,6:1384–96.
15. Kleinman, J. *Maternal weight gain during pregnancy: Determinants and consequences.*

Working Paper No. 33. Hyattsville, MD: National Center for Health Statistics, 1990.

16. Luke, B., Dickinson, C., and Petrie, R. H. Intrauterine growth: Correlations and maternal nutritional status and rate of gestational weight gain. *European Journal of Obstetrics, Gynecology, and Reproductive Biology* (1981) 12:113–21.

17. Kramer, M. S., McLean, F. H., Eason, E. L., and Usher, R. H. Maternal nutrition and spontaneous preterm birth. *American Journal of Epidemiology* (1992) 136:574–83.

18. Kramer, M. S., Coates, A. L., Michoud, M., and Hamilton, E. F. Maternal nutrition and idiopathic preterm labor. *Pediatric Research* (1994) 35,4:277A.

19. National Center for Health Statistics. *Advance report of maternal and infant health data from the birth certificate, 1990.* Monthly Vital Statistics Report, Vol. 42, No. 2, Suppl. Hyattsville, MD: Public Health Service, July 8, 1993.

20. Carruth, B. R., and Skinner, J. D. Practitioners beware: Regional differences in beliefs about nutrition during pregnancy. *Journal of American Dietetic Association* (1991) 91, 4:435–40.

21. Chez, R. Weight gain during pregnancy. *American Journal of Public Health* (1986) 76:1390–91.

22. Keppel, K. G., and Taffel, S. M. Pregnancy-related weight gain and retention: Implications of the 1990 Institute of Medicine Guidelines. *American Journal of Public Health* (1993) 83:1100–1103.

23. Klein, L. Premature birth and maternal prenatal anemia. *American Journal of Obstetrics and Gynecology* (1962) 83,5:588–90.

24. Klebanoff, M. A., Shiono, P. H., Selby, J. V., et al. Anemia and spontaneous preterm birth. *American Journal of Obstetrics and Gynecology* (1991) 164:59–63.

25. Lieberman, E., Ryan, K., Monson, R. R., and Schoenbaum, S. C. Association of maternal hematocrit with premature labor. *American Journal of Obstetrics and Gynecology* (1988) 159:107–14.

26. Klebanoff, J., and Shiono, P. H. Facts and artifacts about anemia and preterm birth. *Journal of the American Medical Association* (1989) 262:511–15.

27. Institute of Medicine, Subcommittee on Nutritional Status and Weight Gain During Pregnancy. *Nutrition during pregnancy.* Washington, DC: National Academy Press, 1990.

28. Dwyer, J. Impact of maternal nutrition on infant health. *Medical Times* (1983) 111:30–38.

29. U.S. Department of Health, Education, and Welfare. *The health consequences of smoking.* DHEW/HSM 73–8704. Washington, DC: DHEW, 1973.

30. Kleinman, J., and Madans, J. H. The effects of maternal smoking, physical stature, and educational attainment on the incidence of low birth weight. *American Journal of Epidemiology* (1985) 121:832–55.

31. National Center for Health Statistics. *Advance report of new data from the 1989 birth certificate, 1989: Final data from the National Center for Health Statistics.* Monthly Vital Statistics Report, Vol. 40, No. 12. Hyattsville, MD: Public Health Service, April 15, 1992.

32. National Center for Health Statistics. *Advance report of final mortality statistics, 1989: Final data from the National Center for Health Statistics.* Monthly Vital Statistics Report, Vol. 40, No. 8, Suppl. 2. Hyattsville, MD: Public Health Service, January 7, 1992.

33. U.S. Department of Health and Human Services. *The health benefits of smoking cessation: A report of the Surgeon General.* DHHS/CDC 90–8416. Washington, DC: DHHS, 1990.

34. Cardoza, L. D., Gibb, D. M. F., Studd, J. W. W., and Cooper, D. J. Social and obstetric features associated with smoking in pregnancy. *British Journal of Obstetrics and Gynecology* (1982) 89:622–27.

35. See note no. 32, National Center for Health Statistics, for mortality statistics in 1989.

36. Butler, N., Goldstein, H., and Ross, E. Cigarette smoking in pregnancy: Its influence on birth weight and perinatal mortality. *British Medical Journal* (1972) 2:127–30.

37. Kramer, M. S. Determinants of low birth weight: Methodological assessment and meta-analysis. *Bulletin of the World Health Organization* (1987) 65:663–737.

38. Martin, T., and Bracken, M. Association of low birth weight with passive smoke exposure in pregnancy. *American Journal of Epidemiology* (1986) 124:633–42.

39. Rush, D., and Cassano, P. Relationship of cigarette smoking and social class to birth weight and perinatal mortality among all births in Britain, 5–11 April 1970. *Journal of Epidemiology and Community Health* (1983) 37:249–55.

40. Wilner, S., Secker-Walker, R. H., Flynn, B. S., et al. How to help the pregnant woman stop smoking. In *Smoking and reproductive health.* M. J. Rosenberg, ed. Littleton, MA: PSG Publishing, 1987, pp. 215–22.

41. Fingerhut, L. A., Kleinman, J. C., and Kendrick, J. S. Smoking before, during, and after pregnancy. *American Journal of Public Health* (1990) 80:541–44.

42. Waterson, E. J., and Murray-Lyon, I. M. Drinking and smoking patterns amongst women attending an antenatal clinic—II. During pregnancy. *Alcohol and Alcoholism* (1989) 24,2:163–73.

43. Windsor, R. *The handbook to plan, implement and evaluate smoking cessation programs for pregnant women.* White Plains, NY: March of Dimes Birth Defects Foundation, 1990.

44. Condon, J. T., and Hilton, C. A. A comparison of smoking and drinking behaviors in pregnant women: Who abstains and why. *Medical Journal of Australia* (1988) 148:381–85.

45. Burns, D., and Pierce, J. P. *Tobacco use in California 1990–1991.* Sacramento: California Department of Health Services, 1992.

46. Brandt, E. N. Smoking and reproductive health. In *Smoking and reproductive health.* M. J. Rosenberg, ed. Littleton, MA: PSG Publishing, 1987, pp 1–3.

47. Weitzman, M., Gortmaker, S., Walker, D. K., and Sobol, A. Maternal smoking and childhood asthma. *Pediatrics* (1990) 85:505–11.

48. U.S. Department of Health and Human Services. *Reducing the health consequences of smoking: A report of the Surgeon General.* DHHS/CDC 89–8411. Rockville, MD: DHHS, 1989.

49. Samet, J. M., Lewit, E. M., and Warner, K. E. Involuntary smoking and children's health. *The Future of Children (Winter 1994)* 4,3:94–114.

50. Serdula, M., Williamson, D., Kendrick, J., et al. Trends in alcohol consumption by pregnant women. *Journal of the American Medical Association* (1991) 265:876–79.

51. Ouellette, E. M., Rosett, H. L., Rosman, N. P., and Weiner, L. Adverse effects on offspring of maternal alcohol abuse during pregnancy. *New England Journal of Medicine* (1977) 297,10:528–30.

52. Abel, E. L., and Sokol, R. J. Incidence of fetal alcohol syndrome and economic impact of FAS-related anomalies. *Drug and Alcohol Dependence* (1987) 19:51–70.

53. Day, N. L., Jasperse, D., Richardson, G., et al. Prenatal exposure to alcohol: Effect on infant growth and morphologic characteristics. *Pediatrics* (1989) 84,3:536–41.

54. Mills, J. L., Graubard, B. I., Harley, E. E., et al. Maternal alcohol consumption and birth weight: How much drinking during pregnancy is safe? *Journal of the American Medical Association* (1984) 252,14:1875–79.

55. Larroque, B., Kaminski, M., Lelong, N., et al. Effects on birth weight of alcohol and caffeine consumption during pregnancy. *American Journal of Epidemiology* (1993) 137:941–50.

56. Halmesmaki, E., Raivio, K., and Ylikorkala, O. Patterns of alcohol consumption during pregnancy. *Obstetrics and Gynecology* (1987) 69:594–97.

57. Little, R., Asker, R. L., Sampson, P. D., and Renwick, J. H. Fetal growth and moderate drinking in early pregnancy. *American Journal of Epidemiology* (1986) 123,2:270–78.

58. Streissguth, A. P., Bookstein, F. L., Sampson, P. D., and Barr, H. M. Neurobehavioral effects of prenatal alcohol: Part III. PLS analyses of neuropsychologic tests. *Neurotoxicology and Teratology* (1989) 11,5:493–507.

59. Streissguth, A. P., Barr, H. M., and Sampson, P. D. Moderate prenatal alcohol exposure: Effects on child IQ and learning problems at age 7½ years. *Alcoholism, Clinical and Experimental Research* (1990) 14,5:662–69.

60. Walpole, I., Zubrick, S., and Pontre, J. Is there a fetal effect with low to moderate alcohol use before or during pregnancy? *Journal of Epidemiology and Community Health* (1990) 44,4:297–301.

61. Ernhart, C. B., Sokol. R. J., Ager, J. W., et al. Alcohol-related birth defects: Assessing the risk. *Annals of the New York Academy of Sciences* (1989) 562:159–72.

62. Johnson, S. F., McCarter, R. J., and Ferencz, C. Changes in alcohol, cigarette, and recreational drug use during pregnancy: Implications for intervention. *American Journal of Epidemiology* (1987) 126,4:695–702.

63. Little, R. Schultz, F., and Mandell, W. Alcohol consumption during pregnancy. *Journal of Studies on Alcohol* (1976) 37:375–79.

64. Russell, M. Drinking and pregnancy: A review of current research. *New York State Journal of Medicine* (1983) 8:1218–21.

65. See note no. 56, Halmesmaki, Raivio, and Ylikorkala, for more information about alcohol consumption patterns during pregnancy.

66. Lecos, C. Caffeine jitters: Some safety questions remain. *FDA Consumer* (December 1987/January 1988) 21:22.

67. Shiono, P. H., and Klebanoff, M. A. Invited commentary: Caffeine and birth outcomes. *American Journal of Epidemiology* (1993) 137:951–54.

68. Zuckerman, B., Frank, D. A., Hingson, R., et al. Effects of maternal marijuana and cocaine use on fetal growth. *New England Journal of Medicine* (1989) 320:762–68.

69. Zelson, C., Rubio, E., and Wasserman, E. Neonatal narcotic addiction: 10 year observation. *Pediatrics* (1971) 48,2:178–89.

70. Fricker, H., and Segal, S. Narcotic addiction, pregnancy, and the newborn. *American Journal of Diseases of Children* (1978) 132:360–66.

71. Lifschitz, M., Wilson, G., Smith, E., et al. Fetal and postnatal growth of children born to narcotic-dependent women. *Journal of Pediatrics* (1983) 102:686–91.

72. Robins, L. N., and Mills, J. L., Krulewitch, C., and Herman, A. A. Effects of in utero exposure to street drugs. *American Journal of Public Health* (December 1993) 83,12:S9.

73. Oleske, J. Experiences with 118 infants born to narcotic-using mothers. *Clinical Pediatrics* (1977) 16:418–23.

74. Dattel, B. J. Substance abuse in pregnancy. *Seminars in Perinatology* (1990) 14,2:179–87.

75. Bateman, D. A., Ng, S. K. C., Hansen, C. A., and Heagarty, M. C. The effects of intrauterine cocaine exposure in newborns. *American Journal of Public Health* (1993) 83,2:190–93.

76. Office for Substance Abuse Prevention. *Alcohol and other drugs can harm an unborn baby: Fact sheet and resource list.* Rockville, MD: National Clearinghouse for Alcohol and Drug Information, 1989, pp 1–19.

77. Fried, P. A., and Makin, J. E. Neonatal behavioral correlates of prenatal exposure to marijuana, cigarettes and alcohol in a low risk population. *Neurotoxicology and Teratology* (1986) 9:1–7.

78. Chasnoff, I. J., Landress, H. J., and Barrett, M. E. The prevalence of illicit-drug or alcohol use during pregnancy and discrepancies in mandatory reporting in Pinellas County, Florida. *New England Journal of Medicine* (1990) 322:1202–6.

79. Centers for Disease Control and Prevention. Statewide prevalence of illicit drug use by pregnant women—Rhode Island. *Morbidity and Mortality Weekly Report* (1990) 39,14:225–27.

80. Handler, A., Kistin, N., Davis, F., and Ferré, C. Cocaine use during pregnancy: Perinatal outcomes. *American Journal of Epidemiology* (1991) 133:818–25.

81. Zeitel, L., Bauer, T. A., and Brooks, P. *Infants at risk: Solutions within our reach.* New York: Greater New York March of Dimes/United Hospital Fund of New York, 1991.

82. U.S. General Accounting Office. *Drug abuse: The crack cocaine epidemic: Health consequences and treatment.* HRD-91–55FS. Washington, DC: GAO, 1991.

83. McCaul, M. E., Svikis, D. S., and Feng, T. Pregnancy and addition: Outcomes and interventions. *Maryland Medical Journal* (1991) 40:995–1001.

84. Newberger, E. H., Barkan, S. E., Leiberman, E. S., et al. Abuse of pregnant women and adverse birth outcome: Current knowledge and implications for practice. *Journal of the American Medical Association* (1992) 267,17:2370–72.

85. McAnarney, E. R., and Stevens-Simon, C. Maternal psychological stress/depression and low birth weight. *American Journal of Diseases of Children* (1990) 144:789–92.

86. Katch, F. I., and McArdle, W. E. *Introduction to nutrition, exercise and health.* 4th ed. Philadelphia: Lea and Febiger, 1993.

87. Dewey, K. G., and McCrory, M. A. Effects of dieting and physical activity on pregnancy and lactation. *American Journal of Clinical Nutrition* (1994) 59:446S–53S.

88. Jovanovic-Peterson, L., Durak, E. P., and Peterson, C. M. Randomized trial of diet versus diet plus cardiovascular conditioning on glucose levels in gestational diabetes. *American Journal of Obstetrics and Gynecology* (1989) 161:415–19.

89. Hall, D. C., and Kaufmann, D. A. Effects of aerobic and strength conditioning on pregnancy outcomes. *American Journal of Obstetrics and Gynecology* (1987) 157:1199–1203.

90. U.S. Bureau of the Census. *Work and family patterns of American women.* Current Population Reports, Series P-23, No. 165. Washington, DC: U.S. Government Printing Office, 1990.

91. Poerksen, A., and Petitti, D. B. Employment and low birth weight in black women. *Social Science and Medicine* (1991) 33:1281–96.

92. Simpson, J. L., Are physical activity and employment related to preterm birth and low birth weight? *American Journal of Obstetrics and Gynecology* (1993) 168:1231–38.

93. Helton, A. S., McFarlane, J., and Anderson, E. T. Battered and pregnant: A prevalence study. *American Journal of Public Health* (1987) 77,10:1337–39.

94. Mcfarlane, J., Parker, B., Soeken, K., and Bullock, L. Assessing for abuse during pregnancy: Severity and frequency of injuries and associated entry into prenatal care. *Journal of the American Medical Association* (1992) 267,23:3176–78.

95. Bullock, L. F., and Mcfarlane, J. The birthweight/battering connection. *American Journal of Nursing* (September 1989):1153–55.

96. Gibbs, R. S., Romero, R., Hillier, S. L., et al. A review of premature birth and subclinical infection. *American Journal of Obstetrics and Gynecology* (1992) 166:1515–28.

97. Carroll, J. C. Chalmaydia trachomatis during pregnancy: To screen or not to screen? *Canadian Family Physician* (1993) 39:97–102.

98. Kramer, M. S. The etiology and prevention of low birthweight: Current knowledge and priorities for future research. In *Advances in the prevention of low birthweight: An international symposium.* H. Berendes, S. Kessel, and S. Yaffe, eds. Washington, DC: National Center for Education in Maternal and Child Health, 1991, pp. 25–39.

99. Zygmunt, D. J. Toxoplasma gondii. *Infection Control and Hospital Epidemiology* (1990) 11,4:207–11.

100. Wegman, M. E. Annual summary of vital statistics—1992. *Pediatrics* (1993) 92,6:743–54.

# A State of the Art
## *Pregnancy*

**New prenatal tests detect problems earlier and more accurately. They may even foretell the health of the adult the baby will become. By Karen Springen**

WHEN SHE WAS NEARLY halfway into her pregnancy, Lisa Lahti, now 31, got the news that every parent-to-be dreads: a routine blood-screening test showed that she was at increased risk of delivering a child with Down syndrome. To learn conclusively, both Lahti's OB-GYN and a geneticist recommended amniocentesis. In the amnio, a doctor would insert a thin needle through Lahti's abdomen to extract two tablespoons of fluid from the sac holding the fetus. A lab would analyze the fluid, which contains the baby's cells and chromosomes, and make a definitive diagnosis. But Lahti turned down the amnio: she and her husband, Daryl, "wouldn't abort in any situation," she explains. Her son, Jacob, now 18 months, was born completely healthy. It turns out that the $50 blood test she took has a false-positive rate of one in 20.

More than half of the 3.9 million pregnant women in the United States will nevertheless take this blood test, and 125,000 will undergo an amnio. But the popularity of the tests belies their shortcomings. First and foremost: neither the blood-screening test nor amniocentesis can be done before the second trimester. Amnios performed earlier than 15 weeks into pregnancy put women at higher risk of miscarrying, leaking amniotic fluid and delivering a baby with a severe clubfoot. Even chorionic villus sampling, in which a highly trained doctor extracts tiny parts of the placenta for chromosomal testing, cannot be done earlier than 10 weeks into pregnancy—and results take at least seven days to come back. "If you're going to end pregnancies, earlier is better," says Arthur Caplan, director of the Center of Biomedical Ethics at the University of Pennsylvania. That's why the push is on for more accurate, earlier prenatal tests. They are just one of the high-tech tools that are giving women a better chance than ever of having a safe pregnancy and a healthy newborn.

Parents in the new millennium will trade their current blurry ultrasound pictures for clearer, three-dimensional photos of their fetuses. But the goal isn't to start the baby album with a better picture. Rather, the new 3-D machines should provide more precise images of the fetal brain and heart, and detect hard-to-spot abnormalities such as cleft lip and palate (one in 930 births) and clubfeet (one in 735).

Ultrasound can also be combined with a blood test for an even clearer crystal ball. Scientists are studying whether the combination can tell if a 10- to 14-week fetus is likely to have either Down syndrome or a form of severe mental retardation called trisomy 18. The ultrasound looks for loose skin in the neck of the fetus, which indicates the presence of three chromosome 21s, and hence Down syndrome. It detects more cases, and can be done earlier, than existing tests for these conditions. "The vast majority of women are going to leave [after the test] feeling good about their pregnancy," says Eugene Pergament, director of reproductive genetics at Northwestern University.

Another test that will be done early in pregnancy analyzes maternal blood. Fetal cells, it turns out, leak into the mother's circulatory system. Although the cells are few and far between, "for the past several years [we have] been trying to find these needles in the haystack," says Mark I. Evans, acting chairman of OB-GYN at Wayne State University in Detroit. Now researchers are getting better at it. Within a decade, fetal DNA analysis "could replace everything" from blood-screening tests to amnios, says Dr. Ronald Wapner, director of maternal fetal medicine at Jefferson Medical Col-

# Ten Tips to a Healthy Start

*Most of the 3.9 million women in the United States who gave birth last year had healthy babies. Here are some steps to increase the excellent odds that you will, too.*

**1** Nutrition: Sorry, you're still eating for one, not two. An average pregnant woman needs only 300 more calories per day than her usual 2,200. Make every calorie count. Folic acid, starting at least a month before conception, helps prevent neural-tube defects. Get 400 micrograms a day, from leafy greens like spinach (130 micrograms per half cup, boiled) or supplements. To make sure the fetus gets plenty of oxygen, choose iron-rich foods, such as red meat and enriched cereals. Vitamin C helps iron absorption. Try to get 1,000 mg of calcium a day (a cup of nonfat plain yogurt contains 450).

**2** Vitamins: Avoid megadoses. More than 10,000 IUs of vitamin A, for example, can cause birth defects.

**3** Alcohol: Abstain. No one knows how much alcohol is safe to drink during pregnancy. Alcohol reaches the fetus through the placenta and can restrict growth and cause cardiac defects and facial malformations. It's the most common nongenetic causes of mental retardation.

**4** Smoking: Stop. Tobacco users are more likely to miscarry and to deliver small, preterm babies with a higher risk of ear infections, colds, heart problems, upper respiratory infections and sudden infant death syndrome (SIDS).

**5** Weight gain: Most women should gain 25 to 35 pounds. Underweight women should gain 28 to 40; overweight women, 15 to 25. Women who gain too little are more likely to have smaller babies.

**6** Exercise: Avoid sports such as racquetball that expose the abdomen to potential trauma. Many doctors advise against Rollerblading, skiing or bicycling after 20 weeks, since growing bellies make it easier to fall and damage the uterus. Walk, swim, run. But check your pulse to make sure your heart isn't beating more than 140 times a minute for more than 20 minutes; that can divert too much blood from the fetus.

**7** Sex: Enjoy it. Amniotic fluid cushions the fetus.

**8** Medicine: Acetaminophen is fine, but ibuprofen in the third trimester may increase the risk of prolonged gestation and labor, and can in rare instances cause pulmonary hypertension in newborns. The acne drug Accutane can cause cleft palate, small ears and brain malformations. Tetracycline in the second half of pregnancy can yellow a baby's teeth.

**9** STDs: Get checked for HIV, syphilis and gonorrhea—ideally before conception. Gonorrhea can infect the baby's eyes at birth; syphilis can cause congenital malformations. Medications can significantly cut the risk of transmitting AIDS to a baby.

**10** Seat belts: Not wearing them is a leading cause of fetal death. In an accident, a belt is far less likely than a windshield to hurt the baby.

SOURCES: DR. LARRY C. GILSTRAP; ACOG

---

lege in Philadelphia. Parents would learn about chromosomal abnormalities weeks earlier than now.

And that's not all they would learn. Fetal DNA holds the child's genetic blueprint, and with a new invention physicians will be able to read it. The device is called a DNA chip, or "biochip." It consists of thousands of strands of DNA. When a sample of blood is dropped onto the chip, DNA in the blood matches up with DNA on the chip. A laser reads the chip, and thus can tell whether the fetus carries virtually any gene that scientists have identified. That means physicians will be able to tell if a fetus is at risk for disorders such as Down syndrome, as well as hundreds of genetic diseases that strike only in adulthood, such as Alzheimer's and cancer.

Eventually embryos conceived through in vitro fertilization could be tested before being implanted in the mother-to-be. Couples could opt not to implant ones at high risk for, say, juvenile diabetes or breast cancer. Yet this "advance" raises troublesome ethical issues. "I could see society saying, 'We don't want to pay [to treat] any babies with genetic diseases. You could have prevented them'," says Caplan.

Even more important than detecting problems is treating them. Highly trained surgeons now operate on fetuses about a dozen times a year, repairing hernias, lung malformations, urinary-tract obstructions and spina bifida, a condition that leaves an opening near the spinal cord and causes paralysis. Working with cameralike "endoscopes" and instruments that pass through the uterine wall without making an incision, doctors hope to correct cleft lip and palate, too. Some surgeons even foresee performing open-heart surgery on fetuses. Still, fetal surgery remains controversial largely because it can cause preterm birth. "It really hasn't revolutionized obstetrics in terms of changing overall outcome for any great number of people," cautions OB-GYN Fredric Frigoletto, chief of obstetrics at Massachusetts General Hospital. But advocates say it's far cheaper to correct birth defects before delivery than to provide a lifetime of care.

When all the tests point to a healthy fetus, just about the only worry left is preterm labor, the No.

1 problem in obstetrics. Some 10 percent of U.S. babies are born less than 37 weeks into pregnancy, which increases the risk of everything from blindness and deafness to cerebral palsy. "The damage that preterm birth causes can last for life," says James McGregor, professor of OB-GYN at the University of Colorado at Denver. "If you can get close to 37 weeks, you're kind of in the clear. You don't get brain damage. You don't get lung damage. You don't have increased risk of cerebral palsy." To avoid all that, a $90 test measures the amount of a form of estrogen called estriol in a pregnant woman's saliva. Estriol levels usually start climbing three weeks before labor. Women at risk for early delivery (because of cramping, illness, a fetal abnormality or a previous early delivery) can now simply provide about a tablespoon of saliva and learn their estriol level within two days. If the level indicates they are about to go into labor, and if it's not time for that, the obstetrician can try to figure out why and treat the cause. To help detect other conditions that can trigger early delivery, some doctors are also performing a $100 test for high levels of a molecule called fibronectin. (They collect it from the cervix with a Q-Tip.) A high level of fibronectin means the uterus is separating from the (probably inflamed) amniotic sac. Moms are vigorously treated for the infection, which can otherwise precipitate early labor.

And who would have guessed that the space program would help prevent preterm deliveries? Scientists at NASA have created a 1½-inch pill-shaped transmitter—implanted into the uterus about 27 weeks into pregnancy—that measures contractions. They're also working on transmitters to measure fetal acidity, temperature and heart rate, all of which reflect the fetus's health. If the transmitter costs $1,000 and saves $300,000 in medical costs from problems caused by a preterm birth, it's well worth it, argues John Hines of NASA's Ames Research Center.

Expect changes even in electronic fetal monitoring, used to detect babies' heart rate during labor. Now the monitors are used on 98 percent of pregnant women. The heart rate supposedly shows whether the baby is getting enough oxygen. If he is not, most obstetricians order an emergency Caesarean section. But a device under development would directly measure how much oxygen the fetus is receiving, rather than making an educated guess based on the heart rate, which can raise false alarms. If the fetus is getting plenty of oxygen after all, despite a high heart rate, the mom could continue natural labor instead of undergoing a C-section. For that's the goal of all these tests anyway: making sure that the fetus is developing normally and setting the mother-to-be's mind at ease.

# pFsSEYTcAHLOLOGY

> **Behaviorally speaking, there's little difference between a newborn baby and a 32-week-old fetus. A new wave of research suggests that the fetus can feel, dream, even enjoy *The Cat in the Hat*. The abortion debate may never be the same.**
>
> **By Janet L. Hopson**

The scene never fails to give goose bumps: the baby, just seconds old and still dewy from the womb, is lifted into the arms of its exhausted but blissful parents. They gaze adoringly as their new child stretches and squirms, scrunches its mouth and opens its eyes. To anyone watching this tender vignette, the message is unmistakable. Birth is the beginning of it all, ground zero, the moment from which the clock starts ticking. Not so, declares Janet DiPietro. Birth may be a grand occasion, says the Johns Hopkins University psychologist, but "it is a trivial event in development. Nothing neurologically interesting happens."

Armed with highly sensitive and sophisticated monitoring gear, DiPietro and other researchers today are discovering that the real action starts weeks earlier. At 32 weeks of gestation—two months before a baby is considered fully prepared for the world, or "at term"—a fetus is behaving almost exactly as a newborn. And it continues to do so for the next 12 weeks.

As if overturning the common conception of infancy weren't enough, scientists are creating a startling new picture of intelligent life in the womb. Among the revelations:

• By nine weeks, a developing fetus can hiccup and react to loud noises. By the end of the second trimester it can hear.

• Just as adults do, the fetus experiences the rapid eye movement (REM) sleep of dreams.

• The fetus savors its mother's meals, first picking up the food tastes of a culture in the womb.

## A fetus spends hours in the rapid eye movement sleep of dreams.

• Among other mental feats, the fetus can distinguish between the voice of Mom and that of a stranger, and respond to a familiar story read to it.

• Even a premature baby is aware, feels, responds, and adapts to its environment.

• Just because the fetus is responsive to certain stimuli doesn't mean that it should be the target of efforts to enhance development. Sensory stimulation of the fetus can in fact lead to bizarre patterns of adaptation later on.

The roots of human behavior, researchers now know, begin to develop early—just weeks after conception, in fact. Well before a woman typically knows she is pregnant, her embryo's brain has already begun to bulge. By five weeks, the organ that looks like a lumpy inchworm has already embarked on the most spectacular feat of human development: the creation of the deeply creased and convoluted cerebral cortex, the part of the brain that will eventually allow the growing person to move, think, speak, plan, and create in a human way.

At nine weeks, the embryo's ballooning brain allows it to bend its body, hiccup, and react to loud sounds. At week ten, it moves its arms, "breathes" amniotic fluid in and out, opens its jaw, and stretches. Before the first trimester is over, it yawns, sucks, and swallows as well as feels and smells. By the end of the second trimester, it can hear; toward the end of pregnancy, it can see.

## FETAL ALERTNESS

Scientists who follow the fetus' daily life find that it spends most of its time not exercising these new abilities but sleeping. At 32 weeks, it drowses 90 to 95% of the day. Some of these hours are spent in deep sleep, some in REM sleep, and some in an indeterminate state, a product of the fetus' immature brain that is different from sleep in a baby, child, or adult. During REM sleep, the fetus' eyes move back and forth just as an adult's eyes do, and many researchers believe that it is dreaming. DiPietro speculates that fetuses dream about what they know—the sensations they feel in the womb.

Closer to birth, the fetus sleeps 85 to 90% of the time, the same as a newborn. Between its frequent naps, the fetus seems to have "something like an awake alert period," according to developmental psychologist William Fifer, Ph.D., who with his Columbia University colleagues is monitoring these sleep and wakefulness cycles in order to identify patterns of normal and abnormal brain development, including potential predictors of

sudden infant death syndrome. Says Fifer, "We are, in effect, asking the fetus: 'Are you paying attention? Is your nervous system behaving in the appropriate way?'"

## FETAL MOVEMENT

Awake or asleep, the human fetus moves 50 times or more each hour, flexing and extending its body, moving its head, face, and limbs and exploring its warm wet compartment by touch. Heidelise Als, Ph.D., a developmental psychologist at Harvard Medical School, is fascinated by the amount of tactile stimulation a fetus gives itself. "It touches a hand to the face, one hand to the other hand, clasps its feet, touches its foot to its leg, its hand to its umbilical cord," she reports.

Als believes there is a mismatch between the environment given to preemies in hospitals and the environment they would have had in the womb. She has been working for years to change the care given to preemies so that they can curl up, bring their knees together, and touch things with their hands as they would have for weeks in the womb.

Along with such common movements, DiPietro has also noted some odder fetal activities, including "licking the uterine wall and literally walking around the womb by pushing off with its feet." Laterborns may have more room in the womb for such maneuvers than first babies. After the initial pregnancy, a woman's uterus is bigger and the umbilical cord longer, allowing more freedom of movement. "Second and subsequent children may develop more motor experience in utero and so may become more active infants," DiPietro speculates.

Fetuses react sharply to their mother's actions. "When we're watching the fetus on ultrasound and the mother starts to laugh, we can see the fetus, floating upside down in the womb, bounce up and down on its head, bum-bum-bum, like it's bouncing on a trampoline," says DiPietro. "When mothers watch this on the screen, they laugh harder, and the fetus goes up and down even faster. We've wondered whether this is why people grow up liking roller coasters."

## FETAL TASTE

Why people grow up liking hot chilies or spicy curries may also have something to do with the fetal environment. By 13 to 15 weeks a fetus' taste buds already look like a mature adult's, and doctors know that the amniotic

**By 15 weeks, a fetus has an adult's taste buds and may be able to savor its mother's meals.**

# What's the Impact on Abortion?

Though research in fetal psychology focuses on the last trimester, when most abortions are illegal, the thought of a fetus dreaming, listening and responding to its mother's voice is sure to add new complexity to the debate. The new findings undoubtedly will strengthen the convictions of right-to-lifers—and they may shake the certainty of pro-choice proponents who believe that mental life begins at birth.

Many of the scientists engaged in studying the fetus, however, remain detached from the abortion controversy, insisting that their work is completely irrelevant to the debate.

"I don't think that fetal research informs the issue at all," contends psychologist Janet DiPietro of Johns Hopkins University. "The essence of the abortion debate is: When does life begin? Some people believe it begins at conception, the other extreme believes that it begins after the baby is born, and there's a group in the middle that believes it begins at around 24 or 25 weeks, when a fetus can live outside of the womb, though it needs a lot of help to do so.

"Up to about 25 weeks, whether or not it's sucking its thumb or has personality or all that, the fetus cannot survive outside of its mother. So is that life, or not? That is a moral, ethical, and religious question, not one for science. Things

can behave and not be alive. Right-to-lifers may say that this research proves that a fetus is alive, but it does not. It cannot."

"Fetal research only changes the abortion debate for people who think that life starts at some magical point," maintains Heidelise Als, a psychologist at Harvard University. "If you believe that life begins at conception, then you don't need the proof of fetal behavior." For others, however, abortion is a very complex issue and involves far more than whether research shows that a fetus hiccups. "Your circumstances and personal beliefs have much more impact on the decision," she observes.

Like DiPietro, Als realizes that "people may use this research as an emotional way to draw people to the pro-life side, but it should not be used by belligerent activists." Instead, she believes, it should be applied to helping mothers have the healthiest pregnancy possible and preparing them to best parent their child. Columbia University psychologist William Fifer, Ph.D., agrees. "The research is much more relevant for issues regarding viable fetuses—preemies."

Simply put, say the three, their work is intended to help the babies that live—not to decide whether fetuses should.—*Camille Chatterjee*

---

fluid that surrounds it can smell strongly of curry, cumin, garlic, onion and other essences from a mother's diet. Whether fetuses can taste these flavors isn't yet known, but scientists have found that a 33-week-old preemie will suck harder on a sweetened nipple than on a plain rubber one.

"During the last trimester, the fetus is swallowing up to a liter a day" of amniotic fluid, notes Julie Mennella, Ph.D., a biopsychologist at the Monell Chemical Senses Center in Philadelphia. She thinks the fluid may act as a "flavor bridge" to breast milk, which also carries food flavors from the mother's diet.

## FETAL HEARING

Whether or not a fetus can taste, there's little question that it can hear. A very premature baby entering the world at 24 to 25 weeks responds to the sounds around it, observes Als, so its auditory apparatus must already have been functioning in the womb. Many pregnant women report a fetal jerk or sudden kick just after a door slams or a car backfires.

Even without such intrusions, the womb is not a silent place. Researchers who have inserted a hydrophone into the uterus of a pregnant woman have picked up a noise level "akin to the background noise in an apartment," according to DiPietro. Sounds include the whooshing of blood in the mother's vessels, the gurgling and rumbling of her stomach and intestines, as well as the tones of her

voice filtered through tissues, bones, and fluid, and the voices of other people coming through the amniotic wall. Fifer has found that fetal heart rate slows when the mother is speaking, suggesting that the fetus not only hears and recognizes the sound, but is calmed by it.

## FETAL VISION

Vision is the last sense to develop. A very premature infant can see light and shape; researchers presume that a fetus has the same ability. Just as the womb isn't completely quiet, it isn't utterly dark, either. Says Fifer: "There may be just enough visual stimulation filtered through the mother's tissues that a fetus can respond when the mother is in bright light," such as when she is sunbathing.

Japanese scientists have even reported a distinct fetal reaction to flashes of light shined on the mother's belly. However, other researchers warn that exposing fetuses (or premature infants) to bright light before they are ready can be dangerous. In fact, Harvard's Als believes that retinal damage in premature infants, which has long been ascribed to high concentrations of oxygen, may actually be due to overexposure to light at the wrong time in development.

A six-month fetus, born about 14 weeks too early, has a brain that is neither prepared for nor expecting signals from the eyes to be transmitted into the brain's visual cortex, and from there into the executive-branch frontal

A fetus prefers hearing Mom's voice over a stranger's—speaking in her native, not a foreign tongue—and being read aloud familiar tales rather than new stories.

lobes, where information is integrated. When the fetus is forced to see too much too soon, says Als, the accelerated stimulation may lead to aberrations of brain development.

## FETAL LEARNING

Along with the ability to feel, see, and hear comes the capacity to learn and remember. These activities can be rudimentary, automatic, even biochemical. For example, a fetus, after an initial reaction of alarm, eventually stops responding to a repeated loud noise. The fetus displays the same kind of primitive learning, known as habituation, in response to its mother's voice, Fifer has found.

But the fetus has shown itself capable of far more. In the 1980s, psychology professor Anthony James DeCasper, Ph.D., and colleagues at the University of North Carolina at Greensboro, devised a feeding contraption that allows a baby to suck faster to hear one set of sounds through headphones and to suck slower to hear a different set. With this technique, DeCasper discovered that within hours of birth, a baby already prefers its mother's voice to a stranger's, suggesting it must have learned and remembered the voice, albeit not necessarily consciously, from its last months in the womb. More recently, he's found that a newborn prefers a story read to it repeatedly in the womb—in this case, *The Cat in the Hat*—over a new story introduced soon after birth.

DeCasper and others have uncovered more mental feats. Newborns can not only distinguish their mother from a stranger speaking, but would rather hear Mom's voice, especially the way it sounds filtered through amniotic fluid rather than through air. They're xenophobes, too: they prefer to hear Mom speaking in her native language than to hear her or someone else speaking in a foreign tongue.

By monitoring changes in fetal heart rate, psychologist Jean-Pierre Lecanuet, Ph.D., and his colleagues in Paris have found that fetuses can even tell strangers' voices apart. They also seem to like certain stories more than others. The fetal heartbeat will slow down when a familiar French fairy tale such as *"La Poulette"* ("The Chick") or *"Le Petit Crapaud"* ("The Little Toad"), is read near the mother's belly. When the same reader delivers another unfamiliar story, the fetal heartbeat stays steady.

The fetus is likely responding to the cadence of voices and stories, not their actual words, observes Fifer, but the conclusion is the same: the fetus can listen, learn, and remember at some level, and, as with most babies and children, it likes the comfort and reassurance of the familiar.

## FETAL PERSONALITY

It's no secret that babies are born with distinct differences and patterns of activity that suggest individual temperament. Just when and how the behavioral traits originate in the womb is now the subject of intense scrutiny.

In the first formal study of fetal temperament in 1996, DiPietro and her colleagues recorded the heart rate and movements of 31 fetuses six times before birth and compared them to readings taken twice after birth. (They've since extended their study to include 100 more fetuses.) Their findings: fetuses that are very active in the womb tend to be more irritable infants. Those with irregular sleep/wake patterns in the womb sleep more poorly as young infants. And fetuses with high heart rates become unpredictable, inactive babies.

"Behavior doesn't begin at birth," declares DiPietro. "It begins before and develops in predictable ways." One of the most important influences on development is the fetal environment. As Harvard's Als observes, "The fetus gets an enormous amount of 'hormonal bathing' through the mother, so its chronobiological rhythms are influenced by the mother's sleep/wake cycles, her eating patterns, her movements."

The hormones a mother puts out in response to stress also appear critical. DiPietro finds that highly pressured mothers-to-be tend to have more active fetuses—and more irritable infants. "The most stressed are working pregnant women," says DiPietro. "These days, women tend to work up to the day they deliver, even though the implications for pregnancy aren't entirely clear yet. That's our cultural norm, but I think it's insane."

Als agrees that working can be an enormous stress, but emphasizes that pregnancy hormones help to buffer both mother and fetus. Individual reactions to stress also matter. "The pregnant woman who chooses to work is a different woman already from the one who chooses not to work," she explains.

She's also different from the woman who has no choice but to work. DiPietro's studies show that the fetuses of poor women are distinct neurobehaviorally—less active, with a less variable heart rate—from the fetuses of middle-class women. Yet "poor women rate themselves as less stressed than do working middle-class women," she notes. DiPietro suspects that inadequate nutrition and exposure to pollutants may significantly affect the fetuses of poor women.

Stress, diet, and toxins may combine to have a harmful effect on intelligence. A recent study by biostatistician Bernie Devlin, Ph.D., of the University of Pittsburgh, suggests that genes may have less impact on IQ than previously thought and that the environment of the womb may account for much more. "Our old notion of nature influencing the fetus before birth and nurture after birth needs an update," DiPietro insists. "There is an antenatal environment, too, that is provided by the mother."

Parents-to-be who want to further their unborn child's mental development should start by assuring that the antenatal environment is well-nourished, low-stress, drug-free. Various authors and "experts" also have suggested poking the fetus at regular intervals, speaking to it through a paper tube or "pregaphone," piping in classical music, even flashing lights at the mother's abdomen.

Does such stimulation work? More importantly: Is it safe? Some who use these methods swear their children are smarter, more verbally and musically inclined, more physically coordinated and socially adept than average. Scientists, however, are skeptical.

"There has been no defended research anywhere that shows any enduring effect from these stimulations," asserts Fifer. "Since no one can even say for certain when a fetus is awake, poking them or sticking speakers on the mother's abdomen may be changing their natural sleep patterns. No one would consider poking or prodding a newborn baby in her bassinet or putting a speaker next to her ear, so why would you do such a thing with a fetus?"

Als is more emphatic: "My bet is that poking, shaking, or otherwise deliberately stimulating the fetus might alter its developmental sequence, and anything that affects the development of the brain comes at a cost."

Gently talking to the fetus, however, seems to pose little risk. Fifer suggests that this kind of activity may help parents as much as the fetus. "Thinking about your fetus, talking to it, having your spouse talk to it, will all help prepare you for this new creature that's going to jump into your life and turn it upside down," he says—once it finally makes its anti-climactic entrance.

# Drug-Exposed Infants

Lucy Salcido Carter
Carol S. Larson

### Abstract

The problem of drug-exposed infants has been a societal concern for more than a decade. *The Future of Children* devoted its first journal issue in spring 1991[1] to this topic and has provided information updates in subsequent journal issues.[2] The 1991 issue reviewed the major trends in judicial, legislative, and treatment responses to this problem, reporting that, for the most part, appellate courts were rejecting attempts to prosecute pregnant substance-abusing women, and state and federal legislative efforts were creating more treatment programs for, rather than punishment of, these women. With only limited exceptions, these trends continue today. Evaluations of treatment programs funded through the federal initiatives of the late 1980s and early 1990s show some level of treatment effectiveness. However, they also highlight the continuing need for rigorous evaluations of treatment outcomes.

*Lucy Salcido Carter, J.D., is a legal research analyst at the Center for the Future of Children.*

*Carol S. Larson, J.D., is director of foundation programs for the David and Lucile Packard Foundation, and special advisor to the Center for the Future of Children.*

This update reviews recent judicial and legislative responses, and includes preliminary results from the major federal funding initiatives for treatment programs and evaluations. A local community treatment program funded under one of these initiatives is described briefly.

## Judicial Activity

In 1997, it continues to be true that no state statute has created criminal laws specifically applicable to pregnant women who use illicit drugs. However, prosecutors continue to use other statutes protecting children to charge women for actions that potentially harm the fetus. Appellate courts reviewing guilty verdicts have typically ruled in favor of the mothers, finding that legislatures did not intend these stat-

From *The Future of Children*, Summer/Fall 1997, pp. 121-138. © 1997 by the Center for the Future of Children of the David and Lucile Packard Foundation. Reprinted by permission. *The Future of Children* journals and executive summaries are available free of charge by faxing mailing information to: Circulation Department (650) 948-6498.

utes to apply to fetuses. A significant exception to this is the South Carolina Supreme Court case *Whitner v. State* decided on July 15, 1996.[3] In this case, the court affirmed conviction of the mother for criminal child neglect because her baby was born with cocaine in her system after the mother used cocaine in the third trimester of pregnancy. The court held that the broad language of South Carolina's criminal neglect statute and its underlying policy of prevention supported the legislature's intent to include viable fetuses within the definition of persons under the statute. The South Carolina Supreme Court did not address federal and state constitutional issues relating to due process and privacy, because these issues were not raised in the lower court. Attorneys for the mother have filed a motion for rehearing, claim-

---

*In the late 1980s and early 1990s, heightened attention to perinatal substance abuse prompted significant federal efforts to increase the availability of drug abuse prevention and treatment programs for women.*

---

ing that the South Carolina Supreme Court must reach a decision on the constitutional claims. At this time, the court has neither granted nor denied the motion for rehearing.[4]

## Legislative Activity

State legislative activity continues to focus on increasing opportunities for treatment and creating task forces to further explore solutions to the problem of perinatal substance abuse.[5] For example, a law enacted in Arizona[6] in 1995 created an Advisory Council on Perinatal Substance Abuse to develop a statewide strategy for addressing substance abuse by pregnant women and mothers. A 1994 Michigan statute[7] requires that substance-abusing pregnant women and women with dependent children have priority in receiving treatment for substance abuse in state-funded facilities. And a 1995 Illinois statute[8] now permits counties in that state to retain revenues from drug-related fines to support community-based treatment for pregnant women addicted to alcohol and/or drugs. The American Academy of Pediatrics tracks such legislative developments.[5]

## Federal Initiatives

In the late 1980s and early 1990s, heightened attention to this issue prompted significant federal efforts to increase the availability of drug abuse prevention and treatment programs for women.[9] The following describes briefly the four major federal initiatives and reports available to date for each.

### Programs for Pregnant and Postpartum Women and Their Infants

Between 1989 and 1992, the federal Center for Substance Abuse Prevention initiated five-year grants for 147 Pregnant and Postpartum Women and Their Infants (PPWI) projects.[10] These projects provide comprehensive prevention, intervention, and treatment services to substance-abusing pregnant and postpartum women, as well as health and related services to their infants. An example of a PPWI program in Santa Clara County, California, is described in Box 1.

A 1997 evaluation of 90 PPWI demonstrations[11] claims that these programs have been highly successful in improving the coordination, availability, and accessibility of health care and alcohol and drug treatment for pregnant and postpartum women. The study also found that at least one-third of the women served by these programs reduced their drug use.[12]

### The Perinatal 20 Projects

The National Institute on Drug Abuse (NIDA) funded a total of 20 projects in 1989 and 1990 to create new treatment opportunities for women with children and to conduct treatment research. These projects, which are no longer funded, were research driven; treatment approaches were designed to answer hypothetical research questions posed by the grantees.

Compilations of findings from project evaluations primarily address methodological issues related to research.[13] Individual program evaluators were encouraged to publish treatment outcomes in peer-review journals. An annotated bibliography on treatment outcomes for women lists many of these published studies.[14]

### The Abandoned Infants Assistance Act

In 1988, Congress passed the Abandoned Infants Assistance Act (AIA)[15] to support comprehensive intervention programs to serve drug-exposed and HIV-affected infants and their families. Approximately 30 programs are funded annually. They provide a variety of services, including case

Box 1

## One Community Treatment Response:
## The Perinatal Substance Abuse Program (PSAP)

The Perinatal Substance Abuse Program (PSAP) is a county-administered, long-term outpatient treatment program with facilities in a hospital complex.[a] The program follows a one-stop shopping model of providing to substance-abusing pregnant women and mothers[b] a comprehensive array of services at one location. These services include individual case management and counseling, 12-step program meetings to help clients combat their addictions, parenting and prevocational skills (such as reading, math, and GED) classes, and on-site child care while mothers are in program activities. A program physician is available two days a week to all clients for consultation and to monitor the clients on methadone maintenance.

The treatment program is designed to take 18 months to complete; however, clients can remain in the program for a longer period of time if they are motivated and it is clear that they need extra time. In the program's first five years, 535 women were enrolled, and 177 births occurred.

Toxicological tests taken from July 1992 through June 1995 revealed that 84% of the women enrolled in the treatment program reduced their substance use. Eighty-two percent of infants born to 71 women (for whom data were available) had negative toxicological screens at birth. Seventy-five percent of births to women in treatment produced infants of normal birth weight. The designers of this program believe, based on their experience, that the number of drug-exposed infants and low birth weight infants would have been higher if the program had not been available to these pregnant women. However, it was beyond the scope of the evaluation to examine comparative birth weights and toxicology results for infants born to drug-abusing women who were not in treatment during pregnancy.

[a]For more information about this program, see the final report for CSAP grant #SPO1498–01, available through the Office of Women's Treatment Services, Perinatal Substance Abuse Program, Anthony J. Puentes Center, 2425 Enborg Lane, San Jose, CA 95128, telephone (408) 885–4060.

[b]Though self-referred women are welcome, most of PSAP's clients were either referred by child protective services or ordered by a court to attend a treatment program.

management, pediatric health care, housing assistance, and respite care for primary caregivers.[16]

Data on AIA programs compiled in annual reports are largely descriptive, rather than evaluative. Individual program evaluations have been conducted, and a monograph summarizing services outcomes for eight of the programs is forthcoming.[17] In October 1996, the collection of client-level outcome data was begun to better assess and refine AIA programs.[18]

### Residential Treatment Grants

The federal Center for Substance Abuse Treatment (CSAT) initiated two demonstration residential programs in 1993: the Residential Treatment Grants for Pregnant and Postpartum Women and Their Infants (PPWI) and the Residential Treatment Grants for Women and Their Children (RWC). Both were designed to support comprehensive residential treatment services, including primary health care, mental health assessments and counseling, and other social services for substance-abusing women and their children. In 1996, some 74 residential programs were

funded and approximately 2,700 women and 2,900 children received services. In 1997, another 65 residential programs were funded.

A summary of evaluation data for both programs is available.[19] One of the key findings was that between October 1993 and June 1996 the number of women who reported the use of illicit drugs decreased by 73% to 80% from intake to postdischarge.[20]

## Conclusion

Since the early 1990s, there has been considerably more experience in providing treatment to substance-abusing pregnant women and mothers. Although the results discussed above suggest some level of effectiveness, for the most part they rely on incomplete data. They demonstrate how difficult it is to study program effectiveness in a rigorous way.

There are many variations of community treatment programs; PSAP, described in Box 1, is just one example. The need for treatment services for substance-abusing pregnant women and mothers remains great. It is hoped that more experience in providing such services, as well as sound evaluations, will help to improve treatment approaches and the lives of these women and their children.

1. Behrman, R. E., ed. Drug Exposed Infants. *The Future of Children* (Spring 1991) 1,1:1–120.
2. Barth, R. P. Revisiting the issues: Adoption of drug-exposed children. *The Future of Children* (Spring 1993) 3,1:167–75; Revisiting the issues: Drug-exposed infants. *The Future of Children* (Summer/Fall 1993) 3,2:208–14; Shiono, P. H. Revisiting the issues: Prevalence of drug-exposed infants. *The Future of Children* (Summer/Fall 1996) 6,2:159–63.
3. *Whitner v. State*, WL 393164 (S.C. 1996). The mother was sentenced to eight years in prison.
4. Priscilla Smith, Center for Reproductive Law and Policy, New York City. Telephone conversation, March 11, 1997. CRLP staff represented the mother in the appellate case.
5. Seven such state bills were enacted from 1993 through 1995. See American Academy of Pediatrics. *Drug-exposed infants*. Elk Grove Village, IL: AAP, Division of State Government and Chapter Affairs, 1996.
6. Arizona Session Laws, 1995. Chapter 215, p. 1688.
7. Michigan Public Act Appropriation Bill for 1993–94, No. 201.
8. See 720 Illinois Compiled Statutes Annotated § 570/411.2 (Public Act 89-215, effective January 1, 1996).
9. Kumpfer, K. Treatment programs for drug-abusing women. In *The Future of Children*. R. E. Behrman, ed. (Spring 1991) 1,1:50–60. See especially the description of federal initiatives on pages 56 and 57.
10. Center for Substance Abuse Prevention, Division of Demonstrations for High Risk Populations. Executive summary: CSAP—PPWI demonstration program findings. Unpublished report. CSAP, October 1996.
11. See note no. 10, Center for Substance Abuse Prevention, pp. 1, 4. This evaluation included the 26 fully implemented PPWI programs that met data collection criteria. In on-site visits, evaluators collected both quantitative and qualitative data on more than 80 variables. Client outcome data on 3,641 women and 2,757 infants were collected by program grantees.
12. See note no. 10, Center for Substance Abuse Prevention, p. 9. Data on maternal drug use were limited to women who had positive toxicology test results at intake. These women were retested after having received program services.
13. Rahdert, E. R., ed. *Treatment for drug-exposed women and their children: Advances in research methodology*. NIDA Research Monograph 166. Rockville, MD: National Institute on Drug Abuse, 1996; Kilbey, M. M., and Asghar, K. *Methodological issues in epidemiological, prevention, and treatment research on drug-exposed women and their children*. NIDA Research Monograph 117. Rockville, MD: National Institute on Drug Abuse, 1992.
14. For more information about the results of the Perinatal Twenty project, contact Dr. E. R. Rahdert, NIDA, Division of Clinical and Service Research, 5600 Fishers Lane, Rockville, MD 20857, (310) 442–0107.
15. Abandoned Infants Assistance Act of 1988, Public Law 100–505, 42 U.S.C. § 670. This funding was reauthorized in 1991 under the Abandoned Infants Assistance Act Amendments of 1991, Public Law 102–236, 42 U.S.C. § 670 note.
16. Goldberg, S., Barth, R. P., and Hernandez, C. S. *Abandoned Infants Assistance programs: 1995 annual report*. Berkeley, CA: National Abandoned Infants Assistance Resource Center, Family Welfare Research Group, School of Social Welfare, University of California, December 1996.
17. For more information regarding this monograph, write to Reneé Robinson at the National Abandoned Infants Assistance Resource Center, Family Welfare Research Group, 1950 Addison, Suite 104, Berkeley, CA 94704, or call (510) 643–7020.
18. Sheryl Goldberg, National Abandoned Infants Assistance Resource Center. Personal communication, March 14, 1997.
19. Center for Substance Abuse Treatment, Department of Health and Human Services. Women and children's program accomplishments. Unpublished internal federal agency report. January 13, 1997. For more information, contact Maggie Wilmore at the Department of Health and Human Services' Center for Substance Abuse Treatment, Clinical Intervention Branch, in Rockville, MD, (301) 443–8216.
20. The analysis used *CSAT Quarterly Report Tracking System* data collected at intake, discharge, and postdischarge on 800 women from 45 programs. Only women with an intake record, discharge record, and at least one postdischarge record were included. On average, follow-up data were collected six months after discharge. All postdischarge records were aggregated. See note no. 19, Center for Substance Abuse Treatment, pp. 8–9.

# SPERM UNDER SIEGE

## MORE THAN WE EVER GUESSED, HAVING A HEALTHY BABY MAY DEPEND ON DAD

### Anne Merewood

IT DIDN'T MAKE SENSE. Kate Malone's* first pregnancy had gone so smoothly. Yet when she and her husband Paul* tried to have a second child, their efforts were plagued by disaster. For two years, Kate couldn't become pregnant. Then she suffered an ectopic pregnancy, in which the embryo began to grow in one of her fallopian tubes and had to be surgically removed. Her next pregnancy heralded more heartache—it ended in miscarriage at four months and tests revealed that the fetus was genetically abnormal. Within months, she became pregnant and miscarried yet again. By this point, some four years after their troubles began, the couple had adopted a son; baffled and demoralized by the string of apparent bad luck, they gave up trying to have another child. "We had been to the top doctors in the country and no one could find a reason for the infertility or the miscarriages," says Kate.

Soon, however, thanks to a newspaper article she read, Kate uncovered what she now considers the likely cause of the couple's reproductive woes. When it all started, Paul had just been hired by a manufacturing company that used a chemical called paradichlorobenzene, which derives from benzene, a known carcinogen. The article discussed the potential effects of exposure to chemicals, including benzene, on a man's sperm. Kate remembered hearing that two other men in Paul's small office were also suffering from inexplicable infertility. Both of their wives had gone through three miscarriages as well. Kate had always considered their similar misfortunes to be a tragic coincidence. Now she became convinced that the chemical (which has not yet

been studied for its effects on reproduction) had blighted the three men's sperm.

Paul had found a new job in a chemical-free workplace, so the couple decided to try once more to have a baby. Kate conceived immediately—and last August gave birth to a healthy boy. The Malones are now arranging for the National Institute for Occupational Safety and Health (NIOSH), the federal agency that assesses work-related health hazards for the public, to inspect Paul's former job site. "Our aim isn't to sue the company, but to help people who are still there," says Kate.

The Malones' suspicions about sperm damage echo the concerns of an increasing number of researchers. These scientists are challenging the double standard that leads women to overhaul their lives before a pregnancy—avoiding stress, cigarettes and champagne—while men are left confident that their lifestyle has little bearing on their fertility or their future child's health. Growing evidence suggests that sperm is both more fragile and potentially more dangerous than previously thought. "There seems to have been both a scientific resistance, and a resistance based on cultural preconceptions, to accepting these new ideas," says Gladys Friedler, Ph.D., an associate professor of psychiatry and pharmacology at Boston University School of Medicine.

But as more and more research is completed, sperm may finally be stripped of its macho image. For example, in one startling review of data on nearly 15,000 newborns, scientists at the University of North Carolina in Chapel Hill concluded that a father's drinking and smoking habits, and even his age, can increase his child's risk of birth defects—ranging from cleft palates to *hydrocephalus*, an abnormal accumulation of spinal fluid in the brain. Other new and equally worrisome

---

*These names have been changed.

From *Health*, April 1991, pp. 53–57, 76–77. © 1991 by Anne Merewood. Reprinted by permission.

studies have linked higher-than-normal rates of stillbirth, premature delivery and low birthweight (which predisposes a baby to medical and developmental problems) to fathers who faced on-the-job exposure to certain chemicals. In fact, one study found that a baby was more likely to be harmed if the father rather than the mother worked in an unsafe environment in the months before conception.

The surprising news of sperm's delicate nature may shift the balance of responsibility for a newborn's well-being. The research may also have social and economic implications far beyond the concerns of couples planning a family. In recent years a growing number of companies have sought to ban women of childbearing age from jobs that entail exposure to hazardous substances. The idea is to protect the women's future children from defects—and the companies themselves from lawsuits. Already, the "fetal protection policy" of one Milwaukee-based company has prompted female employees to file a sex discrimination suit that is now before the U.S. Supreme Court. Conversely, if the new research on sperm is borne out, men whose future plans include fatherhood may go to court to *insist* on protection from hazards. Faced with potential lawsuits from so many individuals, companies may be forced to ensure that workplaces are safe for *all* employees.

## SPERM UND DRANG

At the center of all this controversy are the microscopic products of the male reproductive system. Sperm (officially, spermatozoa) are manufactured by *spermatagonia*, special cells in the testes that are constantly stimulated by the male hormone testosterone. Once formed, a sperm continues to mature as it travels for some 80 days through the *epididymis* (a microscopic network of tubes behind the testicle) to the "waiting area" around the prostate gland, where it is expelled in the next ejaculation.

A normal sperm contains 23 chromosomes—the threadlike strands that house DNA, the molecular foundation of genetic material. While a woman is born with all the eggs she will ever produce, a man creates millions of sperm every day from puberty onwards. This awesome productivity is also what makes sperm so fragile. If a single sperm's DNA is damaged, the result may be a mutation that distorts the genetic information it carries. "Because of the constant turnover

of sperm, mutations caused by the environment can arise more frequently in men than in women," says David A. Savitz, Ph.D., an associate professor of epidemiology and chief researcher of the North Carolina review.

If a damaged sperm fertilizes the egg, the consequences can be devastating. "Such sperm can lead to spontaneous abortions, malformations, and functional or behavioral abnormalities," says Marvin Legator, Ph.D., director of environmental toxicology at the department of preventative medicine at the University of Texas in Galveston. And in some cases, sperm may be too badly harmed even to penetrate an egg, leading to mysterious infertility.

Though the findings on sperm's vulnerability are certainly dramatic, researchers emphasize that they are also preliminary. "We have only a very vague notion of how exposure might affect fetal development, and the whole area of research is at a very early stage of investigation," says Savitz. Indeed, questions still far outnumber answers. For starters, there is no hard evidence that a chemical damages an infant by adversely affecting the father's sperm. A man who comes in contact with dangerous substances might harm the baby by exposing his partner indirectly—for example, through contaminated clothing. Another theory holds that the harmful pollutants may be carried in the seminal fluid that buoys sperm. But more researchers are becoming convinced that chemicals can inflict their silent damage directly on the sperm itself.

## THE CHEMICAL CONNECTION

The most well-known—and most controversial—evidence that chemicals can harm sperm comes from research on U.S. veterans of the Vietnam war who were exposed to the herbicide Agent Orange (dioxin), used by the U.S. military to destroy foliage that hid enemy forces. A number of veterans believe the chemical is responsible for birth defects in their children. The latest study on the issue, published last year by the Harvard School of Public Health, found that Vietnam vets had almost twice the risk of other men of fathering infants with one or more major malformations. But a number of previous studies found conflicting results, and because so little is known about how paternal exposure could translate into birth defects, the veterans have been unsuccessful in their lawsuits against the government.

Scientific uncertainty also dogs investigations into other potentially hazardous chemicals and contaminants. "There seem to be windows of vulnerability for sperm: Certain chemicals may be harmful only at a certain period during sperm production," explains Donald Mattison, M.D., dean of the School of Public Health at the University of Pittsburgh. There isn't enough specific data to make definitive lists of "danger chemicals." Still, a quick scan of the research shows that particular substances often crop up as likely troublemakers. Chief among them: lead, benzene, paint solvents, vinyl chloride, carbon disulphide, the pesticide DBCP, anesthetic gases and radiation. Not surprisingly, occupations that involve contact with these substances also figure heavily in studies of sperm damage. For example, men employed in the paper, wood, chemical, drug and paint industries may have a greater chance of siring stillborn children. And increased leukemia rates have been detected among children whose fathers are medical workers, aircraft or auto mechanics, or who are exposed regularly to paint or radiation. In fact, a study of workers at Britain's Sellafield nuclear power plant in West Cambria found a sixfold leukemia risk among children whose fathers were exposed to the plant's highest radiation levels (about 9 percent of all employees).

Workers in "high-risk" industries should not panic, says Savitz. "The credibility of the studies is limited because we have no firm evidence that certain exposures cause certain birth defects." Yet it makes sense to be watchful for warning signs. For example, if pollution levels are high enough to cause skin irritations, thyroid trouble, or breathing problems, the reproductive system might also be at risk. Another danger signal is a clustered outbreak of male infertility or of a particular disease: It was local concern about high levels of childhood leukemia, for instance, that sparked the investigation at the Sellafield nuclear plant.

The rise in industrial "fetal protection policies" is adding even more controversy to the issue of occupational hazards to sperm. In 1984, employees brought a class-action suit against Milwaukee-based Johnson Controls, the nation's largest manufacturer of car batteries, after the company restricted women "capable of bearing children" from holding jobs in factory areas where lead exceeded a specific level. The suit—which the Supreme Court is scheduled to rule on this spring—focuses on the obstacles the policy creates for women's career advancement. Johnson Controls defends its regulation by pointing to "overwhelming" evidence that a mother's exposure to lead can harm the fetus.

In effect, the company's rule may be a case of reverse discrimination against men. Males continue to work in areas banned to women despite growing evidence that lead may not be safe for sperm either. In several studies over the past 10 years, paternal exposure to lead (and radiation) has been connected to Wilms' tumor, a type of kidney cancer in children. In another recent study, University of Maryland toxicologist Ellen Silbergeld, Ph.D., exposed male rats to lead amounts equivalent to levels below the current occupational safety standards for humans. The rats were then mated with females who had not been exposed at all. Results: The offspring showed clear defects in brain development.

Johnson Controls claims that evidence linking fetal problems to a father's contact with lead is insufficient. But further research into chemicals' effects on sperm may eventually force companies to reduce pollution levels, since *both* sexes can hardly be banned from the factory floor. Says Mattison: "The workplace should be safe for everyone who wants to work there, men and women alike!"

## FATHER TIME

Whatever his occupation, man's age may play an unexpected role in his reproductive health. When researchers at the University of Calgary and the Alberta Children's Hospital in Canada examined sperm samples taken from 30 healthy men aged 20 to 52, they found that the older men had a higher percentage of sperm with structurally abnormal chromosomes. Specifically, only 2 to 3 percent of the sperm from men between ages 20 and 34 were genetically abnormal, while the figure jumped to 7 percent in men 35 to 44 and to almost 14 percent in those 45 and over. "The findings are logical," says Renée Martin, Ph.D., the professor of pediatrics who led the study. "The cells that create sperm are constantly dividing from puberty onwards, and every time they divide they are subject to error."

Such mistakes are more likely to result in miscarriages than in unhealthy babies. "When part of a chromosome is missing or broken, the embryo is more likely to abort as a miscarriage [than to carry to term]," Martin says.

Yet her findings may help explain why Savitz's North Carolina study noted a doubled rate of birth defects like cleft palate and hydrocephalus in children whose fathers were over 35 at the time of conception, no matter what the mothers' age.

Currently, there are no tests available to pre-identify sperm likely to cause genetic defects. "Unfortunately there's nothing offered, because [the research] is all so new," says Martin. But tests such as amniocentesis, alpha fetoprotein (AFP) and chorionic villi sampling (CVS) can ferret out some fetal genetic defects that are linked to Mom *or* Dad. Amniocentesis, for example, is routinely recommended for all pregnant women over 35 because with age a woman increases her risk of producing a Down's syndrome baby, characterized by mental retardation and physical abnormalities.

With respect to Down's syndrome, Martin's study provided some good news for older men: It confirmed previous findings that a man's risk of fathering a child afflicted with the syndrome actually drops with age. Some popular textbooks still warn that men over 55 have a high chance of fathering Down's syndrome babies. "That information is outdated," Martin insists. "We now know that for certain."

### THE SINS OF THE FATHERS?

For all the hidden dangers facing a man's reproductive system, the most common hazards may be the ones most under his control.

*Smoking.* Tobacco addicts take note: Smoke gets in your sperm. Cigarettes can reduce fertility by lowering sperm count—the number of individual sperm released in a single ejaculation. "More than half a pack a day can cause sperm density to drop by 20 percent," says Machelle Seibel, M.D., director of the Faulkner Centre for Reproductive Medicine in Boston. One Danish study found that for each pack of cigarettes a father tended to smoke daily (assuming the mother didn't smoke at all), his infant's birthweight fell 4.2 ounces below average. Savitz has found that male smokers double their chances of fathering infants with abnormalities like hydrocephalus, *Bell's palsy* (paralysis of the facial nerve), and mouth cysts. In Savitz's most recent study, children whose fathers smoked around the time of conception were 20 percent more likely to develop brain cancer, lymphoma and leukemia than were children whose fathers did not

smoke (the results still held regardless of whether the mother had a tobacco habit).

This is scary news—and not particularly helpful: Savitz's studies didn't record how frequently the fathers lit up, and no research at all suggests why the links appeared. Researchers can't even say for sure that defective sperm was to blame. The babies may instead have been victims of passive smoking—affected by Dad's tobacco while in the womb or shortly after birth.

*Drinking.* Mothers-to-be are routinely cautioned against sipping any alcohol while pregnant. Now studies suggest that the father's drinking habits just before conception may also pose a danger. So far, research hasn't discovered why alcohol has an adverse effect on sperm, but it does suggest that further investigation is needed. For starters, one study of laboratory rats linked heavy alcohol use with infertility because the liquor lowered testosterone levels. Another study, from the University of Washington in Seattle, discovered that newborn babies whose fathers drank at least two glasses of wine or two bottles of beer per day weighed an average of 3 ounces less than babies whose fathers were only occasional sippers—even when all other factors were considered.

*Illicit Drugs.* Many experts believe that a man's frequent use of substances such as marijuana and cocaine may also result in an unhealthy fetus, but studies that could document such findings have yet to be conducted. However, preliminary research has linked marijuana to infertility. And recent tests at the Yale Infertility Clinic found that long-term cocaine use led to both very low sperm counts and a greater number of sperm with motion problems.

### WHAT A DAD CAN DO

The best news about sperm troubles is that many of the risk factors can be easily prevented. Because the body overhauls sperm supplies every 90 days, it only takes a season to get a fresh start on creating a healthy baby. Most experts advise that men wait for three months after quitting smoking, cutting out drug use or abstaining from alcohol before trying to sire a child.

Men who fear they are exposed to work chemicals that may compromise the health of future children can contact NIOSH. (Write the Division of Standards Development and Technology Transfer, Technical Information

Branch, 4676 Columbia Parkway, Mailstop C-19, Cincinnati, OH 45226. Or call [800] 356-4674.) NIOSH keeps files on hazardous chemicals and their effects, and can arrange for a local inspection of the workplace. Because it is primarily a research institution, NIOSH is most useful for investigating chemicals that haven't been studied previously for sperm effects (which is why the Malones approached NIOSH with their concerns about paradichlorobenzene). For better-known pollutants, it's best to ask the federal Occupational Safety and Health Administration (OSHA) to inspect the job site (OSHA has regional offices in most U.S. cities).

There is also advice for men who are concerned over exposure to radiation during medical treatment. Direct radiation to the area around the testes can spur infertility by halting sperm production for more than three years. According to a recent study, it can also triple the number of abnormal sperm the testes produce. Men who know they will be exposed to testicular radiation for medical reasons should consider "banking" sperm before the treatment, for later use in artificial insemination. Most hospitals use lead shields during radiation therapy, but for routine X-rays, even dental X-rays, protection might not be offered automatically. If it's not offered, patients should be sure to request it. "The risks are really, really low, but to be absolutely safe, patients—male or female—should *always* ask for a lead apron to protect their reproductive organs," stresses Martin.

Though the study of sperm health is still in its infancy, it is already clear that a man's reproductive system needs to be treated with respect and caution. Women do not carry the full responsibility for bearing a healthy infant. "The focus should be on both parents—not on 'blaming' either the mother or the father, but on accepting that each play a role," says Friedler.

Mattison agrees: "Until recently, when a woman had a miscarriage, she would be told it was because she had a 'blighted ovum' [egg]. We never heard anything about a 'blighted sperm.' This new data suggests that both may be responsible. That is not unreasonable," he concludes, "given that it takes both an egg and a sperm to create a baby!"

## Unit Selections

## Key Points to Consider

❖ Is infant reactivity and temperamental style a factor in the development of personal and social behaviors? Explain.

❖ Can talking to infants shape their ability to compute the rules and structural principles of language? How do they discern meaning and decode patterns?

❖ What should infant caregivers know about cultural differences in child rearing practices?

❖ How can parents facilitate language development and recognize signs of possible trouble?

❖ Why is empathy the trait that makes us human? Why is it critical to our survival?

❖ Where do early childhood education programs need more information and support in order to be state-of-the-art for the new millennium?

 **Links**    # www.dushkin.com/online/

10. **Aggression and Cooperation: Helping Young Children Develop Constructive Strategies**
*http://ericps.crc.uiuc.edu/eece/pubs/digests/1992/jewett92.html*

11. **Children's Nutrition Research Center (CNRC)**
*http://www.bcm.tmc.edu/cnrc/*

12. **Early Childhood Care and Development**
*http://www.ecdgroup.com*

13. **Society of Pediatric Psychology (SPP)**
*http://macserv.psy.miami.edu/SPP/*

14. **Zero to Three: National Center for Infants, Toddlers, and Families**
*http://www.zerotothree.org*

These sites are annotated on pages 4 and 5.

Thousands of studies have linked environmental variables to development during infancy and early childhood over the twentieth century. With new technologies (e.g., tomography, magnetic resonance imaging, gene mapping, computational biology), hundreds of new studies are sure to link various biological variables to childhood development during the twenty-first century. The articles selected for inclusion in this unit reflect both the known influences of nurture (environment) and nature (biology) and the relationships and interactions of multiple variables and child outcomes about which we hope to know more in the new millennium.

Newborns are quite well developed in some areas, and incredibly deficient in others. Babies' brains, for example, already have their full complement of neurons (worker cells). The neuroglia (supportive cells) are almost completely developed and will reach their final numbers by age one. In contrast, babies' legs and feet are tiny, weak, and barely functional. Looking at newborns from another perspective, however, makes their brains seem somewhat less superior. The neurons and neuroglia present at birth must be protected. We may discover ways to make neurons regenerate in the future but such knowledge now is in its infancy and may not go very far. By contrast, the cells of the baby's legs and feet (skin, fat, muscles, bones, blood vessels) are able to replace themselves by mitosis indefinitely. Their numbers will continue to grow through early adulthood; then their quantity and quality can be regenerated through old age.

The developing brain in infancy is a truly fascinating organ. At birth it is poorly organized. The lower (primitive) brain parts (brain stem, pons, medulla, cerebellum) are well enough developed to allow the infant to live. The lower brain directs vital organ systems (heart, lungs, kidneys, etc.). The higher (advanced) brain parts (cerebral hemispheres) have all their neurons, but the nerve cells and cell processes (axons, dendrites) are small, underdeveloped, and unorganized. During infancy, these higher (cerebral) nerve cells (that allow the baby to think, reason, and remember) grow at astronomical rates. They migrate to permanent locations in the hemispheres, develop myelin sheathing (insulation), and conduct messages. Jean Piaget, the father of cognitive psychology, wrote that all brain activity in the newborn was reflexive, based on instincts for survival. Now researchers are discovering that fetuses can learn and newborns can think as well as learn.

The role played by electrical activity of neurons in actively shaping the physical structure of the brain is particularly awe-inspiring. The neurons are produced prenatally. After birth, the flood of sensory inputs from the environment (sights, sounds, smells, tastes, touch, balance, and kinesthetic sensations) drives the neurons to form circuits and become wired to each other. Trillions of connections are established in a baby's brain. During childhood the connections that are seldom or never used are eliminated or pruned. The first 3 years are critical for establishing these connections. Environments that provide lots of sensory stimulation really do produce richer, more connected brains.

The first article in the infancy section of this unit discusses the development of social and emotional behaviors in infancy. Author Jerome Kagan is a Harvard professor with a worldwide reputation as an expert in socioemotional aspects of development. In his essay, he contends that babies who are easily aroused and become distressed quickly are likely to grow into fearful and subdued preschoolers. Infants who remain relaxed are apt to become bold and sociable in early childhood. He sees a danger, however, in excusing conduct disorders and unrestrained emotions because they are due to inherited differences in reactivity. Kagan stresses the need for socialization practices that focus on human obligations to be civil and responsible.

The second selection on infancy deals with language development as it is affected by infant perceptions. Shannon Brownlee reviews research that suggests that infants as young as 18 months old can perceive differences in grammatically correct and incorrect speech. This supports the idea that the brain is biologically equipped to learn language before social learning (modeling, imitation) takes place. This article describes how infants decode patterns, discriminate rules, and cobble words together correctly. Deaf infants do this with sign language. Brownlee reminds readers that in order to do this, infants need early and plentiful human language input. Recordings and television talk do not stimulate babies to compute syntax of language.

The third selection on infancy questions the ethnocentric view that the mainstream American way to socialize, care for, and stimulate infants is the only "right" way. It focuses on cultural variations in sleeping routines. What may be considered inappropriate in a typical U.S. home may be normal and useful in a culturally different home. The authors recommend multicultural education for all people working with infants.

The selections about toddlers and preschoolers in this anthology continue the trend of looking at development physically, cognitively, and socioemotionally. Each of the articles focuses on one topic and views the whole child across all three domains, considering both hereditary and environmental factors.

"The Language Explosion" continues a discussion of language development that began in the infancy section article "Baby Talk." Research suggests that each of the world's 6,000 languages have grammatical rules that are discerned by children by age 3. This article gives practical suggestions for facilitating language learning and offers signs of potential language disabilities for which early remediation is available.

The next article, "Defining the Trait That Makes Us Human," focuses on empathy, the identification with and understanding of another person's situation and feelings. This is a cognitive achievement in early childhood. It requires that the preschooler has knowledge that he or she is separate from others, and that those separate others have their own feelings and positions. Researchers believe that a biological instinct for empathy exists, but it also requires environmental reinforcements to be learned well. Parents and other significant caregivers can encourage (or discourage) the development of this all-important trait.

The concluding article in this unit addresses knowledge about raising young children in early childhood education programs in the twenty-first century. How the United States solves the quality crisis in early care and education will be a major factor in the quality of life for American children and families. The Quality 2000 Initiative's recommendations, it is hoped, will provide discussion and spark bold action on behalf of more effective child care. The authors describe the strategies of helpful state-of-the-art technological resources planned to enhance the well-being of young children in early childhood education programs.

# Temperament and the Reactions to Unfamiliarity

*Jerome Kagan*

The behavioral reactions to unfamiliar events are basic phenomena in all vertebrates. Four-month-old infants who show a low threshold to become distressed and motorically aroused to unfamiliar stimuli are more likely than others to become fearful and subdued during early childhood, whereas infants who show a high arousal threshold are more likely to become bold and sociable. After presenting some developmental correlates and trajectories of these 2 temperamental biases, I consider their implications for psychopathology and the relation between propositions containing psychological and biological concepts.

## INTRODUCTION

A readiness to react to events that differ from those encountered in the recent or distant past is one of the distinguishing characteristics of all mammalian species. Thus, the events with the greatest power to produce both an initial orienting and sustained attention in infants older than 3 to 4 months are variations on what is familiar, often called discrepant events (Fagan, 1981; Kagan, Kearsley, & Zelazo, 1980). By 8 months of age, discrepant events can produce a vigilant posture of quiet staring and, occasionally, a wary face and a cry of distress if the event cannot be assimilated easily (Bronson, 1970). That is why Hebb (1946) made discrepancy a major basis for fear reactions in animals, why a fear reaction to strangers occurs in the middle of the first year in children growing up in a variety of cultural settings, and, perhaps, why variation in the initial behavioral reaction to novelty exists in almost every vertebrate species studied (Wilson, Coleman, Clark, & Biederman, 1993).

Recent discoveries by neuroscientists enrich these psychological facts. The hippocampus plays an important role in the detection of discrepant events (Squire & Knowlton, 1995). Projections from the hippocampus provoke activity in the amygdala and lead to changes in autonomic function and posture and, in older children, to reflection and anticipation (Shima-mura, 1995). Because these neural structures and their projections are influenced by a large number of neurotransmitters and neuromodulators, it is reasonable to expect inherited differences in the neurochemistry of these structures and circuits and, therefore, in their excitability. Variation in the levels of, or receptors for, corticotropin releasing hormone, norepinephrine, cortisol, dopamine, glutamate, GABA, opioids, acetylcholine, and other molecules might be accompanied by differences in the intensity and form of responsivity to unfamiliarity (Cooper, Bloom, & Roth, 1991). This speculation is supported by research with infants and children (Kagan, 1994). This article summarizes what has been learned

From *Child Development*, February 1997, pp. 139-143. © 1997 by the Society for Research in Child Development. Reprinted by permission.

about two temperamental types of children who react in different ways to unfamiliarity, considers the implications of these two temperamental categories for psychopathology, and comments briefly on the relation between psychological and biological constructs.

## INFANT REACTIVITY AND FEARFUL BEHAVIOR

About 20% of a large sample of 462 healthy, Caucasian, middle-class, 16-week-old infants became both motorically active and distressed to presentations of brightly colored toys moved back and forth in front of their faces, tape recordings of voices speaking brief sentences, and cotton swabs dipped in dilute butyl alcohol applied to the nose. These infants are called high reactive. By contrast, about 40% of infants with the same family and ethnic background remained motorically relaxed and did not fret or cry to the same set of unfamiliar events. These infants are called low reactive. The differences between high and low reactives can be interpreted as reflecting variation in the excitability of the amygdala and its projections to the ventral striatum, hypothalamus, cingulate, central gray, and medulla (Amaral, Price, Pitkanen, & Carmichael, 1992; Davis, 1992).

When these high and low reactive infants were observed in a variety of unfamiliar laboratory situations at 14 and 21 months, about one-third of the 73 high reactives were highly fearful (4 or more fears), and only 3% showed minimal fear (0 or 1 fear) at both ages. By contrast, one-third of the 147 low reactives were minimally fearful at both ages (0 or 1 fear), and only 4% displayed high levels of fear (Kagan, 1994).

The profiles of high and low fear to unfamiliar events, called inhibited and uninhibited, are heritable, to a modest degree, in 1- to 2-year-old middle-class children (DiLalla, Kagan, & Reznick, 1994; Robinson, Kagan, Reznick, & Corley, 1992). Further, high

reactives show greater sympathetic reactivity in the cardiovascular system than low reactives during the first 2 years (Kagan, 1994; Snidman, Kagan, Riordan, & Shannon, 1995).

As children approach the fourth and fifth years, they gain control of crying to and reflex retreat from unfamiliar events and will only show these responses to very dangerous events or to situations that are not easily or ethically created in the laboratory. Hence, it is important to ask how high and low reactive infants might respond to unfamiliar laboratory situations when they are 4–5 years old. Each species has a biologically preferred reaction to novelty. Rabbits freeze, monkeys display a distinct facial grimace, and cats arch their backs. In humans, restraint on speech seems to be an analogue of the immobility that animals display in novel situations (Panksepp, Sacks, Crepeau, & Abbott, 1991), for children often become quiet as an initial reaction to unfamiliar situations (Asendorpf, 1990; Kagan, Reznick, & Gibbons, 1989; Kagan, Reznick, & Snidman, 1988; Murray, 1971). It is also reasonable to expect that the activity in limbic sites provoked by an unfamiliar social situation might interfere with the brain states that mediate the relaxed emotional state that is indexed by smiling and laughter (Adamec, 1991; Amaral et al., 1992). When the children who had been classified as high and low reactive were interviewed at 4½ years of age by an unfamiliar female examiner who was blind to their prior behavior, the 62 high reactives talked and smiled significantly less often (means of 41 comments and 17 smiles) than did the 94 low reactives (means of 57 comments and 28 smiles) during a 1 hour test battery: $F(1, 152) = 4.51$, $p < .05$ for spontaneous comments; $F(1, 152) = 15.01$, $p < .01$ for spontaneous smiles. Although spontaneous comments and smiles were positively correlated ($r = 0.4$), the low reactives displayed significantly more smiles than would have been predicted from a regression of number of smiles on number of spontaneous comments. The high reactives

displayed significantly fewer smiles than expected. Every one of the nine children who smiled more than 50 times had been a low reactive infant.

However, only a modest proportion of children maintained an extreme form of their theoretically expected profile over the period from 4 months to 4½ years, presumably because of the influence of intervening family experiences (Arcus, 1991). Only 19% of the high reactives displayed a high level of fear at both 14 and 21 months (>4 fears), together with low values (below the mean) for both spontaneous comments and smiles at 4½ years. But not one low reactive infant actualized such a consistently fearful and emotionally subdued profile. By contrast, 18% of low reactive infants showed the opposite profile of low fear (0 or 1 fear) at both 14 and 21 months together with high values for both spontaneous smiles and spontaneous comments at 4½ years. Only one high reactive infant actualized that prototypic, uninhibited profile. Thus, it is uncommon for either temperamental type to develop and to maintain the seminal features of the other type, but quite common for each type to develop a profile that is characteristic of the less extreme child who is neither very timid nor very bold.

The 4½-year-old boys who had been high reactive infants had significantly higher resting heart rates than did low reactives, but the differences between high and low reactive girls at this older age took a different form. The high reactive girls did not show the expected high negative correlation (−0.6 to −0.8) between heart rate and heart rate variability. It is possible that the greater sympathetic reactivity of high reactive girls interfered with the usual, vagally induced inverse relation between heart rate and heart rate variability (Porges, Arnold, & Forbes, 1973; Richards, 1985).

Honest disagreement surrounds the conceptualization of infant reactivity as a continuum of arousal or as two distinct categories. The raw motor activity score at 4 months formed a continuum, but the distribution of distress cries did not. Some infants never fretted or cried; others cried a great deal. A more important defense of the decision to treat high and low reactivity as two distinct categories is the fact that within each of the two categories variation in motor activity and crying was unrelated to later fearfulness or sympathetic reactivity. If reactivity were a continuous trait, then a low reactive infant with extremely low motor and distress scores should be less fearful than one who showed slightly more arousal. But that prediction was not affirmed. Second, infants who showed high motor arousal but no crying or minimal motor arousal with frequent crying showed developmental profiles that were different from those who were categorized as low or high reactive. Finally, high and low reactives differed in physical and physiological features that imply qualitatively different genetic constitutions. For example, high reactives have narrower faces than low reactives in the second year of life (Arcus & Kagan, 1995). Unpublished data from our laboratory reveal that the prevalence of atopic allergies among both children and their parents is significantly greater among high than low reactive infants. Studies of monozygotic and dizygotic same-sex twin pairs reveal significant heritability for inhibited and uninhibited behavior in the second year of life (Robinson et al., 1992). These facts imply that the two temperamental groups represent qualitatively different types and do not lie on a continuum of arousal or reactivity to stimulation.

The decision to regard individuals with very different values on a construct as members of the discrete categories or as falling on a continuum will depend on the scientists' purpose. Scientists who are interested in the relation, across families and genera, between brain size and body mass treat the two measurements as continuous. However, biologists interested in the maternal behavior of mice and chimpanzees regard these two mammals as members of qualitatively different groups. Similarly, if psychologists are interested in the physiological foundations of high and low reactives, it will be more useful to regard the two groups as categories. But those who are giving advice to mothers who complain about the ease of arousal and irritability of their infants may treat the arousal as a continuum.

## IMPLICATIONS

The differences between high reactive-inhibited and low reactive-uninhibited children provoke speculation on many issues; I deal briefly with implications for psychopathology and the relation between psychological and biological propositions.

### Anxiety Disorder

The high reactive infants who became very inhibited 4-year-olds—about 20% of all high reactives—have a low threshold for developing a state of fear to unfamiliar events, situations, and people. It is reasonable to expect that these children will be at a higher risk than most for developing one of the anxiety disorders when they become adolescents or adults. The childhood data do not provide a clue as to which particular anxiety profile will be most prevalent. However, an extensive clinical interview with early adolescents (13–14 years old), who had been classified 11 years earlier (at 21 or 31 months) as inhibited or uninhibited (Kagan et al., 1988), revealed that social phobia was more frequent among inhibited than among uninhibited adolescents, whereas specific phobias, separation anxiety, or compulsive symptoms did not differentiate the two groups (Schwartz, personal communication). This intriguing result, which requires replication, has interesting theoretical ramifications.

Research with animals, usually rats, suggests that acquisition of a fear reaction (e.g., freezing or potentiated startle) to a conditioned stimulus (light or tone) that had been paired with electric shock is mediated by a circuitry that is different from the one that mediates the conditioned response to the context in which the conditioning had occurred (LeDoux, 1995).

Davis (personal communication) has found that a potentiated startle reaction in the rat to the context in which light had been paired with shock involves a circuit from the amygdala to the bed nucleus of the stria terminalis and the septum. The potentiated startle reaction to the conditioned stimulus does not require that circuit. A phobia of spiders or bridges resembles an animal's reaction of freezing to a conditioned stimulus, but a quiet, avoidant posture at a party resembles a fearful reaction to a context. That is, the person who is extremely shy at a party of strangers is not afraid of any particular person or of the setting. Rather, the source of the uncertainty is a situation in which the shy person had experienced anxiety with other strangers. Thus, social phobia may rest on a neurophysiology that is different from that of specific phobia.

### Conduct Disorder

The correlation between social class and the prevalence of conduct disorder or delinquency is so high it is likely that the vast majority of children with these profiles acquired their risk status as a result of life conditions, without the mediation of a particular temperamental vulnerability. However, a small proportion—probably no more than 10%—who began their delinquent careers before age 10, and who often committed violent crimes as adolescents, might inherit a physiology that raises their threshold for the conscious experience of anticipatory anxiety and/or guilt over violating community standards for civil behavior (Tremblay, Pihl, Vitaro, & Dubkin, 1994). Damasio (1994) and Mountcastle (1995) have suggested that the surface of the ventromedial prefrontal cortex receives sensory information (from the amygdala) that originates in the peripheral targets, like heart, skin, gut, and muscles. Most children and adults who think about committing a crime experience a subtle feeling that accompanies anticipation of the consequences of an antisocial act. That feeling, which might be called anticipatory anxiety, shame, or guilt, provides an effective restraint on the action. However, if a small proportion of children possessed a less excitable amygdala, or a ventromedial surface that was less responsive, they would be deprived of the typical intensity of this feeling and, as a result, might be less restrained than the majority (Kochanska, Murray, Jacques, Koenig, & Vandegeest, 1996; Zahn-Waxler, Cole, Welsh, & Fox, 1995). If these children are reared in homes and play in neighborhoods in which antisocial behavior is socialized, they are unlikely to become delinquents; perhaps they will become group leaders. However, if these children live in families that do not socialize aggression consistently and play in neighborhoods that provide temptation for antisocial behavior, they might be candidates for a delinquent career.

## Biology and Psychology

The renewed interest in temperament has brought some psychologists in closer intellectual contact with neuroscientists. Although this interaction will be beneficial to both disciplines, there is a tension between traditional social scientists who describe and explain behavioral and emotional events using only psychological terms and a smaller group who believe that an acknowledgment of biological events is theoretically helpful. The recent, dramatic advances in the neurosciences have led some scholars to go further and to imply that, in the future, robust generalizations about psychological processes might not be possible without study of the underlying biology (LeDoux, 1995).

Although some neuroscientists recognize that the psychological phenomena of thought, planning, and emotion are emergent—as a blizzard is emergent from the physics of air masses—the media suggest, on occasion, that the biological descriptions are sufficient to explain the psychological events. This publicity creates a misperception that the biological and psychological are competing explanations when, of course, they are not. Vernon Mountcastle notes that although "every mental process is a brain process, ...not every mentalistic sentence is identical to some neurophysiological sentence. Mind and brain are not identical, no more than lung and respiration are identical" (Mountcastle, 1995, p. 294).

Some neuroscientists, sensing correctly the community resistance to a strong form of biological determinism, are emphasizing the malleability of the neuron's genome to environmental events. A few neurobiologists have come close to declaring that the human genome, like Locke's image of the child's mind, is a tabula rasa that is subject to continual change. This position tempts citizens unfamiliar with neuroscience to conclude that there may be a linear cascade that links external events (e.g., loss of a loved one) directly to changes in genes, physiology, and, finally, behavior, with the psychological layer (e.g., a mood of sadness) between brain physiology and apathetic behavior being relatively unimportant. This error is as serious as the one made by the behaviorists 60 years ago when they assumed a direct connection between a stimulus and an overt response and ignored what was happening in the brain. Both corpora of evidence are necessary if we are to understand the emergence of psychological qualities and their inevitable variation. "The phenomena of human existence and experience are always simultaneously biological and social, and an adequate explanation must involve both" (Rose, 1995, p. 380).

## ACKNOWLEDGMENTS

This paper represents portions of the G. Stanley Hall Lecture delivered at the annual meeting of the American Psychological Association, New York City, August 1995. Preparation of this paper was supported, in part, by grants from the John D. and Catherine T. MacArthur Foundation, William T. Grant Foundation, and NIMH grant 47077. The author thanks Nancy Snidman and Doreen Arcus for their collaboration in the research summarized.

## ADDRESS AND AFFILIATION

Corresponding author: Jerome Kagan, Harvard University, Department of Psychology, Cambridge, MA 02138; e-mail: JK@WJH.HARVARD.EDU.

## REFERENCES

Adamec, R. E. (1991). Anxious personality and the cat. In B. J. Carroll & J. E. Barrett (Eds.), *Psychopathology in the brain* (pp. 153–168). New York: Raven.

Amaral, D. J., Price, L., Pitkanen, A., & Carmichael, S. T. (1992). Anatomical organization of the primate amygdaloid complex. In J. P. Aggleton (Ed.), *The amygdala* (pp. 1–66). New York: Wiley.

Arcus, D. M. (1991). *Experiential modification of temperamental bias in inhibited and uninhibited children.* Unpublished doctoral dissertation, Harvard University.

Arcus, D. M., & Kagan, J. (1995). Temperament and craniofacial variation in the first two years. *Child Development, 66,* 1529–1540.

Asendorpf, J. B. (1990). Development of inhibition during childhood. *Developmental Psychology, 26,* 721–730.

Bronson, G. W. (1970). Fear of visual novelty. *Developmental Psychology, 2,* 33–40.

Cooper, J. R., Bloom, F. E., & Roth, R. H. (1991). *Biochemical basis of neuropharmacology.* New York: Oxford University Press.

Damasio, A. (1994). *Descartes' error.* New York: Putnam.

Davis, M. (1992). The role of the amygdala in conditioned fear. In J. P. Aggleton (Ed.), *The amygdala* (pp. 256–305). New York: Wiley.

DiLalla, L. F., Kagan, J., & Reznick, J. S. (1994). Genetic etiology of behavioral inhibition among two year olds. *Infant Behavior and Development, 17,* 401–408.

Fagan, J. F. (1981). Infant intelligence. *Intelligence, 5,* 239–243.

Hebb, D. O. (1946). The nature of fear. *Psychological Review, 53,* 259–276.

Kagan, J. (1994). *Galen's prophecy.* New York: Basic.

Kagan, J., Kearsley, R. B., & Zelazo, P. R. (1980). *Infancy*. Cambridge, MA: Harvard University Press.

Kagan, J., Reznick, J. S., & Gibbons, J. (1989). Inhibited and uninhibited types of children. *Child Development, 60*, 838–845.

Kagan, J., Reznick, J. S., & Snidman, N. (1988). Biological bases of childhood shyness. *Science, 240*, 167–171.

Kochanska, G., Murray, K., Jacques, T. Y., Koenig, A. L., & Vandegeest, K. A. (1996). Inhibitory control in young children and its role in emerging internalization. *Child Development, 67*, 490–507.

LeDoux, J. E. (1995). In search of an emotional system in the brain. In M. S. Gazzinaga (Ed.), *The cognitive neurosciences* (pp. 1049–1062). Cambridge, MA: MIT Press.

Mountcastle, V. (1995). The evolution of ideas concerning the function of the neocortex. *Cerebral Cortex, 5*, 289–295.

Murray, D. C. (1971). Talk, silence, and anxiety. *Psychological Bulletin, 75*, 244–260.

Panksepp, J., Sacks, D. S., Crepeau, L. J., & Abbott, B. B. (1991). The psycho and neurobiology of fear systems in the brain. In M. R. Denny (Ed.), *Fear, avoidance, and phobias* (pp. 17–59). Hillsdale, NJ: Erlbaum.

Porges, S. W., Arnold, W. R., & Forbes, E. J. (1973). Heart rate variability: An index of attention responsivity in human newborns. *Developmental Psychology, 8*, 85–92.

Richards, J. E. (1985). Respiratory sinus arrhythmia predicts heart rate and visual responses during visual attention in 14 to 20 week old infants. *Psychophysiology, 22*, 101–109.

Robinson, J. L., Kagan, J., Reznick, J. S., & Corley, R. (1992). The heritability of inhibited and uninhibited behavior: A twin study. *Developmental Psychology, 28*, 1030–1037.

Rose, R. J. 1995. Genes and human behavior. In J. T. Spence, J. M. Darley, & D. P. Foss (Eds.), *Annual review of psychology* (pp. 625–654). Palo Alto, CA: Annual Reviews.

Shimamura, A. P. (1995). Memory and frontal lobe function. In M. S. Gazzinaga (Ed.), *The cognitive neurosciences* (pp. 803–814). Cambridge, MA: MIT Press.

Snidman, N., Kagan, J., Riordan, L., & Shannon, D. (1995). Cardiac function and behavioral reactivity in infancy. *Psychophysiology, 31*, 199–207.

Squire, L. R., & Knowlton, B. J. (1995). Memory, hippocampus, and brain systems. In M. S. Gazzinaga (Ed.), *The cognitive neurosciences* (pp. 825–838). Cambridge, MA: MIT Press.

Tremblay, R. E., Pihl, R. O., Vitaro, F., & Dubkin, P. L. (1994). Predicting early onset of male antisocial behavior from preschool behavior. *Archives of General Psychiatry, 51*, 732–739.

Wilson, D. S., Coleman, K., Clark, A. B., & Biederman, L. (1993). Shy-bold continuum in pumpkinseed sunfish (*Lepomis gibbosus*): An ecological study of a psychological trait. *Journal of Comparative Psychology, 107*, 250–260.

Zahn-Waxler, C., Cole, P., Welsh, J. D., & Fox, N. A. (1995). Psychophysiological correlates of empathy and prosocial behavior in preschool children with behavioral problems. *Development and Psychopathology, 7*, 27–48.

# BABY TALK

**Learning language, researchers are finding, is an astonishing act of brain computation—and it's performed by people too young to tie their shoes**

## By Shannon Brownlee

Inside a small, dark booth, 18-month-old Karly Horn sits on her mother Terry's lap. Karly's brown curls bounce each time she turns her head to listen to a woman's recorded voice coming from one side of the booth or the other. "At the bakery, workers will be baking bread," says the voice. Karly turns to her left and listens, her face intent. "On Tuesday morning, the people have going to work," says the voice. Karly turns her head away even before the statement is finished. The lights come on as graduate student Ruth Tincoff opens the door to the booth. She gives the child's curls a pat and says, "Nice work."

Karly and her mother are taking part in an experiment at Johns Hopkins University in Baltimore, run by psycholinguist Peter Jusczyk, who has spent 25 years probing the linguistic skills of children who have not yet begun to talk. Like most toddlers her age, Karly can utter a few dozen words at most and can string together the occasional two-word sentence, like "More juice" and "Up, Mommy." Yet as Jusczyk and his colleagues have found, she can already recognize that a sentence like "the people have going to work" is ungrammatical. By 18 months of age, most toddlers have somehow learned the rule requiring that any verb ending in *-ing* must be preceded by the verb *to be*. "If you had asked me 10 years ago if kids this young could do this," says Jusczyk, "I would have said that's crazy.

Linguists these days are reconsidering a lot of ideas they once considered crazy. Recent findings like Jusczyk's are reshaping the prevailing model of how children acquire language. The dominant theory, put forth by Noam Chomsky, has been that children cannot possibly learn the full rules and structure of languages strictly by imitating what they hear. Instead, nature gives children a head start, wiring them from birth with the ability to acquire their parents native tongue by fitting what they hear into a preexisting template for the basic structure shared by all languages. (Similarly, kittens are thought to be hard-wired to learn how to hunt.) Language, writes Massachusetts Institute of Technology linguist Steven Pinker, "is a distinct piece of the biological makeup of our brains." Chomsky, a prominent linguist at MIT, hypothesized in the 1950s that children are endowed from birth with "universal grammar," the fundamental rules that are common to all languages, and the ability to apply these rules to the raw material of the speech they hear—without awareness of their underlying logic.

The average preschooler can't tell time, but he has already accumulated a vocabulary of thousands of words—plus (as Pinker writes in his book, *The Language Instinct,*) "a tacit knowledge of grammar more sophisticated than the thickest style manual." Within a few months of birth, children have already begun memorizing words without knowing their meaning. The question that has absorbed—and sometimes divided—linguists is whether children need a special language faculty to do this or instead can infer the abstract rules of grammar from the sentences they hear, using the same mental skills that allow them to recognize faces or master arithmetic.

The debate over how much of language is already vested in a child at birth is far from settled, but new linguistic research already is transforming traditional views of how the human brain works and how language evolved. "This debate has completely changed the way we view the brain," says Elissa Newport, a psycholinguist at the University of Rochester in New York. Far from being an orderly, computer-like machine that methodically calculates step by step, the brain is now seen as working more like a beehive, its swarm of interconnected neurons sending signals back and forth at lightning speed. An infant's brain, it turns out, is capable of taking in enormous amounts of information and finding the regular patterns contained within it. Geneticists and linguists recently have begun to challenge the common-sense assumption that intelligence and language are inextricably linked, through research on a rare genetic disorder called Williams syndrome, which can seriously impair cognition while leaving language nearly intact (box, Rare Disorder Reveals Split between Language and Thought). Increasingly sophisticated technologies such as magnetic resonance imaging are allowing researchers to watch the brain in action, revealing that language literally sculpts and reorganizes the connections within it as a child grows.

The path leading to language begins even before birth, when a developing fetus is bathed in the muffled sound of its mother's voice in the

## Little polyglots. An infant's brain can perceive every possible sound in every language. By 10 months, babies have learned to screen out foreign sounds and to focus on the sounds of their native language.

---

WILLIAMS SYNDROME

# Rare disorder reveals split between language and thought

Kristen Aerts is only 9 years old, but she can work a room like a seasoned pol. She marches into the lab of cognitive neuroscientist Ursula Bellugi, at the Salk Institute for Biological Studies in La Jolla, Calif., and greets her with a cheery, "Good morning Dr. Bellugi. How are you today?" The youngster smiles at a visitor and says, "My name is Kristen. What's yours?" She looks people in the eye when she speaks and asks questions—social skills that many adults never seem to master, much less a third grader. Yet for all her poise, Kristen has an IQ of about 79. She cannot write her address; she has trouble tying her shoes, drawing a simple picture of a bicycle, and subtracting 2 from 4; and she may never be able to live independently.

Kristen has Williams syndrome, a rare genetic disorder that affects both body and brain, giving those who have it a strange and incongruous jumble of deficits and strengths. They have diminished cognitive capacities and heart problems, and age prematurely, yet they show outgoing personalities and a flair for language. "What makes Williams syndrome so fascinating," says Bellugis, "is it shows that the domains of cognition and language are quite separate."

**Genetic gap.** Williams syndrome, which was first described in 1961, results when a group of genes on one copy of chromosome 7 is deleted during embryonic development. Most people with Williams resemble each other more than they do their families, with wide-set hazel eyes, upturned noses, wide mouths. They also share a peculiar set of mental impairments. Most stumble over the simplest spa-

womb. Newborn babies prefer their mothers' voices over those of their fathers or other women, and researchers recently have found that when very young babies hear a recording of their mothers' native language, they will suck more vigorously on a pacifier than when they hear a recording of another tongue.

At first, infants respond only to the prosody—the cadence, rhythm, and pitch—of their mothers' speech, not the words. But soon enough they home in on the actual sounds that are typical of their parents' language. Every language uses a different assortment of sounds, called phonemes, which combine to make syllables. (In English, for example, the consonant sound "b" and the vowel sound "a" are both phonemes, which combine for the syllable *ba*, as in *banana.*) To an adult, simply perceiving, much less pronouncing, the phonemes of a foreign language can seem impossible. In English, the p of *pat* is "aspirated," or produced with a puff of air; the p of *spot* or *tap* is unaspirated. In English, the two p's are considered the same; therefore it is hard for English speakers to recognize that in many other languages the two p's are two different phonemes. Japanese speak-

ers have trouble distinguishing between the "l" and "r" sounds of English, since in Japanese they don't count as separate sounds.

**Polyglot tots.** Infants can perceive the entire range of phonemes, ac-

cording to Janet Werker and Richard Tees, psychologists at the University of British Columbia in Canada. Werker and Tees found that the brains of 4-month-old babies respond to every phoneme uttered in languages as diverse as Hindi and Nthlakampx, a Northwest American Indian language containing numerous consonant combinations that can sound to

a nonnative speaker like a drop of water hitting an empty bucket. By the time babies are 10 months to a year old, however, they have begun to focus on the distinctions among phonemes of their native language

## Discriminating minds. Toddlers listen for bits of language like <u>the</u>, which signals that a noun will follow. Most 2-year-olds can understand "Find the dog," but they are stumped by "Find gub dog."

and to ignore the differences among foreign sounds. Children don't lose the ability to distinguish the sounds of a foreign language; they simply don't pay attention to them. This allows them to learn more quickly the syllables and words of their native tongue.

An infant's next step is learning to fish out individual words from

tial tasks, such as putting together a puzzle, and many cannot read or write beyond the level of a first grader.

In spite of these deficits, Bellugi has found that children with the disorder are not merely competent at language but extraordinary. Ask normal kids to name as many animals as possible in 60 seconds, and a string of barnyard and pet-store examples will tumble out. Ask children with Williams, and you'll get a menagerie or rare creatures, such as ibex, newt, yak, and weasel. People with Williams have the gift of gab, telling elaborate sto-

ries with unabashed verve and incorporating audience teasers such as "Gadzooks!" and "Lo and behold!"

This unlikely suite of skills and inadequacies initially led Bellugi to surmise that Williams might damage the right hemisphere of the brain, where spatial tasks are processed, while leaving language in the left hemisphere intact. That has not turned out to be true. People with Williams excel at recognizing faces, a job that enlists the visual and spatial-processing skills of the right hemisphere. Using functional brain

imaging, a technique that shows the brain in action, Bellugi has found that both hemispheres of the brains of people with Williams are shouldering the tasks of processing language.

Bellugi and other researchers are now trying to link the outward characteristics of people with Williams to the genes they are missing and to changes in brain tissue. They have begun concentrating on the neocerebellum, a part of the brain that is enlarged in people with Williams and that may hold clues to their engaging personalities and to the evolution

of language. The neocerebellum is among the brain's newest parts, appearing in human ancestors about the same time as the enlargement of the frontal cortex, the place where researchers believe rational thoughts are formulated. The neocerebellum is significantly smaller in people with autism, who are generally antisocial and poor at language, the reverse of people with Williams. This part of the brain helps make semantic connections between words, such as *sit* and *chair*, suggesting that it was needed for language to evolve.

the nonstop stream of sound that makes up ordinary speech. Finding the boundaries between words is a daunting task, because people don't pause . . . between . . . words . . . when . . . they speak. Yet children begin to note word boundaries by the time they are 8 months old, even though they have no concept of what most words mean. Last year, Jusczyk and his colleagues reported results of an experiment in which they let 8-month-old babies listen at home to recorded stories filled with unusual words, like *hornbill* and *python*. Two weeks later, the researchers tested the babies with two lists of words, one composed of words they had already heard in the stories, the other of new unusual words that weren't in the stories. The infants listened, on average, to the familiar list for a second longer than to the list of novel words.

The cadence of language is a baby's first clue to word boundaries. In most English words, the first syllable is accented. This is especially noticeable in words known in poetry as trochees—two-syllable words stressed on the first syllable—which parents repeat to young children (BA-by, DOG-gie, MOM-my). At 6 months, American babies pay equal amounts of attention to words with different stress patterns, like gi-RAFFE or TI-ger. By 9 months, however, they have heard enough of the typical first-syllable-stress pattern of English to prefer listening to trochees, a predilection that will show up later, when they start uttering their first words and mispronouncing giraffe as *raff* and banana as *nana*. At 30 months, children can easily repeat the phrase "TOM-my KISS-ed the MON-key," because it preserves the typical English pattern, but they will leave out the *the* when asked to repeat "Tommy patted the monkey." Researchers are now testing whether French babies prefer words with a second-syllable stress—words like be-RET or ma-MAN.

**Decoding patterns.** Most adults could not imagine making speedy progress toward memorizing words in a foreign language just by listening to somebody talk on the telephone.

That is basically what 8-month-old babies can do, according to a provocative study published in 1996 by the University of Rochester's Newport and her colleagues, Jenny Saffran

## Masters of pattern. Researchers played strings of three-syllable nonsense words to 8-month-old babies for two minutes. The babies learned them by remembering how often syllables occurred together.

and Richard Aslin. They reported that babies can remember words by listening for patterns of syllables that occur together with statistical regularity.

The researchers created a miniature artificial language, which consisted of a handful of three-syllable nonsense words constructed from 11 different syllables. The babies heard a computer-generated voice repeating these words in random order in a monotone for two minutes. What they heard went something like "bidaku-padotigolabubidaku." *Bidaku*, in this case, is a word. With no cadence or pauses, the only way the babies could learn individual words was by remembering how often certain syllables were uttered together. When the researchers tested the babies a few minutes later, they found that the infants recognized pairs of syllables that had occurred together consistently on the recording, such as *bida*. They did not recognize a pair like *kupa*, which was a rarer combination that crossed the boundaries of two words. In the past, psychologists never imagined that young infants had the mental capacity to make these sorts of inferences. "We were pretty surprised we could get this result with babies, and with only brief exposure," says Newport. "Real language, of course, is

much more complicated, but the exposure is vast."

Learning words is one thing; learning the abstract rules of grammar is another. When Noam Chomsky first voiced his idea that language is hard-wired in the brain, he didn't have the benefit of the current revolution in cognitive science, which has begun to pry open the human mind with sophisticated psychological experiments and new computer models. Until recently, linguists could only parse languages and marvel at how quickly children master their abstract rules, which give every human being who can speak (or sign) the power to express an infinite number of ideas from a finite number of words.

There also are a finite number of ways that languages construct sentences. As Chomsky once put it, from a Martian's-eye view, everybody on Earth speaks a single tongue that has thousands of mutually unintelligible dialects. For instance, all people make sentences from noun phrases, like "The quick brown fox," and verb phrases, like "jumped over the fence." And virtually all of the world's 6,000 or so languages allow phrases to be moved around in a sentence to form questions, relative clauses, and passive constructions.

**Statistical wizards.** Chomsky posited that children were born knowing these and a handful of other basic laws of language and that they learn their parents' native tongue with the help of a "language acquisition device," preprogrammed circuits in the brain. Findings like Newport's are suggesting to some researchers that perhaps children can use statistical regularities to extract not only individual words from what they hear but also the rules for cobbling words together into sentences.

This idea is shared by computational linguists, who have designed computer models called artificial neural networks that are very simplified versions of the brain and that can "learn" some aspects of language. Artificial neural networks mimic the way that nerve cells, or neurons, inside a brain are hooked up. The result is a device that shares some basic properties with the brain and that can accomplish some linguistic feats that real children perform. For example, a neural network can make general categories out of a jumble of words coming in, just as a child learns that certain kinds of words refer to objects while others refer to actions. Nobody has to teach kids that words like *dog* and *telephone* are nouns, while *go* and *jump* are verbs; the way they use such words in sentences demonstrates that they know the difference. Neural networks also can learn some aspects of the meaning of words, and they can infer some rules of syntax, or word order. Therefore, a computer that was fed English sentences would be able to produce a phrase like "Johnny ate fish," rather than "Johnny fish ate," which is correct in Japanese. These computer models even make some of the same mistakes that real children do, says Mark Seidenberg, a computational linguist at the University of Southern California. A neural network designed by a student of Seidenberg's to learn to conjugate verbs sometimes issued sentences like "He jumped me the ball," which any parent will recognize as the kind of error that could have come from the mouths of babes.

But neural networks have yet to come close to the computation power of a toddler. Ninety percent of the sentences uttered by the average 3-year-old are grammatically correct. The mistakes they do make are rarely random but rather the result of following the rules of grammar with excessive zeal. There is no logical reason for being able to say "I batted the ball" but not "I holded the rabbit," except that about 180 of the most commonly used English verbs are conjugated irregularly.

## Strict grammarians. Most 3-year-olds rarely make grammatical errors. When they do, the mistakes they make usually are the result of following the rules of grammar with excessive zeal.

Yet for all of grammar's seeming illogic, toddlers' brains may be able to spot clues in the sentences they hear that help them learn grammatical rules, just as they use statistical regularities to find word boundaries. One such clue is the little bits of language called grammatical morphemes, which among other things tell a listener whether a word is being used as noun or as a verb. *The,* for instance, signals that a noun will soon follow, while the suffix *ion* also identifies a word as a noun, as in vibration. Psycholinguist LouAnn Gerken of the University of Arizona recently reported that toddlers know what grammatical morphemes signify before they actually use them. She tested this by asking 2-year-olds a series of questions in which the grammatical morphemes were replaced with other words. When asked to "Find the dog for me," for example, 85 percent of children in her study could point to the right animal in a picture. But when the question was "Find *was* dog for me," they pointed to the dog 55 percent of the time. "Find *gub* dog for me," and it dropped to 40 percent.

**Fast mapping.** Children may be noticing grammatical morphemes when they are as young as 10 months and have just begun making connections between words and their definitions. Gerken recently found that infants' brain waves change when they are listening to stories in which grammatical morphemes are replaced with other words, suggesting they begin picking up grammar even before they know what sentences mean.

Such linguistic leaps come as a baby's brain is humming with activity. Within the first few months of life, a baby's neurons will forge 1,000 trillion connections, an increase of 20-fold from birth. Neurobiologists once assumed that the wiring in a baby's brain was set at birth. After that, the brain, like legs and noses, just grew bigger. That view has been demolished, says Anne Fernald, a psycholinguist at Stanford University, "now that we can eavesdrop on the brain." Images made using the brain-scanning technique positron emission tomography have revealed, for instance, that when a baby is 8 or 9 months old, the part of the brain that stores and indexes many kinds of memory becomes fully functional. This is precisely when babies appear to be able to attach meaning to words.

Other leaps in a child's linguistic prowess also coincide with remarkable changes in the brain. For instance, an adult listener can recognize *eleph* as *elephant* within about 400 milliseconds, an ability called "fast mapping" that demands that the brain process speech sounds with phenomenal speed. "To understand strings of words, you have to identify individual words rapidly," says Fernald. She and her colleagues have found that around 15 months of age, a child needs more than a second to recognize even a familiar word, like *baby*. At 18 months, the child can get the picture slightly before the word is ending. At 24 months, she knows the word in a mere 600 milliseconds, as soon as the syllable *bay* has been uttered.

Fast mapping takes off at the same moment as a dramatic reorganization of the child's brain, in which language-related operations, particularly grammar, shift from both sides of the brain into the left hemisphere. Most adult brains are lopsided when it comes to language, processing grammar almost entirely in the left temporal lobe, just over the left ear. Infants and toddlers, however, treat language in both hemispheres, according to Debra Mills, at the University of California–San Diego, and Helen Neville, at the University of Oregon. Mills and Neville stuck electrodes to toddlers' heads to find that processing of words that serve special grammatical functions, such as prepositions, conjunctions, and articles, begins to shift into the left side around the end of the third year.

From then on, the two hemispheres assume different job descriptions. The right temporal lobe continues to perform spatial tasks, such as following the trajectory of a baseball and predicting where it will land. It also pays attention to the emotional information contained in the cadence and pitch of speech. Both hemispheres know the meanings of many words, but the left temporal lobe holds the key to grammar.

This division is maintained even when the language is signed, not spoken. Ursula Bellugi and Edward Klima, a wife and husband team at the Salk Institute for Biological Studies in La Jolla, Caiif., recently demonstrated this fact by studying deaf people who were lifelong signers of American Sign Language and who also had suffered a stroke in specific areas of the brain. The researchers found, predictably, that signers with damage to the right hemisphere had great difficulty with tasks involving spatial perception, such as copying a drawing of a geometric pattern. What was surprising was that right hemisphere damage did not hinder their fluency in ASL, which relies on movements of the hands and body in space. It was signers with damage to the left hemisphere who found they could no longer express themselves in ASL or understand it. Some had trouble producing the specific facial expressions that convey grammatical information in ASL. It is not just speech that's being processed in the left hemisphere, says MIT's Pinker, or movements of the mouth, but abstract language.

Nobody knows why the left hemisphere got the job of processing language, but linguists are beginning to surmise that languages are constructed the way they are in part because the human brain is not infinitely capable of all kinds of computation. "We are starting to see how the universals among languages could arise out of constraints on how the brain computes and how children learn," says Johns Hopkins linguist Paul Smolensky. For instance, the vast majority of the world's languages favor syllables that end in a vowel, though English is an exception. (Think of a native Italian speaking English and adding vowels where there are none.) That's because it is easier for the auditory centers of the brain to perceive differences between consonants when they come before a vowel than when they come after. Human brains can easily recognize *pad, bad,* and *dad* as three different words; it is much harder to distinguish *tab, tap,* and *tad.* As languages around the world were evolving, they were pulled along paths that minimize ambiguity among sounds.

**Birth of a language.** Linguists have never had the chance to study a spoken language as it is being constructed, but they have been given the opportunity to observe a new sign language in the making in Nicaragua. When the Sandinistas came to power in 1979, they established schools where deaf people came together for the first time. Many of the pupils had never met another deaf person, and their only means of communication at first was the expressive but largely unstructured pantomime each had invented at home with their hearing families. Soon the pupils began to pool their makeshift gestures into a system that is similar to spoken pidgin, the form of communication that springs up in places where people speaking mutually unintelligible tongues come together. The next generation of deaf Nicaraguan children, says Judy Kegl, a psycholinguist at Rutgers University, in Newark, N.J., has done it one better, transforming the pidgin sign into a full-blown language complete with regular grammar. The birth of Nicaraguan sign, many linguists believe, mirrors the evolution of all languages. Without conscious effort, deaf Nicaraguan children have created a sign that is now fluid and compact, and which contains standardized rules that allow them to express abstract ideas without circumlocutions. It can indicate past and future, denote whether an action was performed once or repeatedly, and show who did what to whom, allowing its users to joke, recite poetry, and tell their life stories.

Linguists have a long road ahead of them before they can say exactly how a child goes from babbling to banter, or what the very first languages might have been like, or how the brain transforms vague thoughts into concrete words that sometimes fly out of our mouths before we can stop them. But already, some practical conclusions are falling out of the new research. For example, two recent studies show that the size of toddlers' vocabularies depends in large measure on how much their mothers talk to them. At 20 months, according to a study by Janellen Huttenlocher of the University of Chicago, the children of talkative mothers had 131 more words in their vocabularies than children whose mothers were more taciturn. By age 2, the gap had widened to 295 words.

In other words, children need input and they need it early, says Newport. Parking a toddler in front of the television won't improve vocabulary, probably because kids need real human interaction to attach meaning to words. Hearing more than one language in infancy makes it easier for a child to hear the distinctions between phonemes of more than one language later on.

Newport and other linguists have discovered in recent years that the window of opportunity for acquiring language begins to close around age 6, and the gap narrows with each additional candle on the birthday cake. Children who do not learn a language by puberty will never be fluent in any tongue. That means that profoundly deaf children should be exposed to sign language as early as possible, says Newport. If their parents are hearing, they should learn to sign. And schools might rethink the practice of waiting to teach foreign languages until kids are nearly grown and the window on native command of a second language is almost shut.

Linguists don't yet know how much of grammar children are able to absorb simply by listening. And they have only begun to parse the genes or accidents of brain wiring that might give rise, as Pinker puts it, to the poet, the raconteur, or an Alexander Haig, a Mrs. Malaprop. What is certain is that language is one of the great wonders of the natural world, and linguists are still being astonished by its complexity and its power to shape the brain. Human beings, says Kegl, "show an incredible enthusiasm for discourse." Maybe what is most innate about language is the passion to communicate.

# The Cultural Context of Infant Caregiving

*Navaz Peshotan Bhavnagri and Janet Gonzalez-Mena*

*Navaz Peshotan Bhavnagri is Professor, Early Childhood Education, Wayne State University, Detroit.*
*Janet Gonzalez-Mena is Professor, Napa Valley College, Napa, California.*

*To be prepared for the 21st century, early childhood teacher educators, educators of child care personnel, and early childhood practitioners need an expanded conceptualization of infant caregiving. Instead of preaching "universals" exclusively, cultural relativism should be an equally strong focus when preparing practitioners to work in multiple settings (e.g., early intervention programs, parent-infant centers, parent education programs, infant group care and family child care).*

## Significance of Culture in Caregiving

Teaching about the cultural context is critical in infant care for two reasons. First, the caregiver is a vital influence on infants' ongoing socialization and their personality development. Research indicates enormous cultural variations characterize infant caregiving in developing countries, as well as in industrial countries such as the United States (Abbott, 1992; Bhavnagri, 1986; Field, Sostek, Vietze & Leiderman, 1981; Leiderman, Tulkin & Rosenfeld, 1977). Since the 1970s, immigrants to the United States have been mostly from Asia, Latin America and the Middle East (Jackson, 1980; Kitano & Daniel, 1988). They represent greater ethnic, racial and socioeconomic diversity than immigrants from earlier eras, who were primarily European (Grant, 1995). Therefore, their caregiving practices are usually very different than the prevalent Euro-American practices (Lieberman, 1995).

From *Childhood Education*, Fall 1997, pp. 2-8. © 1998 by the Association for Childhood Education International, 17904 Georgia Avenue, Suite 215, Olney, MD 20832. Reprinted by permission.

Recent empirically developed models on immigrant acculturation (e.g., Garza & Gallegos, 1985; Hareven, 1982; Rueschenberg & Buriel,1989) suggest that immigrant families do not simply shed old values for new ones, as accepted previously (e.g., Gordon, 1964; Handlin,1951); rather, they selectively maintain some of their old values and practices, modify some, and alter others. As a result, these immigrants flexibly operate in at least two cultures. Additionally, these new models view the acculturation as a bi-directional process in which the new immigrants modify the mainstream culture, and at the same time individuals in the mainstream culture also change to effectively adjust the immigrants' ways (Patel, Power & Bhavnagri,1996).

Given this large influx of non-European immigrants who are undergoing rapid but selective acculturation and the non-immigrants also undergoing adjustments, we need to retool early childhood training. Well-intentioned professionals armed with child development research are increasingly baffled by new immigrant parents' very different practices, belief systems, perceptions of their children's capabilities, goals for child rearing, world views and life experiences. Therefore, we need to prepare child care professionals to face these challenges.

Second, a dramatic change affecting infants in the United States further necessitates cultural awareness. Whereas in 1977 only 32 percent of the mothers of infants were employed, the figure increased to 48 percent by 1985 (NICHD Early Child Care Research Network, 1996). Currently, more than 50 percent of mothers with infants are in the workforce (Hofferth, Brayfield, Deitch & Holcomb,1991). It is estimated that 278,000 infants and 791,000 toddlers were in child care arrangements in 1988 (U.S. Bureau of the Census,1992). Institutional group child care is growing, of which infant care is the fastest growing segment (Gonzalez-Mena, 1997). By 1990, more than 50 percent of infants under 12 months were being cared for by adults other than their mothers (e.g., a relative, baby sitter, nanny, family child care provider, or staff in center-based care).

It would be best for these multiple caregivers to work in unison, thereby promoting families' resiliency (Lynch, Fulcher & Ayala,1996). This coordinated approach can occur when all caregivers understand, respect and support each others' efforts, share similar goals and beliefs on infant rearing, and perceive infants' abilities in a similar manner. That is not always the situation, however, especially when multiple caregivers are from different cultures. When professionals do offer culturally consistent caregiving, conflicts and culturally assaultive approaches are minimized (Gonzalez-Mena, 1992, 1995). Therefore, we need to prepare professionals for culturally consistent caregiving and empower them to communicate effectively with each other (Anderson & Fenichel, 1989; Phillips, 1995).

---

# We need to prepare professionals for culturally consistent caregiving and empower them to communicate effectively with each other.

---

Given the above rationale, this article asks professionals first to question the universality of all child development theory and research. Next, it asks readers to reflect on sleeptime practices from a comparative child development perspective. This example will help us reexamine our view of "appropriate," "normal" and/ or "best practices." Finally, the authors will recommend strategies to facilitate a paradigm shift from a universal to a cultural view of child development and care.

## Questioning the Universality of Child Development Theory and Research

Early childhood professionals should be fully cognizant that the generally understood universals (e.g., "developmental tasks," "developmental milestones," and "effective," "optimal" or "best practices") in child development are actually based on an extremely small sample of the world's population. The data for these universal determinations come mainly from the Western world, and principally from middle-class people of European extraction (Levine, 1989; Werner, 1979). Furthermore, this Western research is predominantly from the United States. Lozoff (1977) states that the children studied in the context of modern industrialized societies, such as the United States or Europe, are a select group that is not representative of most other cultures and during most of human history.

New (1994) reports that only 9.3 percent of the studies published in *Child Development* between 1986 to 1990 (i.e., the second half of the International Decade of the Child) were studies on culturally and linguistically diverse populations outside the United States. Of these limited studies, still fewer of them explicitly focused on culture in their research designs or provided ethnographic background material for examining the results. Additionally, less than 3 percent of the studies reported focused on children developing in cultures outside the United States.

Bornstein (1991) states that "... it is a truism of contemporary psychological study that the cultural contexts in which children are reared constitute central, yet often neglected, factors in developmental study" (p. 3). Developmental psychologists are just starting to address this gap, as evidenced by the growing research in comparative child development (e.g., Bornstein,1991; Field, Sostek, Vietze & Leiderman, 1981; Munroe & Munroe, 1975; Rogoff, Mistry, Goncu & Mosier, 1993; Wagner & Stevenson, 1982; Whiting & Edwards, 1988).

Comparative child developmental research provides a unique opportunity to: 1 ) expand the range of normal behavior, 2) raise awareness of how culture contributes divergent pathways to children's development, 3) test specific social science hypotheses, 4) generate new hypotheses, 5) test the generalizability of child development theories, 6) integrate multiple research methodologies and disciplines, 7) develop effective policies for international aid and 8) force us to reflect on our beliefs and practices regarding optimal and normative child development (Bornstein, 1991; Harkness, 1980; Hopkins, 1989; Jahoda, 1986; Levine, 1989; New, 1993, 1994; Rogoff & Morelli,1989).

Given the above arguments, how can early childhood professionals mobilize themselves to challenge their assumptions on "universal" child development principles and practices? According to Dewey (1933), individuals should be encouraged to give active, persistent and careful consideration to any supposed form of knowledge or beliefs in light of the grounds that support it and the conclusions that are drawn from it. He defines this process as reflective thinking, and recommends it for solving real-life problems.

Let us, therefore, reflect on one infant caregiving practice—namely, sleep-time routine. According to Ferber (1985,1986), sleeping is an issue of great concern and a "real problem," even more than feeding and toilet training. At least half of all concerns that American parents raise with their pediatricians involve their children's sleeping habits.

## Cultural Caregiving on Sleeping Routines

Caregivers need to reflect upon the following cultural issues related to sleeping routines:

1. *Early childhood professionals need to realize that while mothers and infants sleeping together may be considered "abnormal" by many in the United States, it has been a common and normal practice in most other societies.* Barry and Paxson (1971) analyzed data from 169 societies and found that none of them practiced putting an infant in a separate room to sleep. Whiting, Kluckhohn and Anthony (1958) reported that out of their sample of 56 world societies, only five had sleeping arrangements similar to those of U.S. Americans, where, typically, parents share a bed and the baby sleeps alone. Their study revealed that less than 10 percent of the ethnography of societies they surveyed have infants sleep in a crib or cradle. In other countries, even when the infant has a cradle or cot, it is generally placed within easy reach of the mother's bed. Cultures that practice cosleeping include both highly technological and less technological communities (Morelli, Rogoff, Oppenheim & Goldsmith,1992). Only in Western societies, notably in the middle class of the U.S., do infants have bedrooms of their own (Whiting & Edwards, 1988).

2. *Professionals need to recognize that sleeping arrangements are strongly mandated by value-laden cultural customs, and upheld by elders or "expert" specialists such as pediatricians or psychologists.* Frequently, nationally known American pediatricians who are also specialists on parenting (e.g., Brazelton, 1978, 1979, 1989; Ferber, 1985; Spock, 1968, 1984) discourage the practice of mothers and infants sleeping together. Spock and Rothenberg (1992) state, "I think it's a sensible rule not to take a child into the parents' bed for any reason" (p. 213). Brazelton (1989) recommends, "A child shouldn't fall asleep in her parent's arms; if she does, then the parents have made themselves part of the child's sleep rituals" (p. 69). Ferber (1985) advises, "Sleeping alone is an important part of [the child's] learning to be able to separate from you without anxiety and to see himself as an independent individual" (p. 39). Eighty-four percent of the pediatricians surveyed in Cleveland asserted that an infant should never sleep with his or her parents (Lozoff, Wolf & Davis,1984). At one time, almost all U.S. hospitals separated the mother from the child at birth. Although neonates in hospitals often stay with their mothers, they still do not share the same bed; instead, they have their own crib.

Trevathan and McKenna (1994) advise, "It is important for parents to know that when pediatricians give advice as to where their infants and children should sleep, they are dispensing cultural judgments and not advice based in scientific findings" (p. 101). To foster "optimal" development some cultures put a high value on promoting individuality (e.g., the United States), while other cultures place greater value on relating to others (e.g., Japan) (Caudill & Plath, 1966; Kawasaki, Nugent, Miyashita, Miyahara & Brazelton,1994; Levine, 1989; Rogoff,1990). Such cultures believe that we need to attend to an infant's need for dependency by allowing a child to sleep with the mother, and thereby creating a secure base from which later independence, autonomy and exploration can grow. Gonzalez-Mena (1991) states that, "The word individual is downplayed in some cultures, and the word private is practically nonexistent" (p. 31).

3. *Early childhood educators need to be informed of the consequences of parents and infants sleeping in the same bed, so that they can confidently discuss this practice with parents.* The proponents of this practice state that infants are vulnerable, immature and poorly regulated. Therefore, human contact during sleep helps infants regulate their body temperature and maintain homeostasis. Research also indicates that Sudden Infant Death Syndrome (SIDS) is infrequent in cultures that accept cosleeping (Gantley, Davies & Murcett,1993; McKenna & Mosko,1993). Moreover, studies show that mother-infant states of sleep are synchronized when they sleep together (McKenna, Mosko, Dungy & McAninch, 1990). Keefe (1987) also reports that newborns who slept in the same room as their parents slept more quietly and cried less compared to those who slept in a separate nursery room. Additionally, sleeping together is more convenient and efficient for breastfeeding. Lastly, children are less likely to need transitional objects (e.g., "security" blankets, teddy bears) as psychological substitutes for human contact when parents cosleep and have frequent daytime contacts (Anders & Taylor, 1994).

Early childhood educators also need to be aware of opposing views on the practice. Opponents believe it interferes with the child's independence, intrudes into parental privacy, sexually arouses the oedipal child, and causes more sleep problems (Wolf, Lozoff, Latz & Paludetto, 1996). Anders and Taylor (1994) report that since most child development literature and professional advice is on how to help the baby sleep through the night, parents have those expectations, and deviations from that practice are viewed as "problems." Nighttime awakenings, however, are not viewed as a "problem" in those cultures where parents are socialized to expect it.

4. *Early childhood educators who want to make "developmentally appropriate" decisions need to reflect on the infant's "development" in relation to other primates' development (i.e., comparative child development from an evolutionary perspective) to determine what is "appropriate."* Trevathan and McKenna (1994) recommend that instead of expecting infants to be independent, caregivers need to accept infants as what they actually are— namely, the least neurologically mature of all mammals at birth. Consequently, human infants have to rely far more on their caregivers for their regulation and survival than infants of other mammalian species. To provide this continuous care all primate adults sleep with their infants, with the exception of human infants, who need the most care. Over centuries, human infants have adapted to sleeping with their mothers, and only recently, in an evolutionary sense, has this adaptive mechanism been disrupted. Even monkey infants show significant detrimental effects (e.g., decrease in body temperature, release of stress hormones, cardiac arrhythmias, sleep disturbances and compromised immune systems) when separated from their mother for only three hours. Therefore, an evolutionist would consider it "developmentally inappropriate" to expect infants to sleep separately from their mothers.

5. *Early childhood educators should not sanctimoniously judge sleeping apart as a totally unacceptable practice, but instead understand the historical roots of this practice in Western cultures.* From the 16th to the 18th centuries, some European countries enacted laws requiring infants to sleep separately from parents, ostensibly in order to prevent suffocation. In reality, these laws were a response to infanticide trends. Parents often killed their children because of food shortages, and then would claim to have accidentally rolled over onto the infant during sleep. Around the same time, the husband-wife bond became more prominent than the parent-child bond. The notion of romantic love gained popularity, contributing to the trend for separate sleeping arrangements for parents and children. Additionally, churches supported separate sleeping, to maintain children's purity (Trevathan & McKenna, 1994).

The cultural development of mother and infant sleeping together also needs to be understood. Levine (1977) explains that infant mortality rates were high in all cultures at one time. Therefore, the parents' overriding goal and concern was the child's survival, which was expressed by keeping the infant in close proximity. This continuous surveillance of the infant's well-being resulted in the mother and infant sleeping together. Over time, this effective survival strategy became encoded as a customary practice within a culture, and was socially transmitted from one generation to the next.

6. *When faced with conflicting values, professionals need to reflect and arrive at creative solutions that are in the child's best interests.* At one child care center where each infant had a crib, for example, a baby who had just arrived from Southeast Asia protested mightily at naptime. The staff discovered that he had never slept apart from his mother and had never even seen a crib. His distress was significant. Noting that he could only go to sleep in the noisy playroom, the staff went along with his inclination. A licensing worker objected to the arrangement after finding the infant asleep on a cushion in the corner, citing a law that read, "each child has the right to quiet undisturbed sleep." She interpreted this regulation to mean that babies must sleep in cribs in a special dark and quiet room, apart from the playroom. Twardosz, Cataldo and Risley's [study] (1974) found, however, that infants can sleep as well in a bright, noisy, common play and sleep room as they can in a darkened, quiet and separate sleep area. The head teacher was able to convince the licensing worker that the only way this particular child could get quiet, undisturbed rest was in the midst of people, and thus the licensing law was not violated. The center was granted a waiver for this child! Early childhood professionals can be helped by discussing such creative resolutions.

7. *When sharing the above-mentioned cross-cultural, evolutionary, historical and medical research perspectives, we need to help students reflect on their own practices.* Reflection will help students understand that what they may have considered "abnormal" and "inappropriate" may be considered "normal" and "appropriate" by others. This awareness itself often makes students feel uncomfortable and generates emotional dissonance. For example, some students reported that they "disobeyed" their doctor's advice and had their baby in bed with them for a very long time, but did not tell others because they felt guilty. They are relieved to know of great variations in infant care. Others view these multidisciplinary research perspectives as eye openers, yet are still uncomfortable in directly questioning their long-held beliefs on infant rearing.

The following are some questions to prompt students' reflection: What if a practice is culturally relevant but somewhat developmentally inappropriate? Where does one draw a line? What cultural practices are benign to infants' development and what practices are unquestionably harmful? What is the criteria and who makes this criteria? How are parents' practices adaptive to the original culture? How adaptive are they to current culture? Should they be practiced exactly as before, or should they be modified? Who should decide? How does one reconcile what one strongly believes in, based on research, with what parents believe, especially when the gap between the two is enormous? Are we acting responsibly and sensitively by saying nothing to parents when we disagree with them, or are we abdicating our responsibilities? How can we be sensitive to differing practices and yet be professionals and share our expertise? On what issues must one take a stand, and which ones must we concede as crucial to the parent's and child's reality?

## Recommendations

Overall, the authors recommend including culture as an integral component of all relevant courses (e.g., parent education, family life education, child development, infant child care, developmentally appropriate curriculum). Multicultural early childhood education courses, which typically and almost exclusively focus on cultures that influence the curriculum during formal schooling, should also reflect how different cultures influence socialization practices in infant rearing. Finally, early childhood faculty should broaden their personal definition of multicultural education to readily incorporate this recommendation.

We recommend including in the coursework comparative developmental data generated by many disciplines, such as anthropology, sociology, medicine, social work, history and linguistics, as well as child development. Ethology and attachment theory, for example, can be used to explain Konner's work (1977) regarding significant changes in infant rearing over time; population psychology to explain Levine's work (1977) on parental goals in infant rearing; and psychocultural theory to explain the Whitings's world famous studies on child rearing in six cultures (Whiting, 1963; Whiting, 1977). Also noteworthy are Brofenbrenner's (1979) ecological theory, Triandris's (1979) cross-cultural model and Lester and Brazelton's (1982) biosocial model (see Bhavnagri,1986, for details on these models). Discussions on Vygotsky's (1978) cultural-historical theory (Wertsch & Tulviste, 1992) as applied by Luria (1976) and Rogoff (e.g., Rogoff, 1990; Rogoff, Malkin & Gilbride,1984; Rogoff, Mistry, Goncu & Mosier, 1993) would explain the cultural context of infant caregiving. Readings from some of the sources cited here and from journals such as *Anthropology and Education Quarterly* and *OMEP-International Journal of Early Childhood* would help students.

The authors earlier recommended a reflective approach to deconstruct the universality of child development theories. This same reflective and dialectic approach is an effective tool for reconstructing culture's contribution to child development. Instead of prescriptively "pouring in" knowledge, we should encourage the co-construction of knowledge on cultural relativism by facilitating student-teacher and student-peer dialogues. Schon (1987) believes that such "reflection-on-action" and "reflection-in-action" helps students to confront unique situations in the real world of practice, when they feel uncertain and have value conflicts. Infant-rearing issues are fettered with uncertainties, value conflicts, and moral and ethical dilemmas for students to reflect upon and question. Finally, reflection could permit students to co-construct a position that is truly accepting of divergent practices.

In addition, when teacher educators use this reflective and dialectical approach, they empower their students to use this same approach with parents of the infants in their care. When students use reflective practices with parents, they empower parents to reflect on their own cultural practices in an enlightened manner and to consider multiple options in infant rearing. Teacher educators should also offer well-guided learning experiences, in which students frequently, meaningfully and reflectively interact with parents of diverse cultures. This practice will reduce students' apprehensions, help them confront their preconceived belief systems about diverse families and offer continuity between the center and home care (Chang & Pulido, 1994; Harry, Torguson, Katkavich & Guerrero, 1993; Whaley & Swadener, 1990). In conclusion, such reflections are necessary for both professionals and parents if they are to work together as a team in the best interests of the child.

# References

Abbott, S. (1992). Holding on and pushing away: Comparative perspectives on an Eastern Kentucky child-rearing practice. *Ethos, 20,* 33–65.

Anders, T. F., & Taylor, T. R. (1994). Babies and their sleep environment. *Children's Environments, 11,* 123–134.

Anderson, P. P., & Fenichel, E. S. (1989). *Serving culturally diverse families of infants and toddlers with disabilities.* Washington, DC: National Center for Clinical Infant Programs.

Barry, H., & Paxson, L. (1971). Infancy and early childhood: Cross-cultural codes 2. *Ethnology, 10,* 466–508.

Bhavnagri, N. (1986). Mother-infant interactions in various cultural settings. In L. G. Katz (Ed.), *Current topics in early childhood: Vol. 6* (pp. 1–32). Norwood, NJ: Ablex.

Bornstein, M. H. (Ed.). (1991). *Cultural approaches to parenting.* Hillsdale, NJ: Lawrence Erlbaum Associates.

Brazelton, T. B. (1978, October). Why your baby won't sleep. *Redbook,* p. 82.

Brazelton, T. B. (1979, June). What parents told me about handling children's sleep problems. *Redbook,* pp. 51–54.

Brazelton, T. B. (1989, February 13). Working parents. *Newsweek,* pp. 66–77.

Bronfenbrenner, U. (1979). *The ecology of human development.* Cambridge, MA: Harvard University Press.

Caudill, W., & Plath, D. W. (1966). Who sleeps by whom? Parent-child involvement in urban Japanese families. *Psychiatry, 29,* 344–366.

Chang, H. N. L., & Pulido, D. (1994). The critical importance of cultural and linguistic continuity for infants and toddlers. *Zero to Three, 15*(2), 13–17.

Dewey, J. (1933). *How we think.* Boston: DC Heath and Company.

Ferber, R. (1985). *Solve your child's sleep problem.* New York: Simon and Schuster.

Ferber, R. (1986). Sleepless child. In C. Guilleminault (Ed.), *Sleep and its disorders in children* (pp. 41–163). New York: Raven Press.

Field, T. M., Sostek, A. M., Vietze, P., & Leiderman, P. H. (Eds.). (1981). *Culture and early interactions.* Hillsdale, NJ: Lawrence Erlbaum Associates.

Gantley, M., Davies, D. P., & Murcett, A. (1993). Sudden infant death syndrome: Links with infant care practices. *British Medical Journal, 306,* 16–20.

Garza, R. T., & Gallegos, P. I. (1985). Environmental influences and personal choice: A humanistic perspective on acculturation. *Hispanic Journal of Behavioral Sciences, 7,* 365–379.

Gonzalez-Mena, J. (1991, July / August). Do you have cultural tunnel vision? *Child Care Information Exchange,* pp. 29–31.

Gonzalez-Mena, J. (1992). Taking a culturally sensitive approach in infant-toddler programs. *Young Children, 47*(2), 4–9.

Gonzalez-Mena, J. (1995). Cultural sensitivity in routine caregiving tasks. In P. Mangione (Ed.), *Infant/toddler caregiving: A guide to culturally sensitive care* (pp. 12–19). Sacramento, CA: Far West Laboratory and California Department of Education.

Gonzalez-Mena, J. (1997). *Multicultural issues in child care* (2nd ed.). Mountainview, CA: Mayfield.

Gordon, M. (1964). *Assimilation in American life.* New York: Oxford University Press.

Grant, R. (1995). Meeting the needs of young second language learners. In E. E. Garcia, B. McLaughlin, B. Spodek, & O.N. Saracho (Eds.), *Meeting the challenge of linguistic and cultural diversity in early childhood education* (pp.1–17). New York: Teachers College Press.

Handlin, O. (1951). *The uprooted.* Boston: Little, Brown.

Hareven, T. (1982). *Family time and industrial time.* New York: Cambridge University Press.

Harkness, S. (1980). The cultural context of child development. In C. M. Super & S. Harkness (Eds.), *Anthropological perspectives on child development: Vol. 8. New direction for child development* (pp. 7–13). San Francisco: Freeman.

Harry, B., Torguson, C., Katkavich, J., & Guerrero, M. (1993). Crossing social class and cultural barriers in working with families. *Teaching Exceptional Children, 26*(1), 48–51.

Hofferth, S., Brayfield, A., Deitch, S., & Holcomb, P. (1991). *National child care survey, 1990.* Washington, DC: Urban Institute.

Hopkins,B. (1989). Culture,infancy and education. *European Journal of Psychology of Education, IV,* 289–293.

Jackson, K. (1980). The old minorities and the new: Understanding a new cultural idiom in U.S. history. In M. Kritz (Ed.), *U.S. immigration and refugee policy: Global and domestic issues* (pp. 313–335). Lexington, MA: Lexington Books.

Jahoda, G. (1986). A cross-cultural perspective on developmental psychology. *International Journal of Behavioral Development, 9,* 417–437.

Kawasaki, C. Nugent, J. K., Miyashita, H., Miyahara, H., & Brazelton, T. B. (1994). The cultural organization of infants' sleep. *Children's Environments, 11,* 135–141.

Keefe, M. R. (1987). Comparison of neonatal night-time sleep-wake patterns in nursery versus rooming-in environments. *Nursing Research, 36,* 140–144.

Kitano, H. L., & Daniel, R. (1988). *Asian Americans: Emerging minorities.* Englewood Cliffs, NJ: Prentice-Hall.

Konner, M. (1977). Evolution of human behavior development. In P. Leiderman, S. Tulkin, & A. Rosenfeld (Eds.), *Culture and infancy: Variations in the human experience* (pp. 69–109). New York: Academic Press.

Leiderman, P. H., Tulkin, S. R., & Rosenfeld, A. (Eds.). (1977). *Culture and infancy: Variations in the human experience.* New York: Academic Press.

Lester, B. M., & Brazelton, T. B. (1982). Cross cultural assessment of neonatal behavior. In D. A. Wagner & H. W. Stevenson (Eds.), *Cultural perspectives on child development* (pp. 20–53). San Francisco: W. H. Freeman.

Levine, R. A. (1977). Child rearing as cultural adaptation. In P. Leiderman, S. Tulkin, & A. Rosenfeld (Eds.), *Culture and infancy: Variations in the human experience* (pp.15–27). New York: Academic Press.

Levine, R. A. (1989). Cultural environments in child development. In W. Damon (Ed.), *Child development today and tomorrow* (pp. 52–68). San Francisco: Jossey-Bass.

Lieberman, A. F. (1995). Concerns of immigrant families. In P. Mangione (Ed.), *Infant/toddler caregiving: A guide to culturally sensitive care* (pp. 28–37). Sacramento, CA: Far West Laboratory and California Department of Education.

Lozoff, B. (1977, March). *The sensitive period: An anthropological view.* Paper presented at the Biennial Meeting of the Society for Research in Child Development, New Orleans.

Lozoff, B., Wolf, A., & Davis, N. (1984). Cosleeping in urban families with young children in the United States. *Pediatrics, 74,* 171–182.

Luria, A. R. (1976). *Cognitive development: Its cultural and social foundations* (M. Lopez-Morillas & L. Solotaroff, Trans.). Cambridge, MA: Harvard University Press.

Lynch, E. W., Fulcher, J. L., & Ayala, E. (1996). Cross-cultural competence in infant care and intervention: Recognizing resilience. *Focus on Infancy, 8*(3), 1–4.

McKenna, J. J., & Mosko, S. (1993). Evolution and infant sleep: An experimental study of infant-parent cosleeping

and its implications for SIDS. *Acta Paediatrica Supplement, 389,* 31–36.

McKenna, J. J., Mosko, S., Dungy, C., & McAninch, P. (1990). Sleep and arousal patterns of co-sleeping human mothers/infant pairs: A preliminary physiological study with implications for the study of Sudden Infant Death Syndrome (SIDS). *American Journal of Physical Anthropology, 83,* 331–347.

Morelli, G. A., Rogoff, B., Oppenheim, D., & Goldsmith, D. (1992). Culture variation in infants' sleeping arrangements: Questions of independence. *Developmental Psychology, 28,* 604–613.

Munroe, R. L., & Munroe, R. H. (1975). *Cross-cultural human development.* Belmont, CA: Wadsworth.

New, R. (1993). Cultural variations on developmentally appropriate practice. In C. Edwards, L. Gandini, & G. Forman (Eds.), *The hundred languages of children: The Reggio Emilia approach to early childhood education* (pp. 215– 231). Norwood, NJ: Ablex.

New, R. (1994). Culture, child development, and developmentally appropriate practices: Teachers as collaborative researchers. In B. Mallory and R. New (Eds.), *Diversity and developmentally appropriate practices* (pp. 2–9). New York: Teachers College Press.

NICHD Early Child Care Research Network, The. (1996, Spring). Child care and the family: An opportunity to study development in context. *SRCD Newsletter,* pp. 4–6.

Patel, N., Power, T., & Bhavnagri, N. P. (1996). Socialization values and practices of Indian immigrant parents: Correlates of modernity and acculturation. *Child Development, 67,* 302–313.

Phillips, C. B. (1995). Culture: A process that empowers. In P. Mangione (Ed.), *Infant/toddler caregiving: A guide to culturally sensitive care* (pp. 2–9). Sacramento, CA: Far West Laboratory and California Department of Education.

Rogoff, B. (1990). *Apprenticeship in thinking: Cognitive development in social context.* New York: Oxford University Press.

Rogoff, B., Malkin, C., & Gilbride, K. (1984). Interaction with babies as guidance in development. *New Directions for Child Development, 23,* 31–44.

Rogoff, B., Mistry, J., Goncu, A., Mosier, C. (1993). Guided participation in cultural activity by toddlers and caregivers. *Monographs of the Society for Research in Child Development, 58,* (8, Serial No. 236).

Rogoff, B., & Morelli, B. (1989). Perspectives on children's development from cultural psychology. *American Psychologist, 44,* 343–348.

Rueschenberg, E., & Buriel, R. (1989). Mexican American family functioning and acculturation: A family systems perspective. *Hispanic Journal of Behavioral Sciences, 11,* 232–244.

Schon, D. S. (1987). *Educating the reflective practitioner.* San Francisco: Jossey-Bass.

Spock, B. (1968). *Baby and child care.* New York: Meredith Press. (Originally published in 1945).

Spock, B., & Rothenberg, M. B. (1992). *Dr. Spock's baby and child care.* New York: Pocket Books.

Spock, B. J. (1984, December). Mommy, can I sleep in your bed? *Parents Magazine,* p. 129.

Trevathan, W. R., & McKenna, J. J. (1994). Evolutionary environments of human birth and infancy: Insights to apply to contemporary life. *Children's Environments, 11,* 88–104.

Triandis, H. C. (1979). Cross-cultural psychology. In M. E. Meyer (Ed.), *Foundations of contemporary psychology* (pp. 544–579). New York: Oxford: Press.

Twardosz, S., Cataldo, M. F., & Risley, T. R. (1974). Open environment design for infant and toddler day care. *Journal of Applied Behavior, Anal., 7,* 529–546.

U.S. Bureau of the Census. (1992). *Who's minding the kids? Child care arrangements: Fall 1988.* (Current Population Report, 30). Washington, DC: Author.

Vygotsky, L. S. (1978). *Mind in society: The development of higher mental processes.* Cambridge, MA: Harvard University Press.

Wagner, D. A., & Stevenson, H. W. (Ed.). (1982). *Cultural perspectives on child development.* San Francisco: W. H. Freeman.

Werner, E. E. (1979). *Cross-cultural child development.* Belmont, CA: Wadsworth.

Wertsch, J. V., & Tulviste, P. (1992). L. S. Vygotsky and contemporary developmental psychology. *Developmental Psychology, 28,* 548–557.

Whaley, K., & Swadener, E. (1990). Multicultural education in infant and toddler settings. *Childhood Education, 66,* 238–240.

Whiting, B. B. (Ed.). (1963). *Six cultures: Studies of child-rearing.* New York: Wiley.

Whiting, B. B., & Edwards, C. P. (1988). *Children of different worlds: The formation of social behavior.* Cambridge, MA: Harvard University Press.

Whiting, J. W. M., Kluckhohn, R., & Anthony, A. S. (1958). The function of male initiation ceremonies at puberty. In E. E. Maccoby, T. Newcomb, & E. Hartley (Eds.), *Readings in social psychology* (pp.359–370). New York: Holt.

Whiting, J. W. M. (1977). A model of psychocultural research. In P. Leiderman, S. Tulkin, & A. Rosenfeld (Eds.), *Culture and infancy: Variations in the human experience* (pp. 29–48). New York: Academic Press.

Wolf, A. W., Lozoff, B., Latz, S., & Paludetto, R. (1996). Parental theories in the management of sleep routines in Japan, Italy and the United States. In S. Harkness & C. M. Super (Eds.), *Parents' cultural belief systems* (pp. 364–385). New York: Guilford.

YOUR CHILD'S FIRST STEPS

# The Language Explosion

By Geoffrey Cowley

**B**ARRY IS A PIXIE-FACED 3-YEAR-OLD who can't yet draw a circle or stack his blocks in a simple pattern. There is little chance he will ever live independently. He may never learn to tie his own shoes. Yet Barry is as chatty and engaging a person as you could ever hope

## Whether they emerge speaking English, Spanish, Czech or Hindi, children all travel the same road as they learn to speak and understand words

to meet. He knows his preschool classmates—and their parents—by name. When he wakes his mom in the morning, he strokes her cheek and tells her how beautiful she is. Then he asks her how she slept. Barry has Williams syndrome, a rare congenital disorder caused by abnormalities on chromosome 7. Children with the condition share an array of distinctive traits, including weak hearts, elfin faces and extremely low IQs. But they're unusually sociable, and often display an extraordinary feeling for language. Ask a Williams child to name an animal, says Dr. Ursula Bellugi of the Salk Institute's Laboratory for Cognitive Neuroscience, and you may get a fanciful discourse on yaks, koalas or unicorns.

If we learned language in the same way that we learn to add, subtract or play cards, children like Barry would not get much be-

yond hello and goodbye. Nor, for that matter, would normal toddlers. As anyone who has struggled through college French can attest, picking up a new language as an adult is as simple as picking up a truck. Yet virtually every kid in the world succeeds at it and without conscious effort. Children attach meanings to sounds long before they shed their diapers. They launch into grammatical analysis before they can tie their shoes. And by the age of 3, most produce sentences as readily as laughter or tears.

Scholars have bickered for centuries over how kids accomplish this feat, but most now agree that their brains are wired for the task. Like finches or sparrows, which learn to sing as hatchlings or not at all, we're designed to acquire certain kinds of knowledge at particular stages of development. Children surrounded by words almost always become fluent by 3, whatever their general intelligence. And people deprived of language as children rarely master it as adults, no matter how smart they are or how intensively they're trained. As MIT linguist Steven Linker observes in his acclaimed 1994 book "The Language Instinct," "Language is not a cultural artifact that we learn the way we learn to tell time or how the federal government works. It is a distinct piece of [our] biological makeup." Whether they emerge speaking Spanish, Czech or Hindi, kids all acquire language on the same general schedule. And as a growing body of research makes clear, they all travel the same remarkable path.

## Sound

THE JOURNEY TOWARD LANGUAGE STARTS NOT in the nursery but in the womb, where the fetus is continually bathed in the sounds of its mother's voice. Babies just 4 days old can distinguish one language from another. French newborns suck more vigorously when they hear French spoken than when they hear Russian—and Russian babies show the opposite preference. At first, they notice only general rhythms and melodies.

But newborns are also sensitive to speech sounds, and they home in quickly on the ones that matter.

Each of the world's approximately 6,000 languages uses a different assortment of phonemes, or distinctive sounds, to build words. As adults, we have a hard time even hearing phonemes from foreign languages. The French don't notice any real difference between the *th* sounds in *thick* and *thin*—and

## Kids attach meanings to sounds before they shed their diapers and analyze grammar by age 3

to most English speakers, the vowel in the French word *tu* (*ee* through rounded lips) is just another *oo*. Researchers have found that month-old infants register both of those distinctions and countless others from the world's languages. But at 6 and 10 months, they start to narrow their range. They grow oblivious to foreign phonemes while staying attuned to whatever sounds the speakers around them are using.

Acquiring a set of phonemes is a first step toward language, but just a baby step. To start decoding speech, you have to recognize words. And as anyone listening to a foreign conversation quickly discovers, people don't talk one . . . word . . . at . . . a . . . time. Real-life language—even the melodious "parentese" that parents use with infants—consists mainly of nonstop streams of sound. So how do babies suss out the boundaries? Long before they recognize words, says Peter Jusczyk, a cognitive scientist at Johns Hopkins University, they get

 From *Newsweek*, Spring/Summer 1997, pp. 16-17, 20-22. © 1997 by Newsweek, Inc. All rights reserved. Reprinted by permission.

a feel for how their language uses phonemes to launch syllables. By the time they're 7 months old, American babies are well accustomed to hearing t joined with *r* (as in *tram*) and c with *l* (as in *clam*), but they've been spared combinations like *db, gd, kt, ts* and *ng*, all of which occur in other languages. And once they have an ear for syllables, word boundaries become less mysterious. *Ten / groaning / deadbeats / are / cleaning / a / train on / blacktop* makes acoustic sense in English, even if you don't know the words. *Te / ngroanin / gdea / dbea / tsare / cleani / nga / traino / nbla / cktop* isn't an option.

As children start to recognize and play with syllables, they also pick up on the metrical patterns among them. French words tend to end with a stressed syllable. The majority of English words—and virtually all of the *mommy-daddy-baby-doggie* diminutives that parents heap on children—have the accented syllable up front. Until they're 6 months old, American babies are no more responsive to words like *bigger* than they are to words like *guitar*. But Jusczyk has found that 6- to 10-month-olds develop a clear bias for words with first-syllable accents. They suck more vigorously when they hear such words, regardless of whether they're read from lists or tucked into streams of normal speech. The implication is that children less than a year old hear speech not as a blur of sound but as a series of distinct but meaningless words.

## Meaning

BY THEIR FIRST BIRTHDAY, MOST KIDS START linking words to meanings. Amid their streams of sweet, melodic gibberish they start to name things—ball, cup, bottle, doggie. And even those who don't speak for a while often gesture to show off their mastery of the nose, eyes, ears and toes. These may seem small steps; after all, most 1-year-olds are surrounded by people who insist on pointing and naming every object in sight. But as Pinker observes, making the right connections is a complicated business. How complicated? Imagine yourself surrounded by people speaking a strange language. A rabbit runs by, and someone shouts, *"Gavagai!"* What does the word mean? "Rabbit" may seem the obvious inference, but it's just one of countless logical alternatives. *Gavagai* could refer to that particular creature, or it could have a range of broader meanings, from "four-legged plant eater" to "furry thing in motion." How do kids get to the right level of generalization? Why don't they spend their lives trying to figure out what words like "rabbit" mean?

Because, says Stanford psychologist Ellen Markman, they come to the game with innate mental biases. Markman has shown that instead of testing endless hypotheses

## How to Talk 'Parentese' to Your Child

PEOPLE THE WORLD OVER alter their way of speaking when they address infants and toddlers. The effects of "parentese" (originally called "motherese") continue to be hotly debated, but "a number of [its] features are likely to facilitate language learning," says linguist Naomi Baron of The American University. Among them:

Higher **pitch** captures a child's attention. Speaking more slowly, and with careful enunciation, makes it easier for the baby to distinguish individual words; emphasizing or repeating one word ("Isn't that a huuuuuge doggie?") also helps.

**Short utterances** help the child grasp grammar more readily than Faulknerian monologues. Don't abandon complex sentences entirely, though: toddlers whose parents use many dependent clauses ("because . . ." and "which . . .") learn to do so earlier than the children of parents who do not.

**Repeating** a child's utterances ("That's right! It's a birdie") assures her she's been understood. Recasting what the child says ("Want cookie?" "Would you like a cookie?") expands her repertoire. The only aspect of parentese that may impede language development: substituting proper nouns for **pronouns** ("Does Billy want to swing?"). These are tricky to master (your you is my "I"), and toddlers should be exposed to them.

### Red Flags

Even normal children whose ears are filled with parentese may refuse to speak. Some delays can be harmless, but those after the age of 3 may well affect how well a child will read, write and even think.

- **0–3 months** Does not turn when you speak or repeat sounds like coos.
- **4–6 months** Does not respond to "no" or changes in tone of voice, look around for sources of sound like a doorbell, or babble in speech-like sounds such as p, b and m.
- **7–12 months** Does not recognize words for common items, turn when you call her name, imitate speech sounds or use sounds other than crying to get your attention.
- **1–2 years** Cannot point to pictures in a book that you name or understand simple questions ("Where is your Teddy?").
- **2–3 years** Can't understand differences in meaning ("up" vs. "down"), follow two requests ("please pick up the bottle and give it to me"), string together two or three words or name common objects.
- **3–4 years** Does not answer simple "who," "what" and "where" questions. Cannot be understood by people outside the family, use four-word sentences or pronounce most phonemes correctly. If delays persist until kindergarten, most pediatricians recommend speech therapy.

## Using innate linguistic software, kids assume that labels refer to wholes rather than parts, and to classes (cups, balls), not individual items

about each word's meaning, kids start from three basic assumptions. First, they figure that labels refer to whole objects, not parts or qualities. Second, they expect labels to denote classes of things (cups, balls, rabbits) rather than individual items. Third, they assume that anything with a name can have only one. These assumptions don't always lead directly to the right inference ("I'm not a noying," Dennis the Menace once told Mr. Wilson, "I'm a cowboy"). But they vastly simplify word learning. In keeping with the "whole object" assumption, a child won't consider a label for "handle" until she has one for "cup." And thanks to the "one label per object" assumption, a child who has mastered the word *cup* never assumes that *handle* is just another way of saying the same thing. "In that situation," says Markman, "the child accepts the possibility that the new word applies to some feature of the object."

Words accrue slowly at first. But around the age of 18 months, children's abilities explode. Most start acquiring new words at the phenomenal rate of one every two hours—and for the first time, they start combining them. Children don't all reach these milestones on exactly the same schedule; their development rates can vary by a year or more, and there's no evidence that late talkers end up less fluent than early talkers. But by their second birthdays, most kids have socked away 1,000 to 2,000 words and started tossing around two-word strings such as "no nap," "all wet" or "bottle juice."

## Grammar

ONCE KIDS CAN PASTE TWO WORDS TOGETHER, it's not long before they're generating sentences. Between 24 and 30 months, "no nap" may become "I don't want nap," and "bottle juice" may blossom into "I want juice." When kids hit that stage, their repertoires start expanding exponentially. Between 30 and 36 months, most acquire rules for expressing tense (*walk* versus *walked*) and number (*house* versus *houses*), often overextending them to produce statements like "I bringed home three mouses." They also start using "function words"—the *somes, woulds, whos, hows* and *afters* that enable us to ask either "Do you like milk?" or "Would you like some milk?"

More fundamentally, they discover that words can have radically different meanings depending on how they're strung together. Even before children start combining words on their own, most know the difference between "Big Bird is tickling Cookie Monster" and "Cookie Monster is tickling Big Bird." That awareness marks the zenith of language development. A chimp can learn to label things, and a high-powered computer can process more information in a minute than any person could handle in a lifetime. But neither a chimp nor a mainframe is any match for a runny-nosed 3-year-old when it comes to reporting who did what to whom. When a chimp with a signboard signals "Me banana you banana you," chances are he wants you to give him one, but the utterance could mean almost anything. Three-year olds don't talk that way. The reason, most linguists agree, is that natural selection has outfitted the human brain with software for grammatical analysis. As MIT linguist Noam Chomsky realized more than 30 years ago, the world's languages all build sentences from noun phrases ("The big dog") and verb phrases ("ate my homework"). And toddlers who have never heard of grammar identify them effortlessly.

To confirm that point, psycholinguists Stephen Cram and Mineharu Nakayama once invited 3-, 4- and 5-year-olds to interview a talking "Star Wars" doll (Jabba the Hutt). With a child at his side, one researcher would pull out a picture and suggest asking Jabba about it. For example: "Ask Jabba if the boy who is unhappy is watching Mickey Mouse." You can't compose the right sentence—"Is the boy who is unhappy watching Mickey Mouse?"—unless you recognize *the-boy-who-is-unhappy* as a single noun phrase. As Chomsky would have predicted, the kids got it right every time.

If children's minds were open to all the possible relationships among words, they would never get very far. No one could memorize 140 million sentences, but a kid who masters 25 common recipes for a noun phrase can produce more than that number from scratch. Too much mental flexibility would confine children, Pinker observes; innate constraints set them free." Not everyone is blessed with those constraints. Kids with a hereditary condition known as Specific Language Impairment, or SLI, never develop certain aspects of grammar, despite their normal IQs. But those are rare exceptions. Most kids are so primed for grammatical rules that they'll invent them if necessary.

Consider hearing adults who take up American Sign Language so they can share it with their deaf children. They tend to fracture phrases and leave verbs unconjugated. Yet their kids still become fluent, grammatical signers. "Children don't need good teachers to master language," says Elissa Newport, a cognitive scientist at the University of Rochester. "They pick up whatever rules they can find, and sharpen and extend them." That, according to University of Hawaii linguist Derek Bickerton, is why the crude pidgins that crop up in mixed-language communities quickly evolve into fully grammatical creoles. When language lacks a coherent granular, children create one.

That's not to say language requires no nurture. Children raised in complete silence grow deaf to grammar. "Chelsea," whose correctable hearing problem went untreated until she was 31, eventually learned enough words to hold a job in a vet's office. Yet her expressive powers have never surpassed those of a chimp with a signboard. She says things like "The woman is bus the going" or "I Wanda be drive come." Fortunately, Chelsea is a rare exception. Given even a few words to play with, most kids quickly take flight. "You don't need to have left the Stone Age," Pinker says. "You don't need to be middle class." All you need to be is young.

---

*With* DONNA FOOTE *in Los Angeles*

# Defining the trait that makes us human

**The ability to empathize with others is critical to our survival as a species, behavioral researchers say.**

**By Beth Azar**
*Monitor* staff

When a content newborn baby hears another baby crying, it also begins to wail. It's not just the loud noise, but also the sound of a fellow human in distress that triggers the baby's crying, researchers find.

New York University psychologist Martin Hoffman, PhD, believes this reflexive crying of newborns is a precursor to human empathy—the ability to observe the anguish or joy of another person and take it on as your own.

This ability has allowed humans to live as a communal species, say social scientists. The trait allows us to move beyond mere survival to helping our fellow humans.

"Empathy serves several major functions," says psychologist Janet Strayer, PhD, of Simon Fraser University. "It is a form of nonverbal communication, letting us know when others are distressed or in danger. It allows us to understand another's feelings, motivating a desire to help. And it gives people a sense of 'I am like

Nita Winter

**Empathy develops along with a child's ability to understand the internal lives of others.**

you and you are like me.' In short, we wouldn't be able to live without it."

Several developmental psychologists, including Carolyn Zahn-Waxler, PhD, of the National Institute of Mental Health, and Nancy Eisenberg, PhD, of the University of Arizona,

have begun to piece together the development of empathy, from basic biological instincts to the roles parents and society play in fostering empathy.

The precise definition of empathy varies depending on whom you talk to. But most psychologists agree that there are two aspects of empathy: an affective aspect—a person *feels* what another is feeling (either the exact emotion or a congruent emotion)—and a cognitive aspect—a person understands what another person is feeling and why.

**Toward an outward focus**

More than 20 years ago, Hoffman developed a five-stage model of empathy development based on anecdotal evidence from several children. Today, his theory is gaining support from empirical research.

"It turns out he was right on target," says Zahn-Waxler, who has been studying empathy for as long as Hoffman's been theorizing about it.

According to the model, empathy develops along with the ability to distinguish the self from others. Newborns

> ## There is . . . a lot of social scaffolding and experiences that can influence how empathy develops, which means we can do something about it."
>
> *Janet Strayer*
> *Simon Fraser University*

make no distinction between themselves and others. When they hear another infant cry, they start to cry far more from that than when they hear any other loud noise.

Sometime late in the first year, babies begin to understand that they are separate from others. When they hear or observe someone in distress, they understand that it's someone else who's upset. Even so, they often look upset and might run to their mothers.

As the self-other distinction becomes clearer—some time after the first year—babies begin trying to help people in distress, often using strategies they themselves find comforting. For example, they might offer their teddy bear or bring a crying child to their own mothers.

By the end of the second year, children are beginning to understand that everyone has their own internal feelings. They're able to use cognitively complex empathic mechanisms, including very early forms of role-taking (see sidebar). By age 4 or 5, children can understand the social situations that can cause people distress. This process continues to evolve throughout life.

"Self-recognition increases along with the development of a concern for others," says Zahn-Waxler, who, along with her colleagues, has followed more than 500 children over time to learn how they respond to distress in others.

These longitudinal studies provide strong support for the early stages described in Hoffman's model. Between

the ages of 1 and 2, children develop empathic concern, cognitive understanding and a repertoire of helpful, comforting behaviors, says Zahn-Waxler.

Eisenberg, Richard Fabes, PhD, and their colleagues believe that whether people feel sympathy or personal distress—which stems from empathy, according to their model—when they observe someone else in distress depends, in part, on how well they can regulate their own emotions.

They've found that children who become overaroused when they witness others in distress show less sympathy than children who are able to regulate their emotional responses.

Children who feel personal distress are less likely to help a person in distress, while those who feel sympathy are more likely to help.

### Nature *and* nurture

Most empathy researchers agree there's some biological disposition toward empathy. By 14 months, identical twins are more similar to each other on measures of empathy than fraternal twins, according to a study by Zahn-Waxler, JoAnn Robinson, PhD, of the University of Colorado Health Sciences Center, and their colleagues. Researchers also find significant individual differences in

## Can your dog empathize with you?

Some researchers would say empathy is one of the emotions that sets humans apart from animals. It's an act of great sophistication requiring a complex cognitive analysis of another person's experience. But others argue that primordial empathy developed in all mammals as an instinctive reaction needed to rear young that require around-the-clock care.

New York University psychologist Martin Hoffman, PhD, believes both arguments might be right. At least five mechanisms are known to trigger empathy, he says. Some are more like reflexes, while others require complex cognition. They include:

• **Newborn cry:** Happy, content newborns will begin to cry when they hear another infant crying. This automatic reaction seems to be an inborn response to another human's distress.

• **Mimicry:** People automatically mimic the facial expressions and postures of others. When their facial and torso muscles move, nerves send the information to the brain, which triggers the emotions that correspond to the expression or posture. This mechanism is fairly automatic, dealing with relatively simple, universal emotions such as sadness and fear, and might be the basis of empathy in young children.

• **Simple classical conditioning:** When people observe others' experiences, they associate them with their own past experiences. That association automatically triggers an emotional reaction in the observer like that of the person having the experience.

• **Mediated association:** When people hear about another person's tragedy or good fortune the words remind them of a similar personal experience and trigger an emotional reaction. This is a more cognitive version of simple conditioning.

• **Role taking:** There are two types. With **self-focused role-taking** people put themselves in another person's place and imagine that what's happening to that person is happening to them. With **other-focused role-taking** people use what they know about the person—past, that individual's fears, financial situation—and imagine how he or she must feel in the situation.

Some researchers and philosophers argue that empathy is a purely human emotion. Others claim that many animals, from chimpanzees to dogs, show sure signs of empathic behavior. It depends on which empathetic mechanism you're talking about, says Hoffman.

There is evidence that some mammals—including chimpanzees and dolphins—mimic the postures and facial expressions of their peers. And many animals respond to conditioning. So, on that level, it's possible that some nonhuman animals have rudimentary versions of empathy, says Hoffman.

In contrast, few would argue that nonhuman animals have the cognitive abilities to experience role-taking or mediated association. Those forms of empathy may be restricted to humans, he says.

—Beth Azar

empathic reactions among children, beginning as early as age 2.

But, many studies also find that environment plays a significant role in shaping empathy, says Robinson. Parents can encourage empathy or discourage it.

For example, greater maternal warmth is associated with increases in empathy during the second year of life, Robinson and Strayer found in separate studies.

Also, mothers who provide forceful, clear messages about the consequences for others of hurtful behaviors tend to have more empathic children. And parents who discuss emotions tend to have children with high sympathy, find Eisenberg and Fabes.

In contrast, children whose mothers control them with anger tend to show decreases in empathy as they age, says Robinson.

Parents are more likely to explain to girls than boys the negative consequences for others of their harmful behaviors, even though young girls typically hurt others less often and show more empathy than boys, says Zahn-Waxler.

"Because empathic caregiving is important for survival, parents may begin early to prepare their girls for this role," she says.

With that said, it's not surprising that boys consistently score lower than girls on measures of empathy.

"Everyone is born with the capacity for empathy—it's part of our biological and cognitive wiring," says Strayer. "But there is also a lot of social scaffolding and experiences that can influence how empathy develops, which means we can do something about it."

### The dark side of empathy

According to Hoffman's model, when parents point out the harmful consequences of hurtful behavior, children learn to pay attention to their empathic tendencies and feel empathy-based guilt—good guilt, says Hoffman. Some experimental evidence links guilt and empathy when children know they're the cause of another person's hurt, says Zahn-Waxler.

But too much empathy can be maladaptive, she adds. Children may begin to blur the distinction between empathy and guilt and begin to blame themselves for others' suffering, even if they are not the cause.

People tend to feel more empathy for people who are similar to themselves, says Hoffman, a potential down side to empathy. Men empathize more with men and women empathize more with women; members of an ethnic group empathize more with their group members; and people from one social stratum empathize more with others from their set.

And even if researchers give people a false sense of kinship, they are more empathic toward each other than if they view themselves as dissimilar, says Hoffman.

On the other side, Strayer and her colleague William Roberts, PhD, found that the more empathy a person feels for another person, the more similar that person seems.

In a study, they showed 73 children, ages 6 to 13, a video of people in distress. The children then had to place a picture of each person in the video on a grid, showing how similar they felt each person was to them. The more empathy a child had for a person, the more similar the children rated the person in the video, Strayer found.

"When we are empathic with somebody, it makes our dissimilarities similar," says Strayer.

# Highlights of the Quality 2000 Initiative:

## Not by Chance

## Sharon L. Kagan and Michelle J. Neuman

**Sharon L. Kagan,** Ed.D., senior associate at Yale University's Bush Center in Child Development and Social Policy in New Haven, Connecticut, is recognized nationally and internationally for her work related to the care and education of young children and their families and investigation of issues, including policy development, family support, early childhood pedagogy, strategies for collaboration and service integration, and evaluation of social programs.

**Michelle J. Neuman** was recently a research assistant at the Yale Bush Center in Child Development and Social Policy. Her research has focused on issues related to children and families, including early care and education policy, family support, children's transitions to school, school readiness, and French family policy.

## The quality crisis in early care and education

Each day 13 million children spend time in early care and education centers or family child care homes. This should be heartening given that quality early care and education contributes to the healthy cognitive, social, and emotional development of all young children (CQ&O Study Team 1995) and in particular children from low-income families (Schweinhart, Barnes, & Weikart 1993; Barnett 1995; Gomby et al. 1995; Phillips 1995; Yoshikawa 1995). Yet we know that the quality of a majority of these settings does not optimize children's healthy development; in fact, many settings seriously jeopardize it (Galinsky et al. 1994; CQ&O Study Team 1995).

We well understand many of the reasons for low quality: underfinanced services, poorly compensated teachers, precarious turnover rates, inadequate and inconsistent regulation and enforcement, fragmented training and delivery mechanisms—the litany goes on. We understand less well how to alter the situation and what it would *really* take to reverse the pattern of neglect and provide quality early care and education to all young children.

## The Quality 2000 initiative

For the past four years, hundreds of experts in early childhood education and allied fields have been examining these very questions under the auspices of an inventive initiative, Quality 2000: Advancing Early Care and Education. The primary goal of this initiative is that by the year 2010, high-quality early care and education programs will be available and accessible to all children from birth to age five whose parents choose to enroll them. Funded by the Carnegie Corporation of New York, with supportive funding from the David and Lucile Packard, W.K. Kellogg, A.L. Mailman Family, and Ewing Marion Kauffman foundations, the initiative carried out its work through a series of commissioned papers, cross-national literature reviews, task forces, and working groups. Informed by national and international research, the fruit of that work, *Not by Chance: Creating an Early Care and Education System for America's Children,* offers a comprehensive, long-range vision for the field.

The vision is not about adding more services or disparate programs to what exists, although additional funds and services are essential to the vision. Rather, consisting of eight recommendations, the vision sets forth new patterns of thinking and pathways for action. Some of the recommendations seem familiar; others may

From *Young Children,* September 1997, pp. 54-62. © 1997 by the National Association for the Education of Young Children. Reprinted by permission.

sound bold, if not audacious. However they are interpreted, the recommendations are not modest or quick fixes; they will take time and energy to accomplish. That is why we set them in the context of the year 2010, not the year 2000 as the project's name suggests.

## Recommendations for eight essential functions

The Quality 2000 recommendations are broad and represent eight essential functions or areas where action to improve quality is needed; each recommendation is accompanied by suggested strategies to be tailored to fit individual community needs. Finally, the recommendations, although individualized to reflect each of the eight essential functions, need to be read in the aggregate—as a set of linked ideas.

### 1. Program quality

*Imagine a time when we expect and support quality in all family child care and center-based programs (Head Start, for-profit and nonprofit child care centers, prekindergartens, nursery schools), allowing staff flexibility in using state-of-the-art strategies, technologies, and resources creatively and cost effectively.*

To address the quality crisis, early care and education programs need the flexibility to explore and implement fresh ideas and strategies—strategies that consider changing demographic and technological realities as well as strategies that focus on the total program and individual classrooms or settings.

### STRATEGIES

*Promote cultural sensitivity and cultural pluralism.* Children, staff, and families need opportunities to better understand and express their own cultural values and beliefs and to learn about other cultures (Derman-Sparks & the A.B.C. Task Force 1989; Phillips 1994; Phillips & Crowell 1994; Chang, Pulido-Tobiassen, &

Muckelroy 1996). Staff should be trained to promote cultural sensitivity and cultural pluralism, and where possible, staff should come from the communities they serve. Children should be encouraged to cherish diversity.

*Encourage pedagogical inventiveness in family child care and centers.* Quality may result from a variety of strategies, including working with children in mixed-age groups (Katz, Evangelou, & Hartman 1990) and working inventively with families, grouping children in new ways, and considering ways of adapting child-staff ratios to capitalize on staff abilities to meet preschoolers' needs.

*Focus on improving the overall organizational climate.* The organizational climate of the total early care and education program—not only classrooms—must be considered as we create positive environments for all staff, parents, and families. Such environments should focus on the program as a learning organization ready to experiment, adapt, and grow.

*Increase the number of accredited programs.* Research indicates that accreditation—a voluntary process of self-assessment—significantly raises program quality. Because accredited centers provide higher quality services than nonaccredited programs (Bredekamp & Glowacki 1995; Bloom 1996; Whitebook, Sakai, & Howes 1997) and because the process promotes professionalism in the field, concerted efforts must be made to significantly increase the numbers of accredited programs.

*Link programs to networks, supportive services, or other community resources.* Linking early care and education programs with other services, especially resource-and-referral agencies, can help address unmet needs, expedite service delivery, minimize duplication of services, ensure smooth transitions for children, and help parents navigate through the social services maze (NACCRRA 1996). In addition, by creating family child care systems or networks, family child care providers can reduce their isolation

and be more effectively linked to each other and community services.

### 2. Results for children

*Imagine a time when clear results and expectations are specified and used to guide individual planning for all three- and four-year-old children, based on all domains of development (social/emotional, physical/motor, cognitive, language) and approaches to learning.*

Traditionally, researchers have focused on inputs (e.g., child-staff ratios, group size, staff training and education) and on the manner in which services are delivered (e.g., the nature of adult-child interactions) (Hofferth & Chaplin 1994). Recently, however, there has been mounting interest in gauging quality in terms of the results that programs or interventions produce for preschool-age children and their families (Schorr 1994; CCSSO 1995). A focus on results for three- and four-year-olds can assist teachers with pedagogical planning and improvement as well as for purposes of evaluation and accountability. By defining desired goals and results, practitioners who work with young children can plan and tailor their activities to foster individual children's development. In addition, specified goals and results can provide programs with the feedback they need to evaluate their effectiveness and identify areas for improvement. Results also can be used to help assess the overall status of young children in communities, states, and the nation (Schorr 1994). With this information in hand, parents, practitioners, and the public can hold decisionmakers at all levels accountable for investing in early care and education (Kagan, Rosenkoetter, & Cohen 1997).

### STRATEGIES

*Identify appropriate results.* To move toward a results-focused approach and to safeguard children from the misuses of results, parents, practitioners, policymakers, and the public need to come together to define results and expectations for three- and four-year-old children, taking into consideration the child, family, and community conditions that promote healthy development. In particular, results should be considered from the perspective of children—across programs and over time. Results should be specified at the local, state, and national levels, increasing the customization and specificity at each level.

*Develop appropriate strategies and instruments.* Developmentally appropriate and culturally sensitive instruments should be developed to evaluate progress toward the achievement of specified results in all domains of development. These strategies should include capturing children's development via portfolios and other documentation of children's work.

*Share results effectively, ensuring safeguards for children.* Demonstration projects, evaluation, and basic research will expand the knowledge base of what helps children achieve positive results. This information needs to be shared in ways that increase public understanding of the connection among child results, effective services, and the expenditure of public funds, not in ways that may label or stigmatize children. Guidelines for the effective use of results should be developed.

### 3. Parent and family engagement

*Imagine a time when parents of young children are actively involved in their children's programs and when programs provide diverse opportunities for such involvement. Imagine a time when parents have the user-friendly information and support they need to be effective consumers in choosing programs for their children. Imagine a time when employers provide policies that enable parents to become involved in their children's early learning and education.*

Research shows that parent and family engagement in early care and education programs improves re-

sults for children, increasing the likelihood of children's success and achievement and decreasing the likelihood of negative outcomes, both in school and later in life (Bronfenbrenner 1974; Bronson, Pierson, & Tivnan 1984; Powell 1989).

### STRATEGIES

*Support parents as partners in early care and education programs.* By focusing on developing regular communication among practitioners and parents (Weissbourd 1987), parents can be more effectively engaged as equals, with valuable information and resources. To that end, programs can offer multiple activities to involve parents (Henderson, Marburger, & Ooms 1986; Epstein 1995), taking into consideration how parents' interests, needs, and work and family responsibilities may influence their participation. Parents also should be engaged in governance opportunities (Kagan 1994).

*Support parents as effective consumers.* Parents can benefit from objective information about programs so they can make educated decisions that will promote their children's early development and learning. Well-funded resource-and-referral agencies, along with other parenting education efforts, can assist parents in learning about and evaluating their early care and education options. Such efforts must acknowledge and respect parents' diverse backgrounds, cultures, and needs.

*Increase the family-friendliness of workplaces.* Parents need support from their employers so they can fulfill their roles as partners in their children's programs, as effective consumers of early care and education services, and as productive employees (Staines & Galinsky 1991; Galinsky, Bond, & Friedman 1993). Employers should consider offering significantly greater employee benefits, at a minimum providing time for parents to find a program and monitor and participate in their children's early care and education. Corporations should offer parents the

choice of working part-time, paid sick days to care for sick children, and job-protected paid maternity and parental leave.

### 4. Staff credentialing

*Imagine a time when all individuals working with children in early care and education programs have—or are actively in the process of obtaining—credentials related to the position they hold or seek. Imagine a time when all staff are encouraged to pursue ongoing training and education—a course of lifelong learning.*

Because individuals who work with children in early care and education programs have a major impact on children's early development and learning experiences, their credentialing/licensing is critical. Licensing individual early childhood educators has many benefits. Licensing

• holds promise for increasing the compensation of staff,

• increases professionalization in the field,

• promotes the creation and coordination of quality training and education as well as career mobility, and

• helps prevent harm to children and ensure the quality of programs (APHA & AAP 1992).

The model for individual licensing can be found in Western European nations and Japan, which require significantly more training and education of practitioners and a more coordinated and sequenced training delivery system (Pritchard 1996). Structures to support licensing individuals are well established in many other occupations in the United States, including helping professionals (e.g., social workers, registered and licensed practical nurses, teachers), technical professionals (e.g., architects, engineers), tradespeople (e.g., electricians), and even service workers (e.g., cosmetologists) (Mitchell 1996).

Individual licenses should be distinct from, but complementary to, facility licenses. They should specify the preparatory and ongoing train-

# An Approach to Licensing Individuals:
# Requirements for Early Care and Education Staff

## Administrator license
For center directors and directors of family child care support services,
- at least a bachelor's or master's degree in early childhood education or child development from an accredited institution, including at least 15 credits in early childhood administration
- certification in pediatric first aid
- demonstration of competency in management and in working with children and families

## Educator license
For center teachers and public school teachers of children ages three and four,
- at least an associate's or bachelor's degree in early childhood education or child development from an accredited institution
- practicum with the age of children with whom individuals would work
- certification in pediatric first aid
- demonstration of competency in working with children and families

## Associate educator license
For lead providers in large family child care homes and assistant teachers in centers,
- at least a Child Development Associate (CDA) credential, the revised National Association for Family Child Care (NAFCC) accreditation or equivalent—meaning at least 120 clock hours of formal education in child development/early childhood education and the demonstration of competency in working with children and families
- practicum with the age group with which individuals would work
- certification in pediatric first aid

## Entry-level position requirement
For aides in centers and in large family child care homes and for family child care providers in small family child care homes,
- interest in and aptitude for working with children and families
- commitment to participating in ongoing training leading to licensure

ing that staff need to work with children in a variety of roles. While there are many approaches to individual licensing, Quality 2000 offers one that calls for a series of three licenses for early care and education workers (see "An Approach to Licensing Individuals" chart).

## STRATEGIES

*Create early childhood administrator licenses.* All center directors and directors of family child care support services would be required to have early childhood administrator licenses. To obtain this license, an individual would need at least a bachelor's or master's degree in early childhood education or child development from an accredited institution, including at least 15 credits in early childhood administration, certification in first aid, and demonstrated competency in management and in working with children and families.

*Create early childhood educator licenses.* All teachers in centers would be required to have early childhood educator licenses. Teachers of three- and four-year-old children in public schools would have the option of obtaining public school teacher certification/licenses or the early childhood educator license. To obtain the early childhood educator license, individuals would need to have at least an associate's or bachelor's degree in early childhood education or child development from an accredited institution; have practicum experience with the age group with which they would work; be certified in pediatric first aid; and pass a competency-based assessment in working with children and families.

*Create early childhood associate educator licenses.* All assistant teachers in centers, as well as lead providers in large family child care homes, would be required to have early childhood associate educator licenses. To obtain the license, an individual working in a center would need to have a Child Development Associate (CDA) credential or the equivalent; an individual working in a family child care home would need to have a CDA, the revised National Association for Family Child Care (NAFCC) accreditation, or equivalent certification. Each of these certifications requires at least 120 clock hours of formal education in early childhood development and education and the demonstration of the competencies needed to work with young children and their families. Assistant teachers and lead providers also would need to have practicum experience with the age group with which they would work and certification in pediatric first aid.

*Maintain access to entry-level positions.* Individuals who do not have training or education in child development or early childhood education, but who have an interest in and aptitude for working with young children and families and a commitment to seeking training in the field, would have access to entry-level jobs as aides in child care centers and in large-group family child care homes or as providers in small family child care homes. These individuals would be considered an integral part of the profession as long as they are actively pursuing training to achieve licensure as early childhood associate educator or educator.

## 5. Staff training and preparation

*Imagine a time when all training for early childhood positions is child and family focused, reflecting and respecting cultural and linguistic diversity. Imagine a time when all approved training bears credit, leads to increased credentials and compensation, and equips individuals for diverse and advanced roles.*

The quality of the credentials just discussed is contingent upon the quality of the training individuals receive. All training and education sequences should, at a minimum, address the CDA competency areas (establishing and maintaining a safe, healthy learning environment; advancing physical and intellectual competence; supporting social and emotional development and provid-

ing positive guidance; establishing positive and productive relationships with families; ensuring a well-run, purposeful program that is responsive to participant needs; and maintaining a commitment to professionalism [Council for Early Childhood Professional Recognition 1992]). More preservice and inservice training, particularly at intermediate and advanced levels, needs to be developed and made available to practitioners in the following areas (Morgan et al. 1993): engaging and supporting families; developing cultural competency; observing and assessing children; working with mixed-age groups and larger groups, and team teaching; working with infants and toddlers; working with children with special needs; promoting ethics; working across human service disciplines; and developing management and leadership skills.

### STRATEGIES

*Revise and develop staff training/preparation curricula and sequences.* Revamping the content of and opportunities for practitioner training/preparation will necessitate the participation of many stakeholders. State licensing boards for early care and education should require staff to have appropriate ranges of skills to earn and maintain licenses, including appropriate preparatory and ongoing course work. Colleges and community organizations that educate and train early care and education staff should revise and develop curricula and sequences to address the broad-based knowledge (early childhood pedagogy and content from allied disciplines) and skills that practitioners need to be competent in today's early care and education programs.

*Promote the development of leaders and managers.* To promote the development of leaders and managers at the local, state, and national levels, program administrators with strong leadership potential should be supported through fellowships and training and mentoring oppor-

tunities. Such mentoring programs are an effective strategy to support staff as they acquire knowledge and skills and to enhance the professional development of more skilled and experienced mentor-teachers (Whitebook, Hnatiuk, & Bellm 1994; Breunig & Bellm 1996).

## 6. Program licensing

*Imagine a time when all early care and education programs are licensed, without any legal exemptions. Imagine a time when facility licensing procedures are streamlined and enforced to ensure that all programs promote children's safety, health, and development. Imagine a time when incentives exist for programs to continually enhance their facilities.*

Research demonstrates that about 40% of center-based programs—including many part-day, school-based, and church-based programs (Adams 1990)—and as many as 80 to 90% of family child care providers (Willer et al. 1991) are legally exempt from regulation despite the fact that states with more stringent regulation yield higher quality programs (CQ&O Study Team 1995).

### STRATEGIES

*Eliminate exemptions.* All programs available to the general public should be required to meet basic safeguards that protect children's well-being and foster equity in the early care and education field; there should be no legal exemptions. For example, programs should not be legally exempt from facility regulations because of their size, hours of operation, location, or auspices.

*Streamline facility licensing.* State facility licensing should be streamlined to focus on essential safeguards of safety, health, and development and to complement the system of individual licensing described earlier (U.S. ACIR 1994; Gormley 1995; Gwen Morgan, personal communication, 22 March 1996). Standards for staffing levels should allow programs the flexibility to group children and organize staff in ways that maximize quality.

*Enforce requirements.* To fully promote children's safety, health, and development, states must not only eliminate exemptions and streamline regulations but also enforce requirements. Licensing agencies must have the appropriate resources to carry out enforcement functions. State monitoring and enforcement systems should employ positive, incentive-based strategies to enable programs to meet licensing requirements. State licensing systems also should provide incentives for programs to invest in facility enhancement to increase capacity for meeting the increasing demand for early care and education services.

*Develop national licensing guidelines.* Although the main responsibility for the development and issue of facility licensing requirements should remain at the state level, national licensing guidelines should be developed to promote regulatory consistency across the country.

## 7. Funding and financing

*Imagine a time when young children's early care and education is funded by the public and private sectors at per-child levels commensurate with funding for elementary-age children and when 10% of the funds are set aside for professional and staff development, enhanced compensation, parent information and engagement, program accreditation, resource-and-referral services, evaluation, research, planning, and licensing and facility enhancement.*

Adequate funding is essential to ensuring that all children have access to quality early care and education services and that their parents have choice in selecting services. The costs must be shared by the public at large, parents (according to income), employers, government, and community organizations. While parents need access to and choice of quality early care and education services, they also need the option of caring for their own very young children; therefore, paid parental leave for parents of very

young children should be provided. These efforts to increase investment necessitate additional research and planning.

### STRATEGIES

*Estimate the actual cost of a quality early care and education system.* The field needs to estimate the actual cost of mounting and sustaining a comprehensive quality early care and education system. In making such estimates, early care and education professionals need to work closely with funding and financing experts, using cost-calculation approaches that other fields have found useful. Such an analysis also should estimate the revenues that the early care and education system would generate in both the short and long term. Longer-term cost-benefit accounting should be used to determine the extended benefits of a quality early care and education system, benefits that include savings in special education, corrections, public assistance, and other social services.

*Identify several revenue-generation mechanisms.* Several revenue-generation options for funding for a comprehensive early care and education system—including increased staff compensation—need to be considered and implemented. Some possible mechanisms include establishing individual and corporate income taxes, federal payroll taxes, and new sales or excise taxes; expanding the populations eligible to receive the school aid formula; cutting other government expenditures to raise some of the needed funds; and procuring funds as part of a larger revenue-generation package designed to support a range of social services that families need. None of these approaches are easy to sell to the public or policymakers, but each would help improve the amount of funding available to support early care and education.

*Develop model approaches for distributing funds to parents.* State-level agencies may be best suited for

administering funds to parents. Mechanisms to distribute funds to parents should promote parent choice, such as vouchers, direct payments to programs of parents' choice, and/or tax credits. Parents should receive assistance in paying for early care and education programs based on a sliding scale linked to parents' income. (As family income increases over time, public assistance for early care and education would decrease proportionately but not be completely cut off [Stangler 1995]).

*Create a targeted, coordinated funding initiative.* Scholarship and knowledge of how to generate increased revenues for the development of a comprehensive early care and education system is emerging but remains piecemeal and embryonic. Focused research is needed to carry out the analyses mentioned above. Therefore, it will be necessary to create a targeted, coordinated initiative focused on funding a quality early care and education system.

## 8. Governance structures

*Imagine a time when early care and education is governed rationally. Imagine a time when mechanisms (councils, boards) are established or built upon in every community and state to carry out planning, governance, and accountability roles in early care and education.*

To increase coordination, efficiency, and continuity of services for young children and their families, it is critical to establish a rational governance system. Quality 2000 recommends establishing governance entities in every state and locality—to be called State Early Care and Education Board and Local Early Care and Education Board, respectively. Where these governing boards or coordinating councils already exist, the State or Local Early Care and Education Board could be built from the existing body or created in collaboration with it.

## STRATEGIES

*Establish state boards.* State boards should be responsible for ensuring quality and achieving agreed-upon results for children. They should engage in planning, collecting, and analyzing data; defining eligibility and subsidy levels and parental-leave conditions; and determining how to allocate funds to parents. They would also develop state standards for results to align with national goals. As with other governance entities, state boards would facilitate collaboration, service integration, and comprehensive services delivery. State boards would be composed of appointed or elected board members, including equal numbers of parents/consumers; practitioners; community and state leaders, including clergy; and municipal or government agency representatives.

*Establish local boards.* Local boards would have responsibility for both the governance and the coordination of early care and education for children birth to age five. They could be geographically aligned with school districts, but would be distinct entities. Like their state counterparts, they should be composed of a broad-based group of appointed or elected board members who would be responsible for developing performance benchmarks for child results, taking into consideration local strengths, needs, priorities, and resources. Local boards would involve consumers and citizens in comprehensive needs assessment and planning.

*Support effective federal governance.* To support these efforts, the federal government will need to provide mandates and incentives to these boards. In addition, the federal government will guide states as they develop standards and communities as they develop benchmarks to meet state standards and national goals. The federal government also will collect national data, provide funding for evaluating demonstration efforts, and offer technical assistance to states and localities. Their well-

being, and the nation's, simply cannot be left to chance.

The quality of daily life for millions of American children and families depends on how the United States solves—or fails to solve—the quality crisis in early care and education. Quality 2000 and the *Not by Chance* report address this crisis by recommending that the nation make a planned, significant, and immediate advance to improve quality and to create a system of services. It is the hope of those involved in the Quality 2000 initiative that the ideas put forth in these recommendations will provoke discussion, advance our collective thinking, and spark bold, new action on behalf of our nation's children. Their well-being, and the nation's, simply cannot be left to chance.

## References

Adams, G. 1990. *Who knows how safe? The status of state efforts to ensure quality child care.* Washington, DC: Children's Defense Fund.

APHA (American Public Health Association), & AAP (American Academy of Pediatrics). 1992. *Caring for our children: National health and safety performance standards—Guidelines for out-of-home child care programs.* Washington, DC: APHA.

Barnett, W.S. 1995. Long-term effects of early childhood programs on cognitive and school outcomes. *The Future of Children* 5 (3): 25–50.

Bloom, P.J. 1996. The quality of work life in early childhood programs: Does accreditation make a difference? In *NAEYC accreditation: A decade of learning and the years ahead,* eds. S. Bredekamp & B.A. Willer, 13–24. Washington, DC: NAEYC.

Bredekamp, S., & S. Glowacki. 1995. The first decade of NAEYC accreditation: Growth and impact on the field. Paper prepared for an invitational conference sponsored by the Robert McCormick Tribune Foundation and NAEYC, 18–20 September, Wheaton, Illinois.

Breunig, G.S., & D. Bellm. 1996. *Early childhood mentoring programs: A survey of community initiatives.* Washington, DC: National Center for the Early Childhood Work Force.

Brofenbrenner, U. 1974. *A report on longitudinal evaluations of preschool programs, Vol. 2: Is early intervention effective?* Washington, DC: Office of Child Development, U.S. Department of Health, Education, and Welfare.

Bronson, M.B., D.E. Pierson, & T. Tivnan. 1984. The effects of early education on children's competence in elementary school. *Evaluation Review* 8: 615–29.

Chang, H.N., D. Pulido-Tobiassen, & A. Muckelroy. 1996. *Looking in, looking out: Redefining care and early education in a di-*verse society. San Francisco: California Tomorrow.

CCSSO (Council of Chief State School Officers). 1995. *Moving toward accountability for results: A look at ten states' efforts.* Washington, DC: Author.

Council for Early Childhood Professional Recognition. 1992. *Child Development Associate assessment system and competency standards.* Washington, DC: Author.

CQ&O (Cost, Quality, & Outcomes) Study Team. 1995. *Cost, quality, and child outcomes in child care centers.* Denver: Department of Economics, University of Colorado at Denver.

Derman-Sparks, L., & the A.B.C. Task Force. 1989. *Anti-bias curriculum: Tools for empowering young children.* Washington, DC: NAEYC.

Epstein, J.L. 1995. School/family/community partnerships: Caring for the children we share. *Phi Delta Kappan* (May): 701–12.

Galinsky, E., J.T. Bond, & D.E. Friedman. 1993. *The changing workforce: Highlights of the National Study.* New York: Families and Work Institute.

Galinsky, E., C. Howes, S. Kontos, & M. Shinn. 1994. *The study of children in family child care and relative care.* New York: Families and Work Institute.

Gomby, D.S., M.B. Larner, C.S. Stevenson, E.M. Lewit, & R.E. Behrman. 1995. Long-term outcomes of early childhood programs: Analysis and recommendations. *The Future of Children* 5 (3): 6–24.

Gormley, W.T. 1995. *Everybody's children: Child care as a public problem.* Washington, DC: Brookings Institution.

Henderson, A.T., C.L. Marburger, & T. Ooms. 1986. *Beyond the bake sale: An educator's guide to working with parents.* Columbia, MD: National Committee for Citizens in Education.

Hofferth, S.L., & D. Chaplin. 1994. *Child care quality versus availability: Do we have to trade one for the other?* Washington, DC: Urban Institute Press.

Kagan, S.L. 1994. *Defining America's commitments to parents and families. An historical-conceptual perspective.* Kansas City, MO: Ewing Marion Kauffman Foundation.

Kagan, S.L., S. Rosenkoetter, & N.E. Cohen, eds. 1997. *Considering child-based outcomes for young children: Definitions, desirability, feasibility, and next steps.* New Haven, CT: Bush Center in Child Development and Social Policy, Yale University.

Katz, L.G., D. Evangelou, & J.A. Hartman. 1990. *The case for mixed-age grouping in early education.* Washington, DC: NAEYC.

Mitchell, A. 1996. Licensing: Lessons from other occupations. In *Reinventing early care and education: A vision for a quality system,* eds. S.L. Kagan & N.E. Cohen, 101–123. San Francisco: Jossey-Bass.

Morgan, G., S.L. Azer, J.B. Costley, A. Genser, I.F. Goodman, J. Lombardi, & B. McGimsey. 1993. *Making a career of it: The state of the states report on career development in early care and education.* Boston: Center for Career Development in Early Care and Education, Wheelock College.

NACCRRA (National Association of Child Care Resource and Referral Agencies). 1996. *Creating and facilitating health linkages: The role of child care resource and referral.* Washington, DC: Author.

Phillips, C.B. 1994. The movement of African-American children through sociocultural contexts: A case of conflict resolution. In *Diversity and developmentally appropriate practices: Challenges for early childhood education*, eds. B.L. Mallory & R.S. New, 137–54. New York: Teachers College Press.

Phillips, D.A., ed. 1995. *Child care for low-income families: Summary of two workshops.* Washington, DC: National Academy Press.

Phillips, D.A., & N.A. Crowell, eds. 1994. *Cultural diversity in early education: Results of a workshop.* Washington, DC: National Academy Press.

Powell, D.R. 1989. *Families and early childhood programs.* Washington, DC: NAEYC.

Pritchard, E. 1996. Training and professional development: International approaches. In *Reinventing early care and education: A vision for a quality system*, eds. S.L. Kagan & N.E. Cohen, 124–41. San Francisco: Jossey-Bass.

Schorr, L.B. 1994. The case for shifting to results-based accountability. In *Making a difference: Moving to outcome-based accountability for comprehensive service reforms*, eds. N. Young, S. Gardner, S. Coley, L. Schorr, & C. Bruner, 13–28. Falls Church, VA: National Center for Service Integration.

Schweinhart, L.J., H.V. Barnes, & D.P. Weikart, with W.S. Barnett, & A.S. Epstein. 1993. *Significant benefits: The High/Scope Perry Preschool Study through age 27.* Ypsilanti, MI: High/Scope Press.

Staines, G.L., & E. Galinsky. 1991. *Parental leave and productivity: The supervisor's view.* New York: Families and Work Institute.

Stangler, G. 1995. Lifeboats vs. safety nets: Who rides . . . who swims? In *Dollars and sense: Diverse perspectives on block grants and the Personal Responsibility Act*, 67–72. Washington, DC: The Finance Project and Institute for Educational Leadership.

U.S. ACIR (Advisory Commission on Intergovernmental Relations). 1994. *Child care: The need for federal-state-local coordination.* Washington, DC: Author.

Weissbourd, B. 1987. A brief history of family support programs. In *America's family support programs*, eds. S.L. Kagan, D.R. Powell, B. Weissbourd, & E.F. Zigler, 38–56. New Haven, CT: Yale University Press.

Whitebook, M., P. Hnatiuk, & D. Bellm: 1994. *Mentoring in early care and education: Refining an emerging career path.* Washington, DC: National Center for the Early Childhood Work Force.

Whitebook, M., L. Sakai, &, C. Howes. 1997. *NAEYC accreditation as a strategy for improving child care quality, executive summary.* Washington, DC: National Center for the Early Childhood Work Force.

Willer, B., ed. 1990. *Reaching the full cost of quality in early childhood programs.* Washington, DC: NAEYC.

Willer, B., S. Hofferth, E. Kiskar, P. Divine-Hawkins, E. Farquhar, & F. Glantz. 1991. *The demand and supply of child care in 1990: Joint findings from the National Child Care Survey 1990 and a profile of child care settings.* Washington, DC: NAEYC.

Yoshikawa, H. 1995. Long-term effects of early childhood programs on social outcomes and delinquency. *The Future of Children* 5 (3): 51–75.

# Unit 3

## Unit Selections

## Key Points to Consider

❖ How much do genes and environment matter for specific cognitive abilities and disabilities? Explain.

❖ Why should Piaget's cognitive constructivism be used to shape lesson plans for students?

❖ How does Howard Gardner justify multiple intelligences? What is naturalist intelligence?

❖ Why is *The Bell Curve* so controversial? Is it a scandalous idea? Explain.

❖ What is the postmodern conception of children? How can education best serve children today?

❖ What is brain-based education? Does scientific research support it? Why or why not?

❖ Can praise be dangerous? If so, what kind of praise is helpful and what kind of praise is harmful?

 **Links**     # www.dushkin.com/online/

15. **Children Now**
    *http://www.childrennow.org*

16. **Council for Exceptional Children**
    *http://www.cec.sped.org*

17. **Educational Resources Information Center (ERIC)**
    *http://www.ed.gov/pubs/pubdb.html*

18. **Federation of Behavioral, Psychological, and Cognitive Science**
    *http://www.am.org/federation/*

19. **The National Association for the Education of Young Children (NAEYC)**
    *http://www.naeyc.org*

20. **Project Zero**
    *http://pzweb.harvard.edu*

These sites are annotated on pages 4 and 5.

gnition is the mental process of knowing. It includes
ects such as awareness, perception, reasoning, and
gement. Many kinds of achievement that require
gnitive processes (awareness, perception, reasoning,
gment) cannot be measured with intelligence tests or
h achievement. Intelligence is the capacity to acquire
d apply knowledge. It is usually assumed that
elligence can be measured. The ratio of tested mental
e to chronological age is expressed as an
elligence quotient (IQ). For years, schoolchildren have
en classified and tracked educationally by IQ scores.
is practice has been both obsequiously praised and
nomously opposed. The links between IQ scores and
hool achievement are positive, but no significant
rrelations exist between IQ scores and life success.
nsider, for example, the motor coordination and
esthetic abilities of a baseball player such as Cal
ken Jr. He has an intelligence about the use of his
dy that surpasses the capacity of most nonathletes. A
arvard psychologist, Howard Gardner, has suggested
at there are at least eight different kinds of
elligences. These include the body movement skills of
hletes and dancers as well as musical, linguistic,
gical/mathematical, spatial, naturalist,
lf-understanding, and social understanding types. The
990s have been host to a spate of research about the
st two types of intelligences: self-understanding and
cial understanding.

Some psychologists have suggested that measuring
e's emotional quotient (EQ) might make more sense
an measuring one's intelligence quotient (IQ). The
pical tests of intelligence only measure achievement
d abilities in the logical/mathematical, spatial, and
guistic areas of intelligence. Jean Piaget, the Swiss
under of cognitive psychology, was involved in the
eation of the world's first intelligence test, the
net-Simon Scale. He became disillusioned with trying
quantify how much children knew at different
ronological ages. He was much more intrigued with
hat they did not know, what they knew incorrectly,
d how they came to know the world in the ways in
hich they knew it. Piaget discovered qualitative, rather
an quantitative, differences in cognitive processes over
e life span. Infants know the world through their
nses and their motor responses. After language
evelops, toddlers and preschoolers know the world
rough their language/symbolic perspectives. Piaget
kened early childhood cognitive processes to bad
ought, or thought akin to daydreams. By school age,
ildren know things in concrete terms, which allows
em to number, seriate, classify, conserve, think
ackwards and forwards, and to think about their own
inking (metacognition). They are able to use reason.
owever, Piaget believed that children do not acquire
e cognitive processes necessary to think abstractly
nd to use clear, consistent, logical patterns of thought
ntil early adolescence.

In the first article in this unit, Robert Plomin and
hn DeFries review the role of genetic potentialities in
etermining how easily and in what ways (e.g.,
rbally, spatially) people process information. The
uthors have researched and written about behavioral
enetics for more than 20 years. They support the idea
at learning affects cognitive processes. However, they
ggest that psychologists and educators should take a
alanced view and acknowledge that babies come into

the world with different genetic attributes for learning.
A teaching style that works for one child may be all
wrong for another child. An appreciation of each
child's cognitive heritabilities will make it easier to
develop an appropriate learning environment and
teaching modality. This could lessen or prevent many
so-called learning disabilities, which might rather be
viewed as learning differences.

The second article in this subsection on cognition
explains Piaget's theory that learning originates from
inside the child. Constance Kamii and Janice Ewing
believe that school teaching should be based on
Piaget's view of cognitive constructivism. Piaget makes
a distinction between three kinds of knowledge:
physical knowledge, social (conventional) knowledge,
and logico-mathematical knowledge. These cognitions
are constructed very differently inside the child. The
sources of each and their modes of being structured
are very important building blocks for education.
Teaching based on scientific theories of how children
construct knowledge is more potent than teaching
based on fads, pendulum swings, or superficial
impressions of what works.

The third article highlights the theory of multiple
intelligences espoused by Howard Gardner. In this
interview with Karen Checkley, he defines intelligence
as the human ability to solve problems or to make
something that is valued in one or more cultures.
Gardner believes that any ability should be considered
an intelligence if it solves a problem or creates a
product that is valued. In the 1990s, Dr. Gardner
rewrote his theory of seven intelligences to include an
eighth type, naturalist intelligence. It is the ability to
understand different species and recognize and classify
objects in nature. In this article he defends the inclusion
of naturalist intelligence in his list of intelligences and
discusses how to help children learn.

The first article in the schooling subsection of this
unit addresses the issue of defining and testing
intelligence for purposes of school placement and
educational programming. Politicians play with rhetoric
about what our children should and should not learn in
school. "Bell, Book, and Scandal" gives a historic
overview of IQ testing and the use of IQ tests to
differentiate children by achievement in the logical/
mathematical type of intelligence. To what extent is
this placement practice discriminating against other
children who demonstrate high motivation and
potential to achieve but have different types of
intelligences?

The second article on schooling, by David Elkind,
presents his belief that an educational system that
believes every child is "regular" is a barrier to progress
in a postmodern society. Behavioral geneticists have
enlightened us about the reality of irregular learning
styles. Different subjects require different learning
strategies. Educational innovators who view learning as
creative and interactional are more effective as teachers.

The third schooling article discusses brain-based
education, how much left/right brain differences should
be used to guide teaching. John Bruer suggests that the
sensitive-period for learning may be overstated.

In "Caution—Praise Can Be Dangerous," Carol
Dweck address the question, "Can praising a child's
intelligence decrease motivation to learn?" The answer
may surprise readers.

# The Genetics of Cognitive Abilities and Disabilities

*Investigations of specific cognitive skills can help clarify how genes shape the components of intellect*

by Robert Plomin and John C. DeFries

People differ greatly in all aspects of what is casually known as intelligence. The differences are apparent not only in school, from kindergarten to college, but also in the most ordinary circumstances: in the words people use and comprehend, in their differing abilities to read a map or follow directions, or in their capacities for remembering telephone numbers or figuring change. The variations in these specific skills are so common that they are often taken for granted. Yet what makes people so different?

It would be reasonable to think that the environment is the source of differences in cognitive skills—that we are what we learn. It is clear, for example, that human beings are not born with a full vocabulary; they have to learn words. Hence, learning must be the mechanism by which differences in vocabulary arise among individuals. And differences in experience—say, in the extent to which parents model and encourage vocabulary skills or in the quality of language training provided by schools—must be responsible for individual differences in learning.

Earlier in this century psychology was in fact dominated by environmental explanations for variance in cognitive abilities. More recently, however, most psychologists have begun to embrace a more balanced view: one in which nature and nurture interact in cognitive development. During the past few decades, studies in genetics have pointed to a substantial role for heredity in molding the components of intellect, and researchers have even begun to track down the genes involved in cognitive function. These findings do not refute the notion that environmental factors shape the learning process. Instead they suggest that differences in people's genes affect how easily they learn.

Just how much do genes and environment matter for specific cognitive abilities such as vocabulary? That is the question we have set out to answer. Our tool of study is quantitative genetics, a statistical approach that explores the causes of variations in traits among individuals. Studies comparing the performance of twins and adopted children on certain tests of cognitive skills, for example, can assess the relative contributions of nature and nurture.

In reviewing several decades of such studies and conducting our own, we have begun to clarify the relations among specialized aspects of intellect, such as verbal and spatial reasoning, as well as the relations between normal cognitive function and disabilities, such as dyslexia. With the help of molecular genetics, we and other investigators have also begun to identify the genes that affect these specific abilities and disabilities. Eventually, we believe, knowledge of these genes will help reveal the biochemical mechanisms involved in human intelligence. And with the insight gained from genetics, researchers may someday develop environmental interventions that will lessen or prevent the effects of cognitive disorders.

Some people find the idea of a genetic role in intelligence alarming or, at the very least, confusing. It is important to understand from the outset, then, what exactly geneticists mean when they talk about genetic influence. The term typically used is "heritability": a statistical measure of the genetic contribution to differences among individuals.

### Verbal and Spatial Abilities

Heritability tells us what proportion of individual differences in a population—known as variance—can be ascribed to genes. If we say, for example, that a trait is 50 percent heritable, we are in effect saying that half of the variance in that trait is linked to heredity. Heritability, then, is a way of explaining what makes people different, not what constitutes a given individual's intelligence. In general, however, if heritability for a trait is high, the influence of genes on the trait in individuals would be strong as well.

Attempts to estimate the heritability of specific cognitive abilities began with family studies. Analyses of similarities between parents and their children and between siblings have shown that cognitive abilities run in families. Results of the largest family study done on specific cognitive abilities, which was conducted in Hawaii in the 1970s, helped to quantify this resemblance.

The Hawaii Family Study of Cognition was a collaborative project between researchers at the University of Colorado at Boulder and the University of Hawaii and involved more than 1,000 families and sibling pairs. The study determined correlations (a statistical measure of resemblance) between relatives on tests of verbal and spatial ability. A correlation of 1.0 would mean that the scores of family members were identical; a correlation of zero would indicate that the scores were no more similar than those of two people picked at random. Because children on average share half their genes with each parent and with siblings, the highest correlation in test scores that could be expected on genetic grounds alone would be 0.5.

The Hawaii study showed that family members are in fact more alike than unrelated individuals on measures of specific cognitive skills. The actual correlations for both verbal and spatial tests were, on average, about 0.25. These correlations alone, however, do not disclose whether cognitive abilities run in families because of genetics or because of environmental effects. To explore this distinction, geneticists rely on two "experiments": twinning (an experiment of nature) and adoption (a social experiment).

Twin studies are the workhorse of behavioral genetics. They compare the resemblance of identical twins, who have the same

---

**TESTS OF VERBAL ABILITY**

1. VOCABULARY: In each row, circle the word that means the same or nearly the same as the underlined word. There is only one correct choice in each line.

|   | a. arid | coarse | clever | modest | dry |
|---|---------|--------|--------|--------|-----|
|   | b. piquant | fruity | pungent | harmful | upright |

2. VERBAL FLUENCY: For the next three minutes, write as many words as you can that start with F and end with M.

3. CATEGORIES: For the next three minutes, list all the things you can think of that are FLAT.

(Answers appear on last page of this article.)

---

genetic makeup, with the resemblance of fraternal twins, who share only about half their genes. If cognitive abilities are influenced by genes, identical twins ought to be more alike than fraternal twins on tests of cognitive skills. From correlations found in these kinds of studies, investigators can estimate the extent to which genes account for variances in the general population. Indeed, a rough estimate of heritability can be made by doubling the difference between identical-twin and fraternal-twin correlations.

Adoption provides the most direct way to disentangle nature and nurture in family resemblance, by creating pairs of genetically related individuals who do not share a common family environment. Correlations among these pairs enable investigators to estimate the contribution of genetics to family resemblance. Adoption also produces pairs of genetically un- related individuals who share a family environment, and their correlations make it possible to estimate the contribution of shared environment to resemblance.

Twin studies of specific cognitive abilities over three decades and in four countries have yielded remarkably consistent results [see illustration, "Twin Studies"]. Correlations for identical twins greatly exceed those for fraternal twins on tests of both verbal and spatial abilities in children, adolescents and adults. Results of the first twin study in the elderly—reported last

---

# How Do Cognitive Abilities Relate to General Intelligence?

## by Karen Wright

Since the dawn of psychology, experts have disagreed about the fundamental nature of intelligence. Some have claimed that intelligence is an inherent faculty prescribed by heredity, whereas others have emphasized the effects of education and upbringing. Some have portrayed intelligence as a global quality that permeates all facets of cognition; others believe the intellect consists of discrete, specialized abilities—such as artistic talent or a flair for mathematics—that share no common principle.

In the past few decades, genetic studies have convinced most psychologists that heredity exerts considerable influence on intelligence. In fact, research suggests that as much as half of the variation in intelligence among individuals may be attributed to genetic factors.

And most psychologists have also come to accept a global conceptualization of intelligence. Termed general cognitive ability, or "g," this global quality is reflected in the apparent overlap among specific cognitive skills. As Robert Plomin and John C. DeFries point out, people who do well on tests of one type of cognitive skill also tend to do well on tests of other cognitive abilities. Indeed, this intercorrelation has provided the rationale for IQ (intelligence quotient) tests, which yield a single score from combined assessments of specific cognitive skills.

Because specific and general cognitive abilities are related in this manner, it is not surprising that many of the findings regarding specific abilities echo what is already known about general ability. The heritabilities found in studies of specific cognitive abilities, for example, are comparable with the heritability determined for g. The developmental trend described by the authors—in which genetic influence on specific cognitive abilities seems to increase throughout childhood, reaching adult levels by the mid-teens—is also familiar to researchers of general cognitive ability.

And because measures of g are derived from intercorrelations of verbal and spatial abilities, a gene that is linked with both those traits is almost guaranteed to have some role in general cognitive ability as well—and vice versa. This month in the journal *Psychological Science*, Plomin and various collaborators report the discovery of the first gene associated with general cognitive ability. Although the finding should further understanding of the nature of cognition, it is also likely to reignite debate. Indeed, intelligence research may be one realm where understanding does little to quell disagreement.

*KAREN WRIGHT is a freelance writer living in New Hampshire.*

year by Gerald E. McClearn and his colleagues at Pennsylvania State University and by Stig Berg and his associates at the Institute for Gerontology in Jönköping, Sweden—show that the resemblances between identical and fraternal twins persist even into old age. Although gerontologists have assumed that genetic differences become less important as experiences accumulate over a lifetime, research on cognitive abilities has so far demonstrated otherwise. Calculations based on the combined findings in these studies imply that in the general population, genetics accounts for about 60 percent of the variance in verbal ability and about 50 percent of the variance in spatial ability.

Investigations involving adoptees have yielded similar results. Two recent studies of twins reared apart—one by Thomas J. Bouchard, Jr., Matthew McGue and their colleagues at the University of Minnesota, the other an international collaboration headed by Nancy L. Pedersen at the Karolinska Institute in Stockholm—have implied heritabilities of about 50 percent for both verbal and spatial abilities.

In our own Colorado Adoption Project, which we launched in 1975, we have used the power of adoption studies to further characterize the roles of genes and environment, to assess developmental trends in cognitive abilities and to explore the extent to which specific cognitive skills are related to one another. The ongoing project compares the correlations between more than 200 adopted children and their birth and adoptive parents with the correlations for a control group of children raised by their biological parents [see illustration, "Colorado Adoption Project"].

These data provide some surprising insights. By middle childhood, for example, birth mothers and their children who were adopted by others are just as similar as control parents and their children on measures of both verbal and spatial ability. In contrast, the scores of adopted children do not resemble those of their adoptive parents at all. These results join a growing body of evidence suggesting that the common family environment generally does not contribute to similarities in family members. Rather family resemblance on such measures seems to be controlled almost entirely by genetics, and environmental factors often end up making family members different, not the same.

The Colorado data also reveal an interesting developmental trend. It appears that genetic influence increases during childhood, so that by

## TESTS OF SPATIAL ABILITY

1. IMAGINARY CUTTING: Draw a line or lines showing where the figure on the left should be cut to form the pieces on the right. There may be more than one way to draw the lines correctly.

2. MENTAL ROTATIONS: Circle the two objects on the right that are the same as the object on the left.

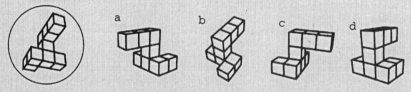

3. CARD ROTATIONS: Circle the figures on the right that can be rotated (without being lifted off the page) to exactly match the one on the left.

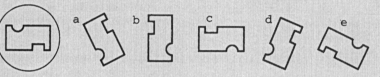

4. HIDDEN PATTERNS: Circle each pattern below in which the figure appears. The figure must always be in this position, not upside down or on its side.

the mid-teens, heritability reaches a level comparable with that seen in adults. In correlations of verbal ability, for example, resemblance between birth parents and their children who were adopted by others increases from about 0.1 at age three to about 0.3 at age 16. A similar pattern is evident in tests of spatial ability. Some genetically driven transformation in cognitive function seems to take place in the early school years, around age seven. The results indicate that by the time people reach age 16, genetic factors account for 50 percent of the variance for verbal ability and 40 percent for spatial ability—numbers not unlike those derived from twin studies of specific cognitive abilities.

The Colorado Adoption Project and other investigations have also helped clarify the differences and similarities among cognitive abilities. Current cognitive neuroscience assumes a modular model of intelligence, in which different cognitive processes are isolated anatomically in discrete modules in the brain. The modular model implies that specific cognitive abilities are also genetically distinct—that genetic effects on verbal abil-

TESTS OF SPECIFIC ABILITIES administered to adolescents and adults include tasks resembling the ones listed here. The tests gauge each cognitive ability in several ways, and multiple tests are combined to provide a reliable measure of each skill. (Answers appear on last page of this article.)

ity, say, should not overlap substantially with genetic effects on spatial ability.

Psychologists, however, have long recognized that most specialized cognitive skills, including verbal and spatial abilities, intercorrelate moderately. That is, people who perform well on one type of test also tend to do well on other types. Correlations between verbal and spatial abilities, for example, are usually about 0.5. Such intercorrelation implies a potential genetic link.

### From Abilities to Achievement

Genetic studies of specific cognitive abilities also fail to support the modu-

# What Heritability Means

The implications of heritability data are commonly misunderstood. As the main text indicates, heritability is a statistical measure, expressed as a percentage, describing the extent to which genetic factors contribute to variations on a given trait among the members of a population.

The fact that genes influence a trait does not mean, however, that "biology is destiny." Indeed, genetics research has helped confirm the significance of environmental factors, which generally account for as much variance in human behavior as genes do. If intelligence is 50 percent heritable, then environmental factors must be just as important as genes in generating differences among people.

Moreover, even when genetic factors have an especially powerful effect, as in some kinds of mental retardation, environmental inter-

ventions can often fully or partly overcome the genetic "determinants." For example, the devastating effects of phenylketonuria, a genetic disease that can cause mental retardation, can often be nullified by dietary intervention.

Finally, the degree of heritability for a given trait is not set in stone. The relative influence of genes and environment can change. If, for instance, environmental factors were made almost identical for all the members of a hypothetical population, any differences in cognitive ability in that population would then have to be attributed to genetics, and heritability would be closer to 100 percent than to 50 percent. Heritability describes what is, rather than what can (or should) be.

*—R.P. and J.C.D.*

---

ar model. Instead it seems that genes are responsible for most of the overlap between cognitive skills. Analysis of the Colorado project data, for example, indicates that genetics governs 70 percent of the correlation between verbal and spatial ability. Similar results have been found in twin studies in childhood, young adulthood and middle age. Thus, there is a good chance that when genes associated with a particular cognitive ability are identified, the same genes will be associated with other cognitive abilities.

Research into school achievement has hinted that the genes associated with cognitive abilities may also be relevant to academic performance. Studies of more than 2,000 pairs of high school–age twins were done in the 1970s by John C. Loehlin of the University of Texas at Austin and Robert C.

Nichols, then at the National Merit Scholarship Corporation in Evanston, Ill. In these studies the scores of identical twins were consistently and substantially more similar than those of fraternal twins on all four domains of the National Merit Scholarship Qualifying Test: English usage, mathematics, social studies and natural sciences. These results suggest that genetic factors account for about 40 percent of the variation on such achievement tests.

Genetic influence on school achievement has also been found in twin studies of elementary school–age children as well as in our work with the Colorado Adoption Project. It appears that genes may have almost as much effect on school achievement as they do on cognitive abilities. These results are surprising in and of themselves, as educa-

tors have long believed that achievement is more a product of effort than of ability. Even more interesting, then, is the finding from twin studies and our adoption project that genetic effects overlap between different categories of achievement and that these overlapping genes are probably the very same genetic factors that can influence cognitive abilities.

This evidence supports a decidedly nonmodular view of intelli- gence as a pervasive or global quality of the mind and underscores the relevance of cognitive abilities in real-world perfor- mance. It also implies that genes for cognitive abilities are likely to be genes involved in school achievement, and vice versa.

Given the evidence for genetic influence on cognitive abilities and achievement, one might

---

TWIN STUDIES have examined correlations in verbal *(top)* and in spatial (bottom) skills of identical twins and of fraternal twins. When the results of the separate studies are put side by side, they demonstrate a substantial genetic influence on specific cognitive abilities from child-

hood to old age; for all age groups, the scores of identical twins are more alike than those of fraternal twins. These data seem to counter the long-standing notion that the influence of genes wanes with time.

Jennifer C. Christiansen

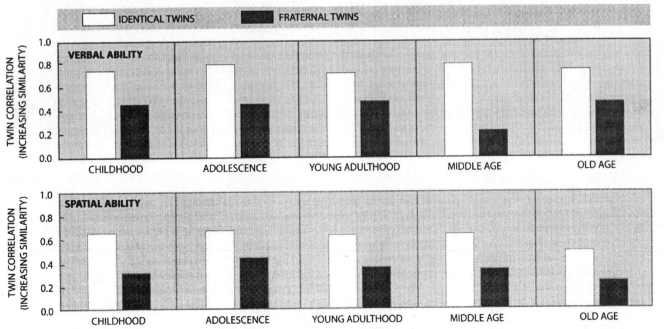

suppose that cognitive disabilities and poor academic achievement must also show genetic influence. But even if genes are involved in cognitive disorders, they may not be the same genes that influence normal cognitive function. The example of mental retardation illustrates this point. Mild mental retardation runs in families, but severe retardation does not. Instead severe mental retardation is caused by genetic and environmental factors—novel mutations, birth complications and head injuries, to name a few—that do not come into play in the normal range of intelligence.

Researchers need to assess, rather than assume, genetic links between the normal and the abnormal, between the traits that are part of a continuum and true disorders of human cognition. Yet genetic studies of verbal and spatial disabilities have been few and far between.

### Genetics and Disability

**M**ost such research has focused on reading disability, which afflicts 80 percent of children diagnosed with a learning disorder. Children with reading disability, also known as dyslexia, read slowly, show poor comprehension and have trouble reading aloud [see "Dyslexia," by Sally E. Shaywitz, SCIENTIFIC AMERICAN, November 1996]. Studies by one of us (DeFries) have shown that reading disability runs in families and that genetic factors do indeed contribute to the resemblance among family members. The identical twin of a person diagnosed

with reading disability, for example, has a 68 percent risk of being similarly diagnosed, whereas a fraternal twin has only a 38 percent chance.

Is this genetic effect related in any way to the genes associated with normal variation in reading ability? That question presents some methodological challenges. The concept of a cognitive disorder is inherently problematic, because it treats disability qualitatively—you either have it or you don't—rather than describing the degree of disability in a quantitative fashion. This focus creates an analytical gap between disorders and traits that are dimensional (varying along a continuum), which are by definition quantitative.

During the past decade, a new genetic technique has been developed that bridges the gap between dimensions and disorders by collecting quantitative information about the relatives of subjects diagnosed qualitatively with a disability. The method is called DF extremes analysis, after its creators, DeFries and David W. Fulker, a colleague at the University of Colorado's Institute for Behavioral Genetics.

For reading disability, the analysis works by testing the identical and fraternal twins of reading-disabled subjects on quantitative measures of reading, rather than looking for a shared diagnosis of dyslexia [see illustration, "Reading Scores"]. If reading disability is influenced by genes that also affect variation within the normal range of reading performance, then the reading scores of the identical twins of dyslexic children should be closer to

those of the reading-disabled group than the scores of fraternal twins are. (A single gene can exert different effects if it occurs in more than one form in a population, so that two people may inherit somewhat different versions. The genes controlling eye color and height are examples of such variable genes.)

It turns out that, as a group, identical twins of reading-disabled subjects do perform almost as poorly as dyslexic subjects on these quantitative tests, whereas fraternal twins do much better than the reading-disabled group (though still significantly worse than the rest of the population). Hence, the genes involved in reading disability may in fact be the same as those that contribute to the quantitative dimension of reading ability measured in this study. DF extremes analysis of these data further suggests that about half the difference in reading scores between dyslexics and the general population can be explained by genetics.

For reading disability, then, there could well be a genetic link between the normal and the abnormal, even though such links may not be found universally for other disabilities. It is possible that reading disability represents the extreme end of a continuum of reading ability, rather than a distinct disorder—that dyslexia might be quantitatively rather than qualitatively different from the normal range of reading ability. All this suggests that if a gene is found for reading disability, the same gene is likely to be associated with the normal range of variation in reading ability. The definitive test will come when a specific gene is identified that is associated

**COLORADO ADOPTION PROJECT, which followed subjects over time, finds that for both verbal (top) and spatial (bottom) abilities, adopted children come to resemble their birth parents (white bars) as much as children raised by their birth parents do (gray bars). In contrast, adopted** children do not end up resembling their adoptive parents (black bars). The results imply that most of the family resemblance in cognitive skills is caused by genetic factors, not environment.

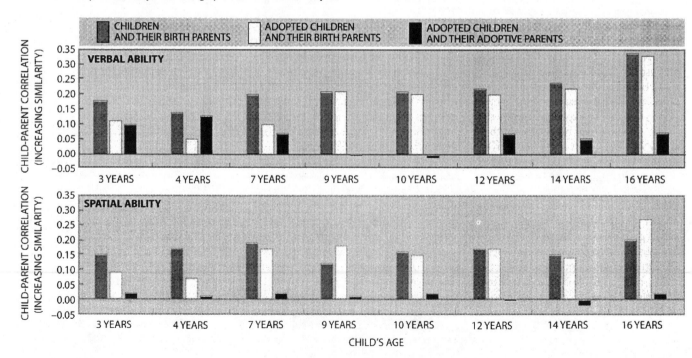

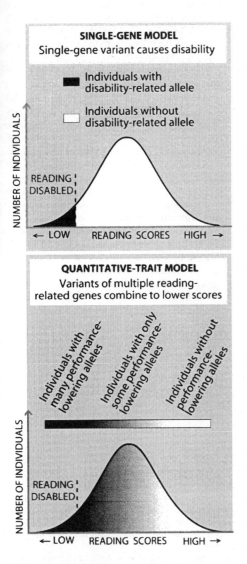

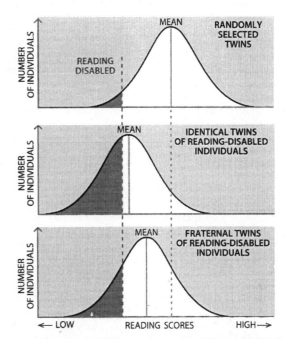

READING SCORES of twins suggest a possible genetic link between normal and abnormal reading skills. In a group of randomly selected members of twin pairs *(top)*, a small fraction of children were reading disabled *(gray)*. Identical *(middle)* and fraternal *(bottom)* twins of the reading-disabled children scored lower than the randomly selected group, with the identical twins performing worse than the fraternal ones. Genetic factors, then, are involved in reading disability. The same genes that influence reading disability may underlie differences in normal reading ability.

**TWO MODELS illustrate how genetics may affect reading disability. In the classic view *(top)*, a single variant, or allele, of a gene is able to cause the disorder; everyone who has that allele becomes reading disabled *(graph)*. But evidence points to a different model *(bottom)*, in which a single allele cannot produce the disability on its own. Instead variants of multiple genes each act subtly but can combine to lower scores and increase the risk of disability.**

with either reading ability or disability. In fact, we and other investigators are already very close to finding such a gene.

### The Hunt for Genes

Until now, we have confined our discussion to quantitative genetics, a discipline that measures the heritability of traits without regard to the kind and number of genes involved. For information about the genes themselves, researchers must turn to molecular genetics—and increasingly, they do. If scientists can identify the genes involved in behavior

and characterize the proteins that the genes code for, new interventions for disabilities become possible.

Research in mice and fruit flies has succeeded in identifying single genes related to learning and spatial perception, and investigations of naturally occurring variations in human populations have found mutations in single genes that result in general mental retardation. These include the genes for phenylketonuria and fragile X syndrome, both causes of mental retardation. Single-gene defects that are associated with Duchenne's muscular dystrophy, Lesch-Nyhan syndrome, neurofibromatosis type 1 and Williams syndrome may also be linked to the specific cognitive disabilities seen in these disorders [see "Williams Syndrome and the Brain," by Howard M. Lenhoff, Paul P. Wang, Frank Greenberg and Ursula Bellugi; SCIENTIFIC AMERICAN, December 1997].

In fact, more than 100 single-gene mutations are known to impair cognitive development. Normal cognitive functioning, on the other hand, is almost certainly orchestrated by many subtly acting genes working

together rather than by single genes operating in isolation. These collaborative genes are thought to affect cognition in a probabilistic rather than a deterministic manner and are called quantitative trait loci, or QTLs. The name, which applies to genes involved in a complex dimension such as cognition, emphasizes the quantitative nature of certain physical and behavioral traits. QTLs have already been identified for diseases such as diabetes, obesity and hypertension as well as for behavioral problems involving drug sensitivity and dependence.

But finding QTLs is much more difficult than identifying the single-gene mutations responsible for some cognitive disorders. Fulker addressed this problem by developing a method, similar to DF extremes analysis, in which certain known variations in DNA are correlated with sibling differences in quantitative traits. Because genetic effects are easier to detect at the extremes of a dimension, the method works best when at least one member of each sibling pair is known to be extreme for a trait. Investigators affiliated with the Colorado Learning Disabilities Research Center at the University of Colorado first used this technique, called QTL linkage, to try to locate a QTL for reading disability—and succeeded. The discovery was reported in 1994 by collaborators at Boulder, the University of Denver and Boys Town National Research Hospital in Omaha.

Like many techniques in molecular genetics, QTL linkage works by identifying differences in DNA markers: stretches of DNA that are known to occupy particular sites on chromosomes and that can vary somewhat from person to person. The different versions of a marker, like the different versions of a gene, are called alleles. Because people have two copies of all chromosomes (except for the gender-determining X and Y chromosomes in males), they have two alleles for any given DNA marker. Hence, siblings can share one, two or no alleles of a marker. In other words, for each marker, siblings can either be like identical twins (sharing both alleles), like fraternal twins (sharing half their alleles) or like adoptive siblings (sharing no alleles).

The investigators who found the QTL for reading disability identified a reading-dis-

abled member of a twin pair and then obtained reading scores for the other twin—the "co-twin." If the reading scores of the co-twins were worse when they shared alleles of a particular marker with their reading-disabled twins, then that marker was likely to lie near a QTL for reading disability in the same chromosomal region. The researchers found such a marker on the short arm of chromosome 6 in two independent samples, one of fraternal twins and one of non-twin siblings. The findings have since been replicated by others.

It is important to note that whereas these studies have helped point to the location of a gene (or genes) implicated in reading disability, the gene (or genes) has not yet been characterized. This distinction gives a sense of where the genetics of cognition stand today: poised on the brink of a new level of discovery. The identification of genes that influence specific cognitive abilities will revolutionize researchers' understanding of the mind. Indeed, molecular genetics will have far-ranging consequences for the study of all human behavior. Researchers will soon be able to investigate the genetic connections between different traits and between behav-

iors and biological mechanisms. They will be able to better track the developmental course of genetic effects and to define more precisely the interactions between genes and the environment.

The discovery of genes for disorders and disabilities will also help clinicians design more effective therapies and to identify people at risk long before the appearance of symptoms. In fact, this scenario is already being enacted with an allele called Apo-E4, which is associated with dementia and cognitive decline in the elderly. Of course, new knowledge of specific genes could turn up new problems as well: among them, prejudicial labeling and discrimination. And genetics research always raises fears that DNA markers will be used by parents prenatally to select "designer babies."

We cannot emphasize too much that genetic effects do not imply genetic determinism, nor do they constrain environmental interventions. Although some readers may find our views to be controversial, we believe the benefits of identifying genes for cognitive dimensions and disorders will far outweigh the potential abuses.

---

TEST ANSWERS    VERBAL: 1a. dry;  1b. pungent    SPATIAL: 1.     2. b, c;   3. a, c, d;   4. a, b, f

---

## The Authors

ROBERT PLOMIN and JOHN C. DeFRIES have collaborated for more than 20 years. Plomin, who worked with DeFries at the University of Colorado at Boulder from 1974 to 1986, is now at the Institute of Psychiatry in London. There he is research professor of behavioral genetics and deputy director of the Social, Genetic and Developmental Psychiatry Research Center. DeFries directs the University of Colorado's Institute for Behavioral Genetics and the university's Colorado Learning Disabilities Research Center. The ongoing Colorado Adoption Project, launched by the authors in 1975, has so far produced three books and more than 100 research papers. Plomin and DeFries are also the lead authors of the textbook *Behavioral Genetics*, now in its third edition.

## Further Reading

NATURE, NURTURE AND PSYCHOLOGY. Edited by Robert Plomin and Gerald E. McClearn. American Psychological Association, Washington, D.C., 1993.
GENETICS OF SPECIFIC READING DISABILITY. J. C. DeFries and Maricela Alarcón in *Mental Retardation and Developmental Disabilities Research Reviews*, Vol. 2, pages 39–47; 1996.
BEHAVIORAL GENETICS. Third edition. Robert Plomin, John C. DeFries, Gerald E. McClearn and Michael Rutter. W. H. Freeman, 1997.
SUSCEPTIBILITY LOCI FOR DISTINCT COMPONENTS OF DEVELOPMENTAL DYSLEXIA ON CHROMOSOMES 6 AND 15. E. L. Grigorenko, F. B. Wood, M. S. Meyer, L. A. Hart, W. C. Speed, A. Schuster and D. L. Pauls in *American Journal of Human Genetics*, Vol. 60, pages 27–39; 1997.

# Basing Teaching on Piaget's Constructivism

**Constance Kamii and Janice K. Ewing**

Constance Kamii is Professor, Department of Curriculum and Instruction, University of Alabama at Birmingham. Janice K. Ewing is Assistant Professor, Department of Social Sciences and Education, Colby-Sawyer College, New London, New Hampshire.

Constructivism, the view that much of learning originates from *inside* the child, has become increasingly popular in recent years. Many educators, however, use the term "construct" loosely without knowing, for example, that children construct a system of writing very differently from how they construct mathematical understanding. And some people think that Piaget had nothing to do with constructivism, crediting him only with discovering the stages of children's development.

The purpose of this article is to explain three main reasons for basing teaching on Piaget's constructivism: 1) it is a scientific theory that explains the nature of human knowledge, 2) it is the only theory in existence that explains children's construction of knowledge from birth to adolescence and 3) it informs educators of how Piaget's distinction among the three kinds of knowledge changes the way we should teach many subjects.

From *Childhood Education*, Annual Theme Issue, 1996, pp. 260-264. © 1996 by the Association for Childhood Education International, 17904 Georgia Avenue, Suite 215, Olney, MD. Reprinted by permission.

## A Scientific Explanation of Human Knowledge

Philosophers have debated for centuries about how human beings attain truth, or knowledge. The two main views—the empiricist and rationalist views—developed in answer to this question differ, especially in the way philosophers thought about the role of experience.

Empiricists (such as Locke, Berkeley and Hume) argued, in essence, that knowledge has its source outside the individual, and that it is acquired by internalization through the senses. Empiricists further argued that the individual at birth is like a clean slate on which experiences are "written" as he or she grows up. As Locke wrote in 1690, "The senses at first let in particular ideas, and furnish the yet empty cabinet, and the mind by degrees growing familiar with some of them, they are lodged in the memory..." (1690/1947, p. 22).

Although rationalists such as Descartes, Spinoza and Kant did not deny the necessity of experience, they argued that reason is more important than sensory experience because reason enables us to know with certainty many truths that observation can never ascertain. We know, for example, that every event has a cause, in spite of the fact that we cannot examine every event in the entire past and future of the universe. Rationalists also pointed out that since our senses often deceive us through perceptual illusions, the senses cannot be trusted to provide reliable knowledge. The rigor, precision and certainty of mathematics, a purely deductive system, was the rationalists' prime example supporting the power of reason. When asked to explain the origin of reason, many proclaimed it was innate in human beings.

As a biologist trained in scientific methods, Piaget decided that the way to resolve the debate between empiricism and rationalism was to study knowledge scientifically, rather than continuing to argue on the basis of speculation. Piaget also believed that to understand the nature of knowledge, we must study its formation rather than examining only the end product. This is why he wanted to study the evolution of science from its prehistoric beginning, to examine the roles of sensory information and reason. Prehistoric evidence did not exist anymore, however, and the closest data available to him were babies' and children's knowledge. For Piaget, the study of children was thus a means of explaining the nature of human knowledge (Bringuier, 1977/1980).

The outcome of more than 50 years of research was Piaget's sharp disagreement with empiricism. Although he did not agree completely with rationalism, he did align himself with rationalism when required to place himself in a broad sense in one tradition or the other. With regard to the empiri-

cist belief that we know objects through our senses, he argued that we never know objects as they are "out there" in external reality. Objects can be known only by assimilation into the schemes that we bring to each situation.

The famous conservation-of-liquid task offers an example of Piaget's opposition to empiricism. Until children construct a certain level of logic from the inside, they are nonconservers because they can base their judgment only on what they can *see*. Their *reason* later enables them to *interpret* the empirical data and deduce that the amount

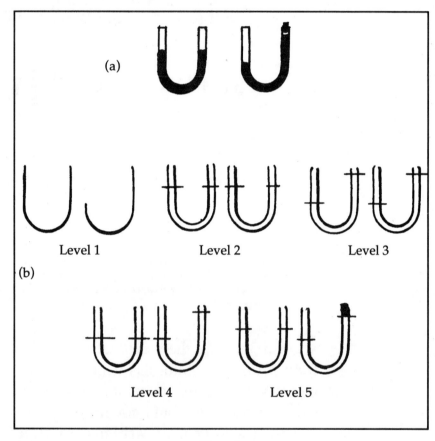

*Figure 1*

of liquid is the same even if one glass appears to have more than the other.

## The Construction of Knowledge from Birth to Adolescence

To teach 3-year-olds, 7-year-olds or any other age group, educators must understand how children have acquired the knowledge they already have, and how this knowledge is related to that of adolescents and adults. The only theory in existence that shows this development from birth to adolescence is Piaget's. In his books about babies (Piaget, 1936/1952, 1937/1954, 1945,/1962), especially *The Construction of Reality in the*

*Child,* we can read in meticulous detail about infants' construction of objects and of object permanence and the roots of logico-mathematical knowledge.

Although gaps are still being filled in Piaget's theory, we can clearly see children's subsequent construction of logic at ages 4–16 in *The Growth of Logical Thinking from Childhood to Adolescence* (Inhelder & Piaget, 1955/1958) and *The Early Growth of Logic in the Child* (Inhelder & Piaget, 1959/1964). An example related to the conservation-of-liquid task is given below to illustrate older children's construction of knowledge (Piaget & Inhelder, 1968/1973).

Children between 4 and 15 years of age were shown two U-shaped glass tubes (Figure 1a) mounted on a board and containing colored water. The subjects were asked to take a good look at the objects because they would later be asked to describe and draw them from memory.

Figure 1b shows examples of the children's drawings. At level 1, they drew only the containers (tubes) or the substance contained therein (liquid). At level 2, they made the water level the same everywhere. At level 3, while the water level became unequal, both tubes looked the same. The drawings became more accurate at level 4, but the children did not notice that the water level in the second tube went up on one side as much as it went down on the other side. At level 5, however, they inferred the initial equality of quantity in the two tubes, conserved this equality and noticed the significance of the stopper. As can be seen in Table 1, only the oldest children were frequently at levels 4 and 5.

*Table 1*

## Relationship Between Ages and Levels in a Memory Task

| | Levels | | | | | |
|---|---|---|---|---|---|---|
| Ages | 1 | 2 | 3 | 4 | 5 | Total number |
| 4–5 | 12(54%) | 6(27%) | 2(9%) | 2(9%) | 0(0%) | 22 |
| 6–7 | 4(22%) | 4(22%) | 1(5%) | 8(44%) | 1(5%) | 18 |
| 8–15 | 0(0%) | 1(5%) | 1(5%) | 9(45%) | 9(45%) | 20 |

This task is one of the countless examples that enable us to trace the roots of adolescents' knowledge all the way back to infancy. It again supports Piaget's view that we do not know objects as they are "out there" in external reality. Six-year-olds cannot even *see* the inequality of the water level in one of the tubes. When they can make more precise spatial relationships, they become able to notice what is obvious to older children.

Hundreds of other tasks can be found in Piaget's books that reveal the surprising process of children's construction of knowledge. In this process, children go from one level of being "wrong" to another, rather than simply accumulating more and more knowledge quantitatively. Nonconservation may be "wrong," but basing one's judgment on water level is an enormous achievement compared to what babies do, without even understanding the word "more."

The roles of sensory information and reason discussed earlier can be understood only in light of the distinction Piaget made among three kinds of knowledge. We, therefore, now turn to a discussion of the three kinds of knowledge and the difference this distinction can make to teaching.

## Three Kinds of Knowledge

The three kinds of knowledge are physical, social (conventional) and logico-mathematical knowledge. Piaget's distinction among the three is based on their ultimate sources and modes of structuring.

*Physical knowledge* is knowledge of objects in external reality. The color and weight of a block are examples of physical properties that are in objects in external reality and can be known empirically by observation.

Examples of *social knowledge* are holidays, written and spoken languages, and the rule of saying "Good morning" under certain circumstances. The ultimate source of physical knowledge is partly in objects, and the ultimate source of social knowledge is partly in man-made conventions. The reason for saying "partly" is clarified shortly.

*Logico-mathematical knowledge* consists of relationships created by each individual and is the hardest kind to understand. When we are presented with a red block and a blue block and think that they are *similar*, for instance, the similarity is an example of logico-mathematical knowledge. Almost everybody thinks that the similarity between the blocks is observable, but this is not true. The blocks themselves are observable, but the similarity between them is not. The similarity exists neither *in* the red block nor *in* the blue one. If a person did not put the objects into this relationship, the similarity would not exist for him or her. The source of logico-mathematical knowledge, therefore, is *in* each child's mind. Other relationships the individual can create between the same blocks are *different, the same in weight* and *two*. Mathematical knowledge such as $2 + 2 = 4$ and $3 \times 4 = 12$ is constructed by each child by making new relationships out of previously created relationships.

It was stated earlier that the source of physical knowledge is only *partly* in objects. Piaget's reason for saying "partly" was that a logico-mathematical framework, or a classificatory framework, is necessary even to recognize a block as a block or to recognize water as a liquid. Classification is also necessary to think about the color of an object and to recognize the color as blue. Without classification, it would be impossible to construct physical knowledge. Likewise, it would be impossible to construct social (conventional) knowledge without a logico-mathematical framework. To recognize a certain word as a "bad one," for example, the child has to categorize words into "good ones" and "bad ones."

The conservation of amount of liquid mentioned earlier is an example of the child's logico-mathematization of physical knowledge. The conservation of quantity of liquid involves spatio-temporal and other relationships, which belong to logico-mathematical knowledge. This is why we say that conservation is a logical deduction and not empirical knowledge.

> *Armed with Piaget's theory about the nature of logico-mathematical knowledge, Kamii set out to test the hypothesis that children can invent their own procedures for the four arithmetical operations . . .*

The memory task described earlier also illustrates children's logico-mathematization of physical knowledge. We do not see facts only with our eyes. To the extent that we can make higher-level relationships and have more physical knowledge about contents such as air pressure, we obtain higher-level knowledge from the objects we see. In other

# The Hindu Scratch Method for Solving 278 + 356 by Proceeding from Left to Right

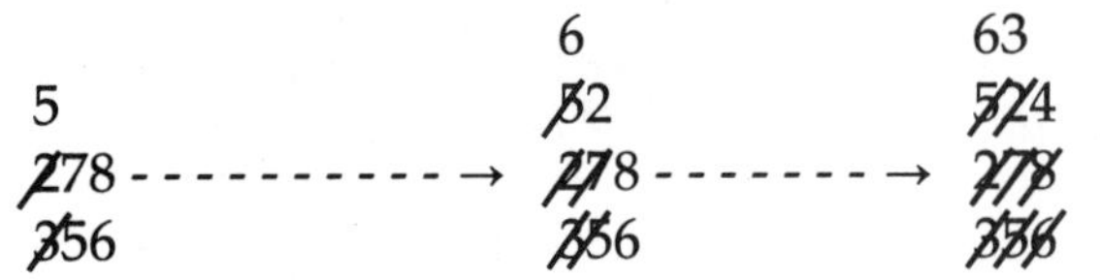

The rules followed:

1. Add 200 and 300, write the result (5 in the hundreds place), and cross out the 200 and 300.

2. Add 70 and 50, write the result (120), and cross out the 70 and 50. Because there was already a 5 in the hundreds place, this 5 was crossed out and changed to 6.

3. Add 8 and 6, write the result (14), and cross out the 8 and the 6. Because there was already a 2 in the tens place, this 2 was crossed out and changed to 3.

*Figure 2*

words, we observe the stopper in the task only if we bring a certain level of knowledge to it.

Physics and all the other branches of science involve the logico-mathematization of objects that are observable. Educators who understand the nature of science focus science education on children's reasoning about observable phenomena, rather than on transmission of scientific facts and terminology (social knowledge). An example of this emphasis on reasoning in physics can be found in Kamii and DeVries (1978/1993).

The teaching of mathematics also changes drastically when we understand the nature of logico-mathematical knowledge. Since 1980, Kamii (1985, 1989, 1994) has been developing an approach to primary mathematics based on Piaget's constructivism. This approach is described below as an example of how Piaget's theory can change the way we teach.

## Elementary Mathematics Education

Traditional mathematics educators are usually not aware of Piaget's distinction among the three kinds of knowledge. Much of traditional elementary mathematics is therefore taught according to associationist-behavioristic principles, as if mathematics were social (conventional) knowledge. Teaching rules such as "carrying" and "borrowing" is an example of this social-knowledge approach.

Armed with Piaget's theory about the nature of logico-mathematical knowledge, Kamii set out to test the hypothesis that children can invent their own procedures for the four arithmetical operations, without any teaching of conventional rules. While this hypothesis was amply confirmed, an unexpected finding surfaced. The rules that are now taught in almost all the elementary schools throughout the United States are harmful to children's development of numerical reasoning.

Two reasons can be given to explain the harm. First, children have to give up their own thinking to use the rules of "carrying," "borrowing" and so forth. These rules make children proceed from right to left; that is, from the column of ones to those of tens, hundreds and so on. When children are free to do their own thinking, however, they invariably proceed in the opposite direction, from left to right. To add 38 + 16, for example, they typically do 30 + 10 = 40, 8 + 6 = 14, and 40 + 14 = 54. To subtract 18 from 32, they often say, "30 − 10 = 20. I can take only 2 from 2; so I have to take 6 more away from 20; so the answer is 14." In multiplication, likewise, children's typical way of doing 5 × 234, for example, is: 5 × 200 = 1,000, 5 × 30 = 150, 5 × 4 = 20, and 1,000 + 150 + 20 = 1170. Because a compromise is not possible between going from left to right and going from right to left, children have to give up their own thinking to obey their teachers.

The second reason for saying that algorithms are harmful is that these rules "unteach" place value and prevent children from developing number sense. While solving the preceding multiplication problem, for example, children who are taught algorithms say, "Five times four is twenty, put down the zero, and carry the two. Five times three is fifteen, plus two is seventeen, put down the seven, and carry the one. Five times two is ten," and so on. Treating every digit as ones is efficient for adults, who already know that the 2 in 234 is 200. For primary-age children, who have a tendency to think that the 2 in 234 means *two,* however, algorithms reinforce their "errors."

The history of computation is full of methods that are similar to the way today's children think. The Hindu Scratch Method shown in Figure 2 is an example of a method our ancestors used. It illustrates the constructive process through which the human species created knowledge (see Kamii, 1994, for other examples). Educators who impose algorithms on primary-age children think that mathematics is a cultural heritage that they must *transmit* to children. While their intentions are good, they impose on children in ready-made form the results of centuries of construction by adult mathematicians. An example of the outcome of this teaching is that the great majority of 4th-graders who had been taught algorithms gave outlandish answers such as 848, 783, 194 and 134 when asked to do 6 + 53 + 185 without paper and pencil (Kamii, 1994).

## Conclusion

Education entered a scientific era when it embraced associationism and behaviorism. While both these theories are scientific, Piaget's constructivism has gone beyond them. Many educators cannot accept constructivism, however, because associationism and behaviorism seem too valid to reject.

It is not necessary to reject associationism and behaviorism completely to embrace constructivism. The reason is that Piaget's constructivism surpassed associationism and behaviorism in a way similar to the way Copernicus's theory went beyond the geocentric theory. Copernicus proved the geocentric theory wrong not by eliminating it, but by encompassing it. This is why even today we speak of sunrise and sunset, knowing perfectly well that the sun does not revolve around the earth. From the limited perspective of earth, it is still true that the sun rises and sets.

In a similar way, associationism and behaviorism still remain true from the limited perspective of surface behavior and specific bits of knowledge. In certain situations, therefore, associationism and behaviorism can still be used by educators. Science, too, advances by going through one level after another of being "wrong." Older, "wrong" knowledge is not eliminated completely. It is *modified* when we construct more adequate theories.

Although education has entered a scientific era, much of it remains at a stage of folk art based on opinions and trial-and-error. Because education is based mainly on opinions, it remains vulnerable to fads and the swinging of the pendulum. Progressive Education went out of fashion by the 1950s, for example, and came back in part in the 1960s as Open Education. But Open Education was quickly defeated by the forces of "back to basics."

Constructivist teaching has the potential of becoming another resurrection of Progressive Education. It is true that education cannot be based on scientific knowledge alone. But if education is to keep advancing and free itself from bandwagons and the swinging of the pendulum, we must study human knowledge with scientific rigor. Teaching will always remain an art, just as medicine is an art. But teaching must become an art based on scientific knowledge because science advances only in one direction and does not return to obsolete theories.

## References

Bringuier, J.-C. (1980). *Conversations with Jean Piaget.* Chicago: University of Chicago Press. (Original work published 1977)

Inhelder, B., & Piaget, J. (1958). *The growth of logical thinking from childhood to adolescence.* New York: Basic Books. (Original work published 1955)

Inhelder, B., & Piaget, J. (1964). *The early growth of logic in the child.* New York: Harper & Row. (Original work published 1959)

Kamii, C. (1985). *Young children reinvent arithmetic.* New York: Teachers College Press.

Kamii, C. (1989). *Young children continue to reinvent arithmetic, 2nd grade.* New York: Teachers College Press.

Kamii, C. (1994). *Young children continue to reinvent arithmetic, 3rd grade.* New York: Teachers College Press.

Kamii, C., & DeVries, R. (1993). *Physical knowledge in preschool education.* New York: Teachers College Press. (Original work published 1978)

Locke, J. (1947). *Essay concerning human understanding.* Oxford, England: Oxford University Press. (Original work published 1690)

Piaget, J. (1952). *The origins of intelligence in children.* New York: Basic Books. (Original work published 1936)

Piaget, J. (1954). *The construction of reality in the child.* New York: Basic Books. (Original work published 1937)

Piaget, J. (1962). *Play, dreams, and imitation in childhood.* New York: Norton. (Original work published 1945)

Piaget, J., & Inhelder, B. (1973). *Memory and intelligence.* New York: Basic Books. (Original work published 1968)

# The First Seven . . . and the Eighth

## A Conversation with Howard Gardner

**Human intelligence continues to intrigue psychologists, neurologists, and educators. What is it? Can we measure it? How do we nurture it?**

**Kathy Checkley**

*Howard Gardner's theory of multiple intelligences, described in* Frames of Mind *(1985), sparked a revolution of sorts in classrooms around the world, a mutiny against the notion that human beings have a single, fixed intelligence. The fervor with which educators embraced his premise that we have multiple intelligences surprised Gardner himself. "It obviously spoke to some sense that people had that kids weren't all the same and that the tests we had only skimmed the surface about the differences among kids," Gardner said.*

*Here Gardner brings us up-to-date on his current thinking on intelligence, how children learn, and how they should be taught.*

*How do you define intelligence?*

Intelligence refers to the human ability to solve problems or to make something that is valued in one or more cultures. As long as we can find a culture that values an ability to solve a problem or create a product in a particular way, then I would strongly consider whether that ability should be considered an intelligence.

First, though, that ability must meet other criteria: Is there a particular representation in the brain for the

ability? Are there populations that are especially good or especially impaired in an intelligence? And, can an evolutionary history of the intelligence be seen in animals other than human beings?

I defined seven intelligences (see box) in the early 1980s because those intelligences all fit the criteria. A decade later when I revisited the task, I found at least one more ability that clearly deserved to be called an intelligence.

*That would be the naturalist intelligence. What led you to consider adding this to our collection of intelligences?*

Somebody asked me to explain the achievements of the great biologists, the ones who had a real mastery of taxonomy, who understood about different species, who could recognize patterns in nature and classify objects. I realized that to explain that kind of ability, I would have to manipulate the other intelligences in ways that weren't appropriate.

So I began to think about whether the capacity to classify nature might be a separate intelligence. The naturalist ability passed with flying colors. Here are a couple of reasons: First, it's an ability we need to survive as human beings. We need, for example, to know which animals to hunt and which to run away from. Second, this ability isn't restricted to human beings. Other animals need to have a naturalist intelligence to survive. Finally, the big selling point is that brain evidence supports the existence of the naturalist intelligence. There are certain parts of the brain particularly dedicated to the recognition and the naming of what are called "natural" things.

*How do you describe the naturalist intelligence to those of us who aren't psychologists?*

The naturalist intelligence refers to the ability to recognize and classify plants, minerals, and animals, including rocks and grass and all variety of flora and fauna. The ability to recognize cultural artifacts like cars or sneakers may also depend on the naturalist intelligence.

Now, everybody can do this to a certain extent—we can all recognize dogs, cats, trees. But, some people from an early age are extremely good at recognizing and classifying artifacts. For example, we all know kids who, at age 3 or 4, are better at recognizing dinosaurs than most adults.

Darwin is probably the most famous example of a naturalist because he saw so deeply into the nature of living things.

*Are there any other abilities you're considering calling intelligences?*

Well, there may be an existential intelligence that refers to the human inclination to ask very basic questions about existence. Who are we? Where do we come from? What's it all about? Why do we die? We might say that existential intelligence allows us to know the invisible, outside world. The only reason I haven't given a seal of approval to the existential intelligence is that I don't think we have good brain evidence yet on its existence in the nervous system—one of the criteria for an intelligence.

*You have said that the theory of multiple intelligences may be best understood when we know what it critiques. What do you mean?*

The standard view of intelligence is that intelligence is something you are born with; you have only a certain amount of it; you cannot do much about how much of that intelligence you have; and tests exist that can tell you how smart you are. The theory of multiple intelligences challenges that view. It asks, instead,

© Susie Fitzhugh

"Given what we know about the brain, evolution, and the differences in cultures, what are the sets of human abilities we all share?"

My analysis suggested that rather than one or two intelligences, all human beings have several (eight) intelligences. What makes life interesting, however, is that we don't have the same strength in each intelligence area, and we don't have the same amalgam of intelligences. Just as we look different from one another and have different kinds of personalities, we also have different kinds of minds.

This premise has very serious educational implications. If we treat everybody as if they are the same, we're catering to one profile of intelligence, the lan-

# School matters, but only insofar as it yields something that can be used once students leave school.

guage-logic profile. It's great if you have that profile, but it's not great for the vast majority of human beings who do not have that particular profile of intelligence.

*Can you explain more fully how the theory of multiple intelligences challenges what has become known as IQ?*

The theory challenges the entire notion of IQ. The IQ test was developed about a century ago as a way to determine who would have trouble in school. The test measures linguistic ability, logical-mathematical ability, and, occasionally, spatial ability.

What the intelligence test does not do is inform us about our other intelligences; it also doesn't look at other virtues like creativity or civic mindedness, or whether a person is moral or ethical.

We don't do much IQ testing anymore, but the shadow of IQ tests is still with us because the SAT—arguably the most potent examination in the world—is basically the same kind of disembodied language-logic instrument.

The truth is, I don't believe there is such a general thing as scholastic aptitude. Even so, I don't think that the SAT will fade until colleges indicate that they'd rather have students who know how to use their minds well—students who may or may not be good test takers, but who are serious, inquisitive, and know how to probe and problem-solve. That is really what college professors want, I believe.

*Can we strengthen our intelligences? If so, how?*

We can all get better at each of the intelligences, although some people will improve in an intelligence area more readily than others, either because biology gave them a better brain for that intelligence or because their culture gave them a better teacher.

Teachers have to help students use their combination of intelligences to be successful in school, to help them learn whatever it is they want to learn, as well as what the teachers and society believe they have to learn.

Now, I'm not arguing that kids shouldn't learn the literacies. Of course they should learn the literacies. Nor am I arguing that kids shouldn't learn the disciplines. I'm a tremendous champion of the disciplines. What I argue against is the notion that there's only one way to learn how to read, only one way to learn how to compute, only one way to learn about biology. I think that such contentions are nonsense.

It's equally nonsensical to say that everything should be taught seven or eight ways. That's not the point of the MI theory. The point is to realize that any topic of importance, from any discipline, can be taught in more than one way. There are things people need to know, and educators have to be extraordinarily imaginative and persistent in helping students understand things better.

*A popular activity among those who are first exploring multiple intelligences is to construct their own intellectual profile. It's thought that when teachers go through the process of creating such a profile, they're more likely to recognize and appreciate the intellectual strengths of their students. What is your view on this kind of activity?*

My own studies have shown that people love to do this. Kids like to do it, adults like to do it. And, as an activity, I think it's perfectly harmless.

I get concerned, though, when people think that determining your intellectual profile—or that of someone else—is an end in itself.

You have to use the profile to understand the ways in which you seem to learn easily. And, from there, determine how to use those strengths to help you become more successful in other endeavors. Then, the profile becomes a way for you to understand yourself better, and you can use that understanding to catapult yourself to a better level of understanding or to a higher level of skill.

*How has your understanding of the multiple intelligences influenced how you teach?*

# As long as you can lose one ability while others are spared, you cannot just have a single intelligence.

My own teaching has changed slowly as a result of multiple intelligences because I'm teaching graduate students psychological theory and there are only so many ways I can do that. I am more open to group work and to student projects of various sorts, but even if I wanted to be an "MI professor" of graduate students, I still have a certain moral obligation to prepare them for a world in which they will have to write scholarly articles and prepare theses.

Where I've changed much more, I believe, is at the workplace. I direct research projects and work with all kinds of people. Probably 10 to 15 years ago, I would have tried to find people who were just like me to work with me on these projects.

I've really changed my attitude a lot on that score. Now I think much more in terms of what people are good at and in putting together teams of people whose varying strengths complement one another.

*How should thoughtful educators implement the theory of multiple intelligences?*

Although there is no single MI route, it's very important that a teacher take individual differences among kinds very seriously. You cannot be a good MI teacher if you don't want to know each child and try to gear how you teach and how you evaluate to that particular child. The bottom line is a deep interest in children and how their minds are different from one another, and in helping them use their minds well.

Now, kids can be great informants for teachers. For example, a teacher might say, "Look, Benjamin, this obviously isn't working. Should we try using a picture?" If Benjamin gets excited about that approach, that's a pretty good clue to the teacher about what could work.

The theory of multiple intelligences, in and of itself, is not going to solve anything in our society, but linking the multiple intelligences with a curriculum focused on understanding is an extremely powerful intellectual undertaking.

When I talk about understanding, I mean that students can take ideas they learn in school, or anywhere for that matter, and apply those appropriately in new situations. We know people truly understand something when they can represent the knowledge in more than one way. We have to put understanding up front in school. Once we have that goal, multiple intelligences can be a terrific handmaiden because understandings involve a mix of mental representations, entailing different intelligences.

*People often say that what they remember most about school are those learning experiences that were linked to real life. How does the theory of multiple intelligences help connect learning to the world outside the classroom?*

The theory of multiple intelligences wasn't based on school work or on tests. Instead, what I did was look at the world and ask, What are the things that people do in the world? What does it mean to be a surgeon? What does it mean to be a politician? What does it mean to be an artist or a sculptor? What abilities do you need to do those things? My theory, then, came from the things that are valued in the world.

So when a school values multiple intelligences, the relationship to what's valued in the world is patent. If you cannot easily relate this activity to something that's valued in the world, the school has probably

© Susie Fitzhugh

lost the core idea of multiple intelligences, which is that these intelligences evolved to help people do things that matter in the real world.

School matters, but only insofar as it yields something that can be used once students leave school.

# The Intelligences, in Gardner's Words

■ Linguistic intelligence is the capacity to use language, your native language, and perhaps other languages, to express what's on your mind and to understand other people. Poets really specialize in linguistic intelligence, but any kind of writer, orator, speaker, lawyer, or a person for whom language is an important stock in trade highlights linguistic intelligence.

■ People with a highly developed logical-mathematical intelligence understand the underlying principles of some kind of a causal system, the way a scientist or a logician does; or can manipulate numbers, quantities, and operations, the way a mathematician does.

■ Spatial intelligence refers to the ability to represent the spatial world internally in your mind—the way a sailor or airplane pilot navigates the large spatial world, or the way a chess player or sculptor represents a more circumscribed spatial world. Spatial intelligence can be used in the arts or in the sciences. If you are spatially intelligent and oriented toward the arts, you are more likely to become a painter or a sculptor or an architect than, say, a musician or a writer. Similarly, certain sciences like anatomy or topology emphasize spatial intelligence.

■ Bodily kinesthetic intelligence is the capacity to use your whole body or parts of your body—your hand, your fingers, your arms—to solve a problem, make something, or put on some kind of a production. The most evident examples are people in athletics or the performing arts, particularly dance or acting.

■ Musical intelligence is the capacity to think in music, to be able to hear patterns, recognize them, remember them, and perhaps manipulate them. People who have a strong musical intelligence don't just remember music eas-

ily—they can't get it out of their minds, it's so omnipresent. Now, some people will say, "Yes, music is important, but it's a talent, not an intelligence." And I say, "Fine, let's call it a talent." But, then we have to leave the word *intelligent* out of *all* discussions of human abilities. You know, Mozart was damned smart!

■ Interpersonal intelligence is understanding other people. It's an ability we all need, but is at a premium if you are a teacher, clinician, salesperson, or politician. Anybody who deals with other people has to be skilled in the interpersonal sphere.

■ Intrapersonal intelligence refers to having an understanding of yourself, of knowing who you are, what you can do, what you want to do, how you react to things, which things to avoid, and which things to gravitate toward. We are drawn to people who have a good understanding of themselves because those people tend not to screw up. They tend to know what they can do. They tend to know what they can't do. And they tend to know where to go if they need help.

■ Naturalist intelligence designates the human ability to discriminate among living things (plants, animals) as well as sensitivity to other features of the natural world (clouds, rock configurations). This ability was clearly of value in our evolutionary past as hunters, gatherers, and farmers; it continues to be central in such roles as botanist or chef. I also speculate that much of our consumer society exploits the naturalist intelligences, which can be mobilized in the discrimination among cars, sneakers, kinds of makeup, and the like. The kind of pattern recognition valued in certain of the sciences may also draw upon naturalist intelligence.

*How can teachers be guided by multiple intelligences when creating assessment tools?*

We need to develop assessments that are much more representative of what human beings are going to have to do to survive in this society. For example, I value literacy, but my measure of literacy should not be whether you can answer a multiple-choice question that asks you to select the best meaning of a paragraph. Instead, I'd rather have you read the paragraph and list four questions you have about the paragraph and figure out how you would answer those questions. Or, if I want to know how you can write, let me give you a stem and see whether you can write about that topic, or let me ask you to write an editorial in response to something you read in the newspaper or observed on the street.

The current emphasis on performance assessment is well supported by the theory of multiple intelligences. Indeed, you could not really be an advocate of multiple intelligences if you didn't have some dissatisfaction with the current testing because it's so focused on short-answer, linguistic, or logical kinds of items.

MI theory is very congenial to an approach that says: one, let's not look at things through the filter of a short-answer test. Let's look directly at the performance that we value, whether it's a linguistic, logical, aesthetic, or social performance; and, two, let's never pin our assessment of understanding on just one particular measure, but let's always allow students to show their understanding in a variety of ways.

*You have identified several myths about the theory of multiple intelligences. Can you describe some of those myths?*

One myth that I personally find irritating is that an intelligence is the same as a learning style. Learning styles are claims about ways in which individuals purportedly approach everything they do. If you are planful, you are supposed to be planful about everything. If you are logical-sequential, you are supposed to be logical-sequential about everything. My own research and observations suggest that that's a dubious assumption. But whether or not that's true, learning styles are very different from multiple intelligences.

Multiple intelligences claims that we respond, individually, in different ways to different kinds of content, such as language or music or other people. This is very different from the notion of learning style.

You can say that a child is a visual learner, but that's not a multiple intelligences way of talking about things. What I would say is, "Here is a child who very easily represents things spatially, and we can draw upon that strength if need be when we want to teach the child something new."

Another widely believed myth is that, because we have seven or eight intelligences, we should create seven or eight tests to measure students' strengths in each of those areas. That is a perversion of the theory. It's re-creating the sin of the single intelligence quotient and just multiplying it by a larger number. I'm personally against assessment of intelligences unless such a measurement is used for a very specific learning purpose—we want to help a child understand her history or his mathematics better and, therefore, want to see what might be good entry points for that particular child.

*What experiences led you to the study of human intelligence?*

It's hard for me to pick out a single moment, but I can see a couple of snapshots. When I was in high school, my uncle gave me a textbook in psychology. I'd never actually heard of psychology before. This textbook helped me understand color blindness. I'm color blind, and I became fascinated by the existence of plates that illustrated what color blindness was. I could actually explain why I couldn't see colors.

Another time when I was studying the Reformation, I read a book by Erik Erikson called *Young Man Luther* (1958).[1] I was fascinated by the psychological motivation of Luther to attack the Catholic Church. That fascination influenced my decision to go into psychology.

The most important influence was actually learning about brain damage and what could happen to people when they had strokes. When a person has a stroke, a certain part of the brain gets injured, and that injury can tell you what that part of the brain does. Individuals who lose their musical abilities can still talk. People who lose their linguistic ability still might be able to sing. That understanding not only brought me into the whole world of brain study, but it was really the seed that led ultimately to the theory of multiple intelligences. As long as you can lose one ability while others are spared, you cannot just have a single intelligence. You have to have several intelligences.

---

1. See Erik Erikson, *Young Man Luther* (New York: W. W. Norton, 1958).

---

**Howard Gardner** is Professor of Education at Harvard Graduate School of Education and author of, among other books, *The Unschooled Mind: How Children Think and How Schools Should Teach* (1991). He can be reached at Roy B. Larsen Hall, 2nd Floor, Appian Way, Harvard Graduate School of Education, Cambridge, MA 02138. **Kathy Checkley** is a staff writer for *Update* and has assisted in the development of ASCD's new CD-ROM, *Exploring Our Multiple Intelligences,* and pilot online project on multiple intelligences.

# Bell, book and scandal

**For more than a century intelligence testing has been a field rich in disputed evidence and questionable conclusions. "The Bell Curve", by Charles Murray and Richard Herrnstein, has ensured it will remain so**

THERE is plenty of room for debate about which was the most amusing book of 1994, or which the best written. But nobody can seriously quibble about which was the most controversial. "The Bell Curve: Intelligence and Class Structure in American Life", an 845-page tome by Charles Murray and Richard Herrnstein*, has reignited a debate that is likely to rage on for years yet, consuming reputations and research grants as it goes.

"The Bell Curve" is an ambitious attempt to resuscitate IQ ("intelligence quotient") testing, one of the most controversial ideas in recent intellectual

*The Free Press. New York, 1994

history; and to use that idea to explain some of the more unpalatable features of modern America. Mr Murray, a sociologist, and Herrnstein, a psychologist who died shortly before the book's publication, argue that individuals differ substantially in their "cognitive abilities"; that these differences are inherited as much as acquired; and that intelligence is distributed in the population along a normal distribution curve—the bell curve of the book's title—with a few geniuses at the top, a mass of ordinary Joes in the middle and a minority of dullards at the bottom (see chart).

Then, into this relatively innocuous cocktail, Messrs Murray and Herrnstein mix two explosive arguments.

The first is that different races do not perform equally in the IQ stakes—that, in America, Asians score, on average, slightly above the norm, and blacks, on average, substantially below it. The second is that America is calcifying into impermeable castes. The bright are inter-marrying, spawning bright offspring and bagging well-paid jobs; and the dull are doomed to teenage pregnancy, welfare dependency, drugs and crime.

For the past three months it has been almost impossible to pick up an American newspaper or tune into an American television station without learning more about Mr Murray's views. Dozens of academics are hard at work rebutting (they would say refuting) his arguments.

Thanks to the controversy, "The Bell Curve" has sold more than a quarter of a million copies.

Undoubtedly, Mr Murray has been lucky in his timing. Left-wingers point out that Americans have seldom been so disillusioned with welfare policy: the voters are turning not just to Republicans, but to Republicans who are arguing seriously about the merits of state orphanages and of compulsory adoption. Mr Murray's arguments answer to a feeling that social policies may have failed not because they were incompetently designed or inadequately funded, but because they are incompatible with certain "facts" of human nature.

Right-wingers retort that it is liberals' addiction to "affirmative action" that has supplied Mr Murray with much of his material. Affirmative action has institutionalised the idea that different ethnic groups have different cognitive abilities: "race norming", now *de rigueur* in academia, means that a black can perform significantly less well than, say, an Asian, and still beat him into a university. It has also resulted in America's having a compilation of statistics about race unequalled outside South Africa.

## Differently weird

The regularity with which discussion of IQ testing turns into an argument that ethnic groups differ in their innate abilities, with blacks at the bottom of the cognitive pile, has done more than anything else to make theorists and practitioners of IQ testing into figures of academic notoriety reviled everywhere from Haight-Ashbury to Holland Park. The early 1970s saw a furious argument about "Jensenism", named after Arthur Jensen, a psychologist at the University of California, Berkeley, who published an article arguing, among other things, that the average black had a lower IQ than the average white. William Shockley, also known as a co-inventor of the transistor, drew the anti-Jensenists' fire by saying that blacks' and whites' brains were "differently wired".

But, even if it could be extricated from arguments about ethnic differences, IQ testing would remain controversial. One reason is that few people like the idea that inequality might be inevitable, the result of natural laws rather than particular circumstances (and the more so, perhaps, when economic inequalities seem likely to widen as labour markets put an ever-higher

premium on intelligence). The implication is that egalitarian policies are self-defeating: the more inherited prejudices are broken down, the more society resolves into intellectual castes.

A second reason for controversy is that IQ testers are all too prone to the fatal conceit of thinking that their discipline equips them to know what is best for their fellow men. To most parents the idea that a man with a book of tests and a clipboard can divine what is best for their children is an intolerable presumption (who can know a child as well as its parents?) and an insupportable invasion of lib-

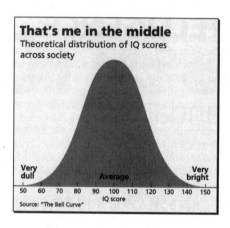

**That's me in the middle**
Theoretical distribution of IQ scores across society

Very dull — Average — Very bright
50  60  70  80  90  100  110  120  130  140  150
IQ score
Source: "The Bell Curve"

erty (surely people should be free to choose the best school for their children?). Nor has the IQ testers' image been helped by their having often been asked—as in England in the days of the 11-plus school entry examination—to help make already contentious decisions.

A third reason IQ testers excite concern is that they seem to make a fetish of intelligence. Many people feel instinctively that intelligence is only one of the qualities that make for success in life—that looks, luck and charm also play their part; they also like to feel that intelligence is less important than what they call "character", which can turn even a dull person into a useful citizen.

But the thing which, in the end, really frightens people about IQ testing is its message of genetic Calvinism: that IQ both determines one's destiny, and is dictated by one's genes. This flies in the face of the liberal notion that we are each responsible for fashioning our own fate. It also upsets two beliefs held particularly firmly in America: that anybody can win out, provided they have "the right stuff"; and that everybody

should be given as many educational chances as possible, rather than sorted out and classified at the earliest possible opportunity. (Thus "Forrest Gump", a film that appeared shortly before publication of "The Bell Curve", enjoyed great popularity and critical acclaim for its portrayal of a well-meaning simpleton who won all America's glittering prizes.)

## Hunting down Sir Humphrey

How, then, did so widely distrusted a discipline originate? To answer that question means a trip to a rather unexpected place, the Whitehall of the mid-19th century. Traditionally, jobs in the British civil service had been handed out on the basis of family connections, in a sort of affirmative-action programme for upper-class twits. But as Britain developed a world-beating economy and a world-spanning empire, reformers argued that preferment should go to the most intelligent candidates, their identity to be discovered by competitive examinations.

This innovation proved so successful that policy-makers applied the same principle to the universities and schools. Their aim was to construct an educational system capable of discovering real ability wherever it occurred, and of matching that ability with the appropriate opportunities.

Ironically, it was children at the other end of the ability scale who inspired the first IQ tests as such. The introduction of compulsory schooling for the masses confronted teachers with the full variety of human abilities, and obliged them to distinguish between the lazy and the congenitally dull. Most investigators contented themselves with measuring children's heads. But in 1905 Alfred Binet, a French psychologist, came up with the idea of assigning an age level to a variety of simple intellectual operations, determined by the earliest age at which the average child could perform them, and ranking children both against their peers and against a normal development curve. Binet's idea was refined soon afterwards by introducing the arithmetical device of dividing mental age by chronological age and multiplying by 100.

Two English psychologists turned intelligence testing into a sort of scientific movement. The first was Francis Galton, a rich and well connected man (Charles Darwin was a cousin) who devoted his life to the nascent sciences of statistics and genetics. His motto was "wherever you can, count", and he measured everything from the distended buttocks of Hottentot women (with a theodolite) to the distribution of "pulchritude" in the British Isles. He compiled family trees of everybody from Cambridge wranglers to West Country wrestlers to prove his belief that "characteristics cling to families" and "ability goes by descent."

Combining his two passions, Galton speculated that abilities in the British population were distributed along a "bell curve", with the upper classes at the top and an underclass at the bottom. He was so worried that those at the bottom of the curve were outbreeding those at the top that he spent most of his fortune bankrolling another "science", eugenics.

Galton's mission was completed by a retired soldier, Charles Spearman. Deciding that the results of certain tests correlated with each other to a remarkable degree, Spearman concluded, in a seminal article published in 1904, that all mental abilities were manifestations of a single general ability, which he called "g": all individuals inherited a fixed quantity of mental energy, which infused every intellectual act they performed and determined what they were capable of in life. The right tests could capture how much "g" each individual possessed and express it as a single number.

Intelligence testing went on to enjoy decades of growing popularity. The American army used it on recruits in the first world war, employing more than 300 psychologists, and other armies followed. Schools used tests to help in streaming or selecting their pupils. Bureaucrats and businessmen used them to identify talented recruits. Tests were thought indispensable for discovering and diagnosing learning problems.

Only in the 1960s did opinion turn sharply against the IQ testers. Educationalists accused them of allowing an obsession with classification to blind them to the full range of human abilities. Sociologists (and sociologically minded psychologists) argued that intellectual differences owed more to social circumstances than to genes. In Britain, disillusionment with IQ tests hastened the introduction of comprehensive schools. In the United States, schools abandoned the use of IQ tests to classify children. In 1978 a district court in San Francisco even ruled unconstitutional the use of IQ tests to place children in classes for the backward if the use of such tests meant that the classes contained a "grossly disproportionate" number of black children.

## Dropping clangers

"The Bell Curve" thus represents an attempt to rehabilitate an idea that had fallen into two or three decades of disfavour. But have Messrs Murray and Herrnstein got their science right?

So far, the debate on "The Bell Curve" has been billed as if it were psychometrists (mind-measurers) versus the rest. In fact, IQ testers divide among themselves on all sorts of key issues, from the structure of the mind to the reliability of tests; moreover, Messrs Murray and Herrnstein occupy a rather eccentric position among psychometrists. They are unabashed supporters of Charles Spearman, believing that intelligence is a unitary quality expressible in a single number, such that people who are good at one thing will also be good at others. Yet this is one of the most hotly disputed topics within psychometry. A British pioneer, Godfrey Thomson, argued that the correlations which so excited Spearman might be explained by the laws of chance. He concluded that the mind had no fixed structure and that intelligence tests gave little more than a hint of a person's mental powers.

Among other psychologists, L.L. Thurstone argued for the existence of dozens of different types of mental abilities, such as mathematical, verbal and visio-spatial abilities. Liam Hudson has found IQ tests to reward a particular type of "convergent" thinker. Howard Gardner thinks there are many sorts of "intelligence".

## Synaptitude

IQ testers have clashed and go on clashing over less arcane issues too. They endorse widely different estimates of the heritability of IQ, ranging from 40% to 80%. They squabble about the accuracy of IQ tests: some argue that such tests are nothing more than estimates that need to be repeated frequently and to be supplemented by personal interviews (and indeed, observably, children can learn, or be taught, to raise their IQ scores). Some of the most illustrious psychometrists are even starting to argue that IQ tests should be replaced by physical tests to measure the speed of reactions, the production of glucose in the brain, the speed of neural transmission and even the size of the brain.

Psychometrists disagree, too, about the validity of generalising about groups in the way that Murray and Herrnstein do. It is widely accepted that differences within groups may reflect hereditary factors; but differences between groups are susceptible to other explanations (just as people in one place may be taller on average than people in another place, for example, but for reasons of nutrition, not genetics).

Oddly, Messrs Murray and Herrnstein have chosen to dispute (or ignore) one of the few arguments on which other psychometrists agree: that children do not necessarily have the same IQ as their parents. "The Bell Curve" argues that society is fixing itself into impermeable castes. But psychometry is a theory of social mobility, not social stasis. It tries to explain why bright people often have dull children and dull people often have bright children. Sex ensures that genes are resorted in each generation.

In fact, it is hereditarianism's sworn enemy, environmentalism, which is really a theory of social stasis: if the rich and educated can pass on their advantages to their children undisturbed by the dance of the chromosomes, then social mobility will always be something of a freak. Messrs Murray and Herrnstein are, perhaps, environmentalists in hereditarian clothing.

Politically, "The Bell Curve" has reinforced the impression that IQ testers are anti-welfare conservatives. Some are. But IQ tests have been invoked in defence of a wide variety of political positions, respectable and otherwise. American psychologists have popped up to support abominations such as compulsory sterilisation and ethnically sensitive immigration laws. Others have been socialists, keen on upward mobility, child-centred education and generous provision for the backward. In Britain between the wars Labour Party intellectuals such as R.H. Tawney argued for IQ testing as a way to ensure educational opportunities were allocated on the basis of innate ability rather than family connections; psychologists such as Cyril Burt have been passionate supporters of nursery-school education and better treatment of backward children. (The fusty T.S. Eliot, on the other hand, thought IQ tests were a plot to promote social mobility and debase education. A particularly crusty Cambridge don, Edward Welbourne, denounced them as "devices invented by Jews for the advancement of Jews.")

## Too clever by half

What makes the IQ debate particularly frustrating is that both sides have long been addicted to exaggeration. The earliest IQ testers were guilty of hubris when they argued that they had invented an infallible technique for measuring mental abilities and distributing educational and occupational opportunities. As if that was not bad enough, they exacerbated their error by claiming that their method contributed to economic efficiency (by making the best use of human resources) and personal happiness (by ensuring that people were given jobs suited to their abilities).

The enemies of IQ testing were also guilty of terrible exaggeration when they accused testers of shoring up capitalism, perpetuating inequality, and justifying sexism, racism, even fascism. In fact, the IQ testers were never anywhere near as influential as they, or their opponents, imagined.

IQ theory played no part in persuading the American Congress to pass the Immigration Restriction Act of 1924; British grammar schools used IQ tests only to supplement other, more traditional selection procedures, such as scholastic examinations and interviews; Hitler and Mussolini had no time for IQ tests that were liable to contradict their own racial prejudices.

What the IQ debate needs now is a dash of cold water. Opponents of testing should forget their over-heated rhetoric about legitimising capitalism and racism. Supporters should fold up their more grandiose blueprints for building the meritocracy, and limit themselves to helping with practical problems. They should point out that IQ tests are useful ways of identifying and diagnosing mental deficiency, just so long as they are administered along with other diagnostic tools by a trained psychologist. They should add that IQ tests can also be useful in helping to allocate places in oversubscribed schools; that, indeed, they are less class-biased than scholastic tests (which favour the well-taught) or personal interviews (which favour the well-brought up). It is a pity that Charles Murray and Richard Herrnstein have chosen to douse the debate not with cold water but with petrol.

# The Death of Child Nature

## Education in the Postmodern World

By David Elkind

*Mr. Elkind reviews the modern and postmodern conceptions of the child and the educational practices that follow from those conceptions. Becoming postmodern in education, he concludes, often means gaining a truer and deeper appreciation of the educational innovators of modernity.*

EVERY CHILD, to paraphrase Clyde Kluckhohn and Henry Murray, is like all other children, like some other children, and like no other child.[1] Children are all alike in that they are members of the same species and share the same biological and physiological characteristics, walk upright, have the potential for speech, and so on. In this species sense, we can reasonably speak of the *biological* child who is like all other children. It is also true that only subgroups of children share the same language, culture, and physical environment. When considering children who are like some other children in this culture/environmental sense, we can speak of the *social* child. Finally, each child is different from every other in his or her unique genetic endowment and in the particular circumstances of his or her upbringing. When we speak of children in this unique, individual sense, we might speak of the *psychological* child.

Although it is unlikely that many would quarrel with this description of the three senses in which the term *child* may be used, the three are often confused, most notably in discussions of education. That is to say, individual psychological characteristics of chil-

*DAVID ELKIND is a professor of child development at Tufts University, Medford, Mass.*

dren are often treated as biological universals. In the past, the belief in a universal psychological child (which I will simply refer to as a belief in *child nature*) had some positive consequences. It contributed, for example, to the provision of free public education. Today, however, this very same belief in a universal child nature has become a barrier to achieving an individually appropriate pedagogy for children in all their personal, ethnic, racial, and cultural diversity. In this article I attempt to substantiate this thesis.

The critique of transcendent realities and overarching generalizations is a major thrust of the movement called *postmodernism*.[2] Although different writers define this movement in different ways, there is general agreement that many of the assumptions that fueled the modern view of the world were romantic ideals that now stand in need of correction. Postmodern critiques are already common in the arts, in architecture, in science, and in industry, but they are only now beginning to be heard in the social sciences and in education.[3]

Even without invoking postmodernism, a few contemporary education reform initiatives challenge the conception of normative education tailored to the needs of a uniform child nature.[4] Likewise, a number of contemporary educational practices reflect postmodern

conceptions. Nonetheless, the modern assumption of an archetypal psychological child dies hard and underlies practices that are contributing to educational dysfunction among large numbers of children. In the succeeding pages, I will try to illustrate some of the educational practices that derive from the modern conception of a common (psychological) child nature and that impede, rather than further, children's academic achievement.

In preparation for that discussion, however, let me first briefly describe the major tenets of modernism and postmodernism and show how these differing paradigmatic assumptions about the world are reflected in the modern and postmodern conceptions of the child and in some of the educational practices that flow from them. That discussion will provide the context for a critique of those contemporary educational practices that remain wedded to a modern conception of a common child nature. Such practices miseducate children in the sense that they place them at risk with no purpose.

## Modernity, Child Nature, And Modern Education

Modernity was built on three unquestioned assumptions about the world. The first idea was that of *progress,* the notion that societies inevitably moved forward in a positive direction from slavery and feudalism to individual freedom and democracy. From its inception in the 16th century, experimental science was the model for the modern conception of progress, with its gradual accumulation of knowledge serving to improve the quality of life for all members of society. Later, Darwin's theory of evolution offered a scientific explanation for this progress, suggesting that societies, like species, evolve by a process of variation and natural selection, with survival of the fittest as the end result.

The notion of progress shaped the modern conception of the child and of education. Although educational philosophers differed as to whether the child's mind was a blank tablet or a full book, none doubted that education was necessary to ensure the child's steady progress toward responsible and productive adulthood. John Locke, for one, saw the child as in need of adult tutelage if he or she was to become a socially responsible and culturally literate human being.[5] In contrast, Jean-Jacques Rousseau argued that experience itself was the best teacher and that adult instruction could well be delayed until children had acquired considerable knowledge on their own.[6] Both Locke and Rousseau, however, talked about children in a universal sense and with little attention to the differential progress that might be observed thanks to dissimilarities in ability, race, ethnicity, or culture.

The notion of progress was extended to pedagogy as well as to the child. It was the rationale for the metaphor of the "ladder" of education. Knowledge, values, and skills, it was assumed, are acquired in a uniform and stepwise fashion. Subject matters were also organized according to what was regarded as a natural progression—for example, arithmetic before algebra and algebra before trigonometry. The same held true for reading, and children were taught simple folk stories and fairy tales before they were introduced to true "literature." Not surprisingly, the rate at which a child ascended this educational ladder became the only measure of individual difference. The mentally "retarded" climbed at less than the average rate, whereas the mentally "gifted" skipped steps and rose more rapidly than the norm.

A second underlying conception of modernity was that of *universality.* The emergence of science, the scientific method, and the reliance on observation and experiment was encouraged by the modern belief that nature, rather than religious or imperial

authority, was the only source of knowledge and truth. Nature was assumed to operate according to universal laws that could be discovered by diligent research. The scientific belief in universal natural laws was supported by such systematic descriptions of regularities as the Newtonian laws of gravitation, the periodic table of the elements, and the Darwinian principles of evolution.

The notion of universality was also incorporated into the modern conception of the child. Educators accepted the doctrine of "formal discipline," according to which the study of Greek, Latin, and mathematics was an effective method of training *all* children to think logically and rationally. Later, with the emergence of the social sciences, universality was given a scientific imprimatur. Educational psychology, like psychology as a whole, assumed that there were universal laws of learning that held across all species and that were the same for rats as they were for children and for adults. Rat psychology led to endless controversies over such issues as the benefits of *mass* versus *distributed learning and the extent of transfer of training.* Using human subjects, memory was studied by means of nonsense syllables so that content would not interfere with observation of the universal memory process. Problem solving was thought to involve only trial and error or insight, inasmuch as these were the processes employed by cats and chimpanzees in their attempts to remove barriers to desired goals.

The last undergirding assumption of the modern world was that of *regularity.* Nature was lawful, and the task of science was to uncover this lawfulness. As Einstein phrased this belief, "God does not play dice with the universe." Unlawful phenomena, from this perspective, were simply phenomena that had yet to be explained or could be explained at another "level." Irregular (unlawful) phenotypes, for example, could be explained by regular (lawful) genotypes. Taking the same "levels" approach to causality, Freud argued that slips of the tongue and pen (unlawful occurrences) could be explained by deeper-level unconscious (lawful) wishes and desires.

The idea of lawfulness was also assimilated into the modern conception of a child nature. Intelligence testing demonstrated that, although children varied considerably in their intellectual abilities, these abilities were nonetheless distributed according to the normal curve of probability. They were thus lawful phenomena. Many of

children's behavior disorders were also explained according to the "levels" notion of causality. Seemingly idiosyncratic learning disabilities were frequently attributed to an underlying lawfulness, namely, "minimal brain damage." Thus children's observable irregular, unpredictable surface behavior could be explained by an underlying lawful relation between the human brain and human action.

## Postmodernity, the Particular Child, and Postmodern Education

Postmodernism arose as a critique of modern ideas and as an effort to correct some of the overly idealistic and romantic views of the world that they created. In this century, after two world wars, the Holocaust, the atom bomb, the degradation of the environment, and the exploitation of the earth's natural resources, it is difficult to hold to the modern conception of progress as an unbroken march toward a better world and a more humane society. Even the progress toward individual freedom and self-fulfillment that did occur was often limited to certain groups (white, Anglo-Saxon males) and did not extend to women or to minorities. To be sure, progress still happens—say, in the conquest of disease—but it is particular and domain-specific rather than holding true for all of humanity.

What has come to the fore in postmodern times is the awareness of the importance of *difference.* In the modern era, difference was often seen from the standpoint of superiority. Non-Western societies, as an illustration, were regarded as inferior to Western "civilizations" because they had not progressed as far. This notion of superiority was implicit in the concept of the United States of America as a "melting pot" in which people (inferior) cultures would be melted down and then poured into a mold from which each would be dropped out as a purified, standard American. Today, however, we recognize that people do not melt and that other cultures, ethnic groups, and races are to be appreciated and valued rather than dissolved into some common amalgam. The postmodern conception of America as a cultural, ethnic, and racial "rainbow" celebrates the valuation of difference, in contrast to the feeling of superiority inherent in the modern conceptions of social progress and of the melting pot.

Unfortunately, the idea of progress is still omnipresent in education. Nonetheless, the appreciation of difference is beginning to make some headway. The new provisions for children with disabilities and for those who come to school with English as a second language are evidence that the needs of these "different" children are at last being recognized—if not fully or properly attended to. In other domains, such as the introduction of multicultural, gender-fair, and anti-bias curricula, the acceptance of difference has met more resistance in the schools and in the local communities. But the very fact that matters of race, gender, and ethnicity are not being openly talked about reflects a new, more accepting climate for a wide range of human differences.

Just as the conception of progress was challenged by the evidence of lack of progress, the assumption of universality has also undergone revision. This is particularly true in the social sciences. When Friedrich Nietzsche, an early postmodernist, proclaimed the death of God, he was railing against metaphysics and those who exploited the belief in universal supernatural beings.[7] In a similar tone, when Michel Foucault wrote about the end of man, he was arguing against the metaphysical idea of a universal human nature and for a fuller and deeper appreciation of human individuality.[8]

And the universals of social science are proving to be less than transcendent. The "grand" social/economic theories such as those of Marx and Engels have turned out to be less than prophetic and universal. Likewise, the "grand" histories of Spengler and Toynbee now appear as flawed individual theories of history rather than as discovered universal principles of societal progression. In a similar way, the recapitulation theory—which posited that the individual in his or her development recapitulates the development of the species—can no longer be maintained. While there are still universals, particularly in the physical and biological sciences, they are much less common in the social sciences, where particularity is more likely to be the rule.

The importance of particularity, as opposed to universals, is already being recognized in education. We now appreciate that different species learn in different ways and that, even within the same species, there are differences in learning *styles*.[9] We also recognize that different subject matters require their own specific learning strategies. The idea that there are "domain-specific" modes of learning has almost completely displaced the universal ideas of "formal discipline" and of "transfer of training." When we do encounter what appear to be universals in human behavior, they are often

closely linked to maturational (biological child) characteristics, such as the Piagetian stages.[10]

Finally, the modern assumption of regularity and lawfulness has been modified by the postmodern acceptance of the normality of *irregularity*. We acknowledge today that some phenomena, such as the weather, are inherently irregular. So too are phenomena such as the dispersion of cream in a coffee cup. Each time we place cream in a coffee cup, the dispersion pattern is different from what it was before. Some phenomena are, by nature, chaotic and have no underlying regularity. The *DSM IV* definition of Attention Deficit Hyperactivity Disorder (ADHD) as involving any four or five out of 18 neurological, behavioral, or attentional symptoms is a recognition that this disorder has no underlying regularity. Likewise, the implementation of multi-age grouping in some schools is tacit acceptance of the fact that development is irregular and that we need flexible classroom arrangements to deal with the "normal irregularity" of growth.

## The Modern Child in the Postmodern World

Although the postmodern conception of the child as different, particular, and irregular has been assimilated into some educational conceptions and practices, the modern conception of the child as progressive, universal, and lawful remains alive and well in many others. The following are but a few examples of the persistence of modern conceptions in contemporary educational practice.

*Progress.* The modern belief that children should progress uniformly through the grades is causing a major problem in kindergarten and first grade. At the heart of the problem is the fact that, in the postmodern world, the majority of children (about 85%) enter school after having been enrolled in one or another early childhood program. As a consequence, schools have tightened standards and now demand that all children know their letters and numbers before being accepted into the first-grade classroom. This demand is based on the modern assumption of a common child nature such that all children of the same age will profit equally from whatever type of early childhood program they have experienced.

Yet the truth lies elsewhere. The early childhood years, roughly from age 3 to age 8, are a period of rapid intellectual growth comparable to the period of rapid physical growth of early adolescence. At such times indi-

vidual differences in growth rates are most evident. With adolescents, for example, some reach their full height at 13, some at 14, some at 15, and some at 16. They may all end up being the same height, but they get there at different rates. The same is true for young children's intellectual growth. Some may attain Piaget's concrete operations at 4, some at 5, some at 6, and some at 7. They will all attain concrete operations, but at different rates—even if they have the same intellectual ability. Because these operations are a necessary prerequisite to learning numbers and letters, children of the same intellectual ability will differ widely in their ability to acquire tool skills. Moreover, different early childhood programs vary widely in the extent to which they work on tool skills.

Because of these wide individual differences in growth rate and early childhood experience, children of school age vary tremendously in their readiness for formal instruction. As a consequence, in many communities some 10% to 20% of the children are being retained or placed in transition classes, and in some school districts the numbers are as high as 50%. This is a case in which a postmodern phenomenon—large numbers of children in early childhood programs—has elicited a modern notion of a common child nature that is having dysfunctional educational outcomes for large numbers of young children.

In a similar way, because of the belief that young people progress in a uniform fashion, there is little or no accommodation of the rather abrupt changes that come about in early adolescence. The middle school concept is supposed to speak more directly to the different needs of this age group,[11] but many middle schools are such in name only. Like the junior high school, misnamed middle schools fail to incorporate the team teaching, extended class times, and integrated curricula envisioned by the inventors of the middle school. The idea that children progress in uniform fashion throughout the grades dies hard, despite abundant knowledge of the differential growth spurts that characterize early adolescence as well as early childhood.

Unfortunately, the postmodern appreciation of difference is sometimes grafted onto modern ideas of progress and, as a result, is completely undermined. A case in point is the current emphasis on "inclusion" of children with special needs in the regular classroom. This practice frequently takes away from the child the special individuality that he or she has just been given. Too often, children are included without sufficient remedial support for teachers and with too little regard to the appropriateness of inclusion of a given child in a particular classroom. Moreover, there is not accommodation to the fact that some children, such as those with spina bifida, may benefit from inclusion when they are young but not when they are teenagers. Nor is sufficient attention being paid to the number and variety of special-needs children in any given classroom. With too many special-needs children in a class, the teacher is overwhelmed and may not be able to meet the needs of other students. With too few special-needs children, the special child may stand out too much. Inclusion can be beneficial, but not for all children in all circumstances at all ages and in all ratios.

*Universality.* The universality component of the modern conception of the child is also difficult to dislodge. The current efforts to establish national standards presuppose that all children can attain the same standards. To be sure, those who are making up the assessment devices are making an effort to include not only quantitative tests but also qualitative measures such as portfolios, products, and performance.[12] Yet qualitative methods of assessment speak to the particularity of achievement rather than to its universality. Different children will attain and express their literacy in different ways. The real challenge of national standards, and one that has yet to be met, is how to reconcile assessments that presuppose individual differences—such as portfolios, projects, and performance—with assessments that presuppose uniformity, namely, standardized tests.

The idea of universality is also taken for granted by educational publishing, which provides standard textbooks with little acknowledgement of individual differences in learning styles, pace of learning, and so on. Publishers assume that it is the teachers' responsibility to individualize, but why should this be so? Those publishers who produce a "teacher-proof" curriculum of complete, day-to-day lesson plans and materials also presuppose a commonality or universality of learning. Yet the assumption of such universality is completely at variance with the diversity within even the most homogeneously grouped class. Educational publishers must begin to address the particularity of teachers and learners and the domain-specific nature of learning strategies. They also need to field-test their materials before they publish them.

*Irregularity.* While the new definition of ADHD and the introduction of multiage grouping in some states and com-

munities are bows to the presence of irregularity, the belief in an underlying regularity is tenacious. Programs such as Benjamin Bloom's mastery learning, Madeline Hunter's model of effective teaching, Arthur Costa's program for teaching critical thinking, and Edward de Bono's CoRT all assume that learning is a regular process or, at least, that its products are.[13] As Richard Gibboney documents, all these innovations have been shown to be no more successful than the programs already in place.[14] One reason is that all these initiatives are founded on modern notions of learning as universal, progressive, and lawful.

From an individual (psychological child) perspective, however, learning is always a creative activity. The learner takes something from himself or herself, something from the external world, and puts them together into a product that cannot be reduced either to the learner or to the experience. Creativity, whether in classroom learning or in the arts or in the sciences, is necessarily chaotic and irregular. The artist cannot fully explain his or her art any more than the scientist can explain his or her insights. Portfolios, projects, and performance make sense only from the perspective of learning as an individual creative process.

To be sure, there are basic skills and common knowledge that all children must acquire. Sometimes the individual must subordinate his or her individual bent to acquire basic tools of the language, concepts and mores of the culture, and so on. But this is only part of learning, not the whole process. And even such learning always has an individual coloration. Put differently, the focus on mastery, skills, and outcomes acknowledges only the accommodative side of learning and totally ignores its assimilative, creative dimension. We need to encourage and to assess both types of learning.

Although we have yet to fully appreciate the fact, the classroom is a chaotic phenomenon as well. Each time a group meets, each member of the group is in some ways different from the time the group met before. Each has had experiences that no other member of the group has encountered. In many ways, every class meeting is like every dispersion of cream in a coffee cup. This does not mean that we cannot or should not study classrooms—only that we should explore them as irregular, chaotic, and social (not as recurring physical) events. Educational research, as long as it operates according to the modern idea of regularity, will fail to capture the true dynamics of classroom interactions.

## Summary and Conclusion

I have briefly reviewed here the modern and postmodern conceptions of the child and the educational practices that follow from those conceptions. The modern conception confused and merged the universal biological child with the individual psychological child. While this identification of the two different conceptions of child nature was probably necessary to the establishment of free public education, it is often a hindrance to effective contemporary educational practice. Despite a growing recognition of children as different, as particular, and as irregular, the modern conception of child nature as progressive, universal, and regular still dominates educational theory and practice. In this article, I have given only a few of the many possible examples to illustrate how modern ideas continue to undermine effective pedagogy and authentic education reform.

For purposes of space, I have limited my discussion to those aspects of education that revolve around the conception of a common child nature. Postmodern ideas, however, have implications for many other educational issues. I have already addressed the issue of school and family from this perspective,[15] but it also has implications for teacher training, curricula, school organization, and so on that cannot be dealt with here. But rethinking the conception of child nature seems a useful starting point for a broader and more wide-ranging critique of modern education.

In closing, it is important to emphasize that I am not arguing that everything postmodern is good and that everything modern is bad. There is much to be valued in modern education. Many of our foremost educational innovators were already quite postmodern. This is certainly true of John Dewey, whose project method foreshadowed the integrated curriculum.[16] It is equality true of Maria Montessori, whose recognition of young children's learning ability is now accepted in our postmodern perception of childhood competence.[17] Likewise, Jean Piaget's contention that children create their reality out of their experiences with the environment[18] is echoed in the postmodern view that all concepts are human constructions, not copies of a preexisting reality. Becoming postmodern in education, therefore, often means gaining a truer and deeper appreciation of the educational innovators of modernity.

1. Clyde Kluckhohn and Henry A. Murray, "Personality Formation: The Determinants,"

in idem, eds., *Personality in Nature, Society, and Culture* (New York: Knopf, 1950), pp. 35–48.

2. See, for example, Steven Connor, *Postmodern Culture* (Oxford: Basil Blackwell, 1989); and Steven Best and Douglas Kellner, *Postmodern Theory* (New York: Guilford, 1991).

3. Henry Giroux, "Postmodernism and the Discourse of Educational Criticism," *Journal of Education,* vol. 170, no. 3, 1988, pp. 6–29; and Stanley Aronowitz and Henry Giroux, *Postmodern Education* (Minneapolis: University of Minnesota Press, 1991).

4. See, for example, James Comer, "Educating Poor Minority Children," *Scientific American,* vol. 295, no. 5, 1988, pp. 42–48; and Theodore Sizer, *Horace's School: Redesigning the American High School* (Boston: Houghton Mifflin, 1992).

5. John Locke, *Some Thoughts Concerning Education,* in Charles Eliot, ed., *The Harvard Classics* (New York: Collier, 1930), pp. 9–200.

6. Jean-Jacques Rousseau, *Emile,* trans. W. Payne (New York: Appleton, 1911).

7. Friedrich Nietzsche, *Thus Spoke Zarathustra* (New York: Viking, 1966).

8. Michel Foucault, *The Order of Things* (New York: Vintage, 1973).

9. Thomas Debello, "Comparison of Eleven Major Learning Style Models: Variables, Appropriate Populations, Validity of Instrumentation, and the Research Behind Them," *Journal of Reading, Writing, and Learning Disabilities International,* vol. 6, 1990, pp. 203–22.

10. Jean Piaget, *The Psychology of Intelligence* (London: Routledge & Kegan Paul, 1950).

11. See, for example, Task Force on Education of Young Adolescents, *Turning Points: Preparing American Youth for the 21st Century* (Washington, D.C.: Carnegie Council on Adolescent Development, 1989); and Jeffrey Wiles and James Bondi, *The Essential Middle School,* 2nd ed. (New York: Macmillan, 1993).

12. Gary Sykes and Phillip Plastrik, *Standard Setting and Educational Reform* (Washington, D.C.: ERIC Clearinghouse on Teacher Education, 1993).

13. Benjamin Bloom, *Human Characteristics and School Learning* (New York: McGraw-Hill, 1976); Madeline Hunter, "Knowing, Teaching, and Supervision," in Peter L. Hosford, 3d., *Using What We Know About Teaching* (Alexandria, Va.: Association for Supervision and Curriculum Development, 1984), pp. 165–76; Arthur L. Costa, *Developing Minds* (Alexandria, Va.: Association for Supervision and Curriculum Development, 1985); and Edward de Bono, *CoRT Program* (San Diego: Pergamon Press, 1988).

14. Richard A. Gibboney, *The Stone Trumpet* (Albany: State University of New York Press, 1994).

15. David Elkind, "School and Family in the Postmodern World," *Phi Delta Kappan,* September 1995, pp. 8–14.

16. John Dewey, *The Child and the Curriculum/The School and Society* (1915; reprint, Chicago: University of Chicago Press, 1956).

17. Maria Montessori, *The Absorbent Mind* (New York: Delta, 1967).

18. Jean Piaget, *Science of Education and the Psychology of the Child* (New York: Viking, 1969).

# In Search of...
# Brain-Based Education

BY JOHN T. BRUER

*The "In Search of..." television series is no way to present history, Mr. Bruer points out, and the brain-based education literature is not the way to present the science of learning.*

WE HAVE almost survived the Decade of the Brain. During the 1990s, government agencies, foundations, and advocacy groups engaged in a highly successful effort to raise public awareness about advances in brain research. Brain science became material for cover stories in our national newsmagazines. Increased public awareness raised educators' always simmering interest in the brain to the boiling point. Over the past five years, there have been numerous books, conferences, and entire issues of education journals devoted to what has come to be called "brain-based education."

Brain-based educators tend to support progressive education reforms. They decry the "factory model of education," in which experts create knowledge, teachers disseminate it, and students are graded on how much of it they can absorb and retain. Like many other educators, brain-based educators favor a constructivist, active learning model. Students should be actively engaged in learning and in guiding their own instruction. Brain enthusiasts see neuroscience as perhaps the best weapon with which to destroy our outdated factory model.[1] They argue that teachers should teach for meaning and understanding. To do so, they claim, teachers should create learning environments that are low in threat and high in challenge, and students

---

*JOHN T. BRUER is president of the James S. McDonnell Foundation, St. Louis.*

From *Phi Delta Kappan*, May 1999, pp. 649-657. © 1999 by John T. Bruer. Reprinted by permission.

# THE DANGER WITH MUCH OF THE BRAIN-BASED EDUCATION LITERATURE IS THAT IT BECOMES EXCEEDINGLY DIFFICULT TO SEPARATE THE SCIENCE FROM THE SPECULATION.

should be actively engaged and immersed in complex experiences. No reasonable parent or informed educator would take issue with these ideas. Indeed, if more schools taught for understanding and if more teachers had the resources to do so, our schools would be better learning environments.

However, there is nothing new in this critique of traditional education. It is based on a cognitive and constructivist model of learning that is firmly rooted in more than 30 years of psychological research. Whatever scientific evidence we have for or against the efficacy of such educational approaches can be found in any current textbook on educational psychology.[2] None of the evidence comes from brain research. It comes from cognitive and developmental psychology; from the behavioral, not the biological, sciences; from our scientific understanding of the mind, not from our scientific understanding of the brain.

To the extent that brain-based educators' recipe for school and classroom change is well grounded in this behavioral research, their message is valuable. Teachers should know about short- and long-term memory; about primacy/recency effects; about how procedural, declarative, and episodic memory differ; and about how prior knowledge affects our current ability to learn. But to claim that these are "brain-based" findings is misleading.

While we know a considerable amount from psychological research that is pertinent to teaching and learning, we know much less about how the brain functions and learns.[3] For nearly a century, the science of the mind (psychology) developed independently from the science of the brain (neuroscience). Psychologists were interested in our mental functions and capacities—how we learn, remember, and think. Neuroscientists were interested in how the brain develops and functions. It was as if psychologists were interested only in our mental software and neuroscientists only in our neural hardware. Deeply held theoretical assumptions in both fields supported a view that mind and brain could, and indeed should, be studied independently.

It is only in the past 15 years or so that these theoretical barriers have fallen. Now scientists called cognitive neuroscientists are

beginning to study how our neural hardware might run our mental software, how brain structures support mental functions, how our neural circuits enable us to think and learn. This is an exciting and new scientific endeavor, but it is also a very young one. As a result we know relatively little about learning, thinking, and remembering at the level of brain areas, neural circuits, or synapses; we know very little about how the brain thinks, remembers, and learns.

Yet brain science has always had a seductive appeal for educators.[4] Brain science appears to give hard biological data and explanations that, for some reason, we find more compelling than the "soft" data that come from psychological science. But seductive appeal and a very limited brain science database are a dangerous combination. They make it relatively easy to formulate bold statements about brain science and education that are speculative at best and often far removed from neuroscientific fact. Nonetheless, the allure of brain science ensures that these ideas will often find a substantial and accepting audience. As Joseph LeDoux, a leading authority on the neuroscience of emotion, cautioned educators at a 1996 brain and education conference, "These ideas are easy to sell to the public, but it is easy to take them beyond their actual basis in science."[5]

And the ideas are far-ranging indeed. Within the literature on the brain and education one finds, for example, that brain science supports Bloom's Taxonomy, Madeline Hunter's effective teaching, whole-language instruction, Vygotsky's theory of social learning, thematic instruction, portfolio assessment, and cooperative learning.

The difficulty is that the brain-based education literature is very much like a docudrama or an episode of "In Search of . . ." in which an interesting segment on Egyptology suddenly takes a bizarre turn that links Tutankhamen with the alien landing in Roswell, New Mexico. Just where did the episode turn from archaeological fact to speculation or fantasy? That is the same question one must constantly ask when reading about brain-based education.

Educators, like all professionals, should be interested in knowing how basic research, including brain science, might contribute to improved professional practice. The danger

with much of the brain-based education literature, as with an "In Search of . . ." episode, is that it becomes exceedingly difficult to separate the science from the speculation, to sort what we know from what we would like to be the case. If our interest is enhancing teaching and learning by applying science to education, this is not the way to do it. Would we want our children to learn about the Exodus by watching "In Search of Ramses' Martian Wife"?

We might think of each of the numerous claims that brain-based educators make as similar to an "In Search of . . ." episode. For each one, we should ask, Where does the science end and the speculation begin? I cannot do that here. So instead I'll concentrate on two ideas that appear prominently in brain-based education articles: the educational significance of brain laterality (right brain versus left brain) and the claim that neuroscience has established that there is a sensitive period for learning.

## Left Brain, Right Brain: One More Time

"Right Brain versus left brain" is one of those popular ideas that will not die. Speculations about the educational significance of brain laterality have been circulating in the education literature for 30 years. Although repeatedly criticized and dismissed by psychologists and brain scientists, the speculation continues.[6] David Sousa devotes a chapter of *How the Brain Learns* to explaining brain laterality and presents classroom strategies that teachers might use to ensure that both hemispheres are involved in learning.[7] Following the standard line, the *left hemisphere* is the logical hemisphere, involved in speech, reading, and writing. It is the analytical hemisphere that evaluates factual material in a rational way and that understands the literal interpretation of words. It is a serial processor that tracks time and sequences and that recognizes words, letters, and numbers. The right hemisphere is the intuitive, creative hemisphere. It gathers information more from images than from words. It is a parallel processor well suited for pattern recognition and spatial reasoning. It is the hemisphere that recognizes faces, places, and objects.

According to this traditional view of laterality, left-hemisphere-dominant individuals tend to be more verbal, more analytical, and better problem solvers. Females, we are told, are more likely than males to be left-hemisphere dominant. Right-hemisphere-dominant individuals, more typically males, paint and draw well, are good at math, and deal with the visual world more easily than with the verbal. Schools, Sousa points out, are overwhelmingly left-hemisphere places in which left-hemisphere-dominant individuals, mostly girls, feel more comfortable than right-hemisphere-dominant individuals, mostly boys. Hemispheric dominance also explains why girls are superior to boys in arithmetic—it is linear and logical, and there is only one correct answer to each problem—while girls suffer math anxiety when it comes to the right-hemisphere activities of algebra and geometry. These latter disciplines, unlike arithmetic, are holistic, relational, and spatial and also allow multiple solutions to problems.

Before we consider how, or whether, brain science supports this traditional view, educators should be wary of claims about the educational significance of gender differences in brain laterality. There are tasks that psychologists have used in their studies that reveal gender-based differences in performance. Often, however, these differences are specific to a task. Although males are superior to females at mentally rotating objects, this seems to be the only spatial task for which psychologists have found such a difference.[8] Moreover, when they do find gender differences, these differences tend to be very small. If they were measured on an I.Q.-like scale with a mean of 100 and a standard deviation of 15, these gender differences amount to around five points. Furthermore, the range of difference within genders is broad. Many males have better language skills than most females; many females have better spatial and mathematical skills than most males. The scientific consensus among psychologists and neuroscientists who conduct these studies is that whatever gender differences exist may have interesting consequences for the scientific study of the brain, but they have no practical or instructional consequences.[9]

Now let's consider the brain sciences and how or whether they offer support for some of the particular teaching strategies Sousa recommends. To involve the right hemisphere in learning, Sousa writes, teachers should encourage students to generate and use mental imagery: "For most people, the left hemisphere specializes in coding information verbally while the right hemisphere codes information visually. Although teachers spend much time talking (and sometimes have their students talk) about the learning objective, little time is given to developing visual cues." To ensure that the left hemisphere gets equal time, teachers should let students "read, write, and compute often."[10]

What brain scientists currently know about spatial reasoning and mental imagery provides counterexamples to such simplistic claims as these. Such claims arise out of a folk theory about brain laterality, not a neuroscientific one.

Here are two simple spatial tasks: 1) determine whether one object is above or below another, and 2) determine whether two objects are more or less than one foot apart. Based on our folk theory of the brain, as spatial tasks both of these should be right-hemisphere tasks. However, if we delve a little

deeper, as psychologists and neuroscientists tend to do, we see that the information-processing or computational demands of the two tasks are different.[11] The first task requires that we place objects or parts of objects into broad categories—up/down or left/right—but we do not have to determine how far up or down (or left or right) one object is from the other. Psychologists call this *categorical* spatial reasoning. In contrast, the second task is a spatial *coordinate* task, in which we must compute and retain precise distance relations between the objects.

Research over the last decade has shown that categorical and coordinate spatial reasoning are performed by distinct subsystems in the brain.[12] A subsystem in the brain's *left* hemisphere performs categorical spatial reasoning. A subsystem in the brain's *right* hemisphere processes coordinate spatial relationships. Although the research does point to differences in the information-processing abilities and biases of the brain hemispheres, those differences are found at a finer level of analysis than "spatial reasoning." It makes no sense to claim that spatial reasoning is a right-hemisphere task.

Based on research like this, Christopher Chabris and Stephen Kosslyn, leading researchers in the field of spatial reasoning and visual imagery, claim that any model of brain lateralization that assigns conglomerations of complex mental abilities, such as spatial reasoning, to one hemisphere or the other, as our folk theory does, is simply too crude to be scientifically or practically useful. Our folk theory can neither explain what the brain is doing nor generate useful predictions about where novel tasks might be computed in the brain.[13] Unfortunately, it is just such a crude folk theory that brain-based educators rely on when framing their recommendations.

Visual imagery is another example. From the traditional, folk-theoretic perspective, generating and using visual imagery is a right-hemisphere function. Generating and using visual imagery is a complex operation that involves, even at a crude level of analysis, at least five distinct mental subcomponents: 1) to create a visual image of a dog, you must transfer long-term visual memories into a temporary visual memory store; 2) to determine if your imagined dog has a tail, you must zoom in and identify details of the image; 3) to put a blue collar on the dog requires that you add a new element to your previously generated image; 4) to make the dog look the other way demands that you rotate your image of the dog; and 5) to draw or describe the imagined dog, you must scan the visual image with your mind's eye.

There is an abundance of neuroscientific evidence that this complex task is not confined to the right hemisphere. There are patients with brain damage who can recognize visual objects and draw or describe visible objects normally, yet these patients cannot answer questions that require them to gen-

erate a mental image. ("Think of a dog. Does it have a long tail?") These patients have long-term visual memories, but they cannot use those memories to generate mental images. All these patients have damage to the rear portion of the left hemisphere.[14]

Studies on split-brain patients, people who have had their two hemispheres surgically disconnected to treat severe epilepsy, allow scientists to present visual stimuli to one hemisphere but not the other. Michael Gazzaniga and Kosslyn showed split-brain patients a lower-case letter and then asked the patients whether the corresponding capital letter had any curved lines.[15] The task required that the patients generate a mental image of the capital letter based on the lower-case letter they had seen. When the stimuli were presented to the patients' left hemispheres, they performed perfectly on the task. However, the patients made many mistakes when the letter stimuli were presented to the right hemisphere. Likewise, brain-imaging studies of normal adult subjects performing imagery tasks show that both hemispheres are active in these tasks.[16] Based on all these data, brain scientists have concluded that the ability to generate visual imagery depends on the left hemisphere.

One of the most accessible presentations of this research appears in *Images of Mind*, by Michael Posner and Mark Raichle, in which they conclude, "The common belief that creating mental imagery is a function of the right hemisphere is clearly false."[17] Again, different brain areas are specialized for different tasks, but that specialization occurs at a finer level of analysis than "using visual imagery." Using visual imagery may be a useful learning strategy, but if it is useful it is not because it involves an otherwise underutilized right hemisphere in learning.

The same problem also subverts claims that one hemisphere or the other is the site of number recognition or reading skills. Here is a simple number task, expressed in two apparently equivalent ways: What is bigger, two or five? What is bigger, 2 or 5? It involves recognizing number symbols and understanding what those symbols mean. According to our folk theory, this should be a left-hemisphere task. But once again our folk theory is too crude.

Numerical comparison involves at least two mental subskills: identifying the number names and then comparing the numerical magnitudes that they designate. Although we seldom think of it, we are "bilingual" when it comes to numbers. We have number words—e.g., *one, two*—to name numbers, and we also have special written symbols, Arabic numerals—e.g., 1, 2. Our numerical bilingualism means that the two comparison questions above place different computational demands on the mind/brain. Using brain-recording techniques, Stanislaus Dehaene found that we identify number words using a system in the brain's left hemisphere,

# The fundamental problem with the right-brain versus left-brain claims in the education literature is that they rely on intuitions and folk theories about the brain.

but we identify Arabic numerals using brain areas in both the right and left hemispheres. Once we identify either the number words or the Arabic digits as symbols for numerical quantities, a distinct neural subsystem in the brain's right hemisphere compares magnitudes named by the two number symbols.[18]

Even for such a simple number task as comparison, both hemispheres are involved. Thus it makes no neuroscientific sense to claim that the left hemisphere recognizes numbers. Brain areas are specialized, but at a much finer level than "recognizing numbers." This simple task is already too complex for our folk theory to handle. Forget about algebra and geometry.

Similar research that analyzes speech and reading skills into their component processes also shows that reading is not simply a left-hemisphere task, as our folk theory suggests. Recognizing speech sounds, decoding written words, finding the meanings of words, constructing the gist of a written text, and making inferences as we read all rely on subsystems in both brain hemispheres.[19]

There is another different, but equally misleading, interpretation of brain laterality that occurs in the literature of brain-based education. In *Making Connections*, Renate Caine and Geoffrey Caine are critical of traditional "brain dichotomizers" and warn that the brain does not lend itself to such simple explanations. In their view, the results of research on split brains and hemispheric specialization are inconclusive—"both hemispheres are involved in all activities"—a conclusion that would seem to be consistent with what we have seen in our brief review of spatial reasoning, visual imagery, number skills, and reading.

However, following the folk theory, they do maintain that the left hemisphere processes parts and the right hemisphere processes wholes. In their interpretation, the educational significance of laterality research is that it shows that, within the brain, parts and wholes always interact. Laterality research thus provides scientific support for one of their principles of brain-based education: the brain processes parts and wholes simultaneously. Rather than number comparison or categorical spatial reasoning, the Caines provide a more global example: "Consider a

poem, a play, a great novel, or a great work of philosophy. They all involve a sense of the 'wholeness' of things and a capacity to work with patterns, often in timeless ways. In other words, the 'left brain' processes are enriched and supported by 'right brain' processes."[20]

For educators, the Caines see the two-brain doctrine as a "valuable metaphor that helps educators acknowledge two separate but simultaneous tendencies in the brain for organizing information. One is to reduce information to parts; the other is to perceive and work with it as a whole or a series of wholes."[21] Effective brain-based educational strategies overlook neither parts nor wholes, but constantly attempt to provide opportunities in which students can make connections and integrate parts and wholes. Thus the Caines number among their examples of brain-based approaches whole-language instruction,[22] integrated curricula, thematic teaching, and cooperative learning.[23] Similarly, because we make connections best when new information is embedded in meaningful life events and in socially interactive situations, Lev Vygotsky's theory of social learning should also be highly brain compatible.[24]

To the extent that one would want to view this as a metaphor, all I can say is that some of us find some metaphors more appealing than others. To the extent that this is supposed to be an attempt to ground educational principles in brain science, the aliens have just landed in Egypt.

Where did things go awry? Although they claim that laterality research in the sense of hemispheric localization is inconclusive, the Caines do maintain the piece of our folk theory that attributes "whole" processing to the right hemisphere and "part" processing to the left hemisphere. Because the two hemispheres are connected in normal healthy brains, they conclude that the brain processes parts and wholes simultaneously. It certainly does—although it probably is not the case that wholes and parts can be so neatly dichotomized. For example, in visual word decoding, the right hemisphere seems to read words letter by letter—by looking at the parts—while the left hemisphere recognizes entire words—the visual word forms.[25]

But again, the parts and wholes to which the brain is sensitive appear to occur at quite a fine-grained level of analysis—categories versus coordinates, generating versus scanning visual images, identifying number words versus Arabic digits. The Caines' example of part/whole interactions—the left-hemisphere comprehension of a text and the right-hemisphere appreciation of wholeness—relates to such a highly complex task that involves so many parts and wholes at different levels of analysis that it is trivially true that the whole brain is involved. Thus their appeal to brain science suffers from the same problem Kosslyn identified in the attempts to use crude theories to understand the brain. The only brain categories that the Caines appeal to are parts and wholes. Then they attempt to understand learning and exceedingly complex tasks in terms of parts and wholes. This approach bothers neither to analyze the brain nor to analyze behaviors.

The danger here is that one might think that there are brain-based reasons to adopt whole-language instruction, integrated curricula, or Vygotskian social learning. There are none. Whether or not these educational practices should be adopted must be determined on the basis of the impact they have on student learning. The evidence we now have on whole-language instruction is at best inconclusive, and the efficacy of social learning theory remains an open question. Brain science contributes no evidence, pro or con, for the brain-based strategies that the Caines espouse.

The fundamental problem with the right-brain versus left-brain claims that one finds in the education literature is that they rely on our intuitions and folk theories about the brain, rather than on what brain science is actually able to tell us. Our folk theories are too crude and imprecise to have any scientific, predictive, or instructional value. What modern brain science is telling us—and what brain-based educators fail to appreciate—is that it makes no scientific sense to map gross, unanalyzed behaviors and skills—reading, arithmetic, spatial reasoning—onto one brain hemisphere or another.

## Brains Like Sponges: The Sensitive Period

A new and popular, but problematic, idea found in the brain-based literature is that there is a critical or sensitive period in brain development, lasting until a child is around 10 years old, during which children learn faster, easier, and with more meaning than at any other time in their lives. David Sousa presented the claim this way in a recent commentary in *Education Week*, titled "Is the Fuss About Brain Research Justified?"

As the child grows, the brain selectively strengthens and prunes connections based on experience. Although this process continues throughout our lives, it seems to be most pronounced between the ages of 2 and 11, as different development areas emerge and taper off.... These so-called "windows of opportunity" represent critical periods when the brain demands certain types of input to create or consolidate neural networks, especially for acquiring language, emotional control, and learning to play music. Certainly, one can learn new information and skills at any age. But what the child learns during that window period will strongly influence what is learned after the window closes.[26]

In a recent *Educational Leadership* article, Pat Wolfe and Ron Brandt prudently caution educators against any quick marriage between brain science and education. However, among the well-established neuroscientific findings about which educators can be confident, they include, "Some abilities are acquired more easily during certain sensitive periods, or 'windows of opportunity.' " Later they continue, "During these years, [the brain] also has a remarkable ability to adapt and reorganize. It appears to develop some capacities with more ease at this time than in the years after puberty. These stages once called 'critical periods' are more accurately described as 'sensitive periods' or 'windows of opportunity.' "[27] Eric Jensen, in *Teaching with the Brain in Mind,* also writes that "the brain learns fastest and easiest during the school years."[28]

If there were neuroscientific evidence for the existence of such a sensitive period, such evidence might appear to provide a biological argument for the importance of elementary teaching and a scientific rationale for redirecting resources, restructuring curricula, and reforming pedagogy to take advantage of the once-in-a-lifetime learning opportunity nature has given us. If teachers could understand when sensitive periods begin and end, the thinking goes, they could structure curricula to take advantage of these unique windows of opportunity. Sousa tells of an experienced fifth-grade teacher who was upset when a mother asked the teacher what she was doing to take advantage of her daughter's windows of opportunity before they closed. Unfortunately, according to Sousa, the teacher was unaware of the windows-of-opportunity research. He warns, "As the public learns more about brain research through the popular press, scenes like this are destined to be repeated, further eroding confidence in teachers and in schools."[29]

This well-established neuroscientific "finding" about a sensitive period for learning originated in the popular press and in advocacy documents. It is an instance where neuroscientists have speculated about the implications of their work for education and where educators have uncritically embraced

that speculation. Presenting speculation as fact poses a greater threat to the public's confidence in teachers and schools than does Sousa's fifth-grade teacher.

During 1993, the *Chicago Tribune* ran Ron Kotulak's series of Pulitzer-Prize-winning articles on the new brain science. Kotulak's articles later appeared as a book titled *Inside the Brain: Revolutionary Discoveries of How the Mind Works.* Kotulak, an esteemed science writer, presented the first explicit statement that I have been able to find on the existence of a sensitive period between ages 4 and 10, during which children's brains learn fastest and easiest.[30] Variations on the claim appear in the Carnegie Corporation of New York's 1996 publication, *Years of Promise: A Comprehensive Learning Strategy for America's Children,* and in *Building Knowledge for a Nation of Learners,* published by the Office of Educational Research and Improvement of the U.S. Department of Education.[31] A report released in conjunction with the April 1997 White House Conference on Early Brain Development stated, "[B]y the age of three, the brains of children are two and a half times more active than the brains of adults—and they stay that way throughout the first decade of life.... This suggests that young children—particularly infants and toddlers—are biologically primed for learning and that these early years provide a unique window of opportunity or prime time for learning.[32]

If the sensitive period from age 4 to age 10 is a finding about which educators can be confident and one that justifies the current fuss about brain science, we would expect to find an extensive body of neuroscientific research that supports the claim. Surprisingly, brain-based enthusiasts appeal to a very limited body of evidence.

In Kotulak's initial statement of the sensitive-period claim, he refers to the brain-imaging work of Dr. Harry Chugani, M.D., at Wayne State University: "Chugani, whose imaging studies revealed that children's brains learned fastest and easiest between the ages of 4 and 10, said these years are often wasted because of lack of input."[33]

*Years of Promise,* the Carnegie Corporation report, cites a speech Kotulak presented at a conference on Brain Development in Young Children, held at the University of Chicago on 13 June 1996. Again referring to Chugani's work, Kotulak said that the years from 4 to about 10 "are the wonder years of learning, when a child can easily pick up a foreign language without an accent and learn a musical instrument with ease."[34] *Years of Promise* also cites a review article published by Dr. Chugani that is based on remarks he made at that Chicago conference.[35] *Rethinking the Brain,* a report based on the Chicago conference, also cites the same sources, as does the U.S. Department of Education document. What's more, Wolfe, Brandt, and Jensen also cite Chugani's work

in their discussions of the sensitive period for learning.

A 1996 article on education and the brain that appeared in *Education Week* reported, "By age 4, Chugani found, a child's brain uses more than twice the glucose that an adult brain uses. Between the ages 4 and 10, the amount of glucose a child's brain uses remains relatively stable. But by age 10, glucose utilization begins to drop off until it reaches adult levels at age 16 or 17. Chugani's findings suggest that a child's peak learning years occur just as all those synapses are forming."[36]

To be fair, these educators are not misrepresenting Chugani's views. He has often been quoted on the existence and educational importance of the sensitive period from age 4 until age 10.[37] In a review of his own work, published in *Preventive Medicine,* Chugani wrote:

The notion of an extended period during childhood when activity-dependent [synapse] stabilization occurs has recently received considerable attention by those individuals and organizations dealing with early intervention to provide "environmental enrichment" and with the optimal design of educational curricula. Thus, it is now believed by many (including this author) that the biological "window of opportunity" when learning is efficient and easily retained is perhaps not fully exploited by our educational system.[38]

Oddly, none of these articles and reports cite the single research article that provides the experimental evidence that originally motivated the claim: a 1987 *Annals of Neurology* article.[39] In that 1987 article, Chugani and his colleagues, M. E. Phelps and J. C. Mazziota, report results of PET (positron emission tomography) scans on 29 epileptic children, ranging in age from five days to 15 years. Because PET scans require the injection of radioactive substances, physicians can scan children only for diagnostic and therapeutic purposes; they cannot scan "normal, healthy" children just out of scientific curiosity. Thus the 1987 study is an extremely important one because it was the first, if not the only, imaging study that attempted to trace brain development from infancy through adolescence.

The scientists administered radioactively labeled glucose to the children and used PET scans to measure the rate at which specific brain areas took up the glucose. The assumption is that areas of the brain that are more active require more energy and so will take up more of the glucose. While the scans were being acquired, the scientists made every effort to eliminate, or at least minimize, all sensory stimulation for the subjects. Thus they measured the rate of glucose uptake when the brain was (presumably) not

NEITHER CHUGANI, HIS CO-AUTHORS,
NOR OTHER NEUROSCIENTISTS
HAVE STUDIED HOW QUICKLY OR
EASILY 5-YEAR-OLDS LEARN AS
OPPOSED TO 15-YEAR-OLDS.

engaged in any sensory or cognitive processing. That is, they measured resting brain-glucose metabolism.

One of their major findings was that, in all the brain areas they examined, metabolic levels reached adult values when children were approximately 2 years old and continued to increase, reaching rates twice the adult level by age 3 or 4. Resting glucose uptake remained at this elevated level until the children were around 9 years old. At age 9, the rates of brain glucose metabolism started to decline and stabilized at adult values by the end of the teenage years. What the researchers found, then, was a "high plateau" period for metabolic activity in the brain that lasted from roughly age 3 to age 9.

What is the significance of this high plateau period? To interpret their findings, Chugani and his colleagues relied on earlier research in which brain scientists had counted synapses in samples of human brain tissue to determine how the number and density of synaptic connections change in the human brain over our life spans. In the late 1970s, Peter Huttenlocher of the University of Chicago found that, starting a few months after birth and continuing until age 3, various parts of the brain formed synapses very rapidly.[40] This early, exuberant synapse growth resulted in synaptic densities in young children's brains that were 50% higher than the densities in mature adult brains. In humans, synaptic densities appear to remain at these elevated levels until around puberty, when some mechanism that is apparently under genetic control causes synapses to be eliminated or pruned back to the lower adult levels.

With this background, Chugani and his colleagues reasoned as follows. There is other evidence suggesting that maintaining synapses and their associated neural structures accounts for most of the glucose that the brain consumes. Their PET study measured changes in the brain's glucose consumption over the life span. Therefore, they reasoned, as the density and number of synapses wax and wane, so too does the rate of brain-glucose metabolism. This 1987 PET study provides important indirect evidence about brain development, based on the study of living brains, that corroborates the direct evidence based on counting synapses in samples of brain tissue taken from patients at autopsy. In the original paper, the scientists stated an important conclusion: "Our findings support the commonly accepted view that brain maturation in humans proceeds at least into the second decade of life."[41]

However, if you read the 1987 paper by Chugani, Phelps, and Mazziota, you will not find a section titled "The Relationship of Elevated Brain Metabolism and Synaptic Densities to Learning." Neither Chugani nor any of his co-authors have studied how quickly or easily 5-year-olds learn as opposed to 15-year-olds. Nor have other neuroscientists studied what high synaptic densities or high brain energy consumption means for the ease, rapidity, and depth of learning.

To connect high brain metabolism or excessive synaptic density with a critical period for learning requires some fancy footwork—or maybe more accurately, sleight of hand. We know that from early childhood until around age 10, children have extra or redundant synaptic connections in their brains. So, the reasoning goes, during this high plateau period of excess brain connectivity, "the individual is given the opportunity to retain and increase the efficiency of connections that, through repeated use during a critical period, are deemed to be important, whereas connections that are used to a lesser extent are more susceptible to being eliminated."[42] This, of course, is simply to assume that the high plateau period is a critical period.

Linking the critical period with learning requires an implicit appeal to another folk belief that appears throughout the history of the brain in education literature. This common assumption is that periods of rapid brain growth or high activity are optimal times, sensitive periods, or windows of opportunity for learning.[43] We get from Chugani's important brain-imaging results to a critical period for learning via two assumptions, neither of which is supported by neuroscientific data, and neither of which has even been the object of neuroscientific research. The claim that the period of high brain connectivity is a critical period for learning, far from being a neuroscientific finding about which educators can be confident, is at best neuroscientific speculation.

Chugani accurately described the scientific state of affairs in his *Preventive Medicine* review. He *believes*, along with some educators and early childhood advocates, that there is a biological window of opportunity when learning is easy, efficient, and easily retained. But there is no neuroscientific evidence to support this belief. And where there is no scientific evidence, there is no scientific fact.

Furthermore, it would appear that we have a considerable amount of research ahead of us if we are to amass the evidence for or against this belief. Neuroscientists have little idea of how experience before puberty affects either the timing or the extent of synaptic elimination. While they have documented that the pruning of synapses does occur, no reliable studies have compared differences in final adult synaptic connectivity with differences in the experiences of individuals before puberty. Nor do they know whether the animals or individuals with greater synaptic densities in adulthood are necessarily more intelligent and developed. Neuroscientists do not know if prior training and education affect either loss or retention of synapses at puberty.[44]

Nor do neuroscientists know how learning is related to changes in brain metabolism and synaptic connectivity over our lifetimes. As the developmental neurobiologist Patricia Goldman-Rakic told educators, "While children's brains acquire a tremendous amount of information during the early years, most learning takes place after synaptic formation stabilizes."[45] That is, a great deal, if not most, learning takes place after age 10 and after pruning has occurred. If so, we may turn into efficient general learning machines only after puberty, only after synaptic formation stabilizes and our brains are less active.

Finally, the entire discussion of this purported critical period takes place under an implicit assumption that children actually do learn faster, more easily, and more deeply between the ages of 4 and 10. There are certainly critical periods for the development of species-wide skills, such as seeing, hearing, and acquiring a first language, but critical periods are interesting to psychologists because they seem to be the exception rather than the rule in human development. As Jacqueline Johnson and Elissa Newport remind us in their article on critical periods in language learning, "In most domains of learning, skill increases over development."[46]

When we ask whether children actually do learn more easily and meaningfully than adults, the answers we get are usually anecdotes about athletes, musicians, and students of second languages. We have not begun to look at the rate, efficiency, and depth of learning across various age groups in a representative sample of learning domains. We are making an assumption about learning behavior and then relying on highly speculative brain science to explain our assumption. We have a lot more research to do.

So, despite what you read in the papers and in the brain-based education literature, neuroscience has *not* established that there is a sensitive period between the ages of 4 and 10 during which children learn more quickly, easily, and meaningfully. Brain-based educators have uncritically embraced neuroscientific speculation.

The pyramids were built by aliens—to house Elvis.

A February 1996 article in *Newsweek* on the brain and education quoted Linda Darling-Hammond: "Our school system was invented in the late 1800s, and little has changed. Can you imagine if the medical profession ran this way?"[47] Darling-Hammond is right. Our school system must change to reflect what we now know about teaching, learning, mind, and brain. To the extent that we want education to be a research-based enterprise, the medical profession provides a reasonable model. We can only be thankful that members of the medical profession are more careful in applying biological research to their professional practice than some educators are in applying brain research to theirs.

We should not shrug off this problem. It is symptomatic of some deeper problems about how research is presented to educators, about what educators find compelling, about how educators evaluate research, and about how professional development time and dollars are spent. The "In Search of . . ." series is a television program that provides an entertaining mix of fact, fiction, and fantasy. That can be an amusing exercise, but it is not always instructive. The brain-based education literature represents a genre of writing, most often appearing in professional education publications, that provides a popular mix of fact, misinterpretation, and speculation. That can be intriguing, but it is not always informative. "In Search of . . ." is no way to present history, and the brain-based education literature is not the way to present the science of learning.

1. Renate Nummela Caine and Geoffrey Caine, Making *Connections: Teaching and the Human Brain* (New York: Addison-Wesley, 1994); idem, "Building a Bridge Between the Neurosciences and Education: Cautions and Possibilities," *NASSP Bulletin*, vol. 82, 1998, pp. 1–8; Eric Jensen, *Teaching with the Brain in Mind* (Alexandria, Va.: Association for Supervision and Curriculum Development, 1998); and Robert Sylwester, *A Celebration of Neurons* (Alexandria, Va.: Association for Supervision and Curriculum Development, 1995).

2. See, for example, Michael Pressley and C. B. McCormick, *Advanced Educational Psychology for Educators*, Researchers, and Policymakers (New York: HarperCollins, 1995).

3. John T. Bruer, *Schools for Thought: A Science of Learning in the Classroom* (Cambridge, Mass.: MIT Press, 1993); and idem, "Education and the Brain: A Bridge Too Far," *Educational Researcher*, November 1997, pp. 4–16.

4. Susan F. Chipman, "Integrating Three Perspectives on Learning," in Sarah L. Friedman, Kenneth A. Klivington, and R. W. Peterson, eds., *The Brain, Cognition, and Education* (Orlando, Fla.: Academic Press, 1986), pp. 203–32.

5. *Bridging the Gap Between Neuroscience and Education: Summary of a Workshop Cosponsored by the Education Commission of the States and the Charles A. Dana Foundation* (Denver: Education Commission of the States, 1996), p. 5.

6. Chipman, op. cit.; Howard Gardner, *Art, Mind, and Brain: A Cognitive Approach to Creativity* (New York: Basic Books, 1982); Mike Rose, "Narrowing the Mind and Page: Remedial Writers and Cognitive Reductionism," *College Composition and Communication*, vol. 39, 1988, pp. 267–302; and Jerre Levy, "Right Brain, Left Brain: Fact and Fiction," *Psychology Today*, May 1985, p. 38.

7. David A. Sousa, *How the Brain Learns: A Classroom Teacher's Guide* (Reston, Va.: National Association of Secondary School Principals, 1995).

8. M. C. Linn and A. C. Petersen, "Emergence and Characterization of Sex Differences in Spatial Ability: A Meta-Analysis," *Child Development*, vol. 56, 1985, pp. 1470–8.

9. Sally Springer and Georg Deutsch, *Left Brain, Right Brain* (New York: W. H. Freeman, 1993).

10. Sousa, pp. 95, 99.

11. Christopher F. Chabris and Stephen M. Kosslyn, "How Do the Cerebral Hemispheres Contribute to Encoding Spatial Relations?," *Current Directions in Psychology*, vol. 7, 1998, pp. 8–14.

12. Ibid.

13. Ibid.

14. Martha Farah, *Visual Agnosias* (Cambridge, Mass.: MIT Press, 1991).

15. Stephen M. Kosslyn et al., "A Computational Analysis of Mental Image Generation: Evidence from Functional Dissociations in Split-Brain Patients," *Journal of Experimental Psychology: General*, vol. 114, 1985, pp. 311–41.

16. Stephen M. Kosslyn et al., "Two Types of Image Generation: Evidence for Left and Right Hemisphere Processes," *Neuropsychologia*, vol. 33, 1995, pp. 1485–1510.

17. Michael I. Posner and Mark E. Raichle, *Images of Mind* (New York: Scientific American Library, 1994), p. 95.

18. Stanislaus Dehaene, "The Organization of Brain Activations in Number Comparison," *Journal of Cognitive Neuroscience*, vol. 8, 1996, pp. 47–68.

19. Mark Jung Beeman and Christine Chiarello, "Complementary Right- and Left-Hemisphere Language Comprehension," *Current Directions in Psychology*, vol. 7, 1998, pp. 2–7.

20. Caine and Caine, p. 37.

21. Ibid., p. 91.

22. Ibid., pp. 9, 48, 91.

23. Ibid., pp. 127–30.

24. Ibid., pp. 47–48.

25. Beeman and Chiarello, op. cit.

26. David A. Sousa, "Is the Fuss About Brain Research Justified?," *Education Week*, 16 December 1998, p. 35.

27. Pat Wolfe and Ron Brandt, "What Do We Know from Brain Research?," *Educational Leadership*, November 1998, p. 12.

28. Jensen, p. 32.

29. Sousa, "Is the Fuss About Brain Research Justified?," p. 35.

30. Ronald Kotulak, *Inside the Brain: Revolutionary Discoveries of How the Mind Works* (Kansas City: Andrews McMeel, 1996), p. 46.

31. *Years of Promise: A Comprehensive Learning Strategy for America's Children* (New York: Carnegie Corporation of New York, 1996), pp. 9–10; and Office of Educational Research and Improvement, *Building Knowledge for a Nation of Learners* (Washington, D.C.: U.S. Department of Education, 1996).

32. Rima Shore, Rethinking the Brain: New Insights into Early Development (New York: Families and Work Institute, 1997), pp. 21, 36.

33. Kotulak, p. 46.

34. Ronald Kotulak, "Learning How to Use the Brain," 1996, available on the Web at http://www.newhorizons.org/ofc_21cliusebrain.html.

35. Harry T. Chugani, "Neuroimaging of Developmental Nonlinearity and Developmental Pathologies," in R. W. Thatcher et al., eds., *Developmental Neuroimaging* (San Diego: Academic Press, 1996), pp. 187–95.

36. Debra Viadero, "Brain Trust," *Education Week*, 18 September 1996, pp. 31–33.

37. *Better Beginnings* (Pittsburgh: Office of Child Development, University of Pittsburgh, 1997); A. DiCresce, "Brain Surges," 1997, available on the Web at www.med.wayne.edu/wmp97/brain.htm; and Lynell Hancock, "Why Do Schools Flunk Biology?," Newsweek, 19 February 1996, pp. 58–59.

38. Harry Chugani, "A Critical Period of Brain Development: Studies of Cerebral Glucose Utilization with PET," *Preventive Medicine*, vol. 27, 1998, pp. 184–88.

39. Harry T. Chugani, M. E. Phelps, and J. C. Mazziota, "Positron Emission Tomography Study of Human Brain Function Development," *Annals of Neurology*, vol. 22, 1987, pp. 487–97.

40. Peter R. Huttenlocher, "Synaptic Density in Human Frontal Cortex—Developmental Changes of Aging," *Brain Research*, vol. 163, 1979, pp. 195–205; Peter R. Huttenlocher et al., "Synaptogenesis in Human Visual Cortex—Evidence for Synapse Elimination During Normal Development," *Neuroscience Letters*, vol. 33, 1982, pp. 247–52; Peter R. Huttenlocher and Ch. de Courten, "The Development of Synapses in Striate Cortex of Man," *Human Neurobiology*, vol. 6, 1987, pp. 1-9; and Peter R. Huttenlocher and A. S. Dabholkar, "Regional Differences in Synaptogenesis in Human Cerebral Cortex," *Journal of Comparative Neurology*, vol. 387, 1997, pp. 167-78.

41. Chugani, Phelps, and Mazziota, p. 496.

42. Chugani, "Neuroimaging of Developmental Nonlinearity," p. 187.

43. Herman T. Epstein, "Growth Spurts During Brain Development: Implications for Educational Policy and Practice," in S. Chall and A. F. Mirsky, eds., Education and the Brain (Chicago: University of Chicago Press, 1978), pp. 343-70; and Chipman, op. cit.

44. Patricia S. Goldman-Rakic, Jean-Pierre Bourgeois, and Pasko Rakic, "Synaptic Substrate of Cognitive Development: Synaptogenesis in the Prefrontal Cortex of the Nonhuman Primate," in N. A. Krasnegor, G. R. Lyon, and P. S. Goldman-Rakic, *Development of the Prefrontal Cortex: Evolution, Neurobiology, and Behavior* (Baltimore: Paul H. Brooks, 1997), pp. 27-47.

45. *Bridging the Gap*, p. 11.

46. Jacqueline S. Johnson and Elissa L. Newport, "Critical Period Effects on Universal Properties," *Cognition*, vol. 39, 1991, p. 215.

47. Hancock, p. 59.

# CAUTION— PRAISE CAN BE DANGEROUS

By Carol S. Dweck

THE SELF-ESTEEM movement, which was flourishing just a few years ago, is in a state of decline. Although many educators believed that boosting students' self-esteem would boost their academic achievement, this did not happen. But the failure of the self-esteem movement does not mean that we should stop being concerned with what students think of themselves and just concentrate on improving their achievement. Every time teachers give feedback to students, they convey messages that affect students' opinion of themselves, their motivation, and their achievement. And I believe that teachers can and should help students become high achievers who also feel good about themselves. But how, exactly, should teachers go about doing this?

In fact, the self-esteem people were on to something extremely important. Praise, the chief weapon in their armory, is a powerful tool. Used correctly it can help students become adults who delight in intellectual challenge, understand the value of effort, and are able to deal with setbacks. Praise can help students make the most of the gifts they have. But if praise is not handled properly, it can become a negative force, a kind of drug that, rather than strengthening students, makes them passive and dependent on the opinion of others. What teachers— and parents—need is a framework that enables them to use praise wisely and well.

*Carol S. Dweck is a professor of psychology at Columbia University, who has carried out research on self-esteem, motivation, and academic achievement for thirty years. Her new book,* Self-Theories: Their Role in Motivation, Personality, and Development, *was just published by The Psychology Press.*

## Where Did Things Go Wrong?

I believe the self-esteem movement faltered because of the way in which educators tried to instill self-esteem. Many people held an intuitively appealing theory of self-esteem, which went something like this: Giving students many opportunities to experience success and then praising them for their successes will indicate to them that they are intelligent. If they feel good about their intelligence, they will achieve. They will love learning and be confident and successful learners.

Much research now shows that this idea is wrong. Giving students easy tasks and praising their success tells students that you think they're dumb.[1] It's not hard to see why. Imagine being lavishly praised for something you think is pretty Mickey Mouse. Wouldn't you feel that the person thought you weren't capable of more and was trying to make you feel good about your limited ability?

But what about praising students' ability when they perform well on challenging tasks? In such cases, there would be no question of students' thinking you were just trying to make them feel good. Melissa Kamins, Claudia Mueller, and I decided to put this idea to the test.

Mueller and I had already found, in a study of the relationship between parents' beliefs and their children's expectations, that 85 percent of parents thought they needed to praise their children's intelligence in order to assure them that they were smart.[2] We also knew that many educators and psychologists thought that praising children for being intelligent was of great benefit. Yet in almost 30 years of research, I had seen over and over that children who had maladaptive achievement patterns were already obsessed with their intelligence—and with proving it to others. The children worried about how smart they looked and feared that failing at some task— even a relatively unimportant one—meant they were dumb. They also worried that having to work hard in order to succeed at a task showed they were dumb. Intelligence seemed to be a label to these kids, a feather in their caps, rather than a tool that, with effort, they could become more skillful in using.

In contrast, the more adaptive students focused on the process of learning and achieving. They weren't worried about their intelligence and didn't consider every task a measure of it. Instead, these students were more likely to concern themselves with the effort and strategies they needed in order to master the task. We wondered if praising children for being intelligent, though it seemed like a positive thing to do, could hook them into becoming dependent on praise.

## Praise for Intelligence

Claudia Mueller and I conducted six studies, with more than 400 fifth-grade students, to examine the effects of praising children for being intelligent.[3] The students were from different parts of the country (a Midwestern town and a large Eastern city) and came from varied ethnic, racial, and socioeconomic backgrounds. Each of the studies involved several tasks, and all began with the students working, one at a time, on a puzzle task that was challenging but easy enough for all of them to do quite well. After this first set, we praised one-third of the children for their *intelligence*. They were told: "Wow, you got x number correct. That's a really good score. You must be smart at this." One-third of the children were also told that they got a very good score, but they were praised for their *effort*: "You must have worked really hard." The final third were simply praised for their *performance*, with no comment on why they were successful. Then, we looked to see the effects of these different types of praise across all six studies.

We found that after the first trial (in which all of the students were successful) the three groups responded similarly to questions we asked them. They enjoyed the task equally, were equally eager to take the problems home to practice, and were equally confident about their future performance.

In several of the studies, as a followup to the first trial, we gave students a choice of different tasks to work on next. We asked whether they wanted to try a challenging task from which they could learn a lot (but at which they might not succeed) or an easier task (on which they were sure to do well and look smart).

The majority of the students who had received praise for being intelligent the first time around went for the task that would allow them to keep on looking smart. Most of the students who had received praise for their effort (in some studies, as many as 90 percent) wanted the challenging learning task. (The third group, the stu-

dents who had not been praised for intelligence or effort, were right in the middle and I will not focus on them.)

These findings suggest that when we praise children for their intelligence, we are telling them that this is the name of the game: Look smart; don't risk making mistakes. On the other hand, when we praise children for the effort and hard work that leads to achievement, they want to keep engaging in that process. They are not diverted from the task of learning by a concern with how smart they might—or might not—look.

## The Impact of Difficulty

Next, we gave students a set of problems that were harder and on which they didn't do as well. Afterwards, we repeated the questions we had asked after the first task: How much had they enjoyed the task? Did they want to take the problems home to practice? And how smart did they feel? We found that the students who had been praised for being intelligent did not like this second task and were no longer interested in taking the problems home to practice. What's more, their difficulties led them to question their intelligence. In other words, the same students who had been told they were smart when they succeeded now felt dumb because they had encountered a setback. They had learned to measure themselves from what people said about their performance, and they were dependent on continuing praise in order to maintain their confidence.

In contrast, the students who had received praise for their effort on the easier task liked the more difficult task just as much even though they missed some of the problems. In fact, many of them said they liked the harder problems even more than the easier ones, and they were even more eager to take them home to practice. It was wonderful to see.

Moreover, these youngsters did not think that the difficulty of the task (and their relative lack of success) reflected on their intelligence. They thought, simply, that they had to make a greater effort in order to succeed. Their interest in taking problems home with them to practice on presumably reflected one way they planned to do this.

Thus, the students praised for effort were able to keep their intellectual self-esteem in the face of setbacks. They still thought they were smart; they still enjoyed the challenge; and they planned to work toward future success. The students who had been praised for their intelligence received an initial boost to their egos, but their view of themselves was quickly shaken when the going got rough. As a final test, we gave students a third set of problems that were equal in difficulty to the first set—the one on which all the students had been successful. The results were striking. Although all three groups had performed equally well on the first trial, the students who had received praise for their intelligence (and who had been discouraged by their poor showing on the second trial) now registered the worst performance of the three groups. Indeed, they did significantly worse than they had on the first trial. In contrast, students who were praised for working hard performed the best of the three groups and significantly better than they had originally. So the different kinds of praise apparently affected not just what students thought and felt, but also how well they were able to perform.

Given what we had already seen, we reasoned that when students see their performance as a measure of their intelligence, they are likely to feel stigmatized when they perform poorly and may even try to hide the fact. If, however, students consider a poor performance a temporary setback, which merely reflects how much effort they have put in or their current level of skill, then it will not be a stigma. To test this idea, we gave students the opportunity to tell a student at another school about the task they had just completed by writing a brief description on a prepared form. The form also asked them to report their score on the second, more difficult trial.

More than 40 percent of the students who had been praised for their intelligence lied about their score (to improve it, of course). They did this even though they were reporting their performance to an anonymous peer whom they would never meet. Very few of the students in the other groups exaggerated their performance. This suggests that when we praise students for their intelligence, failure becomes more personal and therefore more of a disgrace. As a result, students become less able to face and therefore deal with their setbacks.

## The Messages We Send

Finally, we found that following their experiences with the different kinds of praise, the students believed different things about their intelligence. Students who had received praise for being intelligent told us they thought of intelligence as something innate—a capacity that you just had or didn't have. Students who had been praised for effort told us they thought of intelligence more in terms of their skills, knowledge, and motivation—things over which they had some control and might be able to enhance.

And these negative effects of praising for intelligence were just as strong (and sometimes stronger) for the high-achieving students as for their less successful peers. Perhaps it is even easier to get these youngsters invested in looking smart to others. Maybe they are even more attuned to messages from us that tell them we value them for their intellects.

How can one sentence of praise have such powerful and pervasive effects? In my research, I have been amazed over and over again at how quickly students of all ages pick up on messages about themselves—at how sensitive they are to suggestions about their personal qualities or about the meaning of their actions and experiences. The kinds of praise (and criticism) students receive from their teachers and parents tell them how to think about what they do—and what they are.

This is why we cannot simply forget about students' feelings, their ideas about themselves and their motivation, and just teach them the "facts." No matter how objective we try to be, our feedback conveys messages about what we think is important, what we think of them, and how they should think of themselves. These messages, as we have seen, can have powerful effects on many things including performance. And it should surprise no one that this susceptibility starts very early.

Melissa Kamins and I found it in kindergarten children.[4] Praise or criticism that focused on children's personal traits (like being smart or good) created a real vulnerability when children hit setbacks. They saw setbacks as showing that they were bad or incompetent—and they were unable to respond constructively. In contrast, praise or criticism that focused on children's strategies or the efforts they made to succeed left them hardy, confident, and in control when they confronted setbacks. A setback did not mean anything bad about them or their personal qualities. It simply meant that something needed to be done, and they set about doing it. Again, a focus on process allowed these young children to maintain their self-esteem and to respond constructively when things went wrong.

## Ways of Praising

There are many groups whose achievement is of particular interest to us: minorities, females, the gifted, the underachieving, to name a few. The findings of these studies will tell you why I am so concerned that we not try to encourage the achievement of our students by praising their intelligence. When we worry about low-achieving or vulnerable students, we may want to reassure them they're smart. When we want to motivate high-achieving students, we may want to spur them on by telling them they're gifted. Our research says: Don't do that. Don't get students so invested in these labels that they care more about keeping the label than about learning. Instead of empowering students, praise is likely to render students passive and dependent on something they believe they can't control. And it can hook them into a system in which setbacks signify incompetence and effort is recognized as a sign of weakness rather than a key to success.

This is not to say that we shouldn't praise students. We can praise as much as we please when they learn or do well, but should wax enthusiastic about their strategies, not about how their performance reveals an attribute they are likely to view as innate and beyond their control. We can rave about their effort, their concentration, the effectiveness of their study strategies, the interesting ideas they came up with, the way they followed through. We can ask them questions that show an intelligent appreciation of their work and what they put into it. We can enthusiastically discuss with them what they learned. This, of course, requires more from us than simply telling them that they are smart, but it is much more appreciative of their work, much more constructive, and it does not carry with it the dangers I've been describing.

What about the times a student really impresses us by doing something quickly, easily—and perfectly? Isn't it appropriate to show our admiration for the child's ability? My honest opinion is that we should not. We should not be giving students the impression that we place a high value on their doing perfect work on tasks that are easy for them. A better approach would be to apologize for wasting their time with something that was too easy, and move them to something that is more challenging. When students make progress in or master that more challenging work, that's when our admiration—for their efforts—should come through.

## A Challenging Academic Transition

The studies I have been talking about were carried out in a research setting. Two other studies[5] tracked students with these different viewpoints in a real-life situation, as they were making the transition to junior high school and during their first two years of junior high. This is a point at which academic work generally becomes more demanding than it was in elementary school, and many students stumble. The studies compared the attitudes and achievement of students who believed that intelligence is a fixed quantity with students who believed that they could develop their intellectual potential. We were especially interested in any changes in the degree of success students experienced in junior high school and how they dealt with these changes. For the sake of simplicity, I will combine the results from the two studies, for they showed basically the same thing.

First, the students who believed that intelligence is fixed did indeed feel that poor performance meant they were dumb. Furthermore, they reported, in significantly greater numbers than their peers, that if they did badly on a test, they would seriously consider cheating the next time. This was true even for students who were highly skilled and who had a past record of high achievement.

Perhaps even worse, these students believed that having to make an effort meant they were dumb—hardly an attitude to foster good work habits. In fact, these students reported that even though school achievement was very important to them, one of their prime goals in school was to exert as little effort as possible.

In contrast to the hopelessly counterproductive attitude of the first group, the second group of students, those who believed that intellectual potential can be developed, felt that poor performance was often due to a lack of effort, and it called for more studying. They saw effort as worthwhile and important—something necessary even for geniuses if they are to realize their potential.

So once again, for those who are focused on their fixed intelligence and its adequacy, setbacks and even effort bring a loss of face and self-esteem. But challenges, setbacks, and effort are not threatening to the self-esteem of those who are concerned with developing their potential; they represent opportunities to learn. In fact, many of these students told us that they felt smartest when things were difficult; they gained self-esteem when they applied themselves to meeting challenges.

What about the academic achievement of the two groups making the transition to junior high school? In both studies, we saw that students who believed that intelligence was fixed and was manifest in their performance did more poorly than they had in elementary school. Even many who had been high achievers did much less well. Included among them were many students who entered junior high with high intellectual self-esteem. On the other hand, the students who believed that intellectual potential could be developed showed, as a group, clear gains in their class standing, and many blossomed intellectually. The demands of their new environment, instead of causing them to wilt because they doubted themselves, encouraged them to roll up their sleeves and get to work.

These patterns seem to continue with students entering college. Research with students at highly selective universities found that, although they may enter a situation with equal self-esteem, optimism, and past achievement, students respond to the challenge of college differently: Students in one group by measuring themselves and losing confidence; the others by figuring out what it takes and doing it.[6]

## Believing and Achieving

Some of the research my colleagues and I have carried out suggests that it is relatively easy to modify the views of young children in regard to intelligence and effort in a research setting. But is it possible to influence student attitudes in a real-life setting? And do students become set in their beliefs as they grow older? Some exciting new research shows that even college students' views about intelligence and effort can be modified—and that these changes will affect their level of academic achievement.[7] In their study, Aronson and Fried taught minority students at a prestigious university to view their intelligence as a potentiality that could be developed through hard work. For example, they created and showed a film that explained the neural changes that took place in the brain every time students confronted difficulty by exerting effort. The students who were instructed about the relationship between intelligence and effort went on to earn significantly higher grades than their peers who were not. This study, like our intelligence praise studies, shows that (1) students' ideas about their intelligence can be influenced by the messages they receive, and (2) when these ideas change, changes in performance can follow.

But simply getting back to basics and enforcing rigorous standards—which some students will meet and some will not—won't eliminate the pitfalls I have been describing. This approach may convey, even more forcefully, the idea that intelligence is a gift only certain students possess. And it will not, in itself, teach students to value learning and focus on the *process* of achievement or how to deal with obstacles. These students may, more than ever, fear failure because it takes the measure of their intelligence.

## A Different Framework

Our research suggests another approach. Instead of trying to convince our students that they are smart or simply enforcing rigorous standards in the hopes that doing so will create high motivation and achievement, teachers should take the following steps: first, get students to focus on their potential to learn; second, teach them to value challenge and learning over looking smart; and third, teach them to concentrate on effort and learning processes in the face of obstacles.

This can be done while holding students to rigorous standards. Within the framework I have outlined, tasks are challenging and effort is highly valued, required, and rewarded. Moreover, we can (and must) give students frank evaluations of their work and their level of skill, but we must make clear that these are evaluations of their current level of performance and skill, not an assessment of their intelligence or their innate ability. In this framework, we do not arrange easy work or constant successes, thinking that we are doing students a favor. We do not lie to students who are doing poorly so they will feel smart: That would rob them of the information they need to work harder and improve. Nor do we just give students hard work that many can't do, thus making them into casualties of the system.

I am not encouraging high-effort situations in which students stay up studying until all hours every night, fearing they will displease their parents or disgrace themselves if they don't get the top test scores. Pushing students to do that is not about valuing learning or about orienting students toward developing their potential. It is about pressuring students to prove their worth through their test scores.

It is also not sufficient to give students piles of homework and say we are teaching them about the importance of effort. We are not talking about quantity here but about teaching students to seek challenging tasks and to engage in an active learning process.

However, we as educators must then be prepared to do our share. We must help students acquire the skills they need for learning, and we must be available as constant resources for learning. It is not enough to keep harping on and praising effort, for this may soon wear thin. And it will not be effective if students don't know *how* to apply their effort appropriately. It is necessary that we as educators understand and teach students how to engage in processes that foster learning, things like task analysis and study skills.[8]

When we focus students on their potential to learn and give them the message that effort is the key to learning, we give them responsibility for and control over their achievement—and over their self-esteem. We acknowledge that learning is not something that someone gives students; nor can they expect to feel good about themselves because teachers tell them they are smart. Both learning and self-esteem are things that students achieve as they tackle challenges and work to master new material.

Students who value learning and effort know how to make and sustain a commitment to valued goals. Unlike some of their peers, they are not afraid to work hard; they know that meaningful tasks involve setbacks; and they know how to bounce back from failure. These are lessons that cannot help but serve them well in life as well as in school.

These are lessons I have learned from my research on students' motivation and achievement, and they are things I wish I had known as a student. There is no reason that every student can't know them now.

## Endnotes

1. Meyer, W. U. (1982). Indirect communications about perceived ability estimates. *Journal of Educational Psychology, 74,* 888–897.
2. Mueller, C. M., & Dweck, C. S. (1996). Implicit theories of intelligence: Relation of parental beliefs to children's expectations. Paper presented at the Third National Research Convention of Head Start, Washington, D.C.
3. Mueller, C. M., & Dweck, C. S. (1998). Intelligence praise can undermine motivation and performance. *Journal of Personality and Social Psychology; 75,* 33–52.
4. Kamins, M., & Dweck, C. S. (1999). Person vs. process praise and criticism: Implications for contingent self-worth and coping. *Developmental Psychology.*
5. Henderson, V., & Dweck, C. S. (1990). Achievement and motivation in adolescence: A new model and data. In S. Feldman and G. Elliott (Eds.), *At the threshold: The developing adolescent.* Cambridge, MA: Harvard University Press; *and* Dweck, C. S., & Sorich, L. (1999). Mastery-oriented thinking. In C. R. Snyder (Ed.). *Coping.* New York: Oxford University Press.
6. Robins, R. W. & Pals, J. (1998). Implicit self-theories of ability in the academic domain: A test of Dweck's model. Unpublished manuscript, University of California at Davis; *and* Zhao, W., Dweck, C. S., & Mueller, C. (1998). Implicit theories and depression-like responses to failure. Unpublished manuscript, Columbia University.
7. Aronson, J., & Fried, C. (1998). Reducing stereotype threat and boosting academic achievement of African Americans: The role of conceptions of intelligence. Unpublished manuscript, University of Texas.
8. Brown, A. L. (1997). Transforming schools into communities of thinking and learning about serious matters. *American Psychologist, 52,* 399–413.

# Unit 4

## Key Points to Consider

❖ How important are fathers in the lives of their children? What child outcomes are more linked to father love than to mother love?

❖ Do parents really matter? Can they work with children's inherited personalities? Explain.

❖ What is dyssemia? How do adults recognize dyssemia in children? How can dyssemic children be helped to fit in?

❖ What are the effects of poverty on children?

❖ What are the effects of maltreatment on children? How can adults help children develop resiliency?

❖ What wonders are in store for children of the second millennium? How will culture change to adopt to the new technologies available?

 **Links**    **www.dushkin.com/online/**

21. **Childhood Injury Prevention Interventions**
    *http://depts.washington.edu/hiprc/*

22. **Families and Work Institute**
    *http://www.familiesandworkinst.org*

23. **National Committee to Prevent Child Abuse (NCPCA)**
    *http://www.childabuse.org*

24. **The National Parent Information Network (NPIN)**
    *http://ericps.crc.uiuc.edu/npin/*

25. **Parentsplace.com: Single Parenting**
    *http://www.parentsplace.com/family/singleparent/*

These sites are annotated on pages 4 and 5.

# Development during Childhood: Family and Culture

ost people accept the proposition that families and
tures have substantial effects on child outcomes.
 they? New interpretations of behavioral genetic
earch suggest that genetically predetermined child
haviors may be having substantial effects on how
nilies parent and on how cultures are evolved.
ture and nurture are very interactive.

If parents and societies have a significant impact
 child outcomes, is there a set of family values? Is
re a culture that has more correct answers than
other culture? It is often assumed by the layperson
t children's behaviors and personalities have a
ect correlation with the behaviors and personality
the person or persons who provided their
ialization during infancy and childhood. Are you
mirror image of the person or persons who raised
u? Why or why not? How many of their
naviors do you reflect? Do you model your family,
ur peers, your culture, or all of them?

During childhood, a person's family values get
mpared to, and tested against, the values of
ools, community, and culture. Peers, schoolmates,
chers, neighbors, extracurricular activity leaders,
gious leaders, even shopkeepers, play
reasingly important roles. Culture influences and
nfluenced by children through holidays, style of
ss, music, television, movies, slang, games
yed, parents' jobs, transportation, and exposure
sex, drugs, and violence. The ecological theorist,
e Bronfenbrenner, calls these cultural variables
osystem and macrosystem influences. The
veloping personality of a child has multiple
erwoven influences: from genetic potentialities
ough family values and socialization practices to
nmunity and cultural pressures for behaviors.

The first article in the family section of this unit
eals to partnerships in parenting: fathers plus
thers. Fathers have been relegated to "second
nana" position, often viewed as just breadwinners
d disciplinarians. School-age children need
ents who are both responsive and demanding.
cipline is crucial to a healthy personality.
wever, mothers as well as fathers need to be
ciplinarians, and fathers as well as mothers need
provide tender, loving, and responsive caregiving.
 author reviews six types of studies that
nonstrate the power of fathers in their children's
s.

The second article provides both the controversial
ory of Judith Harris that parents do not matter
d many rebuttals of this sentiment. In 1998 Harris
ited a bonfire of controversy with her book, *The
rture Assumption: Why Children Turn Out the
y They Do; Parents Matter Less than You Think
d Peers Matter More*. This selection reviews
vice to parents from Sigmund Freud's heyday at

the beginning of the twentieth century to Harris's
advice at the millennium. It presents the opinions of
currently famous people (for example, Newt
Gingrich, Michael Jordan, Rosie O'Donnell) about
the effects of nature and the effects of nurture.
Scientific research is not on the side of either genes
or environment but rather supports the idea that
both matter very much.

The third article focuses on "Kids Who Don't Fit
In." In April 1999, two students went on an armed
rampage in Littleton, Colorado, to get revenge on
the students who teased them because they did not
fit in. This fomented controversy about bullying and
the maltreatment of children whose behaviors are
different or awkward. The theme of this essay is that
early and appropriate help for children with
dyssemia (difficulty with social skills) is more
beneficial than punishment of the children who tease
them. Advice is given on how to recognize
dyssemia and where to turn for help.

The first article in the culture subsection of unit 4
is a review of recent, detailed, longitudinal data sets
dealing with the effects of poverty on children. It
includes information on the differential effects of
poverty related to timing, depth, and duration of
poverty, and to parental factors such as age and
education.

The second article deals with the question of
maltreatment of children. It reviews some of the
neurological effects of abuse, neglect, and other
traumatic events that affect about 4 million American
children each year. Prolonged abuse is known to
change regions of the brain responsible for memory,
learning, and emotional stability. Barbara Lowenthal
suggests several measures that can promote
resiliency in child victims of maltreatment. Among
her suggestions are availability of alternate
caregivers, social support interventions, informal
support systems, formal support systems, and
intervention programs. Each of these supports are
described in detail.

The third article, "Tomorrow's Child," makes
many predictions about the life and culture of
children in the twenty-first century. It reviews
landmarks of family life from the mid-nineteenth
century through the end of the twentieth century,
showing how rapidly change has taken place in the
past 150 years. Radical new technologies are being
predicted for the future. Among these are brain
scans for instant feedback on what a person is
learning, virtual-reality simulators to practice life
skills, computers for babies under a year old, free
early childhood education programs for toddlers,
health clubs for kids, kids who are more like adults
and vice versa, and clothing designed for survival
rather than for enhancement of physical appearance.

# Father Love and Child Development: History and Current Evidence

*Abstract*

Six types of studies show that father love sometimes explains as much or more of the variation in specific child and adult outcomes as does mother love. Sometimes, however, only father love is statistically associated with specific aspects of offsprings' development and adjustment, after controlling for the influence of mother love. Recognition of these facts was clouded historically by the cultural construction of fatherhood and fathering in America.

*Keywords*

father love; paternal acceptance; parental acceptance-rejection theory

Ronald P. Rohner[1]

Center for the Study of Parental Acceptance and Rejection, School of Family Studies, University of Connecticut, Storrs, Connecticut

Research in every major ethnic group of America (Rohner, 1998b), in dozens of nations internationally, and with several hundred societies in two major cross-cultural surveys (Rohner 1975, 1986, 1998c; Rohner & Chaki-Sircar, 1988) suggests that children and adults everywhere—regardless of differences in race, ethnicity, gender, or culture—tend to respond in essentially the same way when they experience themselves to be loved or unloved by their parents. The overwhelming bulk of research dealing with parental acceptance and rejection concentrates on mothers' behavior, however. Until recently, the possible influence of father love has been largely ignored. Here, I concentrate on evidence

showing the influence of fathers' love-related behaviors—or simply, *father love*—in relation to the social, emotional, and cognitive development and functioning of children, adolescents, and adult offspring. Moreover, I focus primarily, but not exclusively, on families for which information is available about both fathers and mothers—or about youths' perceptions of both their fathers' and mothers' parenting. My principal objective is to identify evidence about the relative contribution to offspring development of father love vis-à-vis mother love.

I define father love in terms of paternal acceptance and rejection as construed in parental acceptance-rejection theory (Rohner, 1986, in press). Paternal

acceptance includes such feelings and behaviors (or children's perceptions of such feelings and behaviors) as paternal nurturance, warmth, affection, support, comfort, and concern. Paternal rejection, on the other hand, is defined as the real or perceived absence or withdrawal of these feelings and behaviors. Rejection includes such feelings as coldness, indifference, and hostility toward the child. Paternal rejection may be expressed behaviorally as a lack of affection toward the child, as physical or verbal aggression, or as neglect. Paternal rejection may also be experienced in the form of undifferentiated rejection; that is, there may be situations in which individuals feel that their fathers (or significant male

From *Current Directions in Psychological Science*, October 1998, pp. 157-161. © 1998 by Ronald P. Rohner and the American Psychological Society. Reprinted by permission of Blackwell Publishers.

caregivers) do not really care about, want, or love them, even though there may not be observable behavioral indicators showing that the fathers are neglecting, unaffectionate, or aggressive toward them. Mother love (maternal acceptance-rejection) is defined in the same way.

# FATHERHOOD AND MOTHERHOOD ARE CULTURAL CONSTRUCTIONS

The widely held cultural construction of fatherhood in America—especially prior to the 1970s—has two strands. Historically, the first strand asserted that fathers are ineffective, often incompetent, and maybe even biologically unsuited to the job of child-rearing. (The maternal counterpoint to this is that women are genetically endowed for child care.) The second strand asserted that fathers' influence on child development is unimportant, or at the very most peripheral or indirect. (The maternal counterpoint here is that mother love and competent maternal care provide everything that children need for normal, healthy development.) Because researchers internalized these cultural beliefs as their own personal beliefs, fathers were essentially ignored by mainstream behavioral science until late in the 20th century. The 1970s through the 1990s, however, have seen a revolution in recognizing fathers and the influence of their love on child development. Three interrelated lines of influence I have discussed elsewhere (Rohner, 1998a) seem to account for this revolution. The net effect of these influences has been to draw attention to the fact that father love sometimes explains a unique, independent portion of the variation in specific child outcomes, over and above the portion explained by mother love. In fact, a few recent studies suggest that father love is the sole significant predictor of specific outcomes, after removing the influence of mother love.

# STUDIES SHOWING THE INFLUENCE OF FATHER LOVE

Six types of studies (discussed at greater length in Rohner, 1998a) demonstrate a strong association between father love and aspects of offspring development.

## Studies Looking Exclusively at Variations in the Influence of Father Love

Many of the studies looking exclusively at the influence of variations in father love deal with one of two topics: gender role development, especially of sons, and father involvement. Studies of gender role development emerged prominently in the 1940s and continued through the 1970s. Commonly, researchers assessed the masculinity of fathers and of sons, and then correlated the two sets of scores. Many psychologists were surprised at first to discover that no consistent results emerged from this research. But when they examined the quality of the father-son relationship, they found that if the relationship between masculine fathers and their sons was warm and loving, the boys were indeed more masculine. Later, however, researchers found that the masculinity of fathers per se did not seem to make much difference because "boys seemed to conform to the sex-role standards of their culture when their relationships with their fathers were warm, regardless of how 'masculine' the fathers were" (Lamb, 1997, p. 9).

Paternal involvement is the second domain in which there has been a substantial amount of research on the influence of variations in father love. Many studies have concluded that children with highly involved fathers, in relation to children with less involved fathers, tend to be more cognitively and socially competent, less inclined toward gender stereotyping, more empathic, psychologically better adjusted, and the like. But "caring for" children is not necessarily the same thing as "caring about" them. And a closer examination of these studies suggests that it was not the simple fact of paternal engagement (i.e., direct interaction with the child), availability, or responsibility for child care that was associated with these positive outcomes. Rather, it appears that the quality of the father-child relationship—especially of father love—makes the greatest difference (Lamb, 1997; Veneziano & Rohner, 1998).

## Father Love Is as Important as Mother Love

The great majority of studies in this category deal with one or a combination of the following four issues among children, adolescents, and young adults: (a) personality and psychological adjustment problems, including issues of self-concept and self-esteem, emotional

stability, and aggression; (b) conduct problems, especially in school; (c) cognitive and academic performance issues; and (d) psychopathology. Recent studies employing multivariate analyses have allowed researchers to conclude that fathers' and mothers' behaviors are sometimes each associated significantly and uniquely with these outcomes. The work of Young, Miller, Norton, and Hill (1995) is one of these studies. These authors employed a national sample of 640 12- to 16-year-olds living in two-parent families. They found that perceived paternal love and caring was as predictive of sons' and daughters' life satisfaction —including their sense of well-being—as was maternal love and caring.

## Father Love Predicts Specific Outcomes Better Than Mother Love

As complex statistical procedures have become more commonplace in the 1980s and 1990s, it has also become more common to discover that the influence of father love explains a unique, independent portion of the variation in specific child and adult outcomes, over and above the portion of variation explained by mother love. Studies drawing this conclusion tend to deal with one or more of the following four issues among children, adolescents, and young adults: (a) personality and psychological adjustment problems, (b) conduct problems, (c) delinquency, and (d) psychopathology. For example, evidence is mounting that fathers may be especially salient in the development of such forms of psychopathology as substance abuse (drug and alcohol use and abuse), depression and depressed emotion, and behavior problems, including conduct disorder and externalizing behaviors (including aggression toward people and animals, property destruction, deceitfulness, and theft) (Rohner, 1998c). Fathers are also being increasingly implicated in the etiology of borderline personality disorder (a pervasive pattern of emotional and behavioral instability, especially in interpersonal relationships and in self-image) and borderline personality organization (a less severe form of borderline personality disorder) (Fowler, 1990; Rohner & Brothers, in press).

Father love appears to be uniquely associated not just with behavioral and psychological problems, however, but also with health and well-being. Amato (1994), for example, found in a national sample that perceived closeness to fathers made a significant contribution—over and above the contribution made by perceived closeness to mothers—to adult sons' and daughters' happiness, life satisfaction, and low psychological distress (i.e., to overall psychological well-being).

## Father Love Is the Sole Significant Predictor of Specific Outcomes

In the 1990s, a handful of studies using a variety of multivariate statistics have concluded that father love is the sole significant predictor of specific child outcomes, after removing the influences of mother love. Most of these studies have dealt with psychological and behavioral problems of adolescents. For example, Cole and McPherson (1993) concluded that father-child conflict but not mother-child conflict (in each case, after the influence of the other was statistically controlled) was positively associated with depressive symptoms in adolescents. Moreover, father-adolescent cohesion was positively associated with the absence of depressive symptoms in adolescents. These results are consistent with Barrera and Garrison-Jones's (1992) conclusion that adolescents' satisfaction with fathers' support was related to a lowered incidence of depressive symptoms, whereas satisfaction with mothers' support was not. Barnett, Marshall, and Pleck (1992), too, found that when measures of the quality of both mother-son and father-son relationships were entered simultaneously into a regression equation, only the father-son relationship was related significantly to adult sons' psychological distress (a summed measure of anxiety and depression).

## Father Love Moderates the Influence of Mother Love

A small but growing number of studies have concluded that fathers' behavior moderates and is moderated by (i.e., interacts with) other influences within the family. Apparently, however, only one study so far has addressed the issue of whether mother love has different effects on specific child outcomes depending on the level of father love. This study, by Forehand and Nousiainen (1993), found that when mothers were low in acceptance, fathers' acceptance scores had no significant impact on youths' cognitive competence. But when mothers were high in acceptance, fathers' acceptance scores made a dramatic difference: Fathers with low acceptance scores tended to have children with poorer cognitive competence, whereas highly accepting fathers tended to have children with substantially better cognitive competence.

## Paternal Versus Maternal Parenting Is Sometimes Associated With Different Outcomes for Sons, Daughters, or Both

Many of the studies in this category were published in the 1950s and 1960s, and even earlier. Many of them may be criticized on methodological and conceptual grounds. Nonetheless, evidence suggests that serious research questions should be raised in the future about the possibility that associations between love-related parenting and child outcomes may depend on the gender of the parent and of the child. Three different kinds of studies tend to be found in this category.

First, some research shows that one pattern of paternal love-related behavior and a different pattern of maternal love-related behavior may be associated with a single outcome in sons, daughters, or both. For example, Barber and Thomas (1986) found that daughters' self-esteem was best predicted by their mothers' general support (e.g., praise and approval) but by their fathers' physical affection. Sons' self-esteem, however, was best predicted by their mothers' companionship (e.g., shared activities) and by their fathers' sustained contact (e.g., picking up the boys for safety or for fun).

Second, other research in this category shows that a single pattern of paternal love-related behavior may be associated with one outcome for sons and a different outcome for daughters. For example, Jordan, Radin, and Epstein (1975) found that paternal nurturance was positively associated with boys' but not girls' performance on an IQ test. Finally, the third type of research in this category shows that the influence of a single pattern of paternal love-related behaviors may be more strongly associated with a given outcome for one gender of offspring than for the other. For example, Eisman (1981) reported that fathers' love and acceptance correlated more highly with daughters' than with sons' self-concept.

## DISCUSSION

The data reported here are but a minuscule part of a larger body of work showing that father love is heavily implicated not only in children's and adults' psychological well-being and health, but also in an array of psychological and behavioral problems. This evidence punctuates the need to include fathers (and other significant males, when appropriate) as well as mothers in future research, and then to analyze separately the data for possible father and mother effects. It is only by separating data in this way that behavioral scientists can discern when and under what conditions paternal and maternal factors have similar or different effects on specific outcomes for children. This recommendation explicitly contradicts a call sometimes seen in published research to merge data about fathers' and mothers' parenting behaviors.

Finally, it is important to note several problems and limitations in the existing research on father love. For example, even though it seems unmistakably clear that father love makes an important contribution to offsprings' development and psychological functioning, it is not at all clear what generative mechanisms produce these contributions. In particular, it is unclear why father love is sometimes more strongly associated with specific offspring outcomes than is mother love. And it is unclear why patterns of paternal versus maternal parenting may be associated with different outcomes for sons, daughters, or children of both genders. It remains for future research to inquire directly about these issues. Until then, we can know only that father love is often as influential as mother love—and sometimes more so.

## Note

1. Address correspondence to Ronald P. Rohner, Center for the Study of Parental Acceptance and Rejection, School of Family Studies, University of Connecticut, Storrs, CT 06269–2058; e-mail: rohner@ uconnvm.uconn.edu or http://vm.uconn. edu/~rohner.

## References

Amato, P. R. (1994). Father-child relations, mother-child relations and offspring psychological well-being in adulthood. *Journal of Marriage and the Family, 56*, 1031–1042.

Barber, B. & Thomas, D. (1986). Dimensions of fathers' and mothers' supportive behavior: A case for physical affection. *Journal of Marriage and the Family, 48*, 783–794.

Barnett, R. C., Marshall, N. L., & Pleck, J. H. (1992). Adult son-parent relationships and the associations with sons' psychological distress. *Journal of Family Issues, 13*, 505–525.

Barrera, M., Jr., & Garrison-Jones, C. (1992). Family and peer social support as specific correlates of adolescent depressive symptoms. *Journal of Abnormal Child Psychology, 20*, 1–16.

Cole, D., & McPherson, A. E. (1993). Relation of family subsystems to adolescent depression: Implementing a new family assessment strategy. *Journal of Family Psychology, 7*, 119–133.

Eisman, E. M. (1981). Sex-role characteristics of the parent, parental acceptance of the child and child self-concept. (Doctoral dissertation, California School of Professional Psychology at Los Angeles, 1981). *Dissertation Abstracts International, 24,* 2062.

Forehand, R., & Nousiainen, S. (1993). Maternal and paternal parenting: Critical dimensions in adolescent functioning. *Journal of Family Psychology, 7,* 213–221.

Fowler, S. D. (1990). *Paternal effects on severity of borderline psychopathology.* Unpublished doctoral dissertation, University of Texas, Austin.

Jordan, B., Radin, N., & Epstein, A. (1975). Paternal behavior and intellectual functioning in preschool boys and girls. *Developmental Psychology, 11,* 407–408.

Lamb, M. E. (1997). Fathers and child development: An introductory overview and guide. In M. E. Lamb (Ed.), *The role of the father in child development* (pp. 1–18). New York: John Wiley & Sons.

Rohner, R. P. (1975). *They love me, they love me not: A worldwide study of the effects of parental acceptance and rejection.* New Haven, CT: HRAF Press.

Rohner, R. P. (1986). *The warmth dimension: Foundations of parental acceptance-rejection theory.* Newbury Park, CA: SAGE.

Rohner, R. P. (1998a). *The importance of father love: History and contemporary evidence.* Manuscript submitted for publication.

Rohner, R. P. (1998b). *Parental acceptance-rejection bibliography* [On-line]. Available: http://vm.unconn.edu/~rohner

Rohner, R. P. (1998c). *Worldwide mental health correlates of parental acceptance-rejection: Review of cross-cultural and intracultural evidence.* Manuscript submitted for publication.

Rohner, R. P. (in press). Acceptance and rejection. In D. Levinson, J. Ponzetti, & P. Jorgensen (Eds.), *Encyclopedia of human emotions.* New York: MacMillan.

Rohner, R. P., & Brothers, S. A. (in press). Perceived parental rejection, psychological maladjustment, and borderline personality disorder. *Journal of Emotional Abuse.*

Rohner, R. P., & Chaki-Sircar, M. (1988). *Women and children in a Bengali village.* Hanover, NH: University Press of New England.

Veneziano, R. A., & Rohner, R. P. (1998). Perceived paternal warmth, paternal involvement, and youths' psychological adjustment in a rural, biracial southern community. *Journal of Marriage and the Family, 60,* 335–343.

Young, M. H., Miller, B. E., Norton, M. C., & Hill, J. E. (1995). The effect of parental supportive behaviors on life satisfaction of adolescent offspring. *Journal of Marriage and the Family, 57,* 813–822.

## Recommended Reading

Biller, H. B. (1993). *Fathers and families: Paternal factors in child development.* Westport, CT: Auburn House.

Booth, A., & Crouter, A. C. (Eds.). (1998). *Men in families: When do they get involved? What difference does it make?* Mahwah, NJ: Erlbaum.

Lamb, M. E. (Ed.). (1997). *The role of the father in child development.* New York: John Wiley & Sons.

Rohner, R. P. (1986). (See References}

# The Parent Trap

Did you think that the way parents treat their children influences how they turn out? Think again, argues a controversial new book, which contends that parents matter a whole lot less than scientists believe. **By Sharon Begley**

SURELY THERE IS NO MORE CHERISHED, YET HUMbling, idea than the conviction that parents hold in their hands the power to shape their child's tomorrows. And the evidence for it is as impossible to ignore as the toddler throwing a tantrum in the grocery store when Daddy refuses to buy him M&Ms: setting reasonable, but firm, limits teaches children self-control and good behavior, but being either too permissive or too dictatorial breeds little brats. Giving your little girl a big hug when she skins her knee makes her feel loved and secure, which enables her to form trusting relationships when she blooms into a young woman. Reading and talking to children fosters a love of reading; divorce puts them at risk of depression and academic failure. Physical abuse makes them aggressive, but patience and kindness, as shown by the parents who soothe their child's frustration at not being able to play a favorite piano piece rather than belittling him, leaves a child better able to handle distress both in youth and in adulthood. Right?

Wrong, wrong and wrong again, contends Judith Rich Harris. In a new book, "The Nurture Assumption: Why Children Turn Out the Way They Do; Parents Matter Less Than You Think and Peers Matter More" (462 *pages. Free Press. $26*), Harris is igniting a bonfire of controversy for her central claim: the belief "that what influences children's development . . . is the way their parents bring

them up . . . is wrong." After parents contribute an egg or a sperm filled with DNA, she argues, virtually nothing they do or say—no kind words or hugs, slaps or tirades; neither permissiveness nor authoritarianism; neither encouragement nor scorn—makes a smidgen of difference to what kind of adult the child becomes. Nothing parents do will affect his behavior, mental health, ability to form relationships, sense of self-worth, intelligence or personality. What genes don't do, peers do.

Although Harris's book lists some 750 scientific papers, articles and books as references, maybe all she really had to do to reach this conclusion was keep good notes about the goings-on in her own suburban New Jersey colonial. Harris and her husband, Charles, had one daughter, Nomi, on New Year's Day, 1966, and adopted a second, Elaine, almost four years later. The girls grew up in the same home "filled to overflowing with books and magazines, where classical music was played, where jokes were told," recalls Harris. Both girls took ballet lessons; both learned the crawl at Mrs. Dee's Swim School. Both were read books by their parents and both delighted in birthday parties with homemade cake. Both experienced the sorrow and stress of a sick mother (Harris developed a mysterious autoimmune illness, part lupus and part systemic sclerosis, when Elaine was 6 and Nomi 10, and was often confined to bed). Yet Nomi was a well-behaved child who "didn't want to do anything

## Do This! Do That! A History of Advice to Parents

Over the last century, pediatricians and scientists who study child development have kept changing the advice that they give parents about the best way to rear children. Some of the major developments:

**The Early Years**

*Sigmund Freud concludes that early childhood shapes adult personality; the ills of adulthood are traceable to childhood. The English biologist Francis Galton uses the phrase "nature vs. nurture."*

**1890:** The first developmental psychologists become interested in studying childhood.

**1914:** "Infant Care," by the U.S. Children's Bureau, urges mothers to battle infants' bad impulses. (Thumb-sucking is disen-

couraged by "pinning sleeves" to beds.)

**1925:** Psychologist John Watson popularizes conditioning and "behaviorism," the idea that environment shapes children's development.

**1935:** Government starts welfare to ease poverty.

we didn't want her to do," says Harris over iced tea in her kitchen. Elaine, adopted at 2 months, was defiant by the age of 11. She angrily announced to her parents that she didn't have to listen to them. When they grounded her once, at 15, she left for school the next morning—and didn't come back that night. Nomi was a model student; Elaine dropped out of high school.

## On the effect of quality time:

'Parenting has been oversold. You have been led to believe that you have more of an influence on your child's personality than you really do.'

It made Harris wonder. Why was she having about as much influence on Elaine as the fluttering wings of a butterfly do on the path of a hurricane? And it made her mad. "All of these studies that supposedly show an influence of parents on children—they don't prove what they purport to," she fumes. Having floated this idea in the scientific journal Psychological Review in 1995, she has now turned it into a book that is becoming the publishing phenom of the season. This week Harris is scheduled for morning television shows, radio interviews and network magazine shows. The Free Press has gone back for a third printing after an initial run of 15,000, and her publicists say every author's dream—Oprah—may be in her future.

This petite, gray-haired grandmother hardly seems the type to be lobbing Molotov cocktails at one of the most dearly held ideas in all of child development. Harris, 60, has no academic affiliation and no Ph.D. In 1961, she was thrown out of Harvard University's graduate department of psychology because her professors believed she showed no ability to do important original research. She got a job writing psych textbooks. Yet in August, Harris shared a $500 prize from the American Psycho-

logical Association, for the paper that best integrates disparate fields of psychology. And she has some big guns on her side. Neuroscientist Robert Sapolsky of Stanford University says her book is "based on solid science." John Bruer, president of the James S. McDonnell Foundation, which funds education programs, praises it as "a needed corrective to this belief that early experiences between the child and parents have a deterministic, lifelong effect." And linguist Steven Pinker of the Massachusetts Institute of Technology predicts that "The Nurture Assumption" "will come to be seen as a turning point in the history of psychology."

So far, though, that's a minority view, and many scientists are nothing short of scathing. "I am embarrassed for psychology," says Harvard's Jerome Kagan, arguably one of the deans of child development. "She's all wrong," says psychologist Frank Farley of Temple University, president of the APA division that honored Harris. "She's taking an extreme position based on a limited set of data. Her thesis is absurd on its face, but consider what might happen if parents believe this stuff! Will it

## On smoking:

'The best predictor of whether a teenager will become a smoker is whether her friends smoke. This is a better predictor than whether her parents smoke.'

free some to mistreat their kids, since 'it doesn't matter'? Will it tell parents who are tired after a long day that they needn't bother even paying any attention to their kid since 'it doesn't matter'?" Psychologist Wendy Williams of Cornell University, who studies how environment affects IQ, argues that "there are many, many good studies that show parents can affect how children turn

### 1940s–1950s

*The baby boom begins and behaviorism dominates thinking.*

**1946:** Dr. Spock's "The Common Sense Book of Baby and Child Care" offers alternative to behaviorism.
**1952:** The research of French psychologist Jean Piaget shows distinct, pre-

dictable stages in the intellectual maturation of children.

### 1960s–1970s

*Studies show nurtured children are more likely to overcome the ills of poverty; Head Start and parent-education programs are started.*
**1969:** English psychiatrist John Bowlby shows babies

seek specific individuals for protection.

### 1980s–1990s

*Parenting advice focuses on strengthening children's emotional development through play. New brain-imaging techniques allow scientists to see how a baby's experience influences the brain's later development.*

**1996:** The federal welfare system is dismantled. Needy families that have children must now rely on the states.

**1997:** The Conference on Early Childhood Development and Learning publicizes the crucial first years of childhood.

RESEARCH BY BRET BEGUN

out in both cognitive abilities and behavior. By taking such an extreme position, Harris does a tremendous disservice."

In fact, neither scholars nor parents have always believed that parents matter. Sure, today rows upon rows of parent-advice books fill stores, parenting magazines clog newsstands, and new parents know the names Penelope Leach and T. Berry Brazelton better than they do their newborns'. But a leading tome on child development published in 1934 didn't even include a chapter on parents. It was only in the 1950s that researchers began to seek the causes of differences among children in the ways that parents raised them (time line). Now Harris is part of a growing backlash against the idea that parents can mold their child like Play-Doh.

With an impish wit and a chatty style, Harris spins a persuasive argument that the 1934 book got it right. Her starting point is behavioral genetics. This field examines how much of the differences between people reflect heredity, the genes they inherit from their parents. Over the years, researchers have concluded that variations in traits like impulsivity, aggression, thrill-seeking, neuroticism, intelligence, amiability and shyness are partly due to genes. "Partly" means anywhere from 20 to 70 percent. The other 30 to 80 percent reflects "environment." "Environment" means influences like an encounter with a

# Born to Win—With a Little Help

*Is there a magic formula for raising a successful child? Or is biology destiny? Some famous names talk about the people who made them what they are.*

## Frank McCourt

*Family was his inspiration*

I think Freud would laugh at the idea of parents' being irrelevant. I know I wasn't affected by my peers as much as by my family, because I went home and there was sitting by the fire and there was breaking of bread. Our experience was very intense. We got the gift of gab from our parents. Everybody told stories because there was nothing else. Son, mother, father, daughter: this is the stuff of literature. Every memoir I know is an exploration of family. It begins with the child at the breast. You can't deny that. You can't say the kid is looking over the mother's shoulder. The baby is completely absorbed in what it's getting from the mother. When can you say that

stops? Who is ever weaned?

## Jamie Lee Curtis

It's a little discouraging to be a parent, because often your efforts don't get you to the goal. The road to hell is paved with good intentions. All of our best intentions with our children often don't lead to the result we want. But I still believe in the process and learned behavior and exampled behavior. Parents are your first role models. I am the mother of adopted children, and I wouldn't deny the nature side of it, but I look at who these children are, and I know who me and my husband are has a lot to do with it. And that is all nurture. Nurture with bumps.

## Newt Gingrich

*A father's love of country*

The man I called "Dad" for half a century adopted me when I

was 3 years old. Even though he passed away two years ago, I still learn from his life and the example he set. It was from him that I first learned about duty and love of country. When I was 16, my parents and I visited the World War I battlefield of Verdun. Watching my father that day, I began to realize the depth of the words he lived by and what it meant that he was willing to die to preserve our country and her ideals. It is a moment I will never forget because it changed by life forever. A parent has tremendous power.

## Chastity Bono

The genetic part is absolutely true. My being more logical, being able to negotiate and educate, that is very similar to my dad. At his funeral, I had people that I had never met before saying to me that they found it almost ghostly how similar we were. I got my rebellious streak

from my mom. In me it's more controlled or subtle. Seeing both my parents achieve great things, having the guts to go for things: that was something I learned from them. When I was young, my mom started acting. That was a huge risk for her, and she was successful. It was the same with my dad and politics.

## Michael Jordan

I know that no one has had a greater impact on me than my parents. Their ethics and morals are my ethics and morals. It's funny, but you don't realize how much they mold until you get older and begin to see them in the things that you do. When I am talking to my kids, I often say things my father said to me or my brothers and sisters, and it hits me again that your parents consciously and unconsciously affect your every move. My father taught me responsibility and so many other things that

ully, a best-friendship that lasts decades, an inspiring math teacher. It also includes, you'd think, how your parents reared you. But Harris argues that "environment" includes a parental contribution of precisely zero (unless you count Mom and Dad's decision about which neighborhood to live in, which we'll get to later). When she says parents don't "matter," she means they do not leave a lasting effect—into adulthood. (She accepts that how parents treat a child affects how that child behaves at home, as well as whether the grown child regards the parents with love, resentment or anger.)

To reach her parents-don't-matter conclusion, Harris first demolishes some truly lousy studies that have become part of the scientific canon. A lot of research, for instance, concludes that divorce puts kids at greater risk of academic failure and problem behavior like drug use and drinking. Other studies claim to show that parents who treat their kids with love and respect, and who get along well with others, have children who also have successful personal relationships. Yet neither sort of study "proves the power of nurture at all," Harris says emphatically. Why? They do not take into account genetics. Maybe the reason some parents are loving or competent or prone to divorce or whatever is genetic. After all, being impulsive and aggressive makes you more likely to divorce; both tendencies are partly genetic, so maybe you

have helped me through a lot.

The peer pressure is a whole different thing today, and parents seem to have less control. The environment seems to shape kids more than family. I think that's the difference in a Grant Hill or a Kobe Bryant. Their families, and their fathers, had a great influence on their lives.

### Deloris Jordan

*Teaching Michael a lesson*

**W**hen Michael was about 13, he went off campus with some friends to get candy and got caught. The principal told us that he was expelled for going off campus. We decided Michael had to learn a lesson about following rules—not friends. So instead of letting him stay home and watch TV, I took him to work with me, left him in the car with his books and windows rolled down. My office was by the parking lot so I could see him, and he hated it.

But he never followed friends again.

### Will Smith

*Parents build self-esteem*

**I** think the reason I've been successful is my family. A lot of people are really unsure whether or not someone loves them. That puts you in a really weird mental place, if you can't point to one person or two people and say, "I know for a *fact* that they love me." There's a certain level of confidence that comes from knowing for a fact that someone loves you. And my parents always made us feel like we were good. From that, succeeding is just, all right, how can I let the world know?

### Cokie Roberts

**I** certainly agree that genes have a great deal to do with it. What's always striking to parents who have more than one child is that children are who they

are from the moment they appear, and you get to know their personalities very quickly. They are very different from each other, and that clearly started before the nurturing began. But I also think that children who have attentive parents learn from their parents all kinds of behavior. Everything from good table manners—which count, by the way—to how to be a good husband or wife. I think children take their examples from their parents even when they don't realize they're doing it. Raise children you like because if you don't like them, nobody else will, and you're going to have to spend the rest of your life with them. Teach them to be likable.

### Rosie O'Donnell
*Adoption is just the beginning*

**Y**ou're born with a personality that's defined by the tenderness, love, support and care you're given. My 3-year-old son, who is

growing up in my family with the values that I show him through example, is so similar to me. And I don't think that's a coincidence. He's learned to quote "The Lion King." I laugh and encourage him. Children could just be born and put in day care and become who they are. But that negates the value of love.

### Mia Farrow

**I** recently lost my mother, and it was one of the hardest things I've ever gone through. I could never minimize or discount what she gave to me. My mother gave me everything that's best in me. All of my survival skills. I went into the same profession. My mom was in my corner cheering me on or providing a shoulder to cry on, loving me unconditionally throughout my life. How can that be minimized? Peers are fickle, and so are spouses. They can leave. But most parents are there for life.

passed them on to your kids. Then it's their genes, and not seeing their parents' marriage fail, that explain the kids' troubles, Harris claims. And if being patient and agreeable makes you more likely to be a loving and patient parent, and if you pass that nice DNA to your kids, then again it is the genes and not the parenting that made the kids nice.

Do your own eyes tell you that being a just-right disciplinarian—not too strict, not too easy—teaches children limits and self-control? Not so fast. Harris points out that children, through their innate temperament, can elicit a particular parenting style. For example, a little hellion will likely make her parents first impatient and then angry and then resigned. It isn't parental anger and resignation that made the kid, say, a runaway and a dropout. Rather, the child's natural, genetic tendencies made her parents behave a certain way; those same tendencies made her a runaway and a dropout. Again, argues Harris, not the parents' fault. By this logic, of course, parents don't get credit, either. You think reading to your toddler made her an academic star? Uh-uh, says Harris. Maybe kids get read to more if they *like* to get read to. If so, liking books is also what makes them good in school, not listening to "Goodnight Moon."

Studies of twins seem to support Harris's demotion of parents. "[I]dentical twins reared in the same home," says Harris," . . . are no more alike than identical twins separated in infancy and reared in different homes." Apparently, being reared by the same parents did nothing to increase twins' alikeness. Same with siblings. "[B]eing reared by the same parents [has] little or no effect on [their] adult personalities," writes Harris. "The genes they share can entirely account for any resemblances between them; there are no leftover similarities for the shared environment to explain." By "shared environment," she means things like parents' working outside the home, battling constantly, being dour or affectionate. A son might be a cold fish like Dad, or react against him and become a warm puppy. "If children can go either way, turning out like their parents or going in the opposite direction," says Harris, "then what you are saying is that parents have no predictable effects on their children. You are saying that *this* parenting style does not produce *this* trait in the adult."

What Harris offers in place of this "nurture assumption" is the idea that peer groups teach children how to behave out in the world. A second-grade girl identifies with second-grade girls and adopts the behavioral norms of that group. Kids model themselves on other kids, "taking on [the group's] attitudes, behaviors, speech, and styles of dress and adornment," Harris says. Later, a child gravitates toward the studious kids or the mischief makers or whomever. Because people try to become more similar to members of their group and more distinct from members of other groups, innate differences get magnified. The jock becomes jockier, the good student more studious. This all begins in elementary school.

## On divorce:

'Heredity . . . makes the children of divorce more likely to fail in their own marriages. . . . Parental divorce has no lasting effects on the way children behave when they're not at home.'

Harris's bottom line: "The world that children share with their peers determines the sort of people they will be when they grow up."

Is there no way parents can shape their children? Harris offers this: have enough money to live in a good neighborhood so your children associate with only the "right" peers. Dress your sons and daughters in the fashions of the moment so they are not ostracized. If their appearance is so odd that they are in danger of being shunned, spring for orthodontia. Or, Harris writes, "if you can afford it, or your health insurance will cover it, plastic surgery."

No one denies that there is *some* truth to her argument. Even her detractors like the way she's blown the lid off dumb studies that can't tell the difference between parents' influencing their kids through genes and influencing them through actions. And they applaud her for pointing out that children of divorce are not necessarily ruined for life, notes psychologist Robert Emery of the University of Virginia. But many of the nation's leading scholars of child development accuse Harris of screwy logic, of misunderstanding behavioral genetics and of ignoring studies that do not fit her thesis. Exhibit A: the work of Harvard's Kagan. He has shown how different parenting styles can shape a timid, shy child who perceives the world as a threat. Kagan measured babies at 4 months and at school age. The fearful children whose parents (over)protected them were still timid. Those whose parents pushed them to try new things—"get into that sandbox and play with the other kids, dammit!"—lost their shyness. A genetic legacy of timidity was shaped by parental behavior, says Kagan, "and these kids became far less fearful."

"Intervention" studies—where a scientist gets a parent to act differently—also undercut Harris. "These show that if you change the behavior of the parents you change the behavior of the kids, with effects outside the home," says John Gottman of the University of Washington. Programs that teach parents how to deal with little monsters produce effects that last for years. "When parents learn how to talk to and listen to kids with the worst aggression and behavior problems, and to deal with the kids' emotions," says Gottman, "the kid becomes less impulsive, less aggressive, and does better in school." Maybe such effects are picked up in the studies Harris cites because such motivated—dare we say saintly?—parents are so rare. Gottman studies children at the age of 4, and then at 8. Some have parents who learned to be good "emotion coaches." They're sensitive, they validate the child's emotion ("I understand, sweetie"), they help her verbalize what she's feeling, they patiently involve her in solving the problem ("What should we do?"). Other parents didn't learn these tough skills. The 8-year-olds of emotionally adept parents can focus their attention better and relate better to other kids. "There is a very strong relationship between parenting style and the social competence of their children," says Gottman. Since the parents learned to be emotion coaches, and the kids changed over the years, the results cannot be easily dismissed as genetic (emotionally intelligent parents pass on emotional-IQ genes).

Critics also slam Harris's interpretation of twins studies. From this research she concludes that "parents do not make siblings any more alike than their genes already made them. . . . [P]arenting has no influence." But some of the leaders in the field say their measurements cannot support that. "The sample sizes we use are so small that you can't detect a 10 percent or even a 20 percent effect of the family environment," says Dr. Kenneth Kendler of the Medical College of Virginia. And as Kagan points out, the vast majority of such studies rely on questionnaires to assess personality, recollections of childhood and descriptions of what goes on in the home. "Questionnaires are totally suspect," Kagan says. "The correlation between reality and what people say is just 30 or 40 percent." Such flaws could be why twin studies fail to detect an influence of parents on kids.

Finally, some researchers take issue with Harris's logic. This one is tricky, but crucial. Harris says studies of twins and siblings find no effect of "shared environment." True. But even children who grow up with the same parents do not have an identical environment. The firstborn does not have the same "environment" as her baby brother: she has younger, less experienced parents, and no midget competitors. Also, parents treat children differently, as Harris admits: she monitored Elaine's homework but not Nomi's. Children, through their innate temperament, elicit different behaviors from their parents; thus they do not share this environment called "parents." Parents, then, arguably belong in the category called "unshared environment"—which behavioral genetics suggests accounts for about half the differences

among people. And besides, even what seems like an identical parenting style may be received differently by different children. One may conform, the other rebel. That does not mean that parents did not influence what their children became. It means that we are not smart enough to figure out *how* parents shape their child. Says psychologist Theodore Wachs of Purdue University, "The data do show that the same [parenting] does not have the *same* effect on kids. But that doesn't mean there is *no* effect."

In person, Harris backs off a bit from her absolutist stance. "I do think there is something to the possibility that parents determine their child's peer group, and children do learn things at home which they take to the peer group," she told NEWSWEEK. She allows that children can retain many of the values and other lessons parents teach despite peer influences. "If the group doesn't care about plans for the future, then the child can retain those ideas from home," she says. "And if things like an interior life aren't discussed by peers, then that wouldn't be affected by the group either." Might different children experience the same parenting differently, and be influenced by it? Harris pauses a few seconds. "I can't eliminate that as a possibility," she says. As for her own daughter, yes, Elaine was a handful and a heartache. But she is now married, a mother and a nurse in New Jersey—and close to her parents.

If "The Nurture Assumption" acts as a corrective to the hectoring message of so many books on child rearing, then it will have served a noble function. It lands at a time when many parents are terrified that failing to lock eyes with their newborn or not playing Mozart in the nursery or—God forbid—losing it when their kid misbehaves will ruin him for life. One of Harris's "primary motivations for writing the book," she says in an e-mail was "to lighten the burden of guilt and blame placed on the parents of 'problem' children." Her timing is perfect: millions of baby boomers, having blamed Mom and Dad for all that ails them, can now be absolved of blame for how their own children turn out. Harris is already receiving their thanks. As one mother wrote, "We parents of the difficult children need all the support and understanding we can get." Clearly, the idea that actions have consequences, that behavior matters and that there is such a thing as personal responsibility to those who trust you is fighting for its life. Near the end of "The Nurture Assumption," Harris bemoans the "tendency to carry things to extremes, to push ideas beyond their logical limits." Everyone who cares about children can only hope that readers bring the same skepticism.

*With* ERIKA CHECK

FOCUS ON

## Your Family

# Kids Who Don't Fit In

**Researchers say that good social skills are critical to success and happiness. How can parents help children who are left out? BY PAT WINGERT**

THE FIRST SIGN OF A PROBLEM WAS 3-year-old William's refusal to hold hands with other children. As he moved through preschool, he made friends but didn't keep them. By first grade, he was isolated and lonely. The other kids, his mother admits, "thought he was weird." William (not his real name) was painfully aware there was a problem. "He'd ask me, 'Why don't the kids like me?' " his mother recalls. Third grade was a crisis; William was falling apart. "His teacher pulled us in and said, 'He's always crying at school and walking around the periphery of the playground. You should have him tested'."

*You should have him tested.* That advice is echoed in classrooms around the country as more and more teachers and parents understand the importance of developing good social skills. Researchers now know that success in life—personal happiness, too—depends to a great degree on an individual's "emotional intelligence," the ability to function well in a group and to form meaningful relationships. "Children who are generally disliked, who are aggressive and disruptive, who are unable to sustain close relationships with other children and who cannot establish a place for themselves in the peer culture are seriously at risk," says psychologist Willard Hartup of the University of Minnesota. That's why kids like William, who run into trouble early, are getting the help they need at an age when the right therapy can really make a difference.

Sometimes the problem is just awkwardness; in other cases, there can be real neurological deficits. In William's case, test results revealed that he was suffering from attention deficit disorder and an inability to read social cues. "He didn't know where his personal space ended and someone else's space began," his mother says. "He couldn't read facial expressions. Sometimes he was nonresponsive when people were talking directly to him. He talked at people, and didn't laugh at the right time."

For three years William attended weekly group therapy, where he would play with other kids with similar problems while the therapist gently prompted and corrected his interactions. He also met with a psychologist for one-on-one help. Now in eighth grade, he continues with individual therapy. He's still "not Mr. Popularity," his mom says, but "he has friends."

Experts agree that the earlier the intervention, the more effective the therapy. But evaluating very young children can be tricky. Many psychologists believe children develop social competence at different rates—just as some children are slow to walk or talk. "On the one hand it's encouraging that more children are getting help early on, " says Jan Wintrol, director of the Ivymount School in suburban Maryland, which diagnoses social, emotional and behavioral problems. "On the other hand, I get concerned about an overemphasis: we think we have to have therapy for everything."

So how does a parent know whether to worry about a kid who's always alone on the playground? The experts advise parents to watch, compare, consult with teachers and, in the end, trust their instincts.

The first hint of trouble often shows up when children are preverbal, between 12 and 24 months, says psychiatrist Stanley Greenspan, author of "The Growth of the Mind." At this stage, children typically "learn to use gestures to get their needs met and express their emotions." Most toddlers learn this automatically. Kids who don't master this skill may also fail to develop in other ways. Parents might begin to notice that their child isn't interacting the way other children do or that playmates avoid their child. Marshall Duke and Steve Nowicki Jr., psychology professors at Emory University and authors of "Helping the Child Who Doesn't Fit In," call this condition "dyssemia." The abilities to interpret and use nonverbal cues "are the building blocks of social skills," Nowicki says.

Tests can reveal that a child is unable to read facial expressions, body language or tone of voice. Other children can't get their bodies and faces to express the right emotions. And some children can do neither. Some stand much too close to people, or touch them inappropriately. They may talk way too loud—or so softly they can't be heard. They may laugh or cry or get angry at the wrong times, or seem to be talking at people rather than conversing with them. "These are the kind of rules that you only notice when they get broken," Duke says.

Some of these kids may have a brain processing problem that makes it difficult for them to sequence or put their thoughts into action. Others may have a speech disability or a form of autism or developmental problems. Some problems may be aggravated by learning disabilities or attention deficit disorder. Others simply haven't had enough experience interacting with people. Children with depressed, alcoholic or drug-using parents can exhibit the same problems, as can youngsters who are not getting enough one-on-one attention from busy parents or overworked child-care providers. Duke and Nowicki's studies indicate that about 10 percent of children have some form of dyssemia. If those estimates are right, that would be equal to double the number of children who have been diagnosed with attention deficit disorder.

TO FIND THE RIGHT KIND OF HELP, parents can start by asking teachers, the school psychologist or an educational counselor. Some kids join "social skill groups" like William's with other children and a trained therapist acting almost as a coach. Others seek help through family or one-on-one counseling. Some therapists act primarily as consultants, observing a kid's behavior at home and in

# The Edge of Kindness

## A veteran kindergarten teacher on what she's learned

VIVIAN PALEY NEVER MISSES the opportunity to tell the tale of Teddy. She was visiting a London preschool when some kids from a nearby school for the severely disabled came to visit. Teddy was pushed into the classroom in a wheelchair, his head protected by a padded helmet, his limbs twitching. Paley watched in wonder as the small children incorporated Teddy—who had trouble speaking more than a word at a time—into their play. To Paley, 70, a longtime Chicago kindergarten teacher and the winner of a MacArthur Fellowship for her writing about children, that moment inspired an insightful new book, "The Kindness of Children." In an interview with NEWSWEEK's Pat Wingert, Paley talked about how adults can nurture empathy.

**WINGERT: Do you think children are always ready to be kind?**
PALEY: Yes, even when they're in a snit. You may have to wait a little and not push. But out of the side of their eye they may see someone, maybe even the child they were fighting with, with a trembling lip, and their eyes filling, and something says to them: "Stop. Do something nice now. This has gone too far." I believe children are always on the edge of committing an act of kindness, always ready to go in that direction.

**By sharing stories of kindness, can we inspire children?**
When children hear a story about kindness, they are very moved. From our earliest school years, we know all we need to know about hurt feelings and how to help someone salvage hurt feelings.

**When does the earliest kindness appear in children?**
Even very young children are moved when they see a baby or a friend crying, and they'll go pull their teacher to help. No one has taught this. No one has said to these 18-month-olds, "If you see any human being struggling or suffering, call me right away."

**Do you think young children are naturally more accepting than older children or adults?**
Absolutely. I've never seen a young child be anything other than very interested in what other children look like, do, say, how they behave—they're fascinated. They have a tremendous, almost scientific interest in each other.

**Is that why you've become such an advocate of diversity?**
When children with problems come into a regular classroom, there are more opportunities for children and teachers to show kindness. Acting out kindness makes us realize what we're capable of. It feels good to be in power, but it feels terrific to see yourself as the giver of kindness.

**You say play helps create a "new life for a wandering soul." What do you mean?**
The lonely child only lacks a role to play because play is the language of children. Play is a story. We don't hear the story when kids are in the sandbox, but we could almost write the story from the noises we hear coming out of it. Play was a brilliant invention of whoever created mankind.

**You say loneliness is the major struggle when children first enter school. Does that experience foster empathy?**
Every child knows loneliness. But because I have been lonely, do I recognize the plight of others who are lonely? That's more subtle, and that's where the artistry comes in, where the modelling comes in. I can't imagine a greater source of satisfaction for a teacher.

**How do you help children who don't know how to play?**
If I saw a child running through the block like a whirlwind and knocking everything down, I would ask the child to sit with me and watch others who find it easy to play well with others. The class then becomes a kind of laboratory where you can point out what works.

**How does the kindness of children inspire us as adults?**
It gives me joy as a teacher to be a witness to these things. It gives me the strength to deal with that other side of life, when people are wounded and disencouraged.

---

school and then advising teachers and parents.

Children struggle with these problems at all ages. Maryland pediatrician Sharon Goldman says she has one new patient who's a senior in high school. "She's never gone on a date," Goldman says. "She's never hung out at the mall with friends. She's so exquisitely afraid of how others will view her that she has no friends. She needs to learn to do these things before she goes off to college by herself."

It's never too late to get that help; some therapists who specialize in social skills work only with adults, and others even consult with corporations that are having difficulties with employees. But children benefit the most. Intervention can help kids with mild to moderate social problems have a normal social life. Those with more severe problems may always be a little stiff or quirky in their social exchanges, but with help they have a much better chance of being able to relate to others. As William's mom says, "This stuff doesn't just disappear. But he's going up the ladder. He's going in the right direction." And his future looks a lot less lonely.

# The Effects of Poverty on Children

Jeanne Brooks-Gunn
Greg J. Duncan

*Jeanne Brooks-Gunn,
Ph.D., is Virginia and
Leonard Marx profes-
sor of child develop-
ment and education,
and is director of the
Center for Young Child-
ren and Families at
Teachers College, Co-
lumbia University.*

*Greg J. Duncan, Ph.D.,
is a professor of edu-
cation and social pol-
icy, and is a faculty
associate at the Insti-
tute for Policy Re-
search, Northwestern
University.*

## Abstract

Although hundreds of studies have documented the association between family poverty and children's health, achievement, and behavior, few measure the effects of the timing, depth, and duration
of poverty on children, and many fail to adjust for other family
characteristics (for example, female headship, mother's age, and
schooling) that may account for much of the observed correlation
between poverty and child outcomes. This article focuses on a recent set of studies that explore the relationship between poverty
and child outcomes in depth. By and large, this research supports
the conclusion that family income has selective but, in some instances, quite substantial effects on child and adolescent well-being.
Family income appears to be more strongly related to children's
ability and achievement than to their emotional outcomes. Children
who live in extreme poverty and who live below the poverty line
for multiple years appear, all other things being equal, to suffer the
worst outcomes. The timing of poverty also seems to be important
for certain child outcomes. Children who experience poverty during
their preschool and early school years have lower rates of school
completion than children and adolescents who experience poverty
only in later years. Although more research is needed on the significance of the timing of poverty on child outcomes, findings to
date suggest that interventions during early childhood may be most
important in reducing poverty's impact on children.

In recent years, about one in five American children—some
12 to 14 million—have lived in families in which cash income failed to exceed official poverty thresholds. Another
one-fifth lived in families whose incomes were no more than
twice the poverty threshold.[1,2] For a small minority of children—4.8% of all children and 15% of children who ever
became poor—childhood poverty lasted 10 years or more.[3]

From *The Future of Children,* Summer/Fall 1997, pp. 55-71. © 1997 by the Center for the Future of Children of the David and
Lucile Packard Foundation. Reprinted by permission. *The Future of Children* journals and executive summaries are available free
of charge by faxing mailing information to: Circulation Department (650) 948-6498.

Income poverty is the condition of not having enough income to meet basic needs for food, clothing, and shelter. Because children are dependent on others, they enter or avoid poverty by virtue of their family's economic circumstances. Children cannot alter family conditions by themselves, at least until they approach adulthood. Government programs, such as those described by Devaney, Ellwood, and Love in this journal issue, have been developed to increase the likelihood that poor children are provided basic necessities. But even with these programs, poor children do not fare as well as those whose families are not poor.[4]

What does poverty mean for children? How does the relative lack of income influence children's day-to-day lives? Is it through inadequate nutrition; fewer learning experiences; instability of residence; lower quality of schools; exposure to environmental toxins, family violence, and homelessness; dangerous streets; or less access to friends, services, and, for adolescents, jobs? This article reviews recent research that used longitudinal data to examine the relationship between income low-poverty and child outcomes in several domains.

Hundreds of studies, books, and reports have examined the detrimental effects of poverty on the well-being of children. Many have been summarized in recent reports such as *Wasting America's Future* from the Children's Defense Fund and *Alive and Well?* from the National Center for Children in Poverty.[5] However, while the literature on the effects of poverty on children is large, many studies lack the precision necessary to allow researchers to disentangle the effects on children of the array of factors associated with poverty. Understanding of these relationships is key to designing effective policies to ameliorate these problems for children.

This article examines these relationships and the consequences for children of growing up poor. It begins with a long, but by no means exhaustive, list of child outcomes (see Table 1) that have been found to be associated with poverty in several large, nationally representative, cross-sectional surveys. This list makes clear the broad range of effects poverty can have on children. It does little, however, to inform the discussion of the causal effects of income poverty on children because the studies from which this list is derived did not control for other variables associated with poverty. For example, poor families are more likely to be headed by a parent who is single, has low educational attainment, is unemployed, has low earning potential and is young. These parental attributes, separately or in combination, might

account for some of the observed negative consequences of poverty on children. Nor do the relationships identified in the table capture the critical factors of the timing, depth, and duration of childhood poverty on children.[6,7]

This article focuses on studies that used national longitudinal data sets to estimate the effects of family income on children's lives, independent of other family conditions that might be related to growing up in a low-income household. These studies attempt to isolate the effect of family income by taking into account, statistically, the effects of maternal age at the child's birth, maternal education, marital status, ethnicity, and other factors on child outcomes.[2,8] Many used data on family income over several years and at different stages of development to estimate the differential effects of the timing and duration of poverty on child outcomes. The data sets analyzed include the Panel Study of Income Dynamics (PSID), the National Longitudinal Survey of Youth (NLSY), Children of the NLSY (the follow-up of the children born to the women in the original NLSY cohort), the National Survey of Families and Households (NSFH), the National Health and Nutrition Examination Survey (NHANES), and the Infant Health and Development Program (IHDP). These rich data sets include multiple measures of child outcomes and family and child characteristics.

This article is divided into four sections. The first focuses on the consequences of poverty across five child outcomes. If income does, in fact, affect child outcomes, then it is important not only to identify these outcomes but also to describe the pathways through which income operates. Accordingly, in the second section, five pathways through which poverty might operate are described. The third section focuses on whether the links between poverty and outcomes can reasonably be attributed to income rather than other family characteristics. The concluding section considers policy implications of the research reviewed.

## Effects of Income on Child Outcomes

### Measures of Child Well-Being

As illustrated in Table 1, poor children suffer higher incidences of adverse health, developmental, and other outcomes than non-poor children. The specific dimensions of the well-being of children and youths considered in some detail in this article include (1) physical health (low birth weight, growth stunting, and lead poisoning), (2) cognitive ability (intelligence, verbal ability, and achievement test scores), (3) school achievement

## Table 1

## Selected Population-Based Indicators of Well-Being for Poor and Nonpoor Children in the United States

| Indicator | Percentage of Poor Children (unless noted) | Percentage of Nonpoor Children (unless noted) | Ratio of Poor to Nonpoor Children |
|---|---|---|---|
| **Physical Health Outcomes** (for children between 0 and 17 years unless noted) | | | |
| Reported to be in excellent health[a] | 37.4 | 55.2 | 0.7 |
| Reported to be in fair to poor health[a] | 11.7 | 6.5 | 1.8 |
| Experienced an accident, poisoning, or injury in the past year that required medical attention[a] | 11.8 | 14.7 | 0.8 |
| Chronic asthma[a] | 4.4 | 4.3 | 1.0 |
| Low birth weight (less than 2,500 grams)[b] | 1.0 | 0.6 | 1.7 |
| Lead poisoning (blood lead levels 10u/dl or greater)[c] | 16.3 | 4.7 | 3.5 |
| Infant mortality[b] | 1.4 deaths per 100 live births | 0.8 death per 100 live births | 1.7 |
| Deaths During Childhood (0 to 14 years)[d] | 1.2 | 0.8 | 1.5 |
| Stunting (being in the fifth percentile for height for age for 2 to 17 years)[e] | 10.0 | 5.0 | 2.0 |
| Number of days spent in bed in past year[a] | 5.3 days | 3.8 days | 1.4 |
| Number of short-stay hospital episodes in past year per 1,000 children[a] | 81.3 stays | 41.2 stays | 2.0 |
| **Cognitive Outcomes** | | | |
| Developmental delay (includes both limited and long-term developmental deficits) (0 to 17 years)[a] | 5.0 | 3.8 | 1.3 |
| Learning disability (defined as having exceptional difficulty in learning to read, write, and do arithmetic) (3 to 17 years)[a] | 8.3 | 6.1 | 1.4 |
| **School Achievement Outcomes** (5 to 17 years) | | | |
| Grade repetition (reported to have ever repeated a grade)[a] | 28.8 | 14.1 | 2.0 |
| Ever expelled or suspended[a] | 11.9 | 6.1 | 2.0 |
| High school dropout (percentage 16- to 24-year olds who were not in school or did not finish high school in 1994)[f] | 21.0 | 9.6 | 2.2 |
| **Emotional or Behavioral Outcomes** (3 to 17 years unless noted) | | | |
| Parent reports child has ever had an emotional or behavioral problem that lasted three months or more[g] | 16.4 | 12.7 | 1.3 |
| Parent reports child ever being treated for an emotional problem or behavioral problem[a] | 2.5 | 4.5 | 0.6 |
| Parent reports child has experienced one or more of a list of typical child behavioral problems in the last three months[h] (5 to 17 years) | 57.4 | 57.3 | 1.0 |
| **Other** | | | |
| Female teens who had an out-of-wedlock birth[i] | 11.0 | 3.6 | 3.1 |
| Economically inactive at age 24 (not employed or in school)[j] | 15.9 | 8.3 | 1.9 |
| Experienced hunger (food insufficiency) at least once in past year[k] | 15.9 | 1.6 | 9.9 |
| Reported cases of child abuse and neglect[l] | 5.4 | 0.8 | 6.8 |
| Violent crimes (experienced by poor families and nonpoor families)[m] | 5.4 | 2.6 | 2.1 |

(years of schooling, high school completion), (4) emotional and behavioral outcomes, and (5) teenage out-of-wedlock childbearing. Other outcomes are not addressed owing to a scarcity of available research, a lack of space, and because they overlap with included outcomes.

While this review is organized around specific outcomes, it could also have been organized around the various ages of childhood.[9–11] Five age groups are often distinguished—prenatal to 2 years, early childhood (ages 3 to 6), late childhood (ages 7 to 10), early adolescence (ages 11

| Indicator | Percentage of Poor Children (unless noted) | Percentage of Nonpoor Children (unless noted) | Ratio of Poor to Nonpoor Children |
|---|---|---|---|
| Afraid to go out (percentage of family heads in poor and nonpoor families who report they are afraid to go out in their neighborhood)[n] | 19.5 | 8.7 | 2.2 |

Note: This list of child outcomes reflects findings from large, nationally representative surveys that collect data on child outcomes and family income. While most data comes from the 1988 National Health Interview Survey Child Health Supplement, data from other nationally representative surveys are included. The rates presented are from simple cross-tabulations. In most cases, the data do not reflect factors that might be important to child outcomes other than poverty status at the time of data collection. The ratios reflect rounding.

[a] Data from the 1988 National Health Interview Survey Child Health Supplement (NHS-CHS), a nationwide household interview survey. Children's health status was reported by the adult household member who knew the most about the sample child's health, usually the child's mother. Figures calculated from Dawson, D.A. *Family structure and children's health: United States, 1988.* Vital Health and Statistics, Series 10, n0. 178. Hyattsville, MD: U.S. Department of Health and Human Services, Public Health Service, June 1991; and Coiro, M.J., Zill, n., and Bloom, B. *Health of our nation's children.* Vital Health and Statistics, Series 10, n0. 191. Hyattsville, MD: U.S. department of Health and Human sErvices, Public Health Service, December 1994.

[b] Data from the National Maternal and Infant Health Survey, data collected in 1989 and 1990, with 1988 as the reference period. Percentages were calculated from the number of deaths and number of low birth weight births per 1,000 live births as reported in Federman, M., Garner, T., Short, K., et al. What does it mean to be poor in America? *Monthly Labor Review* (May 1996) 119, 5:10.

[c] Data from the NHANES III, 1988–1991. Poor children who lived in families with incomes less than 130% of the poverty threshold are classified as poor. All other children are classified as nonpoor.

[d] Percentages include only black and white youths. Percentages calculated from Table 7 in Rogot, E. *A mortality study of 1.3 million persons by demographic, social and economic factors: 1979–1985 follow-up.* Rockville, MD: National Institutes of Health, July 1992.

[e] Data from NHANES II, 1976–1980. For more discussion, see the Child Indicators article in this journal issue.

[f] National Center for Education Statistics. *Dropout rates in the United States: 1994.* Table 7, Status dropout rate, ages 16–24, by income and race ethnicity: October 1994. Available online at: http://www.ed.gov/NCES/pubs/r9410†07.html.

[g] Data from the NHIS-CHS. The question was meant to identify children with common psychological disorders such as attention deficit disorder or depression, as well as more severe problems such as autism.

[h] Data from the NHIS-CHS. Parents responded "sometimes true," "often true,", or "not true" to a list of 32 statements typical of children's behaviors. Each statement corresponded to one of six individual behavior problems—antisocial behavior, anxiety, peer conflict/social withdrawal, dependency, hyperactivity, and headstrong behavior. Statements included behaviors such as cheating or lying, being disobedient in the home, being secretive, and demanding a lot of attention. For a more complete description, see Section P-11 of the NHIS-CHS questionnaire.

[i] Data from the Panel Study of Income Dynamics (PSID). Based on 1,705 children ages 0 to 6 in 1968; outcomes measured at ages 21 to 27. Haveman, R., and Wolfe, B. Succeeding generations: On the effect of investments in children. New York: Russel Sage Foundation, 1994, p. 108, Table 4, 10c.

[j] Data from the PSID. Based on 1,705 children ages 0 to 6 in 1968; outcomes measured at ages 21 to 27. In Succeeding generations: On the effect of investments in children. Haveman, R., and Wolfe, B. New York: Russel Sage Foundation, 1994, p. 108, Table 4, 10d. Economically inactive is defined as not being a full-time student, working 1,000 hours or more per year; attending school part time and working 500 hours; a mother of an infant or mother of two or more children less than five years old; a part-time student and the mother of a child less than five years old.

[k] Data from NHANES III, 1988–1991. Figures reflect food insufficiency, the term used in government hunger-related survey questions. For a more in-depth discussion, see Lewit, E.M., and Kerrebrock, N. Child indicators: Childhood hunger. *The Future of Children* (Spring 1997), 7, 1:128–37.

[l] Data from Study of National Incidence and Prevalence of Child Abuse and Neglect: 1988. In *Wasting America's future.* Children's Defense Fund. Boston: Beacon Press, 1994, pp. 5–29, 87, Tables 5–6. Poor families are those with annual incomes below $15,000.

[m] Data from the National Crime Victimization Interview Survey. Results are for households or persons living in households. Data were collected between January 1992 and June 1993 with 1992 as the reference period. Percentages are calculated from number of violent crimes per 1,000 people per year. Reported in Federman, M., Garner, T., Short, K., et al. What does it mean to be poor in America? *Monthly Labor Review.* (May 1996) 119,5:9.

[n] Data from the Survey of Income and Program Participation. Participation data collection and reference periods are September through December 1992. Reported in Federman, M., Garner, T., Short, K., et al. What does it mean to be poor in America? *Monthly Labor Review* (May 1996) 119,5:9.

to 15), and late adolescence (ages 16 to 19). Each age group covers one or two major transitions in a child's life, such as school entrances or exits, biological maturation, possible cognitive changes, role changes, or some combination of these. These periods are characterized by relatively uni-versal developmental challenges that require new modes of adaptation to biological, psychological, or social changes.[10]

Somewhat different indicators of child and youth well-being are associated with each period. For example, grade retention is more salient in the late childhood years than in adolescence (since most schools do not hold students back once they reach eighth grade[12]). Furthermore, low income might influence each indicator differently. As an illustration, income has stronger effects on cognitive and verbal ability test scores than it has on indices of emotional health in the childhood years.

*Poverty status had a statistically significant effect on both low birth weight and the neonatal mortality rate for whites but not for blacks.*

### Physical Health

Compared with nonpoor children, poor children in the United States experience diminished physical health as measured by a number of indicators of health status and outcomes (see Table 1). In the 1988 National Health Interview Survey; parents reported that poor children were only two-thirds as likely to be in excellent health and almost twice as likely to be in fair or poor health as nonpoor children. These large differences in health status between poor and nonpoor children do not reflect adjustment for potentially confounding factors (factors, other than income, that may be associated with living in poverty) nor do they distinguish between long- or short-term poverty or the timing of poverty. This section reviews research on the relationship of poverty to several key measures of child health, low birth weight and infant mortality, growth stunting, and lead poisoning. For the most part, the focus is on research that attempts to adjust for important confounding factors and/or to address the effect of the duration of poverty on child health outcomes.

### Birth Outcomes

Low birth weight (2,500 grams or less) and infant mortality are important indicators of child health. Low birth weight is associated with an increased likelihood of subsequent physical health and cognitive and emotional problems that can persist through childhood and adolescence. Serious physical disabilities, grade repetition, and learning disabilities are more prevalent among children who were low birth weight as infants, as are lower

levels of intelligence and of math and reading achievement. Low birth weight is also the key risk factor for infant mortality (especially death within the first 28 days of life), which is a widely accepted indicator of the health and well-being of children.[13]

Estimating the effects of poverty alone on birth outcomes is complicated by the fact that adverse birth outcomes are more prevalent for unmarried women, those with low levels of education, and black mothers—all groups with high poverty rates. One study that used data from the NLSY to examine the relationship between family income and low birth weight did find, however, that among whites, women with family income below the federal poverty level in the year of birth were 80% more likely to have a low birth weight baby as compared with women whose family incomes were above the poverty level (this study statistically controlled for mothers' age, education, marital status, and smoking status). Further analysis also showed that the duration of poverty had an important effect; if a white woman was poor both at the time when she entered the longitudinal NLSY sample and at the time of her pregnancy (5 to 10 years later), she was more than three times more likely to deliver a low birth weight infant than a white woman who was not poor at both times. For black women in this sample, although the odds of having a low birth weight baby were twice the odds for white mothers, the probability of having a low birth weight baby was not related to family poverty status.[14]

Other studies that used county level data to examine the effects of income or poverty status and a number of pregnancy-related health services on birth outcomes for white and black women also found that income or poverty status had a statistically significant effect on both low birth weight and the neonatal mortality rate for whites but not for blacks.[15,16]

### Growth Stunting

Although overt malnutrition and starvation are rare among poor children in the United States, deficits in children's nutritional status are associated with poverty. As described more fully in the Child Indicators article in this journal issue, stunting (low height for age), a measure of nutritional status, is more prevalent among poor than nonpoor children. Studies using data from the NLSY show that differentials in height for age between poor and nonpoor children are greater when long-term rather than single-year measures of poverty are used in models to predict stunting. These differentials by poverty status are large even in models that statistically control for many other family and child characteristics associated with poverty.[17]

### Lead Poisoning

Harmful effects of lead have been documented even at low levels of exposure. Health problems vary with length of exposure, intensity of lead in the environment, and the developmental stage of the child—with risks beginning prior to birth. At very young ages, lead exposure is linked to stunted growth,[18] hearing loss,[19] vitamin D metabolism damage, impaired blood production, and toxic effects on the kidneys.[20] Additionally, even a small increase in blood lead above the Centers for Disease Control and Prevention (CDC) current intervention threshold (10 µg/dL) is associated with a decrease in intelligence quotient (IQ).[21]

Today, deteriorating lead-based house paint remains the primary source of lead for young children. Infants and toddlers in old housing eat the sweet-tasting paint chips and breathe the lead dust from deteriorating paint. Four to five million children reside in homes with lead levels exceeding the accepted threshold for safety,[22] and more than 1.5 million children under six years of age have elevated blood lead levels.[23]

Using data from NHANES III (1988–1991), one study found that children's blood lead levels declined as family income increased.[23] All other things being equal, mean blood lead levels were 9% lower for one-to five-year-olds in families with incomes twice the poverty level than for those who were poor. Overall blood levels were highest among one-to five-year-olds who were non-Hispanic blacks from low-income families in large central cities. The mean blood lead level for this group, 9.7 µg/dL, was just under the CDC's threshold for intervention and almost three times the mean for all one- to five-year-olds.

### Cognitive Abilities

As reported in Table 1, children living below the poverty threshold are 1.3 times as likely as non-poor children to experience learning disabilities and developmental delays. Reliable measures of cognitive ability and school achievement for young children in the Children of the NLSY and IHDP data sets have been used in a number of studies to examine the relationship between cognitive ability and poverty in detail.[6,24–26] This article reports on several studies that control for a number of potentially important family characteristics and attempts to distinguish between the effects of long- and short-term poverty.

A recent study using data from the Children of the NLSY and the IHDP compared children in families with incomes less than half of the poverty threshold to children in families with incomes between 1.5 and twice the poverty threshold. The poorer children scored between 6 and 13 points lower on various standardized tests of IQ, verbal ability, and achievement.[25] These differences are very large from an educational perspective and were present even after controlling for maternal age, marital status, education, and ethnicity. A 6- to 13-point difference might mean, for example, the difference between being placed in a special education class or not. Children in families with incomes closer to, but still below, the poverty line also did worse than children in higher-income families, but the differences were smaller. The smallest differences appeared for the earliest (age two) measure of cognitive ability; however, the sizes of the effects were similar for children from three to eight. These findings suggest that the effects of poverty on children's cognitive development occur early.

---

*The effects of long-term poverty on measures of children's cognitive ability were significantly greater than the effects of short-term poverty.*

---

The study also found that duration of poverty was an important factor in the lower scores of poor children on measures of cognitive ability. Children who lived in persistently poor families (defined in this study as poor over a four-year span) had scores on the various assessments six to nine points lower than children who were never poor.[25] Another analysis of the NLSY that controlled for a number of important maternal and child health characteristics showed that the effects of long-term poverty (based on family income averaged over 13 years prior to testing of the child) on measures of children's cognitive ability were significantly greater than the effects of short-term poverty (measured by income in the year of observation).[26]

A few studies link long-term family income to cognitive ability and achievement measured during the school years. Research on children's test scores at ages seven and eight found that the effects of income on these scores were similar in size to those reported for three-year-olds.[25] But research relating family income measured during adolescence on cognitive ability finds relatively smaller effects.[27] As summarized in the next section, these modest effects of income on cognitive ability are consistent with literature showing modest effects of income on schooling attainment, but both sets of studies may be biased by the fact that their measurement of parental income is restricted to the child's adolescent years. It is not yet possible to make conclusive statements regarding the size of the effects of poverty on children's long-term cognitive development.

*For low-income children, a $10,000 increase in mean family income between birth and age 5 was associated with nearly a full-year increase in completed schooling.*

### School Achievement Outcomes

Educational attainment is well recognized as a powerful predictor of experiences in later life. A comprehensive review of the relationship between parental income and school attainment, published in 1994, concluded that poverty limited school achievement but that the effect of income on the number of school years completed was small.[28] In general, the studies suggested that a 10% increase in family income is associated with a 0.2% to 2% increase in the number of school years completed.[28]

Several more recent studies using different longitudinal data sets (the PSID, the NLSY and Children of the NLSY) also find that poverty status has a small negative impact on high school graduation and years of schooling obtained. Much of the observed relationship between income and schooling appears to be related to a number of confounding factors such as parental education, family structure, and neighborhood characteristics.[28–30] Some of these studies suggest that the components of income (for example, AFDC) and the way income is measured (number of years in poverty versus annual family income or the ratio of income to the poverty threshold) may lead to somewhat different conclusions. But all the studies suggest that, after controlling for many appropriate confounding variables, the effects of poverty

per se on school achievement are likely to be statistically significant, yet small. Based on the results of one study, the authors estimated that, if poverty were eliminated for all children, mean years of schooling for all children would increase by only 0.3% (less than half a month).[30]

Why do not the apparently strong effects of parental income on cognitive abilities and school achievement in the early childhood years translate into larger effects on completed schooling? One possible reason is that extrafamilial environments (for example, schools and neighborhoods) begin to matter as much or more for children than family conditions once children reach school age. A second possible reason is that school-related achievement depends on both ability and behavior. As is discussed in the Emotional and Behavioral Outcomes section, children's behavioral problems, measured either before or after the transition into school, are not very sensitive to parental income differences.

A third, and potentially crucial, reason concerns the timing of economic deprivation. Few studies measure income from early childhood to adolescence, so there is no way to know whether poverty early in childhood has noteworthy effects on later outcomes such as school completion. Because family income varies over time,[31] income measured during adolescence, or even middle childhood, may not reflect income in early childhood. A recent study that attempted to evaluate how the timing of income might affect completed schooling found that family income averaged from birth to age 5 had a much more powerful effect on the number of school years a child completes than does family income measured either between ages 5 and 10 or between ages 11 and 15.[7] For low-income children, a $10,000 increase in mean family income between birth and age 5 was associated with nearly a full-year increase in completed schooling. Similar increments to family income later in childhood had no significant impact, suggesting that income may indeed be an important determinant of completed schooling but that only income during the early childhood years matters.

### Emotional and Behavioral Outcomes

Poor children suffer from emotional and behavioral problems more frequently than do nonpoor children (see Table 1). Emotional outcomes are often grouped along two dimensions: externalizing behaviors including aggression, fighting, and acting out, and internalizing behaviors such as anxiety, social withdrawal, and depression. Data regarding emotional outcomes are based on parental and teacher reports. This section reviews studies that distinguish between the effects of long- and short-term poverty on emotional outcomes of children at different ages.

One study of low birth weight five-year-olds using the IHDP data set found that children in persistently poor families had more internalizing and externalizing behavior problems than children who had never been poor. The analysis controlled for maternal education and family structure and defined long-term poverty as income below the poverty threshold for each of four consecutive years. Short-term poverty (defined as poor in at least one of four years) was also associated with more behavioral problems, though the effects were not as large as those for persistent poverty.[6]

Two different studies using the NLSY report findings consistent with those of the IHDP study. Both found persistent poverty to be a significant predictor of some behavioral problems.[26,32] One study used data from the 1986 NLSY and found that for four- to eight-year-olds persistent poverty (defined as a specific percentage of years of life during which the child lived below the poverty level) was positively related to the presence of internalizing symptoms (such as dependence, anxiety, and unhappiness) even after controlling for current poverty status, mother's age, education, and marital status. In contrast, current poverty (defined by current family income below the poverty line) but not persistent poverty was associated with more externalizing problems (such as hyperactivity, peer conflict, and headstrong behavior).[32]

The second study used NLSY data from 1978–1991 and analyzed children ages 3 to 11. On average children living in long-term poverty (defined by the ratio of family income to the poverty level averaged over 13 years) ranked three to seven percentile points higher (indicating more problems) on a behavior problem index than children with incomes above the poverty line. After controlling for a range of factors including mother's characteristics, nutrition, and infant health behaviors, the difference remained though it dropped in magnitude. This study also found that children who experienced one year of poverty had more behavioral problems than children who had lived in long-term poverty.[26]

The above studies demonstrate that problematic emotional outcomes are associated with family poverty. However, it is important to note that the effects of poverty on emotional outcomes are not as large as those found in cognitive outcomes. Also these studies do not show that children in long-term poverty experience emotional problems with greater frequency or of the same type as children who experience only short-term poverty. These studies analyzed data for young children. Few studies have examined the link between emotional outcomes and poverty for adolescents. One small study of 7th- to 10th-graders in the rural Midwest did not find a statistically significant relationship between poverty and emotional problems, either internalizing or externalizing.[33] Self-reporting by the adolescents rather than maternal reporting, as used in the data sets on younger children, may account for the differences found in the effects of

*Problematic emotional outcomes are associated with family poverty; however, the effects of poverty on emotional outcomes are not as large as its effects on cognitive outcomes.*

income on emotional outcomes in this study as compared with the previously reviewed research. It may also be that younger children are more affected by poverty than older children.

These findings point to the need for further research to improve understanding of the link between income and children's emotional outcomes.

### Teenage Out-of-Wedlock Childbearing

The negative consequences for both mothers and children associated with births to unwed teen mothers make it a source of policy concern.[34] Although the rate of out-of-wedlock births among poor teens is almost three times as high as the rate among those from nonpoor families (see Table 1), the literature on linkages between family income and out-of-wedlock childbearing is not conclusive. A recent review of the evidence put it this way: "[P]arental income is negative and usually, but not always, significant. . . . The few reports of the quantitative effects of simulated changes in variables suggest that decreases in parental income . . . will lead to small increases in the probability that teen girls will experience a nonmarital birth."[28]

A recent study, which used data from the PSID to investigate factors in teen out-of-wedlock births, found that variations in income around the poverty threshold were not predictive of a teenage birth but that the probability of a teenager's having an out-of-wedlock birth declined significantly at family income levels above twice the poverty threshold.[35] The duration and timing of poverty had no effect on the probability of a teen out-of-wedlock birth. These findings are somewhat dif-

*A child's home environment accounts for a substantial portion of the effects of family income on cognitive outcomes in young children.*

ferent from those reported for cognitive outcomes and school achievement. In the case of cognitive outcomes for young children, the variation in income mattered most to children at very low levels of income; for school achievement, the timing and duration of poverty seemed to have important differential effects on outcomes.

Why should poverty status matter more for schooling than for childbearing? This difference is consistent with the more general result that parental income appears more strongly linked with ability and achievement than with behavior. The factors influencing teenage out-of-wedlock childbearing are less well understood than the factors influencing schooling completion: interventions have generally been much less successful in altering teen birthrates than in keeping teens in school.[36,37]

## Pathways Through Which Poverty Operates

The research reviewed thus far suggests that living in poverty exacts a heavy toll on children. How-

ever, it does not shed light on the pathways or mechanisms by which low income exerts its effects on children. As the term is used in this discussion, a "pathway" is a mechanism through which poverty or income can influence a child outcome. By implication, this definition implies that a pathway should be causally related to both income and at least one child outcome. Exploration of these pathways is important for a more complete understanding of the effects of poverty on children; moreover, exploration of pathways can lead to the identification of leverage points that may be amenable to policy intervention and remediation in the absence of a change in family income.

Research on the size and strength of the pathways through which income might influence child health and development is still scanty. In this section, five potential pathways are discussed: (1) health and nutrition, (2) the home environment, (3) parental interactions with children, (4) parental mental health, and (5) neighborhood conditions. Space limitations preclude a discussion of other potential pathways such as access to and use of prenatal care, access to pediatric care, exposure to environmental toxins, household stability, provision of learning experiences outside the home, quality of school attended, and peer groups. Further, few studies have tested pathway models using these variables.

### Health and Nutrition

Although health is itself an outcome, it can also be viewed as a pathway by which poverty influences other child outcomes, such as cognitive

© Steven Rubin

ability and school achievement. As discussed previously poor children experience increased rates of low birth weight and elevated blood lead levels when compared with nonpoor children. These conditions have, in turn, been associated with reduced IQ and other measures of cognitive functioning in young children and, in the case of low birth weight, with increased rates of learning disabilities, grade retention, and school dropout in older children and youths.

A 1990 analysis indicated that the poverty-related health factors such as low birth weight, elevated blood lead levels, anemia,[38] and recurrent ear infections and hearing loss contributed to the differential in IQ scores between poor and nonpoor four-year-olds.[39] The findings suggest that the cumulative health disadvantage experienced by poor children on these four health measures may have accounted for as much as 13% to 20% of the difference in IQ between the poor and nonpoor four-year-olds during the 1970s and 1980s.[39]

As discussed in the Child Indicators article in this journal issue, malnutrition in childhood (as measured by anthropometric indicators) is associated with lower scores on tests of cognitive development. Deficits in these anthropometric measures are associated with poverty among children in the United States, and the effects can be substantial. One recent study found that the effect of stunting on short-term memory was equivalent to the difference in short-term memory between children in families that had experienced poverty for 13 years and children in families with incomes at least three times the poverty level.[26]

## Home Environment

A number of studies have found that a child's home environment—opportunities for learning, warmth of mother-child interactions, and the physical condition of the home—account for a substantial portion of the effects of family income on cognitive outcomes in young children. Some large longitudinal data sets use the HOME scale as a measure of the home environment. The HOME scale is made up of items that measure household resources, such as reading materials and toys, and parental practices, such as discipline methods. The HOME scale has been shown to be correlated with family income and poverty, with higher levels of income associated with improved home environments as measured by the scale.[7,40]

Several studies have found that differences in the home environment of higher- and lower-income children, as measured by the HOME scale, account for a substantial portion of the effect of income on the cognitive development of pre-

school children and on the achievement scores of elementary school children.[6,26,37] In one study, differences in the home environment also seemed to account for some of the effects of poverty status on behavioral problems. In addition, the provisions of learning experiences in the home (measured by specific subscales of the HOME scale) have been shown to account for up to half of the effect of poverty status on the IQ scores of five-year-olds.[37,41]

---

*Parents who are poor are likely to be less healthy, both emotionally and physically, than those who are not poor.*

---

## Parental Interactions with Children

A number of studies have attempted to go beyond documentation of activities and materials in the home to capture the effects of parent-child interactions on child outcomes. Much of the work is based on small and/or community-based samples. That work suggests that child adjustment and achievement are facilitated by certain parental practices. There is also some evidence that poverty is linked to lower-quality parent-child interaction and to increased use of harsh punishment. This research suggests that parental practices may be an important pathway between economic resources and child outcomes.

Evidence of such a parental-practice pathway from research using large national data sets of the kind reviewed in this article is less consistent. One NLSY-based study found that currently poor mothers spanked their children more often than nonpoor mothers and that this harsh behavior was an important component of the effect of poverty on children's mental health.[32] Mothers' parenting behavior was not, however, found to be an important pathway by which persistent poverty affected children's mental health. A more recent study using the National Survey of Families and Households found that the level of household income was only weakly related to effective parenting and that differences in parent practices did not account for much of the association between poverty and child well-being.[42]

Among adolescents, family economic pressure may lead to conflict with parents, resulting in lower school grades, reduced emotional health, and impaired social relationships.[33,43] Other work suggests that it may be income loss or economic uncertainty due to unemployment, underemployment, and unstable work conditions, rather than poverty or low income per se, that is a source for conflict between parents and teens leading to emotional and school problems.[33,44]

## Parental Mental Health

Parents who are poor are likely to be less healthy, both emotionally and physically, than those who are not poor.[45] And parental irritability and depressive symptoms are associated with more conflicted interactions with adolescents, leading to less satisfactory emotional, social, and cognitive development.[43,46,47] Some studies have established that parental mental health accounts for some of the effect of economic circumstances on child health and behavior. Additionally, poor parental mental health is associated with impaired parent-child interactions and less provision of learning experiences in the home.[33,41,48]

*Low income may lead to residence in extremely poor neighborhoods characterized by social disorganization and few resources for child development.*

## Neighborhood Conditions

Another possible pathway through which family income operates has to do with the neighborhoods in which poor families reside. Poor parents are constrained in their choice of neighborhoods and schools. Low income may lead to residence in extremely poor neighborhoods characterized by social disorganization (crime, many unemployed adults, neighbors not monitoring the behavior of adolescents) and few resources for child development (playgrounds, child care, health care facilities, parks, after-school programs).[49,50] The affluence of neighborhoods is associated with child and adolescent outcomes (intelligence test scores at ages 3 and 5 and high school graduation rates by age 20) over and above family poverty.[37,51]

Neighborhood residence also seems to be associated with parenting practices, over and above family income and education.[52] Neighborhood effects on intelligence scores are in part mediated by the learning environment in the home.[52,53] Living in neighborhoods with high concentrations of poor people is associated with less provision of learning experiences in the homes of preschoolers, over and above the links seen between family income and learning experiences.

A key issue that has not been fully explored is the extent to which neighborhood effects may be overestimated because neighborhood characteristics also reflect the choices of neighborhood residents. One study that examined the effects of peer groups (as measured by the socioeconomic status of students in a respondent's school) on teenage pregnancy and school dropout behavior found that while student body socioeconomic status seemed to be an important predictor of both dropout and teen pregnancy rates, it did not appear to be related to those outcomes in statistical models that treated this peer characteristic as a matter of family choice.[54]

## How Much Does Income Cause Child Outcomes?

It may seem odd to raise this question after summarizing evidence indicating that family income does matter—across the childhood and adolescent years and for a number of indicators of well-being. However, these associations have been demonstrated when a relatively small set of family characteristics are controlled through statistical analyses. It is possible, therefore, that other important family characteristics have not been controlled for and that, as a result of this omission, the effects of income are estimated incorrectly. . . . Distinguishing between the effects on children of poverty and its related events and conditions is crucial for public policy formulation. Programs that alter family income may not have intended benefits for children if the importance of family income has been mismeasured.

Despite the evidence reviewed in this article and elsewhere, there is an important segment of the population who believes that income per se may not appreciably affect child outcomes. This viewpoint sees parental income mainly as a proxy for other charateristics such as character (a strong work ethic) or genetic endowment that influence both children and parents. A recent book by Susan Mayer, *What Money Can't Buy: The Effect of Parental Income on Children's Outcomes,*[55] presents a series of tests to examine explicitly the effects of income on a set of child outcomes. In one test, measures of income *after* the occurrence of an outcome are added to statistical models of the effects of income and other characteristics on a child outcome. The idea behind this test is that unanticipated future income can capture unmeasured parental characteristics but cannot have caused the child outcome. The inclusion of future income frequently produced a large reduction in the estimated impact of prior parent income. Mayer also tries to estimate the effects on children of components of income (for example, asset income) that are independent of the actions of the family. Although these tests provide some support for the hypothesis that family income may not matter much for child outcomes, even Mayer admits that these statistical procedures are not without their problems. For example, prior income and future income are highly correlated, and if parents take reasonable expectations of future income into consideration in making decisions regarding the well-being of children, then the assumption that child outcomes are independent of future income, which underlies the first test, is violated.

A second approach to the problem that omitted variables may bias the estimation of the effects of income and poverty on children looks at siblings within families. Siblings reared in the same family share many of the same unmeasured family characteristics. Thus, comparing children at the same age within families makes it possible to look at the income of the family at different time points (for example, if a firstborn was five years of age in 1985 and the second child was five years of age in 1988, it is possible to look at their achievement levels at this age and the average family income between 1980 and 1985 for the firstborn and between 1983 and 1988 for the second child). One study that used this approach found that sibling differences in income were associated with sibling differences in completed schooling, which gave support to the notion that family income matters.[7]

Perhaps the most convincing demonstration of the effects of income is to provide poor families with income in the context of a randomized trial. In four Income Maintenance/Negative Income Tax Experiments in the 1960s and 1970s, experimental treatment families received a guaranteed minimum income. (These experiments are discussed in more detail in the article by Janet Currie in this journal issue.) Substantial benefits resulting from increased income effects were found for child nutrition, early school achievement, and high school completion in some sites but not in others. These results might be viewed as inconclusive; however, since

the site with the largest effects for younger children (North Carolina) was also the poorest, one interpretation of the results is that income effects are most important for the very poorest families.[56,57]

## Conclusion

The evidence reviewed in this article supports the conclusion that family income can substantially influence child and adolescent well-being. However, the associations between income and child outcomes are more complex and varied than suggested by the simple associations presented in Table 1. Family income seems to be more strongly related to children's ability and achievement-related outcomes than to emotional outcomes. In addition, the effects are particularly pronounced for children who live below the poverty line for multiple years and for children who live in extreme poverty (that is, 50% or less of the poverty threshold). These income effects are probably not due to some unmeasured characteristics of low-income families: family income, in and of itself, does appear to matter.

The timing of poverty is also important, although this conclusion is based on only a small number of studies. Low income during the preschool and early school years exhibits the strongest correlation with low rates of high school completion, as compared with low income during the childhood and adolescent years.[7,58] Poor-quality schooling, which is correlated with high neighborhood poverty, may exacerbate this effect.[59] These findings suggest that early childhood interventions may be critical in reducing the impact of low income on children's lives.

The pathways through which low income influences children also suggest some general recommendations. Nutrition programs, especially if they target the most undernourished poor, may have beneficial effects on both physical and cognitive outcomes. Lead abatement and parental education programs may improve cognitive outcomes in poor children residing in inner-city neighborhoods where lead is still an important hazard.

Because about one-half of the effect of family income on cognitive ability is mediated by the home environment, including learning experiences in the home, interventions might profitably focus on working with parents. An example is the Learningames curriculum in which parents are provided instruction, materials, and role playing in learning experiences.[60] Other effective learning-oriented programs might also be pursued.[61–63]

Finally, income policies (as discussed by Robert Plotnick in this journal issue) and in-kind support programs (as discussed by Devaney, Ellwood, and Love in this journal issue) can have immediate impact on the number or children living in poverty and on the circumstances in which they live. Most important, based on this review, would be efforts to eliminate deep and persistent poverty especially during a child's early years. Support to families with older children may be desirable on other grounds, but the available research suggests that it will probably not have the same impact on child outcomes as programs focused on younger children.

---

*The authors would like to thank the National Institute of Child Health and Human Development Research Network on Child and Family Well-being for supporting the writing of this article. The Russell Sage Foundation's contribution is also appreciated as is that of the William T. Grant Foundation, and the Canadian Institute for Advanced Research. The authors are also grateful for the feedback provided by Linda Baker, Pamela K. Klebanov, and Judith Smith and would like to thank Phyllis Gyamfi for her editorial assistance.*

---

1. Hernandez, D.J. *America's children: Resources from family government and the economy.* New York: Russell Sage Foundation, 1993.

2. Duncan, G.J., and Brooks-Gunn, J., eds. *Consequences of growing up poor.* New York: Russell Sage Foundation, 1997.

3. Duncan, G.J., and Rodgers, W.L. Longitudinal aspects of childhood poverty. *Journal of Marriage and the Family* (November 1988) 50,4:1007–21.

4. Chase-Lansdale, P.L., and Brooks-Gunn, J., eds. *Escape from poverty: What makes a difference for children?* New York: Cambridge University Press, 1995.

5. Children's Defense Fund. *Wasting America's future.* Boston: Beacon Press, 1994; Klerman, L. *Alive and well?* New York: National Center for Children in Poverty, Columbia University, 1991.

6. Duncan, G.J., Brooks-Gunn, J., and Klebanov, P.K. Economic deprivation and early-childhood development. *Child Development* (1994) 65,2:296–318.

7. Duncan, G.J., Yeung, W., Brooks-Gunn, J., and Smith, J.R. How much does childhood poverty affect the life chances of children? *American Sociological Review,* in press.

8. Hauser R., Brown, B., and Prosser W. *Indicators of children's well-being.* New York: Russell Sage Foundation, in press.

9. Brooks-Gunn,J., Guo, G., and Furstenberg, F.F.Jr. Who drops out of and who continues beyond high school?: A 20-year study of black youth. *Journal of Research in Adolescence* (1993) 37,3:271–94.

10. Graber, J.A., and Brooks-Gunn, J. Transitions and turning points: Navigating the passage from childhood through adolescence. *Developmental Psychology* (1996) 32,4:768–76.

11. Rutter, M. Beyond longitudinal data: Causes, consequences, changes and continuity. *Journal of Counseling and Clinical Psychology* (1994) 62,5:928–90.

12. Guo, G., Brooks-Gunn, J., and Harris, K.M. Parents' labor-force attachment and grade retention among urban black children. *Sociology of Education* (1996) 69,3:217–36.

13. For a review of the causes and consequences of low birth weight in the United States, see Shiono, P., ed. Low Birth Weight. *The Future of Children* (Spring 1995) 5,1:4–231.

14. Starfield, B., Shapiro, S., Weiss, J., et al. Race, family income, and low birth weight. *American Journal of Epidemiology* (1991) 134,10:1167–74.

15. Corman, H., and Grossman, M. Determinants of neonatal mortality rates in the U.S.: A reduced form model. *Journal of Health Economics* (1985) 4,3:213–36.

16. Frank, R., Strobino, D., Salkever, D., and Jackson, C. Updated estimates of the impact of prenatal care on birthweight outcomes by race. *Journal of Human Resources* (1992) 27,4:629–42.

17. Miller, J., and Korenman, S. Poverty and children's nutritional status in the United States. *American Journal of Epidemiology* (1994) 140,3:233–43.

18. Schwartz, J., Angle, C., and Pitcher, H. Relationship between childhood blood lead levels and stature. *Pediatrics* (1986) 77,3:281–88.

19. Schwartz, J., and Otto, D. Lead and minor hearing impairment. *Archives of Environmental Health* (1991) 46,5:300–05.

20. Agency for Toxic Substances and Disease Registry. *The nature and extent of lead poisoning in the US.: A report to Congress.* Washington, DC: U.S. Department of Health and Human Services, 1988, Section II, p. 7.

21. Schwartz, J. Low level lead exposure and children's IQ: A meta-analysis and search for threshold. *Environmental Research* (1994) 65,1:42–55.

22. Ronald Morony, Deputy Director, U.S. Department of Housing and Urban Development, Office of Lead Based Paint Abatement and Poisoning Prevention, Washington, DC. Personal communication, November 20, 1996.

23. Brody, D.J., Pirkle, L., Kramer, R., et al. Blood lead levels in the U.S. population. *Journal of the American Medical Association* (1994) 272,4:277–81.

24. Brooks-Gunn, J., McCarton, C.M., Casey, P.H., et al. Early intervention in low birth weight premature infants: Results through age 5 years from the Infant Health and Development Program. *Journal of the American Medical Association* (1994) 272,16: 1257–62.

25. Smith, J.R., Brooks-Gunn, J., and Klebanov, P. The consequences of living in poverty for young children's cognitive and verbal ability and early school achievement. In *Consequences of growing up poor.* G.J. Duncan and J. Brooks-Gunn, eds. New York: Russell Sage Foundation, 1997.

26. Korenman, S., Miller, J.E., and Sjaastad,J.E. Long-term poverty and child development in the United States: Results from the National Longitudinal Survey of Youth. *Children and Youth Services Review* (1995)17,1/2:127–51.

27. Peters. E., and Mullis, N. The role of the family and source of income in adolescent achievement.

In *Consequences of growing up poor:* G. Duncan and J. Brooks-Gunn, eds. New York: Russell Sage Foundation, 1997.

28. Haveman, R., and Wolfe, B. The determinants of children's attainments: A review of methods and findings. *Journal of Economic Literature* (1995) 33,3:1829–78.

29. Teachman,J., Paasch, K.M., Day, R., and Carver, K.P Poverty during adolescence and subsequent educational attainment. In *Consequences of growing up poor:* G. Duncan and J. Brooks-Gunn, eds. New York: Russell Sage Foundation, 1997.

30. Haveman, R., and Wolfe, B. *Succeeding generations: On the effect of investments in children.* New York: Russell Sage Foundation, 1994.

31. Duncan, G.J. Volatility of family income over the life course. In *Life-span development and behavior.* Vol. 9. P. Baltes, D. Featherman, and R.M. Lerner, eds. Hillsdale, NJ: Erlbaum, 1988, pp. 317–58.

32. McLeod, J.D., and Shanahan, M.J. Poverty, parenting and children's mental health. *American Sociological Review* (June 1993) 58,3:351–66.

33. Conger, R.D., Conger, K.J., and Elder, G.H. Family economic hardship and adolescent adjustment: Mediating and moderating processes. In *Consequences of growing up poor:* G. Duncan and J. Brooks-Gunn, eds. New York: Russell Sage Foundation, 1997.

34. Hotz, V.J., McElroy, S.W., and Sanders, S.G. Costs and consequences of teenage childbearing. *Chicago Policy Review.* Internet: http://www.spc.uchicago.edu/cpr/Teenage_Child.htm.

35. Haveman, R., Wolfe, B., and Wilson, K. Childhood poverty and adolescent schooling and fertility outcomes: Reduced form and structural estimates. In *Consequences of growing up poor.* G.J. Duncan and J. Brooks-Gunn, eds. New York: Russell Sage Foundation, 1997.

36. U.S. Department of Health and Human Services. *Report to Congress on out-of-wedlock childbearing.* PHS-95–1257. Hyattsville, MD: DHHS, September 1995.

37. Brooks-Gunn, J., Duncan, G.J., Klebanov, P.K., and Sealand, N. Do neighborhoods influence child and adolescent behavior? *American Journal of Sociology* (1993) 99,2:335–95.

38. Iron-deficiency anemia is an important health problem that was traditionally identified with child poverty. Iron-deficiency anemia has been associated with impaired exercise capacity, increased susceptibility to lead absorption, and developmental and behavioral problems; see Oski, F. Iron deficiency in infancy and childhood. *The New England Journal of Medicine.* (July 15, 1993) 329,3:190–93. The importance of iron-deficiency anemia and its sequelae among poor children in the United States today is unclear. Increased use of iron-fortified foods and infant formulas along with their provision through public nutrition programs such as the Special Supplemental Food Program for Women, Infants, and Children (see the article by Devaney, Ellwood, and Love in this journal issue) have contributed to a dramatic decline in anemia; see Yip, R., Binkin, N.J., Fleshood, L., and Trowbridge, F.L. Declining prevalence of anemia among low-income children in the U.S. *Journal of American Medical Association* (1987) 258,12:1623. Between 1980 and 1991, the prevalence of ane-

mia among infants and children through age five declined from 7% to 3%. Still, low-income children participating in public health programs have a higher-than-average prevalence of anemia; see Yip, R., Parvanta, I., Scanlon, K., et al. Pediatric Nutrition Surveillance System—United States, 1980–1991. *Morbidity and Mortality Weekly Report* (November 1992) 41,SS-7:1–24. In part, this is because risk of anemia is a criterion for enrollment in these programs and also because these low-income children have low iron levels.

39. Goldstein, N. *Explaining socioeconomic differences in children's cognitive test scores.* Working Paper No. H-90-1. Cambridge, MA: Malcolm Wiener Center for Social Policy, John F. Kennedy School of Government, Harvard University, 1990.

40. Garrett, P., Ng'andu, N., and Ferron, J. Poverty experience of young children and the quality of their home environments. *Child Development* (1994) 65,2:331–45.

41. Bradley, R.H. Home environment and parenting. In *Handbook of parenting:* M. Bornstein, ed. Hillsdale, NJ: Erlbaum, 1995.

42. Hanson, T., McLanahan, S., and Thomson, E. Economic resources, parental practices, and child well-being. In *Consequences of growing up poor:* G.J. Duncan and J. Brooks-Gunn, eds. New York: Russell Sage Foundation, 1997.

43. Conger, R.D., Ge, S., Elder, G.H., Jr., et al. Economic stress, coercive family process and developmental problems of adolescents. *Child Development* (1994) 65,2:541–61.

44. McLoyd, V.C. The impact of economic hardship on black families and children: Psychological distress, parenting, and socioemotional development. *Child Development* (1990) 61,2:311–46.

45. Adler, N.E., Boyce, T., Chesney, M.A., et al. Socioeconomic inequalities in health: No easy solution. *Journal of the American Medical Association* (1993) 269:3140–45.

46. Liaw, F.R., and Brooks-Gunn, J. Cumulative familial risks and low birth weight children's cognitive and behavioral development. *Journal of Clinical Child Psychology* (1995) 23,4:360–72.

47. McLoyd, V.C., Jayaratne, T.E., Ceballo, R., and Borquez, J. Unemployment and work interruption among African American single mothers. Effects on parenting and adolescent socioemotional functioning. *Child Development* (1994) 65,2:562–89.

48. Brooks-Gunn, J., Klebanov, P.K., and Liaw, F. The learning, physical, and emotional environment of the home in the context of poverty: The Infant Health and Development Program. *Children and Youth Services Review* (1995)17,1/2.251–76.

49. Wilson, W.J. *The truly disadvantaged. The inner city, the underclass, and public policy.* Chicago. University of Chicago Press, 1987.

50. Sampson, R., and Morenoff, J. Ecological perspectives on the neighborhood context of urban poverty: Past and present. In *Neighborhood poverty: Conceptual, methodological, and policy approaches to studying neighborhoods.* Vol. 2. J. Brooks-Gunn, G. Duncan, and J.L. Aber, eds. New York: Russell Sage Foundation, in press.

51. Brooks-Gunn, J., Duncan, G.J., and Aber, J.L., eds. *Neighborhood poverty: Context and consequences for*

*children.* Vol. 1. New York: Russell Sage Foundation, in press.

52. Klebanov, P.K., Brooks-Gunn, J., and Duncan, G.J. Does neighborhood and family poverty affect mother's parenting, mental health and social support? *Journal of Marriage and Family* (1994) 56,2:441–55.

53. Klebanov, P.K., Brooks-Gunn, J., Chase-Lansdale, L., and Gordon, R. The intersection of the neighborhood and home environment and its influence on young children. In *Neighborhood poverty: Context and consequences for children.* Vol. 1. J. Brooks-Gunn, G.J. Duncan, and J.L. Aber, eds. New York: Russell Sage Foundation, in press.

54. Evans, W.N.. Oates, W.E., and Schwab, R.M. Measuring peer group effects: A study of teenage behavior. *Journal of Practical Economy* (1992) 100,5:966–91.

55. Mayer S.E. *What money can't buy: The effect of parental income on children's outcomes.* Cambridge, MA: Harvard University Press, 1997.

56. Kershwa, D., and Fair, J. *The New Jersey income maintenance experiment.* Vol. I. New York: Academic Press, 1976.

57. Salkind, N.J., and Haskins, R. Negative income tax: The impact on children from low-income families. *Journal of Family Issues* (1982) 3,2:165–80.

58. Baydar, N., Brooks-Gunn, J., and Furstenberg, E.F., Jr. Early warning signs of functional illiteracy: Predictors in childhood and adolescence. *Child Development* (1993) 64,3:815–29.

59. Alexander, K.L., and Entwisle, D.R. Achievement in the first 2 years of school: Patterns and processes. *Monographs of the Society for Research in Child Development* (1988) 53,2:1–153.

60. Sparling, J.J., and Lewis, J. *Partner for learning.* Lewisville, NC: Kaplan, 1984.

61. Olds, D.L., and Kitzman, H. Review of research on home visiting for pregnant women and parents of young children. *The Future of Children* (Winter 1993) 3,3:53–92.

62. Brooks-Gunn, J., Denner, J., and Klebanov, P.K. Families and neighborhoods as contexts for education. In *Changing populations, changing schools: Ninety-fourth yearbook of the National Society for the Study of Education, Part II.* E. Flaxman and A. H. Passow, eds. Chicago, IL: National Society for the Study of Education, 1995, pp. 233–52.

63. Brooks-Gunn, J. Strategies for altering the outcomes of poor children and their families. In *Escape from poverty: What makes a difference for children?* P.L. Chase-Lansdale and J. Brooks-Gunn, eds. New York: Cambridge University Press, 1996.

# Effects of Maltreatment

## and Ways To Promote Children's Resiliency

**Barbara Lowenthal**

*Barbara Lowenthal is Professor, Department of Special Education, Northeastern Illinois University, Chicago, Illinois.*

Each year, about four million American children are exposed to traumatic events (Schwartz & Perry, 1994) such as physical, sexual, and emotional abuse; neglect; accidents; severe injuries; and natural disasters. Children may develop posttraumatic stress disorder as a result, leaving them vulnerable to phobias, conduct and behavioral difficulties, anxiety disorders, depression, and other neuropsychiatric disorders. This article will focus on the effects of maltreatment, including abuse and neglect, on young children. The author will discuss possible neurological, psychological, and cognitive consequences, as well as interventions that can promote resiliency in children. As concerned professionals, we need toadvocate both for methods of preventing abuse and neglect, and for interventions that will assist maltreated children.

## Neurological Effects of Abuse and Neglect

Recent research provides information about the neurology and development of the brain during the first years of life. At birth, the brain is the most immature organ in the human body; it will continue to develop as a result of both genetics and environmental experiences, which can have both positive or negative effects (Terr, 1991). Different areas of the brain are responsible for specific functions (Terr, 1991). The frontal lobe is responsible for abstract thought. Systems in the limbic area regulate affect, emotion, and the attachment process. Other systems in the brain stem regulate the heart rate, blood pressure, and states of arousal (Tauwer, 1989).

The brain houses millions of nerve cells or neurons, which are connected to each other by synapses. These synapses, or pathways, compose the "wiring" of the brain (Neuberger, 1997), and allow the various regions of the brain to communicate with each other. Brain development after birth consists of a continuous process of wiring the connections among neurons. While new synapses form, those that are not used will be "pruned." A child's brain will develop 1,000 trillion synapses during the first year of life. By age 10, however, the pruning process occurs more frequently than does the formation of new synapses (Nash, 1997). At that point, the child has about 500 trillion synapses, a figure that remains somewhat constant through adulthood.

> As concerned professionals, we need to advocate both for methods of preventing abuse and neglect, and for interventions that will assist maltreated children.

From *Childhood Education*, Summer 1999, pp. 204-209. © 1999 by the Association for Childhood Education International, 17904 Georgia Avenue, Suite 215, Olney, MD 20832. Reprinted by permission.

A young child's neurodevelopment can be disrupted in two ways: through a lack of sensory experiences, which are necessary for the brain's optimal development (Stermer, 1997), and through abnormally active neurons, caused by such negative experiences as maltreatment and neglect (Perry, 1993). Negative environmental events can result in the malfunctioning of those regions of the brain responsible for the regulation of affect, empathy, and emotions. Continual abuse and neglect also can disrupt infants' attachment process with their caregivers, and, consequently, lead children to mistrust their environments (Nash, 1997).

Humans' so-called fight-or-flight response to stress, which prepares individuals to defend themselves against perceived dangers, may actually make the brain malfunction. Under the stress of the fight-or-flight response, the body exhibits a faster heart rate as well as increased production of a steroid hormone called cortisol. High levels of cortisol can kill brain cells and reduce the number of synapses. Studies of adults who experienced continuous abuse as children indicate that the prolonged stress of maltreatment results in a shrinkage of those regions of the brain responsible for memory, learning, and the regulation of affect and emotional expression (Neuberger, 1997). Other studies show that the brains of maltreated children can be 20 to 30 percent smaller than those of their nonmaltreated peers (Perry, 1993).

Maltreated youngsters' brains tend to be attuned to danger. At the slightest threat, these children will track anxiously any signs of further abusive attacks. Such early experiences of stress form templates in the brain in which the fear responses become fixed; thus, their brains become organized purely for survival. The resulting state of constant alert may help them avoid further maltreatment, but it also degrades their development. These youngsters are at great risk for emotional, behavior, learning, and physical difficulties (Herman, 1992; Terr, 1990). Other potential long-term effects include fewer opportunities for comfort, support, and nurturance.

Other ways that abused children cope with fears are "freezing" and dissociative responses. Because physical flight often is not possible for very young children, they freeze when they have no control over threatening events. The freezing response allows a child time to process and evaluate the stressor. Some caretakers, however, often interpret a freezing response as noncompliance to their instructions, which, if frustration arises, may open the door to further mistreatment. The

> Studies of adults who experienced continuous abuse as children indicate that the prolonged stress of maltreatment results in a shrinkage of those regions of the brain responsible for memory, learning, and the regulation of affect and emotional expression.

brain's organization may be further altered if the additional maltreatment lasts long enough. Eventually, youngsters feel anxious and frustrated all the time, even when experiences are nonthreatening. As a result, children may be irritable, hypervigilant, hyperactive, or aggressive; they also might be prone to throwing tantrums and showing a regression in their development (James, 1994).

Dissociation, another common response to maltreatment, occurs when individuals separate their painful experience from conscious awareness. It protects maltreated children against the overwhelming emotions and thoughts connected to their traumatic experiences. When carried to an extreme, however, this response can result in amnesia and hallucinations (Herman, 1992; Terr, 1991). Children also may exhibit personality and self-identity disorders.

## Psychological Effects of Abuse and Neglect

The psychological effects of abuse and neglect may include the disregulation of affect, the avoidance of intimacy, provocative behaviors, and disturbances in the attachment process.

*Disregulation of Affect.* Maltreated children often have difficulty in regulating affect and emotions. They may have intrusive and intensely emotional memories of their maltreatment, which they attempt to control by avoiding displays of their feelings. Sometimes, the only way to identify their emotions is through physiological responses, such as increased heart rates and perspiration. Although these children appear capable of describing other people's feelings, they cannot describe their own.

*Avoidance of Intimacy.* Survivors of child abuse and neglect tend to avoid intimate relationships, because they believe that getting close to someone else increases their vulnerability and lack of control (James, 1994). Intimacy, in fact, represents a threat, rather than nurturance and love. To avoid intimacy, children may withdraw, avoid eye contact, be hyperactive, or exhibit inappropriate behaviors.

*Provocative Behaviors.* If maltreated children are unable to find relief through numbing their feelings, they may instead act provocatively and aggressively. They may inflict harm on others, commit self-mutilation or even suicide, and otherwise behave in antisocial ways. Apparently, the underlying purpose behind these provocative and emotional acts is to produce the numbing responses that can lessen their extreme anxieties.

*Disturbances in the Attachment Process.* Attachment is the bond that young children form with their primary caregivers—usually, their parents (Hanson & Lynch, 1995). Early relationships help shape the development of the child's personality and social-emotional adjustment (Thurman & Widerstrom, 1990). The attachment process is important, as it affects the child's ability to cope with stress, regulate emotions, benefit from social supports, and form nurturing and loving relationships. Maltreated children's attachment processes are disrupted, however (Barnett, 1997). Usually, a caregiver and infant form close, secure emotional bonds, as evident by infants' demonstrably strong preferences for their primary caregivers, and by the enjoyment and comfort that they derive from that closeness. Parents show their attachment in their desire to nurture, comfort, and protect their babies, and by acting uneasy and sad when separated. Because the attachment process promotes a sense of security, trust, and self-esteem, it also furthers the infants' desire to explore and learn from their environments. While secure attachments help children in all areas of development, they are

> On average, abused, maltreated, or neglected children score lower on cognitive measures and demonstrate poorer school achievement compared to their non-abused peers of similar socioeconomic backgrounds.

All types of maltreated children, as they get older, demonstrate more cognitive deficits and are considered more at-risk for school failure and to drop out than their non-maltreated peers.

essential in establishing self-identity and self-worth (Moroz, 1993).

Abuse and neglect can impede the attachment process and diminish children's feelings of security and trust in their caregivers. Maltreated children may feel unworthy or unloved, and they may view the world as a dangerous place. When caregivers are neglectful, uncaring, or abusive, children become more vulnerable to stressors, and will have difficulty forming intimate and positive relationships. The children often become angry and resentful toward their caregivers, a feeling that may transfer to other relationships in their lives (Zeanah, 1993).

*Effects on Cognition and Learning.* Child abuse may adversely affect children's ability to learn. On average, abused, maltreated, or neglected children score lower on cognitive measures and demonstrate poorer school achievement compared to their non-abused peers of similar socioeconomic backgrounds (Barnett, 1997; Vondra, Barnett, & Cicchetti, 1990). Children with uncaring parents or caregivers will learn to view themselves as unworthy, unlovable, and incompetent in school-related and cognitive tasks. Abuse often leads to a loss of self-esteem and a lack of motivation to achieve at school.

Even at a very early age, maltreated children have difficulty adapting to their child care and preschool environments. Abused toddlers respond more negatively, in contrast with non-abused peers, to their mirror images, and they make fewer positive statements about themselves (Vondra, Allen, & Cicchetti, 1990). A study by Erickson, Stroufe, and Pianta (1989) found that physically abused preschoolers were more angry and noncompliant, compared to their non-abused classmates of similar socioeconomic backgrounds. The maltreated children also were more impulsive and disorganized, and were less successful on pre-academic tasks. They lacked the necessary social and work skills for age-appropriate adjustment in their preschool and kindergarten classes. Almost half of the physically abused youngsters were referred for special education or retention by the end of their kindergarten year. Similarly, emotionally abused young children displayed more disruptive, noncompliant behavior and a lack of persistence in their schoolwork, compared to their non-abused peers.

The behavior of the sexually abused children studied by Erickson, Stroufe, and Pianta (1989) was characterized by extreme anxiety, inattentiveness, and difficulty in following directions. Their social behaviors ranged from withdrawal to extreme aggression; consequently, they often were rejected by their classmates. These children commonly depended much more than their peers did on adults, appearing to have a strong need for their teachers' affection and approval. Their dependent behaviors seemed to reflect their roles as victims at home.

Neglected children, compared to children suffering from other forms of abuse, appeared to have the most severe problems, based on a number of investigations (Eckenrode, Laird, & Doris, 1993; Mash & Wolfe, 1991). They were the least successful on cognitive tasks in kindergarten; they were more anxious, inattentive, apathetic; and they had more difficulty concentrating on pre-academic work. Socially, they exhibited inappropriate behaviors and were not accepted by their peers. These youngsters rarely displayed positive affect, humor, or joy. A majority of these neglected children were retained or referred for special education (because of possible learning disabilities and/or social-emotional difficulties) at the end of kindergarten. The lack of stimulation at home might have been an important factor contributing to their poor performances. A lack of opportunities to learn social and pre-academic skills becomes obvious at school.

All types of maltreated children, as they get older, demonstrate more cognitive deficits and are considered more at-risk for school failure and to drop out than their non-maltreated peers (Kurtz, Gaudin, Wodarski, & Howing, 1993; Reyome, 1993). Teachers rated the abused children as being more overactive, inattentive, and impulsive than their non-abused classmates. They appeared less motivated to achieve at school and had difficulty learning. All types of maltreated children behave similarly, because forms of abuse often overlap. In other words, children may suffer from more than one type of abuse, such as a combination of emotional, sexual, and physical maltreatment.

Two studies compared the characteristics of physically abused, sexually abused, and neglected school-age children (Eckenrode, Laird, & Doris, 1993; Kurtz, Gaudin, Wodarski, & Howing, 1993). The physically abused students had significant school problems. Their performance was poor in all academic subjects, especially so in mathematics and language skills. They appeared to be underachievers and were more likely to be retained than their non-maltreated classmates. As adolescents, they were more likely to drop out of school. Both teachers and parents reported that these children had significantly more behavioral problems than their non-abused peers.

Neglect was associated with the poorest academic achievement among the groups of maltreated students. Teachers reported that these pupils were performing below grade level, and that their rate of school absenteeism was nearly five times that of the comparison group of non-neglected students. Neglect appears to have a greater long-term impact on academic performance than other forms of abuse. The neglected children's adaptive functioning ability, however, was within normal limits. Perhaps these children learned the survival skills out of necessity, because of the lack of care in their homes. Sexually abused children, on the other hand, were similar to nonabused youngsters in terms of academic achievement and in the number of discipline problems. They did not differ significantly in any area of academic performance. Although sexual abuse has negative social-emotional consequences, its effects on academic achievement were not evident in these studies. No matter what type of abuse, however, school personnel must intervene—to help prevent further maltreatment, and to assist these children with their learning problems.

## Interventions To Prevent Maltreatment and Promote Resiliency

Abused and neglected children are at high risk for psychological, neurological, and cognitive impairments. Children already may have developed problems by the time they are identified as being maltreated. Consequently, we need to pay greater attention to measures that promote resiliency, including home visits, and to the presence of alternate caregivers, social support interventions, and therapeutic programs.

*Availability of Alternate Caregivers.* Alternate caregivers must step in when children have been abused by their parents or other primary caregivers. These caregivers may be grandparents, other relatives, foster or adoptive parents, and teachers. Alternate caregivers can provide abused or neglected children with the safety, dedication, and nurturance they need to recover from their traumas.

Therapeutic caregiving can help prevent either the fight-or-flight response or dissociation from becoming "fixed" in children's brains. Thus, children can develop a sense of trust, and remain open to positive learning and emotional experiences. Therapeutic caregiving requires, among other attributes, the ability to acknowledge the child's pain; the ability to recognize that some anti-social behaviors are reflections of painful experiences; an understanding of the child's need to process and integrate these experiences; a willingness to be a part of a treatment team; and a strong belief that caregivers' actions will help the youngster, even if the benefits are not immediately apparent. Caregivers must help these children develop positive self-images (Moroz, 1993). Children need warmth, nurturance, empathy, stability, and a sense of belonging in order to promote their resiliency.

*Social Support Interventions.* Social support can "include the emotional, physical, informational, instrumental and material aid provided by others to maintain health and well-being, promote adoptions of life events and foster development in an adaptive manner" (Dunst, Trivette, & Deal, 1988, p. 28). Informal support may be provided by family members, friends, and neighbors, as well as by religious organizations and peer support groups. Formal support systems include home visiting programs, parenting classes, and mental health services.

*Informal Support Systems.* Some of the parents or primary caregivers who abuse their children have suffered from their own maltreatment as children. Poverty and unemployment may increase the likelihood of abuse. Informal support from families, friends, and community members, in the form of providing child care, respite care, counsel during a job search, transportation, or financial aid, for example, can greatly help. Taking advantage of such informal support can help dysfunctional families to end the cycle of abuse and to function more positively (Barnett, 1997).

*Formal Support Systems.* Formal community support systems, such as family therapy, are available (Daro, 1993; Manly, Cicchetti, & Barnett, 1994). Such services may supply basic needs, such as food, clothing, and shelter. The programs that teach basic parenting skills are particularly helpful. Such programs also help reduce family stress and pathology (Barnett, Manley, & Cicchetti, 1993).

*Intervention Programs for Child Victims.* Intervention services, including child care and preschool classes that specialize in the treatment of neglected and abused young children, are increasingly available. Many challenges must be overcome when assisting maltreated children, who may have a combination of language, cognitive, and social-emotional delays (Barnett, 1997). A National Clinical Evaluation study examined the outcomes of 19 separate projects (Daro, 1993) that trained teachers to use therapeutic techniques with maltreated young children, ages 18 months to 8 years. About 70 percent of the abused children demonstrated improvements in their adaptive, cognitive, and social-emotional skills.

Culp, Little, Lefts, & Lawrence (1991) described therapeutic projects that provided services such as play therapy, speech and language therapy, occupational and physical therapies, and home visits. The curriculum was designed to foster children's positive relationships with adults and peers, to increase their abilities to regulate emotions, and to improve self-esteem. Court-mandated services for the maltreating parents consisted of comprehensive group and individual therapy, and home visits by professionals. Positive outcomes were documented for both the maltreated children and their parents. The results of these studies indicate that abused children and their caretakers require individualized treatments for special problems. The duration of treatment also had an effect on the outcomes. Maltreating parents who were in therapy for 18 months made more improvements in their interactions with the children than did parents who were in treatment for shorter periods of time (Culp, Little, Letts, & Lawrence, 1991). Home visits appeared to help parents manage their stress levels, which, in turn, helped to head off further maltreatment. Other preventive measures consisted of mental health services, which enabled some parents to relieve emotional problems.

## Conclusion

Abuse and neglect have many possible negative neurological, psychological, and cognitive effects on young children. More research on childhood traumas and on therapeutic techniques that assist the child victims is needed, and should be advocated by concerned professionals, families, and citizens.

## References

Barnett, D. (1997). *The effects of early intervention on maltreating parents and their children.* In M. J. Guralnick (Ed.), The effectiveness of early intervention (pp. 147–170). Baltimore: Brookes.

Barnett, D., Manley, J. T., & Cicchetti, D. (1993). Defining child maltreatment: The interface between policy and research. In D. Cicchetti & S. Toth (Eds.), *Child abuse, child development, and social policy* (pp. 7–73). Norwood, NJ: Ablex.

Barnett, D., Vondra, J. I., & Shonk, S. (1996). Relations among self perceptions, motivation, and school functioning of low income maltreated and non-maltreated children. *Child Abuse and Neglect, 20,* 397–410.

Culp, R. E., Little, V., Letts, D., & Lawrence, H. (1991). Maltreated children's self-concept. Effects of a comprehensive treatment program. *American Journal of Orthopsychiatry, 61,* 114–121.

Daro, D. (1993). Child maltreatment research: Implications for program design. In D. Cicchetti & S. Toth (Eds.), *Child abuse, child develop-*

*ment, and social policy* (pp. 331–367). Norwood, NJ: Ablex.

Dunst, C., Trivette, C., & Deal, A. (1988). *Enabling and empowering families.* Cambridge, MA: Brookline Books.

Eckenrode, J., Laird, M., & Doris, J. (1993). School performance and disciplinary problems among abused and neglected children. *Developmental Psychology, 29,* 53–62.

Erickson, M. F., Stroufe, L. A., & Pianta, R. (1989). The effects of maltreatment on the development of young children. In D. Cicchetti & V. Carlson (Eds.), *Child maltreatment: Theory and research on the causes and consequences of child abuse and neglect* (pp. 647–684). New York: Cambridge University Press.

Hanson, M. J., & Lynch, E. W. (1995). *Early intervention: Implementing child and family services for infants and toddlers who are at-risk or disabled.* Austin, TX: Pro-Ed.

Herman, J. (1992). *Trauma and recovery.* New York: Basic Books.

James, B. (1994). *Handbook for treatment of attachment-trauma problems in children.* New York: Lexington Books.

Kurtz, P.D., Gaudin, J. M., Wodarski, J. S., & Howing, P. T. (1993). Maltreatment and the school-aged child: School performance consequences. *Child Abuse and Neglect, 17,* 581–589.

Mash, E. J., & Wolfe, D. A. (1991). Methodological issues in research in child abuse. *Criminal Justice and Behavior, 18,* 8–29.

Moroz, K. J. (1993). *Supporting adoptive families with special needs children—A handbook for mental health professionals.* Waterbury, VT: The Vermont Adoptions Project, U.S. Department of Health and Human Services Grant #90–CO–0484.

Nash, J. J. (1997, February 3). Fertile minds. *Time,* 48–56.

Neuberger, J. J. (1997). Brain development research: Wonderful window of opportunity to build public support for early childhood education. *Young Children, 52,* 4–9.

Perry, B. D. (1993). Medicine and psychotherapy: Neurodevelopment and neurophysiology of trauma. *The Advisor, 6,* 13–20.

Reyome, N. D. (1993). A comparison of the school performance of sexually abused, neglected, and non-maltreated children. *Child Study Journal, 23,* 17–38.

Schwartz, E. D., & Perry, B. D. (1994). The post-traumatic response in children and adolescents. *Psychiatric Clinics of North America, 17,* 311–326.

Stermer, J. (1997, July 31). Home visits give kids a chance. *Chicago Tribune, 16.*

Tauwer, C. L. (1989). Critical periods of brain development. *Infants and Young Children, 1,* VII–VIII.

Terr, L. (1990). *Too scared to cry: Psychic trauma in childhood.* New York: Harper and Row.

Terr, L. C. (1991). Childhood traumas: An outline and overview. *American Journal of Psychiatry, 148,* 10–20.

Thurman, S. K., & Widerstrom, A. H. (1990). *Infants and young children with special needs.* Baltimore: Brookes.

Vondra, J. I., Barnett, D., & Cicchetti, D. (1990). Self concept, motivation, and competence among preschoolers from maltreating and comparison families. *Child Abuse and Neglect, 14,* 525–540.

Zeanah, C. H., Jr. (1993). *Handbook of infant mental health.* New York: Guilford Press.

Amazing medical advances, great economic opportunities, earlier schooling and many new kinds of Barbie dolls are among the wonders in store for the first Americans of a new century. BY JERRY ADLER

# TOMORROW'S CHILD

SHE WILL BE CONCEIVED, ALMOST CERtainly, sometime in the next six months, and will tumble headfirst into the world nine months later, wholly unconscious of her uniqueness as the first American of the millennium. Escaping by a stroke of the clock the awful burden of the present century, she (or he) will never hear the screams at Dachau or see the sky burst into flames over Hiroshima; the cold war will be as remote as the epic of Gilgamesh. For that matter, even the re-runs of "Barney" will bear the musty reek of the classics. Some things are eternal, though, and present trends indicate that sometime in the next century the average American girl could have more Barbie dolls than she has classmates. Grandchild of baby boomers! The very phrase boggles the mind—although not so much, perhaps, as the fact that of the 8.9 million American children who will be born in the year 2000, at least 70,000 of them are expected to still be alive in 2100.

First, though, they'll survive being dropped on their heads in the delivery room when the Y2K computer bug shuts off the electricity. To each century belongs its own terrors, and also its own pleasures. The child born in the year 2000 may face epidemics of previously unknown tropical diseases, but he also may be able to eat broccoli Jell-O instead of broccoli. And the toy industry may come to the rescue of lonely kids with a doll designed to remind them of their mothers. "We have so many latchkey children in search of a human connection," muses marketing consultant Faith Popcorn. "They'll be able to carry their mother around in doll form!" A lot has been written lately about the future as the venue for abstract breakthroughs in science, technology and medicine, but much less on the concrete questions of how Americans will actually live in it.

The millennium baby will be born into a nation of approximately 275 million, the third largest in the world, and still growing; the midrange estimate of the Census Bureau is that the population will reach 323 million by 2020 and 394 million by midcentury. Where will all those people live? Mostly in California, Texas and Florida, which among them will account for almost three out of 10 Americans by 2025. They will be squeezed onto proportionately less land: the median lot size of a new single-family house will almost certainly continue the slow, steady drop of the last 20 years. Children born in the year 2000 will live, on average, twice as long as those born in 1900. But they will live in bigger houses; the median floor area will reach 2,000 square feet any year now, a 25 percent increase since 1977. "The 800-square-foot Levittown house—that's a big family room now," says Columbia University historian Kenneth T. Jackson.

The cohort born circa 2000 should also benefit from what some economists are calling "the great asset sell-off" of the 21st century—the liquidation of family homes as the baby boomers start retiring in the second and third decades. "Younger Americans will get some great deals" on real estate, says Teresa Ghilarducci, a specialist in economic forecasting at Notre Dame. And, she adds, "it will be a great time to look for and get great jobs." But boomers will also be liquidating their investments, so stock-market values will stagnate. Except in some favored sunbelt locales, families moving out will create what Ghilarducci ominously calls "suburban wastelands." Downtown neighborhoods that haven't gentrified by then will be just out of luck.

The salient economic fact in the child's life may be the growing gap between the haves and have-nots, says Robert Litan, director of economic studies at the Brookings Institution. As disparities of wealth and income continue to widen, he says, "we could find ourselves living in a winner-take-all society. If people don't see economic opportunity, they drop out" of civil society. These trends will play themselves out in an America increasingly populated by minorities. By 2050, the Census Bureau projects an American population that is one-quarter black, Asian or Native American and one-quarter Hispanic. How the nation fares in the next century will depend on whether those changes widen the socioeconomic gap between races or help close it. And meanwhile, which of the children born in the year 2000 will be chosen for the Harvard class of 2022—bearing in mind that by the time they enroll, the projected cost of a Harvard education will be more than $320,000?

There are a few things we can say with some assurance. Millennium babies will be about the same size as their parents. The long-term trend among Caucasians toward greater size is a factor of better nutrition, but as everyone knows, Americans are already maxed out when it comes to food consumption. Children born in the year 2000 will, however; live longer than ever: 73 years, on average, for a boy, and almost 80 for a girl—approximately double the average life expectancy of a newborn at the turn of the last century. And the figures are expected to rise steadily throughout the first half of the century. Those averages, though, conceal a wide disparity among different races. Whites, interestingly, are about in the middle; the category of Asians and Pacific Islanders will live the longest; blacks the shortest. It is a depressing statistic that a black male born in 2000 will have a life expectancy of 64.6 years—actually *less* than for an older brother born in 1995.

Some of the improvement in life span will come from reducing already low rates

# The reading wars will continue, with increasing reliance on computers, but kids will still be put to bed with 'Goodnight Moon'

of infant death. Dr. James Marks of the Centers for Disease Control estimates that the mortality rate for newborns, around eight per 1,000 live births, could drop to as little as one per 1,000. Premature births account for many newborn deaths, but in the next decade, says bioethicist Arthur Caplan of the University of Pennsylvania, doctors will perform the astonishing feat of keeping alive babies born as early as 19 or 20 weeks after conception, weighing only eight ounces. Preemies younger than about 24 weeks now almost invariably succumb to the failure of their underdeveloped lungs, but techniques are now being developed to allow them to breathe oxygen from a liquid solution until they can sustain themselves in the air.

Even more impressive are advances forecast for in utero surgery. Already doctors can remove fetal tumors and correct conditions such as diaphragmatic hernia—a hole in the diaphragm that can cause serious lung problems. But standard open surgery on a living fetus is a very high-risk procedure. Within the next decade, surgeons will be performing these operations with the help of tiny cameras mounted on needle-like probes, according to Dr. Michael Harrison, head of the Fetal Treatment Center at the University of California, San Francisco. Ultimately, he expects, doctors will be able to do anything on a fetus that can be done after birth. "Heart repairs? We're working on them day and night [in animals]," Harrison says. "It hasn't been done in humans yet, but we will be there in the next century."

The road map to the 21st century is being written now in the Human Genome Project, the monumentally ambitious attempt to catalog the entire complement of a normal person's DNA. When it's completed, in about 2003, researchers will be able to identify the genes responsible for many of mankind's most intractable afflictions—such as cystic fibrosis, muscular dystrophy and congenital immune deficiency. As a first step, doctors will be able to diagnose these diseases in utero, and parents will have the chance—and, consequently, the burden—of deciding whether to end the pregnancy. (Some of these tests are already in use.) But by the early years of the next century doctors will

perform the equivalent of alchemy, curing disease by directly tinkering with patients' DNA. They will synthesize normal copies of the defective gene, or altered genes that counteract it, and attach them to a "vector" such as a benign virus to carry them into the patient's cells. In combination with Harrison's fetal-surgery techniques, it may be possible to cure congenital conditions even before birth.

For most babies born in the year 2000, smoking and overeating obviously will be a bigger threat to health than birth defects. Childhood obesity "is up dramatically since the '80s," says Marks of the CDC, and is expected to increase among kids who lift a finger only to click a mouse button. But routine genetic screening early in the next century will make a difference there, too, by identifying the health risks specific to each individual. The public-health lesson of this century is that people generally change their lifestyles only under the threat of death, which is why those born in the future will probably not have to sit through so many public-service exhortations about fitness from Arnold Schwarzenegger. Instead, doctors will tell them which particular risks they run, and what they have to do to stay alive—including, for example, the nutritional supplements that will do them the most good. On smoking, diet and exercise the advice is probably going to be pretty much the same as it is now—except that there are always people who will live a long time no matter what they eat. One of the great pleasures of living in the next century may be finding out you're one of them.

# A new theory will change our attitudes about child rearing— we don't know what it is yet, but there always is one

In terms of psychological health, a new theory will revolutionize parents' attitudes toward child rearing. No one knows what the new theory will be, but there always is one. The 20th century's succession of mutually contradictory panaceas (more structure; more freedom; it doesn't make a difference) shouldn't obscure the point that until about the 1940s, "most parents didn't give much thought to child development at all," says Jerome Singer, a Yale child psychologist. "From a parenting point of view, children are better off today, and will be better off in

the next few decades. Parents realize children need attention and oversight of what's going on in their lives, and those beliefs are penetrating into the lower socioeconomic groups."

And if kids persist in being maladjusted, there will be lots more ways to treat them. Caplan foresees radical new therapies that will rely on virtual-reality simulators (so the patient can practice, say, controlling his aggression in a mock situation) and brain scans that will tell the therapist on the spot whether the patient was learning. With this technique, he says, "you could look for change in real time," a boon to patients and insurance companies alike. There also will be many more problems to treat. The frontier of therapy in the next century will be "sub-syndromal" conditions such as mild depression, social phobias and anxieties. "We'll be treating emotional disabilities that we don't even label today," says Dr. Solomon H. Snyder, who heads the department of neuroscience at Johns Hopkins University. The debates over Prozac and Ritalin, which some authorities suspect are being prescribed indiscriminately, prefigure what will be two of the most important questions in 21st-century medical ethics: How far should we go in "enhancing" people who are essentially normal? And who will pay for it?

And periodically someone will invent the one and only best method to teach reading, rendering all other techniques hopelessly obsolete. It might well involve computers; there is already a burgeoning market for what's called "lapware," software aimed at children under a year old, who do their computing while sitting on Mommy's lap. "I've seen some that attempt to teach kids to associate letters and sounds with colors," says a very dubious David Elkind, a professor of child development at Tufts University. "That's a skill most children don't have until they're 4 or 5." Whatever the new movement is, it will provoke an equally strong reaction as soon as parents discover that it doesn't automatically turn their toddlers into John Updike. "The reading wars"—basically pitting old-fashioned phonics against everything else—"have been going on for a century and a half, so what chance do we have of ending them by the year 2000?" says Timothy Shanahan, a professor of education at the University of Illinois-Chicago.

The truth, well known to researchers, is that most kids can learn to read with almost any method, and will do it by themselves if left alone with a pile of books. And there will still be books in the next century. As births increased in the 1980s, the number of new children's titles published annually doubled, even as families started buying computers for the first time. Paula Quint, president of the Children's Book Council, expects that as births level off over the next few years the number of new titles will hold steady at about 5,000 a year. A few of these may even turn into classics, but it's safe to say that in the next century and beyond, kids will still be put to bed with "Goodnight Moon."

The change that is likely to make a real difference in the lives of millennium kids is a mundane one: the slow adoption of universal pre-K education. Most of the kids who attend preschool now are from relatively well-off families, even though research shows that the programs most benefit poor children. A few states, in search of a morally unassailable use of gambling proceeds, are dedicating them to providing free programs for 4-year-olds. "In 10 years," predicts Anne Mitchell, a consultant on early-childhood programs, "free preschool will be commonplace."

And in so many other ways, the year 2000 will be a great time to be born. Kids will have terrifically cool ethnic names like Pilar, Selena or Kai—although there may also be a countertrend, fueled by millennial religious fervor, for Biblical names like Isaiah and Elijah. Their mothers are more likely to breast-feed them than has been true for a generation (a quarter of all mothers nursed their children for at least six months last year, up from about 5 percent in 1971). And they will be able, if their parents don't mind, to run around in diapers until they're almost 4. Recognizing a trend toward later toilet training (and bigger kids), Procter & Gamble recently introduced Pampers in size 6, for toddlers 35 pounds and over. Of course, kids who are kept in diapers until

## Babies born as early as 19 weeks after conception may survive, thanks to a technology enabling them to breathe through a liquid

the age of 4 can only help drive up the cost of raising them, which, according to U.S. Department of Agriculture statistics, will amount to approximately $250,000 for the first 18 years of a millennium baby's life.

Inevitably, part of that sum will go toward the purchase of Barbie dolls. In the early 1980s, most girls were content with one Barbie; the average collection is now up to 10 and likely to rise in the future as Mattel expands the line into infinity—adding just this year, for example, Chilean, Thai, Polish and Native American Barbies. Last year Mattel added a wheelchair Barbie, and a spokeswoman suggests "there may be more dolls with other disabilities in the future."

Yes, the kid of the future will be, if anything, even more pampered and catered to

than the fabled baby boomers themselves, at least in part because there's so much money to be made off them. Leaving the house at 7:30 in the morning for 12-hour days of school, restaurants and shopping, they will require ever-more-elaborate "urban survival clothes," like the currently popular cargo pants in whose capacious pockets one can stow a meatball grinder, a palmtop computer and a jar of The Limited's most exciting new cosmetic product, fruit-scented antibacterial glitter gel. In what marketing guru Popcorn regards as one of the most significant social trends of the next millennium, "cross-aging," kids will be more like adults (and vice versa): "We're going to see health clubs for kids, kids as experts on things like the Internet, and new businesses, like Kinko's for Kids, to provide professional quality project presentations." The travel market of the future will increasingly be geared to kids, and not just at theme parks—24 million business trips included children in 1996, up 160 percent from 1991. So, to anyone who may have wondered whether it was right to bring a child into the uncertain world of the 21st century, it's fair to say, your fears are groundless.

The next millennium is going to be great for kids.

It's the adults who will miss the 1990s.

*With* PAT WINGERT, KAREN SPRINGEN, ELIZABETH ANGELL *and* MICHAEL MEYER

# Unit 5

## Unit Selections

## Key Points to Consider

❖ Why is adolescence going on and on?

❖ What factors account for the behavior of teenagers who take guns to school and murder their classmates?

❖ Should parents try to access the secret world of their adolescents? Why or why not?

❖ Are there biological as well as environmental reasons for gender differences in intimacy? Explain.

❖ Why is infertility such a challenge in young adulthood?

❖ What factors are involved in keeping marriages workable, healthy, and happy?

❖ Are dreams useful in the lives of young adults who have multiple stresses and/or traumatic events with which to cope? Defend your answer.

 **Links**     # www.dushkin.com/online/

26. **AMA—Adolescent Health On Line**
   *http://www.ama-assn.org/adolhlth/adolhlth.htm*
27. **American Academy of Child and Adolescent Psychiatry**
   *http://www.aacap.org/web/aacap/*
28. **Ask NOAH About: Mental Health**
   *http://www.noah.cuny.edu/illness/mentalhealth/mental.html*
29. **Biological Changes in Adolescence**
   *http://www.personal.psu.edu/faculty/n/x/nxd10/biologic2.htm*

These sites are annotated on pages 4 and 5.

e limbo between childhood and adulthood is
ollectively known as adolescence, a term coined in
904 by G. Stanley Hall. He saw adolescence as a
screte stage of life bridging the gap between sexual
aturity (puberty) and socioemotional and cognitive
aturity. Adolescence is often marked by the desire to
e independent of parental control as much as by the
eginning of sexual maturation. The end of adolescence
as extended upwards. Although legal maturity is now
sually 18 (voting, enlisting in the armed services,
wning property, marrying without permission are all
ossible), the social norm is to consider persons in their
te teen adolescents, not adults. The years between 18
nd 21 are often problematic for youth tethered
etween adult and not-adult status. They can be
narried, with children, living in homes of their own,
unning their own businesses, yet not be able to drive
heir cars in certain places or at certain times. They
an go to college and participate in social activities,
ut they cannot legally drink. Often the twenty-first
birthday is viewed as a rite of passage into adulthood
n the United States because it signals the legal right to
buy and drink alcoholic beverages. "Maturity" is usually
reserved for those who have achieved full economic as
well as socioemotional independence as adults.

In the first article in the adolescence section, Cynthia
Crossen reviews the milestones of the history of
adolescence with a pictorial time line. She presents
reasons for the lengthening of time it takes to "grow
up" in a technologically complicated and affluent society.

The second article addresses the tragic trend for
angry young children to express themselves with
weapons and mass murder. Sharon Begley looks at
several possible explanations. Biological answers to
"Why the Young Kill" include male sex hormones; the
stress hormones; the maltreatment of children in the
vulnerable early years of life; a genetic predisposition
to an antisocial personality; a difficult temperament at
birth (usually correlated with prenatal physiology);
hyperactivity; and the abuse of drugs or alcohol, which
creates chemical changes in the body. Environmental
answers to "Why the Young Kill" are legion. Begley
concludes that youth who kill have a particular biology
imposed on a particular environment. Neither nature
nor nurture is a sufficient answer in and of itself.

The third article in the adolescence unit describes
"The Secret Life of Teens." John Leland believes that
youth devise secret communications to express their
plans about sex, drugs, parties, and the like, meant to
exclude adults. When adults decipher the code, the
code is changed. The advent of computer technology
with e-mail, the World Wide Web, Web pages, chat
rooms, and so forth, has made the secret life of teens
much more difficult to decode. In fact, the secret world
of adolescents is now inaccessible to many parents.

As adolescence has been extended, so too has
young adulthood. Life expectancy has been extended
into the seventies. Improved health care, diet, exercise,
stress management, and a safer food and water supply
have allowed persons in their sixties and seventies to
enjoy vigorous good health. Young adulthood began
when children reached puberty 100 years ago. Parents
of teenagers were middle-aged between 35 and 55.
With the passage of the Social Security Act in 1935,
the end of middle age and the beginning of old age
was redefined as age 65. Today retirement is usually
postponed until after age 70, which has again
redefined the line between middle age and old age.

Later marriages and delayed childbearing have,
concurrently, redefined the line between young
adulthood and middle age. Many people today do not
appreciate or agree to the label "middle-aged" until
they are well into their fifties.

Erik Erickson, the personal/social personality theorist,
marked the passage from adolescence to young
adulthood by a change in the nuclear conflicts of two
life stages: identity vs. role confusion and intimacy vs.
isolation. Adolescents struggle to answer the question
"Who am I? Young adults struggle to find a place
within the existing social order where they can feel
propinquity rather than isolation. In the 1960s, Erikson
wrote that some females resolve both their conflicts of
identity and intimacy by living vicariously through their
husbands. He did not comment, however, on whether
or not some males resolve their conflicts of identity and
intimacy by living vicariously through their wives. He
felt that true intimacy was difficult to achieve if the
person seeking it had not first become a trusting,
autonomous, self-initiating, industrious, and self-
knowledgeable human being.

The first article in this young adulthood subsection
addresses the Eriksonian nuclear conflict of achieving
intimacy. The author, Robert Nadeau, has an alternate
theory to explain Erikson's belief that women achieve
intimacy by living vicariously through their husbands.
He reviews research that suggests that the female brain
may biologically evoke more emotional responsivity
than the male brain. Women's brains may make them
more aware of nuances, hidden meanings, and/or
sensory clues to meaning. Women use language to
achieve consensus and intimacy. Men use physical
presence and physical movement. Both women and
men also learn that their cultures have gender-specific
behaviors that they then imitate in their "language of
love" or intimacy strivings.

The second article about young adulthood discusses
infertility. It considers the impact of reproductive
technology on the lives of young couples. The
refinement in treatment follows sophistication in
detecting the cause of infertilty. A small percentage of
couples are still left not knowing why they cannot
conceive. Assignment of blame, astronomical costs not
covered by insurance, and the high incidence of
chromosomal mistakes in offspring make treating
infertility a real challenge.

The third article in this subsection addresses "The
Science of a Good Marriage." New research reveals
that the biggest problem in marriage is neither money
nor frequency of sex but rather shared power. The
article reviews new research on happy marriages
conducted in a "love lab" by Dr. John Gottman. He did
not find the emotional differences between the sexes
(Mars vs. Venus) to be as big a factor in relationships
as previously stated. Rather, good communication and a
balance of work and power keeps marriages healthy.
The birth of a first baby is a high-risk time in couples
relationships. Humor, appreciation of each other, and
attempts to prevent negative feelings from taking control
are especially important as child care becomes a reality.

The fourth article dealing with young adults
discusses the uses of dreaming. Dr. Ernest Hartmann
contends that dreams are useful for self-understanding.
Dreams also help people cope with traumatic events by
contextualizing emotions. Also, the next time something
similar happens it will not be as frightening because of
the dream work.

# Growing Up Goes On and On and On

By CYNTHIA CROSSEN

*Staff Reporter of* THE WALL STREET JOURNAL

**T**HERE'S GOOD NEWS and bad news about adolescence, and it's the same: The amount of time Americans spend in limbo between childhood and adulthood is the longest it has ever been—and getting longer.

On the early side, puberty, the physical changes that kick off adolescence, now begins for girls a good two years earlier than it did in the early part of this century. That means the precursors of puberty, the secondary sex characteristics, now appear in girls as young as eight or nine. At the late end, the age of separating from parents—the last and most important task of adolescence—has steadily risen from 16 to 18 to 21 and now often well beyond.

"Alligators drop their eggs, the egg is ready to roll," says David Murray, an anthropologist by training and now director of a statistical research center in Washington, D.C. "We hold on to youth more than any other species."

If you think of adolescents as hormones with feet, as some do, this is troubling news. The baby boom's children are marching toward their teen years; when they arrive, there will be more teenagers than in two decades. Adolescence means drugs, violence and unwed pregnancies, not to mention bad haircuts, big clothes, loud music and pierced everything. Surges of hormones make adolescents emotionally unsteady, and creating their own identities is a mandate to annoy adults, especially their parents. "I think some adults are scared because the bad teenagers are getting 'badder,'" says 14-year-old Sylvia Indyk of Fairway, Kan. Indeed, some experts believe the fact that guns have replaced fists and knives as the weapon of choice among some teens is the single most significant change in adolescence today.

But today's powerful adolescent culture adds zest to a society that is otherwise getting creakier. With the extraordinary increase in life expectancy in this century, every stage of life is longer, and the baby boom will soon begin a very long old age. "Adolescents are delightfully fun, creative and unconstrained people," says Susan Mackey, a clinical psychologist at the Family Institute at Northwestern University. "There's nothing funnier than their sense of humor. They can laugh hysterically for a half hour over one phrase."

Fortunately, youth isn't always wasted on the young. "I enjoy being a teenager," says 16-year-old Jeannie Gardiner of Dayville, Conn. "I get to hang out with my friends, and I don't have to think about major expenses and bills, like house payments and children."

That does sound like a good deal. Which is why a long adolescence is a luxury enjoyed only by societies with money and leisure. In the earliest cultures, where boys and girls could do most adult tasks by their early teens, adolescence was a brief rite of passage: A boy would go away for a few weeks and return a man; girls simply found a mate and began bearing children. Even in early, rural America, few farm families could afford to give their children much in the way of adolescence. In 1879, Henry Ford left his family's farm at the age of 15 to start apprenticing in Detroit machine shops.

In fact, it wasn't until 1904 that adolescence became a recognized and discrete stage of life, instead of simply a brief transition between child and adult. That year G. Stanley Hall, a psychologist and the president of Clark University, declared that youths' minds were too tender to be exposed to the real world's severity—the so-called early ripe, early rot philosophy. Many scholars note the coincidence between Dr. Hall's widely accepted theories and the fact that the industrial economy couldn't absorb as many workers as the rural economy.

The problem of warehousing these able-bodied but impressionable young people was solved by state laws making education compulsory to the age of 16 or 17. In 1900, only 11% of America's high-school age youth were in high school. Today, that figure is over 90%. Some people believe high schools exacerbate the problems of adolescents, confining them to an overcharged world where they are permitted to do far less than they could.

"We now so believe teenagers are... irresponsible, incapable, can't be trusted, can't be left alone that trying to think about what they might do that's productive is really hard," says Nancy Lesko, an associate professor of education at Indiana University.

That's exactly how many teenagers feel. "I feel like I'm mature enough to have more privileges," says Tara Conte, 15, of Haverhill, Mass. Such as? "Like being able to work part time and drive, but I have to wait until the law says I can do these things. And I think I'm mature enough to make most decisions on my own, but my parents have a difference of opinion."

Others say with the world becoming more technological and complicated, it takes longer to train children for adult responsibilities. "The age at which you are truly established and can support yourself keeps lengthening," says Joseph P. Allen, associate professor of clinical and development psychology at the University of Virginia. "I have graduate students who are in their late 20s and are still a ways away from being able to support themselves." Bob Enright, a professor at the University of Wisconsin with a specialty in adolescent psychology, agrees that "part of the reason we have adolescence is to educate people for an increasingly complex society." But, he adds, "there's also only so much room in a work force that is being downsized."

For many people, the lengthening of adolescence today is less worrisome than the fact that it is starting so early for girls. Earlier menstruation is associated with heavier body weight, so girls may not only be sexual before their minds and hearts are ready, but also out of step with the culture of leanness. Meanwhile, puberty is accelerating the growth process at a time when most of the boys are still shrimps. "For a boy, getting taller and larger is good," says Joan Jacobs Brumberg, a historian and author of the forthcoming "The Body Project: An Intimate History of American Girls." "For girls, it's problematic."

Psychologists who work with teenagers say there is no question that girls are

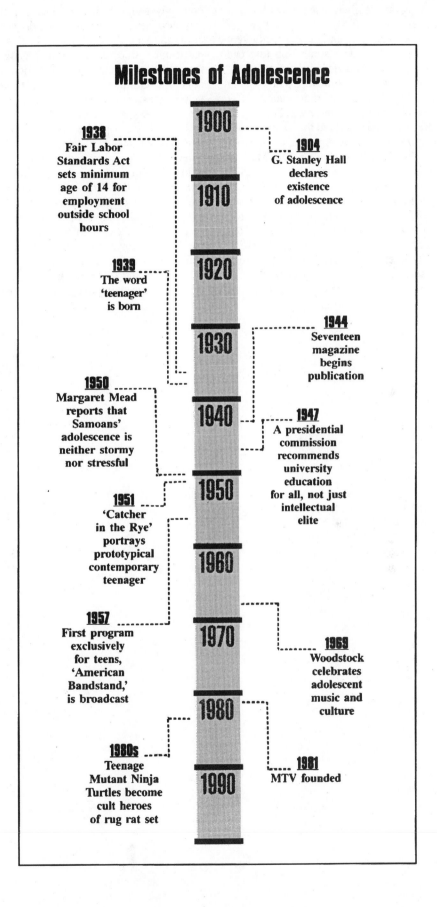

## Milestones of Adolescence

**1900**

**1938**
Fair Labor Standards Act sets minimum age of 14 for employment outside school hours

**1904**
G. Stanley Hall declares existence of adolescence

**1910**

**1939**
The word 'teenager' is born

**1920**

**1944**
Seventeen magazine begins publication

**1930**

**1950**
Margaret Mead reports that Samoans' adolescence is neither stormy nor stressful

**1940**

**1947**
A presidential commission recommends university education for all, not just intellectual elite

**1951**
'Catcher in the Rye' portrays prototypical contemporary teenager

**1950**

**1960**

**1957**
First program exclusively for teens, 'American Bandstand,' is broadcast

**1970**

**1969**
Woodstock celebrates adolescent music and culture

**1980**

**1980s**
Teenage Mutant Ninja Turtles become cult heroes of rug rat set

**1981**
MTV founded

**1990**

having sex earlier, usually with older males. "Kids have sex a lot younger than they used to, and they're really very young to be doing something that can have the consequences it has," says Anthony E. Wolf, a clinical psychologist in Longmeadow, Mass., and author of "Get Out of My Life, But First Could You Drive Me and Cheryl to the Mall?" "They just don't have the emotional maturity."

The Family Institute's Dr. Mackey cites research showing that the earlier girls hit puberty, the more likely they are to have poor body images, more problems in school, more depression and more drug use; they are also more likely to become sexually active earlier.

Furthermore, early development can exact a psychological price from a girl at home, where some parents back off, both physically and emotionally, from this new sexual person living in such close quarters. Psychologists say this is particularly true of fathers and daughters. "We can maintain the fiction of nonerotic children, but when girls develop breasts and boys get facial hair, we can't do that anymore," says Dr. Lesko. "They're right in our face. That's a trigger of major discomfort." When parents stop hugging their children or holding them on their laps, "the kid thinks, 'Now that I'm a sexual person, the only kind of physical contact I can have is sexual,' " says Dr. Mackey.

Linda Bips, a psychologist who runs the counseling center at Muhlenberg College in Allentown, Pa., says the biggest change she sees among adolescents is the increased intensity of their psychological problems. "In the '80s you'd see kids who had a kind of mild, everyday depression that rattled them; it was supportive therapy," she says. "Today they don't get out of bed. They end up eventually needing medication. I almost never used to refer out to medication. Now it's become more of a necessity."

Despite all this, many teenagers say the 1990s are a great time to be an adolescent. "We've got the Internet, the greatest thing to happen to education in a long time," says Daniel Snow, 18, of Tulsa, Okla. And they've always got their hormones. "Some days you can feel on top of the world, and on other days you feel hopeless, you wonder why you're here," says Mr. Snow. "Our emotions go to extremes, so when we have hope, we can do great things."

# WHY THE YOUNG KILL

**Are certain young brains predisposed to violence?
Maybe—but how these kids are raised can either save them
or push them over the brink. The biological roots of violence.**

## BY SHARON BEGLEY

THE TEMPTATION, OF COURSE, IS TO seize on one cause, one single explanation for Littleton, and West Paducah, and Jonesboro and all the other towns that have acquired iconic status the way "Dallas" or "Munich" did for earlier generations. Surely the cause is having access to guns. Or being a victim of abuse at the hands of parents or peers. Or being immersed in a culture that glorifies violence and revenge. But there isn't one cause. And while that makes stemming the tide of youth violence a lot harder, it also makes it less of an unfathomable mystery. Science has a new understanding of the roots of violence that promises to explain why not every child with access to guns becomes an Eric Harris or a Dylan Klebold, and why not *every* child who feels ostracized, or who embraces the Goth esthetic, goes on a murderous rampage. The bottom line: you need a particular environment imposed on a particular biology to turn a child into a killer.

It should be said right off that attempts to trace violence to biology have long been tainted by racism, eugenics and plain old poor science. The turbulence of the 1960s led some physicians to advocate psychosurgery to "treat those people with low violence thresholds," as one 1967 letter to a medical journal put it. In other words, lobotomize the civil-rights and antiwar protesters. And if crimes are disproportionately committed by some ethnic groups, then finding genes or other traits common to that group risks tarring millions of innocent people. At the other end of the political spectrum, many conservatives view biological theories of violence as the mother of all insanity defenses, with biology not merely an explanation but an excuse. The conclusions emerging from interdisciplinary research in neuroscience and psychology, however, are not so simple-minded as to argue that violence is in the genes, or murder in the folds of the brain's frontal lobes. Instead, the picture is more nuanced, based as it is on the discovery that experience rewires the brain. The dawning realization of the constant back-and-forth between nature and nurture has resurrected the search for the biological roots of violence.

Early experiences seem to be especially powerful: a child's brain is more malleable than that of an adult. The dark side of the zero-to-3 movement, which emphasizes the huge potential for learning during this period, is that the young brain also is extra vulnerable to hurt in the first years of life. A child who suffers repeated "hits" of stress—abuse, neglect, terror—experiences physical changes in his brain, finds Dr. Bruce Perry of Baylor College of Medicine. The incessant flood of stress chemicals tends to reset the brain's system of fight-or-flight hormones, putting them on hair-trigger alert. The result is the kid who shows impulsive aggression, the kid who pops the classmate who disses him. For the outcast, hostile confrontations—not necessarily an elbow to the stomach at recess, but merely kids vacating en masse when he sits down in the cafeteria—can increase the level of stress hormones in his brain. And that can have dangerous consequences. "The early environment programs the nervous system to make an individual more or less reactive to stress," says biologist Michael Meaney of McGill University. "If parental care is inadequate or unsupportive, the [brain] may decide that the world stinks—and it better be ready to meet the challenge." This, then, is how having an abusive parent raises the risk of youth violence: it can change a child's brain. Forever after, influences like the mean-spiritedness that schools condone or the humiliation that's standard fare in adolescence pummel the mind of the child whose brain has been made excruciatingly vulnerable to them.

In other children, constant exposure to pain and violence can make their brain's system of stress hormones unresponsive, like a keypad that has been pushed so often it just stops working. These are the kids with antisocial personalities. They typically have low heart rates and impaired emotional sensitivity. Their signature is a lack of empathy, and their sensitivity to the world around them is practically nonexistent. Often they abuse animals: Kip Kinkel, the 15-year-old who killed his parents and shot 24 schoolmates last May, had a history of this; Luke Woodham, who killed three schoolmates and wounded seven at his high school in Pearl, Miss., in 1997, had previously beaten his dog with a club, wrapped it in a bag and set it on fire. These are also the adolescents who do not respond to punishment: nothing hurts. Their ability to feel, to react, has died, and so has their conscience. Hostile, impulsive aggressors usually feel sorry afterward. Antisocial aggressors don't feel at all. Paradoxically, though, they often have a keen sense of injustices aimed at themselves.

Inept parenting encompasses more than outright abuse, however. Parents who are withdrawn and remote, neglectful and passive, are at risk of shaping a child who (absent a compensating source of love and attention) shuts down emotionally. It's important to be clear about this: inadequate parenting short of Dickensian neglect generally has little ill effect on most children. But to a vulnerable baby, the result of neglect can be tragic. Perry finds that neglect impairs the development of the brain's cortex, which controls feelings of belonging and attachment. "When there are experiences in early life that result in an underdeveloped capacity [to form relationships]," says Perry, "kids have a hard time empathizing with people. They tend to be relatively passive, and perceive themselves to be stomped on by the outside world."

These neglected kids are the ones who desperately seek a script, an ideology that fits their sense of being humiliated and ostracized. Today's pop culture offers all too many dangerous ones, from the music of Rammstein to the game of Doom. Historically, most of those scripts have featured males. That may explain, at least in part, why the murderers are Andrews and Dylans rather than Ashleys and Kaitlins, suggests Deborah Prothrow-Smith of the Harvard School of Public Health. "But girls are now 25 percent of the adolescents arrested for violent crime," she notes. "This follows the media portrayal of girl superheroes beating people up," from Power Rangers to Xena. Another reason that the schoolyard murderers are boys is that girls tend to internalize ostracism and shame rather than turning it into anger. And just as girls could be the next wave of killers, so could even younger children. "Increasingly, we're seeing the high-risk population for lethal violence as being the 10- to 14-year-olds," says Richard Lieberman, a school psychologist in Los Angeles. "Developmentally, their concept of death is still magical. They still think it's temporary, like little Kenny in 'South Park'." Of course, there are loads of empty, emotionally unattached girls and boys. The large majority won't become violent. "But if they're in a violent environment," says Perry, "they're more likely to."

## RISK FACTORS

Having any of the following risk factors doubles a boy's chance of becoming a murderer:

- **Coming from a family with a history of criminal violence**
- **Being abused**
- **Belonging to a gang**
- **Abusing drugs or alcohol**

Having any of these risk factors, in addition to the above, triples the risk of becoming a killer:

- **Using a weapon**
- **Having been arrested**
- **Having a neurological problem that impairs thinking or feeling**
- **Having had problems at school**

There seems to be a genetic component to the vulnerability that can turn into antisocial-personality disorder. It is only a tiny bend in the twig, but depending on how the child grows up, the bend will be exaggerated or straightened out. Such aspects of temperament as "irritability, impulsivity, hyperactivity and a low sensitivity to emotions in others are all biologically based," says psychologist James Garbarino of Cornell University, author of the upcoming book "Lost Boys: Why Our Sons Turn Violent and How We Can Save Them." A baby who is unreactive to hugs and smiles can be left to go her natural, antisocial way if frustrated parents become exasperated, withdrawn, neglectful or enraged. Or that child can be pushed back toward the land of the feeling by parents who never give up trying to engage and stimulate and form a loving bond with her. The different responses of parents produce different brains, and thus behaviors. "Behavior is the result of a dialogue between your brain and your experiences," concludes Debra Niehoff, author of the recent book "The Biology of Violence." "Although people are born with some biological givens, the brain has many blank pages. From the first moments of childhood the brain acts as a historian, recording our experiences in the language of neurochemistry."

There are some out-and-out brain pathologies that lead to violence. Lesions of the frontal lobe can induce apathy and distort both judgment and emotion. In the brain scans he has done in his Fairfield, Calif., clinic of 50 murderers, psychiatrist Daniel Amen finds several shared patterns. The structure called the cingulate gyrus, curving through the center of the brain, is hyperactive in murderers. The CG acts like the brain's transmission, shifting from one thought to another. When it is impaired, people get stuck on one thought. Also, the prefrontal cortex, which seems to act as the brain's supervisor, is sluggish in the 50 murderers. "If you have violent thoughts that you're stuck on and no supervisor, that's a prescription for trouble," says Amen, author of "Change Your Brain/ Change Your Life." The sort of damage he finds can result from head trauma as well as exposure to toxic substances like alcohol during gestation.

Children who kill are not, with very few exceptions, amoral. But their morality is aberrant. "I killed because people like me are mistreated every day," said pudgy, bespectacled Luke Woodham, who murdered three students. "My whole life I felt outcasted, alone." So do a lot of adolescents. The difference is that at least some of the recent school killers felt emotionally or physically abandoned by those who should love them. Andrew Golden, who was 11 when he and Mitchell Johnson, 13, went on their killing spree in Jonesboro, Ark., was raised mainly by his grandparents while his parents worked. Mitchell mourned the loss of his father to divorce.

Unless they have another source of unconditional love, such boys fail to develop, or lose, the neural circuits that control the capacity to feel and to form healthy relationships. That makes them hypersensitive to perceived injustice. A sense of injustice is often accompanied by a feeling of abject powerlessness. An adult can often see his way to restoring a sense of self-worth, says psychiatrist James Gilligan of Harvard Medical School, through success in work or love. A child usually lacks the emotional skills to do that. As one killer told Garbarino's colleague, "I'd rather be wanted for murder than not wanted at all."

THAT THE LITTLETON MASSACRE ended in suicide may not be a coincidence.

As Michael Carneal was wrestled to the ground after killing three fellow students in Paducah in 1997, he cried out, "Kill me now!" Kip Kinkel pleaded with the schoolmates who stopped him, "Shoot me!" With suicide "you get immortality," says Michael Flynn of John Jay College of Criminal Justice. "That is a great feeling of power for an adolescent who has no sense that he matters."

The good news is that understanding the roots of violence offers clues on how to prevent it. The bad news is that ever more children are exposed to the influences that, in the already vulnerable, can produce a bent toward murder. Juvenile homicide is twice as common today as it was in the mid-1980s. It isn't the brains kids are born with that has changed in half a generation; what has changed is the ubiquity of violence, the easy access to guns and the glorification

of revenge in real life and in entertainment. To deny the role of these influences is like denying that air pollution triggers childhood asthma. Yes, to develop asthma a child needs a specific, biological vulnerability. But as long as some children have this respiratory vulnerability—and some always will—then allowing pollution to fill our air will make some children wheeze, and cough, and die. And as long as some children have a neurological vulnerability—and some always will—then turning a blind eye to bad parenting, bullying and the gun culture will make other children seethe, and withdraw, and kill.

*With* ADAM ROGERS, PAT WINGERT *and* THOMAS HAYDEN

**Sex, drugs and rock have worried parents for decades. But now the Net, videogames and no-holds-barred-music are creating new worlds that many adults can't enter. BY JOHN LELAND**

# The Secret Life of Teens

**H**I, KIDS, DO YOU LIKE VIOLENCE? WANNA SEE ME STICK NINE-inch nails through each one of my eyelids? Wanna copy me and do exactly like I did?" The bleached-blond pixie could be a refugee from the set of "Friends," all smirk and glimmer. He is Marshall Mathers, better known as Eminem, whose debut rap album has been near the top of the charts for the last two months. In the secret lives of American teenagers, Eminem is large. "By the way," he raps, "when you see my dad, tell him I slit his throat in this dream I had."

Since they first emerged as a demographic entity earlier this century, adolescents of every era have carved out their own secret worlds, inventing private codes of style and behavior designed to communicate only within the in group and to exclude or offend adults. It is a central rite of American passage. But lately this developmental process has come under great strain. "In the past, the toughest decision [teens] had was whether to have sex, or whether to use drugs," says Sheri Parks, who studies families and the media at the University of Maryland. "Those are still

# Voices of a Generation

Teens say their lives are stressful, filled with social pressures—especially about looks and dress—worries about safety and fears of being stereotyped. And, of course, some parents just don't understand.

## ON CLIQUES

**Julia Papastavridis, 15**
Freshman, the Paideia School, Atlanta. Student rep on the disciplinary committee, chorus member.

"I see people who don't allow themselves to grow in certain areas, even though they have talent or skill, because they feel that would be out of character or that people wouldn't like them if they changed. Say you're really good at math, but your friends say, "I hate math. It's such a nerdy stupid subject." You can't be good at it because then you're a nerdy brainiac person. And then you feel like you don't fit in."

## ON MEDIA VIOLENCE

**Chris Haley, 17**
Junior, Lewisville High School, Lewisville, Texas. Founder of philosophy group, loves classical music.

"Our generation is far more densensitized to violence than any other generation. TVs raise children now more than parents do, and television caters to children's violent fantasies. Parents are working more and spending less time with their kids."

## ON FASHION

**Marisol Salguero, 16**
Junior, Alexander Hamilton High School, Los Angeles. AP and honors classes, academic tutor.

"The biggest thing here is wearing name-brand clothes. If you even think of wearing a non-name brand, you have guts. Looks are real important, too. If you're not pretty, people won't want to hang out with you. Even the girls with dark hair usually dye their hair blonde. Everything is just one big competition."

## ON APPEARANCE

**Lauren Barry, 17**
Senior, Glenbrook South High School, Glenview, Ill. National Honor Society, alternative theater group.

"I went to a National Honor Society induction. The parents were just staring at me. I think they couldn't believe someone with pink hair could be smart. I want to be a high-school teacher, but I'm afraid that, based on my appearance, they won't hire me. Don't be afraid of us. Don't stereotype us."

## ON FEAR

**Thomas James, 17**
Senior, Northside High School, Ft. Smith, Ark. Plays trombone in the band; does volunteer work.

"I used to not worry about safety at my school. But after the Jonesboro shootings, I started to think about it more. Jonesboro is just across the state from here. I just started to think, if it can happen there, it can happen here. This year we had two bomb threats. It was a hoax this time, but it makes me think that next time it may not be."

## ON SCHOOL AND PARENTS

**Diane Leary, 17**
Senior, Memorial High School, West New York, N.J. Student council, tennis team.

"The school is divided into different groups of kids: the break-dancers, the people who listen to heavy metal, the pretty girls, the ravers and the hip-hop people. But there's no pressure to be in one group or another. If a person is a break-dancer, they can still chill with the ravers. I'm a hip-hopper. We wear baggy jeans and sweatshirts. But if I'm really good friends with a person in the heavy-metal group; I can go chill with them and it's just like, whatever. I don't really worry about violence. And I don't really worry about peer pressure. Like if you're at a party and you don't drink, that's cool.

"Most kids' parents don't know what they are doing. I talk to my mom about everything. She shows up for every parents' night; sometimes she's the only one there. It makes me feel good that I have a mom who cares about what is going on with me."

# The Good, the Bad and the Ugly

Parents once just had to contend with Elvis's pelvis thrusting on the family TV. Now teens are off in their own garden of electronic delights. Here's what they're doing:

**Shake:** *Teen style has long strived to offend adults. Yesterday's bobby-soxer is today's pierced Goth.*

**Rattle:** *Violent entertainments like the videogame Half-Life and the rapper DMX both reflect and create a harsher cultural climate for adolescents.*

**Roll:** *Teen luv still conquers all. Amid the sour stuff, candy like 'Dawson's Creek' and Britney Spears tally sweet ratings and sales figures.*

there, but on top are piled all these other issues, which are very difficult for parents or children to decipher." New technologies and the entertainment industry, combined with changes in family structure, have more deeply isolated grown-ups from teenagers. The results are what Hill Walker, codirector of the Institute on Violence and Destructive Behavior in Oregon, calls "almost a virtual reality without adults."

With as many as 11 million teenagers now online, more and more of adolescent life is taking place in a landscape that is inaccessible to many parents. "That is apparent in the geography of households, " says Marlene Mayhew, a clinical psychologist who runs an online mental-health newsletter. With the computer often in the teen's bedroom, Mayhew says, the power structure in the family is turned upside down. "Kids are unsupervised, looking at whatever they please." A parent who might eventually notice a stockpile of Guns & Ammo or pornographic magazines has fewer clues to a child's online activities. "We're missing the opportunity for an adult reality check, adult perspective on the stimulation [teens] are getting exposed to. Kids have less access to parents, more access to potentially damaging information."

The pop-culture industry, marketing tribal styles through MTV and the Internet, makes it harder than ever for adults to read their kids, even parents raised on rock and roll. Parents in the '50s could " read" the ripe sexuality of Elvis—they just might not have approved. But what to make of the much more densely encrypted messages and camp nihilism of Eminem or Marilyn Manson, who dare outsiders to take offense? How to distinguish a kid drawn to gangsta rapper DMX for the rhymes from one drawn to the crimes? Making the process harder, teens have long been adept at lying, dissembling and otherwise conniving to hide their secret lives. Robyn Sykes, a senior at Jordan High School in Long Beach, Calif., reports that the skills are still sharp. "Some girls," she says, "leave the house wearing one thing,

and then change into tight, short skirts when they're here."

Mike L., 13, from suburban New York, is one of the unsupervised millions online. A couple years ago his father spied on him through a window, catching him in a chat room where people swapped pirated software. But now Mike has his own laptop and can do what he wants. Like many kids, he mostly sends e-mail and hangs around chat rooms, where he encounters both adults and other teens. "You go in, and someone offers what they've got stored in their computer," he says. "And maybe one of the things is 'The Anarchist Cookbook'," a notorious handbook that includes instructions for building bombs. Though he doesn't have it, he says, "one of my friends gets called down to the guidance counselor every day because somebody told a teacher that he knows how to make bombs. He's not the kind of guy who would do it. But he found out how on the Internet." Andrew Tyler, 13, from Haddonfield, N.J., used his Internet freedom another way: two weeks ago, while his mother tended the family garden, Tyler placed bids on $3.2 million worth of merchandise via the online auction house eBay, including the winning bid on a $400,000 bedroom set. "I thought [eBay] was just a site," he told NEWSWEEK. "It turned out to be a lot more than that."

The vast majority of adolescents' online activity ranges from edifying to harmless. Though hard numbers on Internet use are notoriously suspect, Malcolm Parks, an Internet researcher at the University of Washington in Seattle, says that most teens use the computer to send e-mail or instant messages, visit chat rooms or fan Web sites, do homework or download songs. For the most part, he says, "I worry more about poor quality of information online, and students' lack of skills for evaluating information, than I worry about frequently discussed evils like pornography."

At Neutral Ground in Manhattan on a recent afternoon, other skills are in play. The

drafty, fourth-floor gaming room, undetectable from the street, is a teen oasis, dotted with interconnected computers. By a quarter to four, it is packed with adolescent boys. Robert, one of eight boys glued to the screens, suddenly curses and bangs on the table. "Die, you stupid whore," he shouts. Then, "I'm gonna go kill Sebastian now." Sebastian, three terminals down, calls back, "You take this game way too seriously."

They are playing Half-Life, known in videogame parlance as a multiplayer "first-person shooter" game, or FPS. As Robert pushes a key, a red shell fires from an on-screen shotgun; arms fly off, blood spatters on the walls. "If my parents came down here now," says Mike, pausing from the carnage, "they'd probably drag me out." The best-known FPS is Doom, the game reportedly favored by the Littleton shooters, but to the kids at Neutral Ground, Doom is already passe. A new game, Kingpin, promises even hairier carnal gratifications. "Includes multiplayer gang bang death match for up to 16 thugs!" coos the ad copy. "Target specific body parts and actually see the damage done, including exit wounds."

The videogame business last year topped $6.3 billion, much of it dedicated for play on the home computer. The more violent games are marked for sales to mature buyers only, but like R-rated movies, they are easily accessible to kids. "The people usually tell you you're not old enough," says Eddie, 14, a regular at Neutral Ground, "but they don't stop you from buying it." Eddie says most FPS games "make me dizzy," but he enjoys one called Diablo, which is not just another shoot-'em-up orgy. "It's more like slice 'em up." His parents don't like the games but rarely engage him on it. His mother, he says, "thinks it's too violent, so she doesn't watch."

Most teenagers seem to process the mayhem as mindless pyrotechnics. But not all kids react the same way, warns Dan Anderson, a University of Massachusetts psychologist who has studied the effects of TV on

**47%** of Americans say very few parents really know what their teens are up to; **60%** say the government should restrict access to some Internet material.

children. "It's always been the case that the kids who have been vulnerable to violent messages on television have been a small minority. But a small minority can cause serious havoc. If you're predisposed to violence and aggression, you can find like-minded people who will validate your experience. You can become part of an isolated group that family and friends don't know about, and that group can exchange information on getting or making weapons." Brad Bushman, an Iowa State University psychologist, argues that violent computer games are more harmful than movies, "because the person becomes the aggressor. They're the one that does the killing."

In Santa Monica last week Collin Williams and his friends, a multiracial group of eighth graders, describe a numbing effect. Sure, they shrugged, a tragedy like the one in Littleton could happen in their school. Though they don't spend much time on computers, says Williams, 14, "we see so much violence on TV and in the movies that it just seems like it's everywhere. We don't go to school thinking we're going to be killed. But maybe it's because we're so used to it."

The challenges for parents may be new, but they are not insurmountable. Many psychologists recommend changing the way the computer is used. Put it in a family room, where adults and teens have more opportunities to discuss what's coming into the house. Every Web browser records what sites users visit; parents can monitor their kids' activities with just elementary computer savvy. Filters, such as Net Nanny, restrict which sites users can visit, but smart kids can get around them often by using a friend's computer. Idit Harel, founder of the kid-friendly site MaMaMedia, highly recommends playing videogames along with your kids. Even in violent games, she says, "there is learning, visualization; there is analysis of hints." Likewise, parents can either set limits on their kids' pop-cultural diets or just talk to the teens about what they're consuming. Say: "I don't understand this kid Eminem. What's he about?"

Even with such interaction, the secret lives of teenagers are likely to remain secret. They are as unbounded as the Internet and as plebeian as the Backstreet Boys, a daunting world for any parent to enter. But this remains the job of parenting. Today's teens command an electronic landscape more stimulating, vibrant and mysterious than any before. They are the masters of the new domain. But they still need adult guidance on their travels.

*With* Devin Gordon, Anne Underwood, Tara Weingarten and Ana Figueroa.

# BRAIN SEX AND THE LANGUAGE OF LOVE

Robert L. Nadeau

If we can believe the experts, the standard for healthy intimacy in love relationships between men and women is female, and maleness is a disease in desperate need of a cure. Men, say social scientists, have a "trained incapacity to share" and have learned to overvalue independence and to fear emotional involvement. Female friendships, claim the intimacy experts, are based on emotional bonding and mutual support, and male friendships on competition, emotional inhibition, and aggression.[1] Social scientists have also pathologized maleness because men typically view love as action, or doing things for another, while women view love as talking and acknowledging feelings.

In fairness to the intimacy experts, what they say about differences in the behavior of men and women has been well documented. Numerous studies have shown that men feel close to other men when working or playing side by side, while women feel close to other women when talking face to face.[2] Male group behavior is characterized by an emphasis on space, privacy, and autonomy, and female group behavior by a need to feel included, connected, and attached.[3] Male conversation tends to center around activities (sports, politics, work), and personal matters are discussed in terms of strengths and achievements. Female conversation,

1. Mirra Komarovsky, *Blue-collar Marriage* (New York: Vintage, 1964).

2. D. Goleman, "Two Views of Marriage Explored: His and Hers," *New York Times,* 1 Apr. 1989.

3. C. Gilligan, *In a Different Voice* (Cambridge, Mass.: Harvard University Press, 1982).

This article originally appeared in *The World & I,* November 1997, pp. 330-339. Reprinted by permission of *The World & I,* a publication of the Washington Times Corporation. © 1997.

*The human brain, like the human body, is sexed, and differences in the sex-specific human brain condition a wide range of behaviors that we typically associate with maleness or femaleness.*

in contrast, is more likely to center around feelings and relationships, and there is considerably less reluctance to reveal fears and weaknesses.

Men and women also appear to experience intimacy in disparate ways. In men's relationships with other men, the index of intimacy is the degree of comfort and relaxation felt when engaged in activities, such as helping a friend move furniture or repair cars. Even when men comfort one another in crisis situations, like the loss of a family member or a spouse, it is physical presence, rather than intimate talk, that tends to be most valued.[4]

The index for intimacy among women is the extent to which personal feelings can be shared in a climate of mutual support and trust. What tends to be most valued in these interactions is confirmation of feelings as opposed to constructive criticism and advice. When women are asked to describe the benefits of such conversations with other women, they typically mention relief from anxiety and stress, feeling better, and a more enhanced sense of self-worth. Although women also express intimacy by doing things for other

women, the doing is typically viewed as an occasion for verbal intimacy.[5]

The response of males to depression also favors action, or a tendency to "run" when overcome with sadness, anxiety, or dread. And when men talk about their depression in therapy, they typically "rush through" an account of their emotions and describe depression with action metaphors, such as "running in place," "running wide open," and "pushing the edge."[6] When women are clinically depressed, they are more willing to talk about their feelings, to find opportunities to do so with other women, and to seek help in talk therapy. Women also typically disclose the sources of depression in detailed narratives that represent and analyze experience. And while men tend to respond to clinical depression by running or moving, women tend to respond with sedentary activities like uncontrollable crying, staying in bed, and compulsive eating.

The sex-specific patterns that lie beneath the diversity of these behaviors reduce to a male orientation toward action and a female orientation toward talking. Why is this the case? According to the intimacy experts, it is entirely a product of learning and one of the primary sources of male pathology. As psychologist Carol Tavris puts it, "The doing-versus-talking distinction in the emotional styles of males and females begins in childhood, when boys begin to develop what psychologists call 'side by side' relationships, in which intimacy means sharing the same activity— sports, games, watching a movie

or a sports event together." Girls, in contrast, "tend to prefer 'face to face' relationships, in which intimacy means revealing ideas and emotions in a heart-to-heart exchange."[7]

The problem is not, as a best-selling book would have us believe, that women are from Venus and men from Mars. It is that we have only recently come to realize something about the legacy of the evolution of our species on planet Earth. Throughout virtually all of our evolutionary history, men and women lived in small tribes of hunter-gatherers where the terms for survival were not the same. We have long recognized that the different terms for survival, along with mate selection, account for sexual differences in the human body. But only in the last few decades have we discovered that the legacy of our evolutionary past is also apparent in the human brain. The human brain, like the human body, is sexed, and differences in the sex-specific human brain condition a wide range of behaviors that we typically associate with maleness or femaleness.

## THE LEGACY OF THE HUNTER-GATHERERS

The family album containing the record of our hunter-gatherer evolutionary past is DNA, and the legacy of that past begins to unfold following the union of sperm and ovum. Normal females have two long X chromosomes, contrib-

4. Scott Swain, "Covert Intimacy: Closeness in Men's Friendship," in B. J. Reisman and P. Schwartz, eds., *Gender in Intimate Relations* (Belmont, Calif.: Wadsworth, 1989).

5. Robin Lakoff, *Talking Power: The Politics of Language* (New York: Basic Books, 1990).

6. Catherine Riessman, *Divorce Talk: Women and Men Make Sense of Personal Relationships* (New Brunswick, N.J.: Rutgers University Press, 1990).

7. Carol Tavris, *The Mismeasure of Women* (New York: Simon & Schuster, 1992), 251–52.

*While males talk about their status in terms of simple descriptions of individual skills and achievements, Tannen says, females do so with complicated descriptions of overall character.*

uted by each biological parent, that closely resemble one another. Normal males have a long X chromosome, contributed by the mother, and a short Y chromosome, contributed by the father. Although each sperm and ovum contributes half of the full complement of forty-six chromosomes, the ovum provides all of the cytoplasmic DNA.

A fetus will develop with a female brain unless a gene on the Y chromosome, known as SRY, is expressed about the sixth week of pregnancy and triggers the release of testosterone in the gonads. The testosterone transforms the developing fetus into a male by interacting with genes that regulate or are regulated by the expression of SRY. The result is a kind of chain reaction in which genes involved in the determination of maleness are activated in a large number of cells. But since the levels

of hormones vary across individual brains, the response of brain regions to the presence of hormones is highly variable.

Many of the sex-specific differences in the human brain are located in more primitive brain regions, and they condition male and female copulatory behavior, sexual orientation, and cyclic biological processes like menstruation. Sex-specific differences also exist, however, in the more recently evolved neocortex or in the higher brain regions. The neocortex looks like a redundantly folded sheet and contains 70 percent of the neurons in the central nervous system. It is divided into two hemispheres that process different kinds of information fairly independently, and each communicates with the other via a 200-million-fiber network called the corpus callosum. While the symmetry is not exact, structures in one hemisphere are mirrored in the other. Thus we have two parietal lobes, two occipital lobes, and so on.

In people with normal hemispheric dominance, the left hemisphere has executive control. This hemisphere manages linguistic analysis and expression, as well as sequential motor responses or body movements. The right hemisphere is responsible for perception of spatial relationships, faces, emotional stimuli, and prosody (vocal intonations that modify the literal meaning of a word).[8] The two frontal lobes of each hemisphere, located behind the forehead, integrate inputs from other brain regions and are closely associated with conscious decision mak-

ing. This portion of our brain, which occupies 29 percent of the cortex, has undergone the most recent evolutionary expansion.

One piece of evidence that suggests why the brains of women and men tend to process information differently involves the corpus callosum, or the network of fibers connecting the two hemispheres. A subregion of this network, the splenium, is significantly larger in women than in men and more bulbous in shape.[9] More connections between the hemispheres in female brains could be a partial explanation for another significant discovery—both hemispheres are normally more active in the brains of females.

Computer-based imaging systems, such as positron emission tomography (PET) and magnetic resonance imaging (MRI), allow scientists to assess which areas of the brains of conscious subjects are active. All of these systems use advanced computers to construct three-dimensional images of brains as they process various kinds of information. Studies based on advanced imaging systems have revealed that cognitive tasks in the female brain tend to be localized in both hemispheres,[10] and that the same tasks in the male brain tend to be localized in one hemisphere.[11] Other recent studies using this technology have revealed sex-specific differences in the brain regions used to process language and sex-specific differences in feedback from more-primitive brain regions.[12] What this research suggests is that differences in the

8. S. F. Wietelson, "Neural Sexual Mosaicism: Sexual Differentiation of the Human Temporo-Parietal Region for Functional Asymmetry," *Psychoneuroendochrinology* 16:1–3 (1991): 131–55.

9. Wietelson, "Neural Sexual Mosaicism," 137–38.

10. I. Jibiki, H. Matsuda, et al., "Quantitative Assessment of Regional Blood Flow with 1231–IMP in Normal Adult Subjects," *Acta-Neurol-Napoli* 15:1 (1993): 7–15, and F. Okada, Y. Tokumitsu, et al., "Gender and Handedness-Related Differences of Forebrain Oxygenation and Hemodynamics," *Brain Research* 601:1–2 (1993): 337–47.

11. S. P. Springer and G. Deutsch, *Left Brain, Right Brain* (San Francisco: W. H. Friedman Co., 1985).

12. Ruben Gur, quoted in Gina Kolata, "Men's World, Women's World? Brain Studies Point to Differences," *New York Times*, 28 Feb. 1995, C1.

communication styles of men and women are not simply the product of learning.[13] They are also conditioned by differences in the sex-specific human brain.[14]

## YOU JUST DON'T UNDERSTAND ME

While none of the intimacy experts, to my knowledge, attribute differences in the conversation styles of men and women to the sex-specific human brain, there is a growing consensus that it is extremely difficult to eliminate these differences. In the bestseller *You Just Don't Understand: Women and Men in Conversation*, Deborah Tannen claims that while men use conversation "to preserve their independence and negotiate and maintain status in a hierarchical social order," women use conversation as "a way of establishing connections and negotiating relationships."[15] Based on this assumption, Tannen makes the case that there are some large differences in the languages of men and women.

Men, she says, are more comfortable with public speaking, or "report talk," and women are more comfortable with private or "rapport talk." Men use language that is abstract and categorical, or communicate in "messages," and women use language that conveys subtle nuances and hidden meanings, or communicate in "metamessages." Similarly, men respond to problems with concrete solutions and suggestions, and women respond with empathy and an emphasis on community.

Competitive males, claims Tannen, favor "commands," or statements that indicate what should be done without qualification, while consensus-building females favor "conditional propositions," or statements prefaced with words like "let's," "we could," and "maybe." And while males talk about their status in terms of simple descriptions of individual skills and achievements, Tannen says, females do so with complicated descriptions of overall character.

This sparse theoretical framework, however, does not account for the enormous popularity of Tannen's book. What most impresses readers are the conversations that Tannen uses to illustrate the distinctive character of the languages used by men and women. The following exchange occurs when a husband indicates that he did not get enough sleep:

> **He:** I'm really tired. I didn't sleep well last night.
> **She:** I didn't sleep well either. I never do.
> **He:** Why are you trying to belittle me?
> **She:** I'm not! I'm just trying to show you I understand!

"This woman," says Tannen, "was not only hurt by her husband's reaction; she was mystified by it. How could he think she was belittling him? By 'belittle me,' he meant 'belittle my experience.' He was filtering her attempts to establish connection through his concern with preserving independence and avoiding being put down."[16]

In a discussion of the differences between messages and metamessages, Tannen quotes from Anne Tyler's novel *The Accidental Tourist*. At this point in the narrative the character Macon has left his wife and moved in with a woman named Muriel. The conversation begins when Macon makes an observation about Muriel's son:

> "I don't think Alexander's getting a proper education," he said to her one evening.
> "Oh, he's okay."
> "I asked him to figure what change they'd give back when we bought the milk today, and he didn't have the faintest idea. He didn't even know he'd have to subtract."
> "Well, he's only in second grade," Muriel said.
> "I think he ought to go to private school."
> "Private schools cost money."
> "So? I'll pay."
> She stopped flipping the bacon and looked over at him. "What are you saying?" she said.
> "Pardon?"
> "What are you saying, Macon? Are you saying you're committed?"

Muriel then tells Macon that he must decide whether he wants to divorce his wife and marry her, and that she will not put her son in a new school when he could be forced to leave if Macon returns to his wife. Confused and frustrated by Muriel's attack, Macon responds, "But I just want him to learn to subtract." The problem, writes Tannen, is that "Macon is concerned with the message, the simple matter of Alexander's learning math. But Muriel is concerned with the metamessage. What would it say about the relationship if he began paying for her son's education?"[17]

Some reviewers of Tannen's book have rightly complained that these differences are made to appear too categorical. But they also concede, along with the majority of other reviewers, that Tannen has disclosed some actual disparities in the languages used by men and women. How, then, does Tannen account for these remarkable differences in the manner in which men and women linguistically construct reality? She claims that younger children "learn" these languages from older children in single-sex groups on the playground.

13. Melissa Hines, "Gonadal Hormones and Human Cognitive Development," in Jacques Balthazart, ed., *Hormones, Brain and Behavior in Vertebrates* (Basel, Switz.: Karger, 1990), 51–63.

14. Susan Phillips, Susan Steele, and Christine Tanz, eds., *Language, Gender and Sex in Comparative Perspective* (Cambridge, Eng.: Cambridge University Press, 1987); and David Martin and H. D. Hoover, "Sex Differences in Educational Achievement: A Longitudinal Study," *Journal of Early Adolescence* 7 (1987): 65–83.

15. Deborah Tannen, *You Just Don't Understand: Women and Men in Conversation* (New York: Ballantine Books, 1990), 77.

16. Tannen, *You Just Don't Understand*, 51.

17. Quoted in Tannen, *You Just Don't Understand*, 175.

## WHY MEN CAN'T ALWAYS TALK LIKE WOMEN

When we examine what Tannen says about differences in the languages used by men and women in the light of what we know about the sex-specific human brain, it seems clear the differences are not simply learned. Report talk and messages may reflect the orientation toward action associated with higher reliance on the primitive region of the limbic system in the male brain and with an orientation toward linear movement in abstract map space in the neocortex.

Although the usual biological explanation for the male tendency to give commands is higher levels of aggression, this linguistic habit also seems consistent with the manner in which reality tends to be constructed in the male brain. Commands may reflect the bias toward action and the organization of particulars in terms of movement between points in map space. All of which suggests that men may perceive commands, as opposed to requests, as more consistent with their sense of the real and as a more expedient way to solve problems.

The relationship between the two hemispheres in the female brain tends to be more symmetric, and there is a greater degree of interaction between these hemispheres. Since linguistic reality in the brains of women seems to invoke a wider range of right-brain cognitive functions, this may enhance awareness of emotionally relevant details, visual clues, verbal nuances, and hidden meanings. This suggests that the female brain tends to construct linguistic reality in terms of more extensive and interrelated cognitive and emotional contexts. If this is the case, all aspects of experience may appear more interdependent and interconnected, and this could contribute to the tendency to perceive people and events in a complex web of relation. Perhaps this is why the language of women tends to feature a more profound sense of identification with others, or why this language seems more "consensual."

Rapport talk may reflect this sense of identification and satisfy the need to feel interconnected. And metamessages, which allow analysis of single events to be extended through a complex web of relation, also seem consistent with the manner in which the female brain tends to construct reality. Since this reality seems more consensual, women may be more inclined to regard decision making as consensual and to prefer "us" instead of "I." Higher reliance in the female brain on the portion of the limbic system associated with symbolic action could also contribute to these tendencies.

Since the male brain tends to construct reality in terms of abstract solutions and sequential movements in map space, men probably perceive action as more commensurate with their sense of the real. If action in the reality of males seems more "actual" than talking, this could explain, in part at least, why men are more inclined to associate intimacy with shared activities, to respond to depression with action, and to describe feelings with action metaphors.

Neuroscience also suggests why women seem to believe that emotions are conveyed more through talking than action. If reality as it is constructed in the female brain features a more extended network of perceptions, memories, associations, and feelings, then the real could be more closely associated with language. This could also explain why women favor "rapport talk," or conversations about the personal and the private. If this talk is more commensurate with the actual character of reality in the female brain, women more than men might depend on conversation to reinforce their reality.

More emotional content in female constructions of reality could also explain why women are more inclined to equate talking with feeling, and to view caring actions that are not accompanied by verbal expressions of feeling as less than authentic. And if linguistic constructions of reality in the female brain feature a broader range of emotional experience, women may have less difficulty, on average, disclosing, describing, and contextualizing feelings.

## A NEW VIEW OF THE LANGUAGE OF LOVE

The use of qualifiers like "on average," "tends," "may," "probably," and "might" in the description of behavior associated with the sex-specific human brain is not a concession to political correctness. It is the only way to fairly characterize the differences. There is nothing in this research that argues for a direct causal connection between sex-specific brains and the behavior of men and women. Every human brain is unique and becomes more so as a result of learning, and there is more variation between same-sex brains than opposite-sex brains. What is most striking in virtually all of the research on the sex-specific human brain is not differences between the emotional and cognitive processes of men and women but the amazing degree of overlap, or sameness. And while nature may play a larger role in conditioning same-sex behavior than we previously realized, nurture, or learning, remains the most vital part of the equation.

Although many of the behaviors in the litany of male pathology are obviously learned and subject to change, the tendencies associated with the sex-specific male brain cannot be erased in the learning process. This means that the assumption that love is not love unless men must think, feel, and behave like women in love relationships is not, in the vast majority of instances, realistic. Consider, for example, the primary reason why women seek a divorce. When divorced women are asked to explain the failure of a marriage, the

ommon refrain is "lack of communication," or the unwillingness of
the ex-husband to talk about or
share feelings.[18] In one recent study,
over two-thirds of the women surveyed felt that men would never understand them, or that the men in
their lives would remain forever

clueless about the lives of women.[19]
And yet numerous studies have also
shown that women view men who
deviate from the masculine norm by
displaying or talking openly about
emotions as "too feminine" and
"poorly adjusted."[20]

Recognizing discrepancies in reality as it "tends" to be constructed in
the brains of men and women does
not frustrate the desire of men and
women to communicate better with
their partners. In fact, the opposite
is true. Awareness of the discrepancies makes it much easier to negotiate differences and to communicate
to our partners how they might better satisfy our expectations and desires without recourse to blame and

anger. And this could lead to a
greater willingness to embrace two
additional assumptions about
human reality that have been
grandly reinforced by brain science—the total reality is that of both
men and women, and the overlap or
sameness of the realities of men
and women is far greater than the
differences.

---

*Robert L. Nadeau is a professor at
George Mason University. This article
is based on his most recent book,* S/he
Brain: Science, Sexual Politics and
the Feminist Movement *(Praeger,
1996).*

18. Thomas Wills, Robert Weiss, and Gerald
Patterson, "A Behavioral Analysis of the Determinants of Marital Separation," *Journal of
Consulting and Clinical Psychology* 42 (1974):
802–11.

19. Survey by Yankelovitch Partners, 1993.

20. See, for example, John Robertson and
Louise Fitzgerald, "The (Mis)treatment of
Men: Effects of Client Gender Role and Lifestyle on Diagnosis and Attribution of Pathology," *Journal of Counseling Psychology* 37
(1990): 3–9.

# The Infertility Challenge

**Today's baby makers can't help everyone. But with advances like enhanced embryo freezing, they're getting close. By Annetta Miller and Joan Raymond**

I T HAS BEEN 20 YEARS SINCE LOUISE BROWN, the world's first test-tube baby, was born—20 years in which microchip technology has transformed the computer industry, scientists have almost mapped the entire human genome and Brown herself grew up to become a healthy, well-adjusted day-care worker. The assisted reproductive technology (ART) that brought Brown into the world has matured, too. Although fertility experts from some of the most successful clinics in the United States agree that ART still has a lot of growing up to do, the techniques have come a long way since the 1970s and even the 1980s, when most couples endured round after round of assisted reproduction without receiving a bundle of joy at the end of it all. The chance of taking home a baby using the costly new technologies is now more than 20 percentage points higher than it was in the early 1980s. That still falls short of guaranteeing every infertile couple a baby, but researchers haven't given up. "There's a lot of research going on," says Dr. William Gibbons, chairman of the department of obstetrics and gynecology at the Jones Institute for Reproductive Medicine at Eastern Virginia Medical School, which performed the first successful in vitro fertilization procedure in America. Techniques with futuristic names like cytoplasmic and blastocyst transfer, as well as refinements in established procedures like embryo freezing and intracytoplasmic sperm injection (ICSI), promise new hope to infertile couples. Says Gibbons: "It's an extraordinarily exciting time."

Since Brown's birth in 1978, millions of women have sought treatment for infertility, which most experts define as the inability to become pregnant after one year of regularly timed, unprotected intercourse. The incidence of infertility is evenly split between men and women: in about 40 percent of infertile couples the man is infertile, in 40 percent the woman is and 10 to 20 percent fall into the great abyss termed "unexplained." The most frequent causes include blocked fallopian tubes; poor or absent ovulation, especially in women over 35; endometriosis, a disorder marked by the overgrowth of tissue of the uterine lining; poor cervical mucus, and "male factor" problems such as low sperm count and impeded sperm motility. About 25 percent of infertile couples encounter more than one of these problems.

But fertility doctors say that overall, the most formidable enemy of fertility is what they refer to as AMA: advanced maternal age. With women now routinely attempting pregnancies in their late 30s to mid-40s, the field has made relatively few inroads in reversing the effects of age-related barrenness. Using traditional methods of conception, a woman in her 20s still has a 20 to 25 percent chance of becoming pregnant during any given month. By her 40s, that drops to 10 to 15 percent—a reality even high-tech procedures cannot alter significantly. Older women may continue to ovulate, but the eggs they produce are compromised by chromosomal and structural problems, and often fail to fertilize. If they do fertilize, the resulting embryos often have difficulty implanting in the uterus. Dr. Mark Sauer, head of New York's Columbia-Presbyterian Medical Center's division of reproductive endocrinology, says that as society increasingly celebrates older motherhood, many of his patients are shocked to learn that science often cannot help them conceive using their own eggs. "In school we teach young girls about sex education; we encourage them to defer motherhood until they've finished their education and begun a career," Sauer says. "What we don't teach them is that if they postpone motherhood too long, their chances of having a biological child may be very small."

Overcoming the problems wreaked by age and other factors is now the province of more than 300 fertility clinics around the country. They are refining an alphabet soup of high-tech variations on in vitro fertilization with names like GIFT, ZIFT and IVF with ICSI. In IVF, the procedure that produced Louise Brown, egg and sperm are united in a petri dish and then implanted into a woman's uterus. In GIFT (gamete intrafallopian transfer) and ZIFT (zygote intrafallopian transfer), implantation occurs in the fallopian tubes. In ICSI, a single sperm is manipulated so it fertilizes a woman's egg and creates an embryo. All these treatments require eggs that have matured in the ovaries. This means that women who undergo them need to take costly and difficult-to-administer ovulation-inducing drugs designed to increase the number of eggs available for fertilization. In doing so, they also increase their chances of conceiving twins or triplets—or, in the case of a Houston couple last

# Playing the Fertility Odds

*U.S. clinics made more than 64,000 attempts at assisted reproduction in 1996. Successes—with fresh, non-donor eggs—are given as a percentage of the fertilized egg returned to or created in women.*

- Standard in vitro fertilization (IVF): 45,462 attempts, 25.9 percent successful.
- IVF with intracyctoplasmic sperm injection (ICSI): about 15,000 attempts, 27.8 percent successful
- Gamete intrafallopian transfer (GIFT): 2,892 attempts, 28.7 percent successful
- Zygote intrafallopian transfer (ZIFT): 1,225 attempts, 30.3 percent successful

December, octuplets. Until now the most commonly used induction aids had to be administered via painful intramuscular injections. But recently Serono Laboratories introduced Fertinex, an ovulation inducer that can be self-administered using a very small needle just under the skin, much the way someone with diabetes injects herself with insulin.

One promising experimental technique may do away with ovulation-inducing drugs altogether. Called in vitro maturation (IVM), the procedure involves raising an immature egg in a laboratory dish until it is fertilized by a sperm. Because the egg's maturation occurs in the lab, rather than inside a woman's body, there is no need for fertility drugs.

IVM may still be years away from widespread use. But a new procedure called cytoplasmic transfer may soon help women whose eggs are, according to a microscopic examination, chromosomally or structurally fragile and therefore may fail to implant or grow. In an experimental procedure pioneered by St. Barnabas Medical Center in Livingston, N.J., doctors withdraw a portion of the fluid surrounding the nucleus from a healthy donor egg. This cytoplasm replaces substances in the poorer egg that are "deficient," while still allowing it to retain its own DNA. "This is a big leap forward," says Dr. Richard T. Scott, St. Barnabas's director of assisted reproduction, since using cytoplasmic transfer allows parents to pass their genetic material to a child. The only other available option for these women is using donor eggs, in which another woman's egg is fertilized with sperm from the first woman's partner and then placed in the uterus. Scott believes the patients who will benefit most from cytoplasmic transfer are

those who make an adequate number of eggs during stimulation for in vitro fertilization, but whose eggs are "poor performers" during embryonic development. "This may prove to be an exceptional technique for women in their 30s and those with structural problems with their eggs and embryos," says Scott.

Another technique designed to aid infertility's most difficult cases is autologous endometrial co-culture. In the procedure, doctors grow an embryo in a lab dish along with previously harvested tissue from an infertile woman's own endometrium, or uterine lining. The theory behind the technique is that the tissue provides the embryo with a more natural growing environment than the usual laboratory medium. "We've seen remarkable success rates, even in women who have previously failed three to four IVF cycles," says Dr. Zev Rosenwaks, director of the Center for Reproductive Medicine and Infertility at Cornell University's Weill Medical College.

Many of the most promising fertility treatments are improvements on existing techniques. For years doctors have been able to use cryopreservation—or embryo freezing—to increase the success rates after each retrieval. But frozen embryos were typically less hardy than their fresh counterparts, and they were less successful in creating pregnancies. Now, embryologists are able to make frozen embryos nearly as viable as fresh ones. Doctors at the Mayo Clinic's Division of Reproductive Endocrinology and

them for nearly four years. Worse, doctors could not explain why. "I felt like God was mad at me," recalls Stockwell. Using the Mayo Clinic's improved cryopreservation methods, Stockwell and Hemmila gave birth two years ago to a towheaded baby boy. "I can't believe he was frozen once," says Stockwell. "Not too long ago, he wouldn't have been possible."

Refinements to other existing IVF techniques are also making new babies possible. One promising technique involves transferring embryos to the uterus when they are blastocysts, embryos about five days old that consist of eight or more cells. Until now, most embryos have been transferred to the uterus after only two to three days of development in the petri dish, when they consist of a mere two to eight cells. Blastocyst transfer is designed to more closely mimic what happens in the body during natural conception. It offers the added advantage of allowing doctors to prescreen the embryos that they implant. Thus, embryos that are inadequately developing can be more readily identified—and not transferred. Because blastocyst transfer improves the chances that only healthy embryos will be implanted, doctors can now advise their patients to have only two or three embryos implanted rather than four or five. The results, it is hoped, will be more full-term pregnancies—and fewer multiple births.

For all the promise surrounding new assisted reproductive technology, however, there have been reports of a darker side. A

---

**Did You Know?**

Humans have an estimated 80,000 genes, strung along 23 pairs of chromosomes. The sex chromosomes are the 23d pair. The X, or 'female,' chromosome carries an estimated 5,000 genes. The Y, or 'male,' chromosome has a mere 30.

---

Infertility say frozen embryos result in pregnancies about 40 percent of the time for women under 40 who use their clinic, an exceptionally high rate of success. "Frozen-embryo-transfer technology has come a long way," says Mayo's Dr. Daniel A. Dumesic, chairman of the division. "It's less expensive than creating embryos through another egg retrieval.

Just ask Debbie Stockwell, of Rhinelander, Wis. As an obstetrician, Stockwell spends her days bringing new life into the world. So it was a bitter irony that she and her husband, Robert Hemmila, were unable to conceive a baby of their own. Despite repeated attempts at IVF, a pregnancy eluded

recent study reported in a journal published by the European Society of Human Reproduction and Embryology indicates that babies conceived through ICSI have an eight-in-1,000 chance of having an extra or missing sex (X or Y) chromosome. This is a fourfold higher incidence than seen in the general population. Some of the conditions associated with sex-chromosome abnormalities in affected children include heart problems that may require surgery, learning and behavior difficulties, and adult infertility. The study is preliminary, but doctors like Eldon Schriock, director of the fertility clinic at the University of California, San Francisco, are informing patients of a potential risk. "At present, we do not know why there would be this increased risk for children conceived through ICSI," says Schriock. "Two possibilities are that the sperm being used is abnormal or the procedure itself leads to an increased risk of sex-chromosome abnormalities." Schriock notes that if an ICSI offspring has normal chromosomes, as determined by prenatal testing, the health risks are no greater than those of a child conceived by intercourse.

The greatest deterrent to assisted reproduction, however, is cost. A few rounds of reproductive roulette can run upwards of $40,000 at many clinics, and the tab is rarely covered by insurance. In response to patient demand, fertility clinics and customers are increasingly examining ways to cut costs. For example, many couples opt to bypass IVF in favor of lower-cost procedures that offer very similar returns. A study published in January in The New England Journal of Medicine suggests that pairing ovulation-inducing drugs with relatively low-tech treatments like intrauterine insemination (IUI) may be almost as effective as IVF. According to the study, fertility drugs plus IUI resulted in a 33 percent chance of a couple's conceiving a child in any given cycle.

Sauer is out to make costs more competitive. In 1997 Columbia-Presbyterian became one of the few to offer what's known in the business as "embryo adoption." By adopting embryos created from sperm and eggs donated by others, patients can forgo some of the costs associated with traditional assisted reproduction. Completing an IVF cycle with an adopted embryo, for example, might lop as much as 50 to 75 percent off the price of an IVF procedure. Last year Sauer joined forces with GenCor, Inc., a physician-practice management company that handles the business side of his program. Sauer says the move helped cut the rate for first-time IVF, including medications, cryopreservation and one year's egg storage to $8,600. That's about $4,000 less than the competition, he says. Based on those fees, Sauer has signed preliminary agreements with several insurance companies willing to cover the costs of treatment.

Low cost or not, the word infertility will not be taken out of the dictionary any time soon. Despite all the recent advances, it may be decades before the most complex fertility mysteries are solved. Until then, many of those seeking treatment will continue on a Sisyphean quest for a baby of their own.

# The Science of a Good Marriage

## Psychology is unlocking the secrets of happy couples.

BY BARBARA KANTROWITZ AND PAT WINGERT

THE MYTH OF MARRIAGE goes like this: somewhere out there is the perfect soul mate, the yin that meshes easily and effortlessly with your yang. And then there is the reality of marriage, which, as any spouse knows, is not unlike what Thomas Edison once said about genius: 1 percent inspiration and 99 percent perspiration. That sweaty part, the hard work of keeping a marriage healthy and strong, fascinates John Gottman. He's a psychologist at the University of Washington, and he has spent more than two decades trying to unravel the bewildering complex of emotions that binds two humans together for a year, a decade or even (if you're lucky) a lifetime.

Gottman, 56, comes to this endeavor with the best of qualifications: he's got the spirit of a scientist and the soul of a romantic. A survivor of one divorce, he's now happily married to fellow psychologist Julie Schwartz Gottman (they run couples workshops together). His daunting task is to quantify such intangibles as joy, contempt and tension. Ground zero for this research is the Family Research Laboratory on the Seattle campus (nicknamed the Love Lab). It consists of a series of nondescript offices equipped with video cameras and pulse, sweat and movement monitors to read the hearts and minds of hundreds of couples who have volunteered to be guinea pigs in longitudinal studies of the marital relationship. These volunteers have opened up their lives to the researchers, dissecting everything from the frequency of sex to who takes out

the garbage. The results form the basis of Gottman's new book, "The Seven Principles for Making Marriage Work," which he hopes will give spouses a scientific road map to happiness.

Among his unexpected conclusions: anger is not the most destructive emotion in a marriage, since both happy and miserable couples fight. Many popular therapies aim at defusing anger between spouses, but Gottman found that the real demons (he calls them "the Four Horsemen of the Apocalypse") are criticism, contempt, defensiveness and stonewalling. His research shows that the best way to keep these demons at bay is for couples to develop a "love map" of their spouse's dreams and fears. The happy couples all had such a deep understanding of their partner's psyche that they could navigate roadblocks without creating emotional gridlock.

Gottman's research also contradicts the Mars-Venus school of relationships, which holds that men and women come from two very different emotional worlds. According to his studies, gender differences may contribute to marital problems, but they don't cause them. Equal percentages of both men and women he interviewed said that the quality of the spousal friendship is the most important factor in marital satisfaction.

Gottman says he can predict, with more than 90 percent accuracy, which couples are likely to end up in divorce court. The first seven years are especially precarious; the average time for a divorce in this group is 5.2

years. The next danger point comes around 16 to 20 years into the marriage, with an average of 16.4 years. He describes one couple he first met as newlyweds: even then they began every discussion of their problems with sarcasm or criticism, what Gottman calls a "harsh start-up." Although they professed to be in love and committed to the relationship, Gottman correctly predicted that they were in trouble. Four years later they were headed for divorce, he says.

An unequal balance of power is also deadly to a marriage. Gottman found that a husband who doesn't share power with his wife has a much higher risk of damaging the relationship. Why are men singled out? Gottman says his data show that most wives, even those in unstable marriages, are likely to accept their husband's influence. It's the men who need to shape up, he says. The changes can be simple, like turning off the football game when she needs to talk. Gottman says the gesture proves he values "us" over "me."

Gottman's research is built on the work of many other scientists who have focused on emotion and human interaction. Early studies of marriage relied heavily on questionnaires filled out by couples, but these were often inaccurate. In the 1970s several psychology labs began using direct observation of couples to study marriage. A big boon was a relatively new tool for psychologists: videotape. Having a visual record that could be endlessly replayed made it much easier to study the emotional flow between spouses. In 1978 researchers Paul Ekman and Wallace Freisen devised a coding system for the human face (*See box,* "Know Your Spouse") that eventually provided another way to measure interchange between spouses.

Although early studies focused on couples in trouble, Gottman thought it was also important to study couples whose marriages work; he thinks they're the real experts. The Love Lab volunteers are interviewed about the history of their marriage. They then talk in front of the cameras about subjects that cause conflict between them. One couple Gottman describes in the book, Tim and Kara, argued constantly about his friend Buddy, who often wound up spending the night on Tim and Kara's couch. The researchers take scenes like this and break down every second of interaction to create a statistical pattern of good and bad moments. How many times did she roll her eyes (a sign of contempt) when he spoke? How often did he fidget (indicating tension or stress)? The frequency of negative and positive expressions, combined with the data collected by the heart, sweat and other monitors, provides a multidimensional view of the relationship. (Tim and Kara ultimately decided Buddy could stay, only not as often.)

Gottman and other researchers see their work as a matter of public health. The average couple who seek help have been having problems for six years—long enough to have done serious damage to their relationship. That delay, Gottman says, is as dangerous as putting off regular mammograms. The United States has one of the highest divorce rates in the industrialized world, and studies have shown a direct correlation between marriage and well-being. Happily married people are healthier; even their immune systems work better than those of people who are unhappily married or divorced. Kids suffer as well; if their parents split, they're more likely to have emotional or school problems.

But going to a marriage counselor won't necessarily help. "Therapy is at an impasse," Gottman says, "because it is not based on solid empirical knowledge of what real couples do to keep their marriages happy and stable." In a 1995 Consumer Reports survey, marriage therapy ranked at the bottom of a poll of patient satisfaction with various psychotherapies. The magazine said part of the problem was that "almost anyone can hang out a shingle as a marriage counselor." Even credentialed therapists may use approaches that have no basis in research. Several recent studies have shown that many current treatments produce few long-term benefits for couples who seek help.

One example: the process called "active listening." It was originally used by therapists to objectively summarize the complaints of a patient and validate the way the patient is feeling. ("So, I'm hearing that you think your father always liked your sister

## Know Your Spouse

Test the strength of your marriage in this relationship quiz prepared especially for NEWSWEEK by John Gottman.

TRUE/FALSE

1   I can name by partner's best friends.

2   I can tell you what stresses my partner is currently facing

3   I know the names of some of the people who have been irritating my partner lately

4   I can tell you some of my partner's life dreams

5   I can tell you about my partner's basic philosophy of life

6   I can list the relatives my partner likes the least

7   I feel that my partner knows me pretty well

8   When we are apart, I often think fondly of my partner

9   I often touch or kiss my partner affectionately

10   My partner really respects me

11   There is fire and passion in this relationship

12   Romance is definitely still a part of our relationship

13   My partner appreciates the things I do in this relationship

14   My partner generally likes my personality

15   Our sex life is mostly satisfying

16   At the end of the day my partner is glad to see me

17   My partner is one of my best friends

18   We just love talking to each other

19   There is lots of give and take (both people have influence) in our discussions

20   My partner listens respectfully, even when we disagree

21   My partner is usually a great help as a problem solver

22   We generally mesh well on basic values and goals in life

**Scoring:** GIVE YOURSELF ONE POINT FOR EACH "TRUE" ANSWER. ABOVE 12: YOU HAVE A LOT OF STRENGTH IN YOUR RELATIONSHIP. CONGRATULATIONS. BELOW 12: YOUR RELATIONSHIP COULD STAND SOME IMPROVEMENT AND COULD PROBABLY BENEFIT FROM SOME WORK ON THE BASICS SUCH AS IMPROVING COMMUNICATION.

better and you're hurt by that.") In recent years this technique has been modified for marital therapy—ineffectively, Gottman says. Even highly trained therapists would have a hard time stepping back in the middle of a fight and saying, "So, I'm hearing that you think I'm a fat, lazy slob."

Happily married couples have a very different way of relating to each other during disputes, Gottman found. The partners make frequent "repair attempts," reaching out to each other in an effort to prevent negativity from getting out of control in the midst of conflict. Humor is often part of a successful repair attempt. In his book, Gottman describes one couple arguing about the kind of

car to buy (she favors a minivan; he wants a snazzier Jeep). In the midst of yelling, the wife suddenly puts her hand on her hip and sticks out her tongue—mimicking their 4-year-old son. They both start laughing, and the tension is defused.

In happy unions, couples build what Gottman calls a "sound marital house" by working together and appreciating the best in each other. They learn to cope with the two kinds of problems that are part of every marriage: solvable conflicts and perpetual problems that may represent underlying conflicts and that can lead to emotional gridlock. Gottman says 69 percent of marital conflicts fall into the latter category. Happy spouses

# Facing Your Problems

IN THE LAB, THE WAY A MARRIED COUPLE FIGHTS CAN OFTEN TELL psychologists more than *what* they fight about. The expressions and underlying emotions displayed during a conflict may reveal the strength or weakness of the marriage. During a couple's 15-minute conversation—on a topic known to be a sore point—researchers at the University of Washington measure physiological responses (below) and facial expressions, which can reveal true feelings even when words don't. Videotapes also show how long the partners' emotional responses last—even the happiest of couples has fleeting moments of bad feeling, but if the negative indicators tend to endure, it can signal a marriage in trouble.

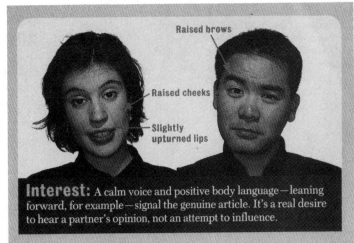

**Interest:** A calm voice and positive body language—leaning forward, for example—signal the genuine article. It's a real desire to hear a partner's opinion, not an attempt to influence.

**Surprise:** A big smile, with popping eyes, indicates a positive surprise. Something unexpected but unpleasant yields the eye-pop only. Either way, a short-lived state.

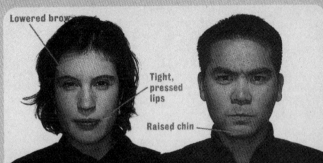

**Anger:** The tone is cold or loud, the wording staccato. But honest anger, an internal state, is different from contempt, directed at the spouse. A fake smile, without raised cheeks, may mask anger.

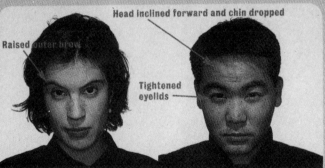

**Domineering:** A "low and slow" voice often signals that one partner is trying to force the other to his or her view. Ranges from lawyerly cross-examination to blatant threats.

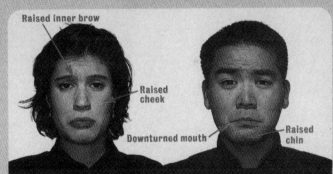

**Sadness:** Passivity and sulking can look like stonewalling or disengaging from a fight, but sad people maintain more eye contact than stonewallers.

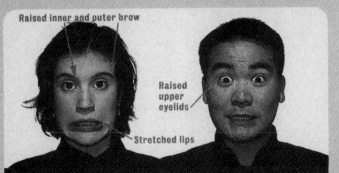

**Fear:** Outright fear is rare; a lower-grade version—tension—is more common. And a wife's tension, if pronounced, can be a predictor for divorce down the road.

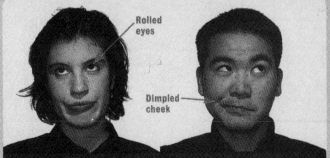

**Contempt:** If prolonged, this expression is a red alert. Especially when accompanied by sarcasm and insults, it suggests a marriage in serious trouble.

deal with these issues in a way that strengthens the marriage. One couple Gottman studied argued constantly about order in their household (she demanded neatness, and he couldn't care less). Over the years they managed to accommodate their differences, acknowledging that their affection for each other was more important than newspapers piled up in the corner of the living room.

As psychologists learn more about marriage, they have begun devising new approaches to therapy. Philip Cowan and Carolyn Pape-Cowan, a husband-and-wife team (married for 41 years) at the University of California, Berkeley, are looking at one of the most critical periods in a marriage: the birth of a first child. (Two thirds of couples experience a "precipitous drop" in marital satisfaction at this point, researchers say.) "Trying to take two people's dreams of a perfect family and make them one is quite a trick," Pape-Cowan says. The happiest couples were those who looked on their spouses as partners with whom they shared household and child-care duties. The Cowans say one way to help spouses get through the transition to parenting would be ongoing group sessions with other young families to provide the kind of support people used to get from their communities and extended families.

## Inside the Love Lab

In the laboratory, video cameras record facial expressions. Motion-sensing jiggle-ometers register fidgeting, and a cluster of sensors reads physiological data.

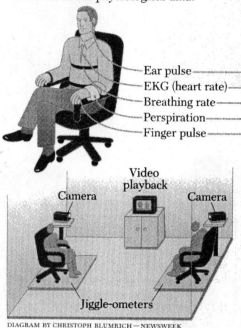

Ear pulse
EKG (heart rate)
Breathing rate
Perspiration
Finger pulse

Video playback
Camera          Camera

Jiggle-ometers

DIAGRAM BY CHRISTOPH BLUMRICH — NEWSWEEK

Two other researchers—Neil Jacobson at the University of Washington and Andrew Christensen at UCLA—have developed what they call "acceptance therapy" after studying the interactions of couples in conflict. The goal of their therapy is to help people learn to live with aspects of their spouse's characters that simply can't be changed. "People can love each other not just for what they have in common but for things that make them complementary," says Jacobson. "When we looked at a clinical sample of what predicted failure in traditional behavior therapy, what we came upon again and again was an inability to accept differences."

Despite all these advances in marital therapy, researchers still say they can't save all marriages—and in fact there are some that *shouldn't* be saved. Patterns of physical abuse, for example, are extremely difficult to alter, Gottman says. And there are cases where the differences between the spouses are so profound and long-standing that even the best therapy is futile. Gottman says one quick way to test whether a couple still has a chance is to ask what initially attracted them to each other. If they can recall those magic first moments (and smile when they talk about them), all is not lost. "We can still fan the embers," says Gottman. For all the rest of us, there's hope.

# The Nature and Uses of
# DREAMING

*"The connections made in dreaming are not random.
They are guided by the dominant emotions of the dreamer."*

## by Ernest Hartmann, M.D.

A 20-YEAR-OLD college student barely escaped with his life from a fire that killed several members of his family. A few nights later, he had a vivid dream: "I was on a beach when a huge tidal wave came along and engulfed me. I was flipped over and over; there was nothing I could do. I was just about to drown when I woke up." On another night, he also dreamt: "I was swept away in a whirlwind. I was helpless, just blown away." These dreams clearly do not picture the details of what happened to him—the fire. Rather, they picture his emotional state—his feeling of fear, terror, and helplessness.

I have collected and studied many series of dreams after major trauma and repeatedly have come across such dreams as tidal waves, whirlwinds, or being chased by gangs of thugs. I am convinced that these dreams are a sort of paradigm, a place where we can see most clearly what is happening in all dreams. Such dreams are by no means nonsense. They picture the emotional state of our minds.

*Dr. Hartmann, professor of psychiatry, Tufts University School of Medicine, and director, Sleep Disorders Center, Newton-Wellesley Hospital, Boston, Mass., is the author of* Dreams and Nightmares: The New Theory on the Nature and Functions of Dreaming.

My collaborators and I have been developing a view of dreams which differs considerably from accepted wisdom on the subject. Nevertheless, it turns out to be very compatible with the commonsense experience of those who remember their dreams and have developed an interest in them.

Over all, dreams have not gotten much respect in the past few decades. There have been two dominant schools of thought. One view championed by some biologists is that dreams basically are random nonsense, the products of a poorly functioning brain during sleep. If there is any meaning to dreams, it is "added on later" as our brains try to "make the best of a bad job." A related view proposed by other biologists is that dreaming may function as an "unlearning" procedure: a dream is garbage being thrown out by a computer to keep itself from being clogged up. In this view, we dream specifically about what we do *not* need to remember.

The other view of dreams, more common among psychoanalysts and therapists, derives broadly from the work of pioneering psychoanalyst Sigmund Freud. He did take dreams seriously in one sense, calling them the "royal road" to the workings of the unconscious. However, Freud felt that his main contribution—his discovery of the secret of dreams—was his finding that, when properly analyzed, every dream turns out to be a fulfillment of a wish. Further, although Freud appears to take dreams much more seriously than the biologists do, he does not place much value on the dream itself, which he calls the "manifest dream." He repeatedly refers to the dream as an irrational mental product, whose value emerges only when one subjects it to a process of free association leading eventually to an underlying "latent dream" containing the underlying wish.

After having spent many years conducting research on the biology of dreaming, I disagree with both these broad views. Indeed, there now is available a tremendous amount of information about the biology of sleep and specifically the biology of REM (rapid eye movement) sleep, the part of sleep in which most of our memorable dreams occur. However, this knowledge of the underlying biology of dreaming does not tell us the true nature or functions of dreaming, and it certainly is not a reason for dismissing the psychological meaning of dreams. Why should the developing understanding of the biology underlying it make dreaming meaningless, any more than the developing understanding of the biology underlying thought makes thought meaningless?

I have spent many years analyzing my own and my patients' dreams in my clinical practice, using Freud's technique of free association as well as somewhat different techniques developed by psychologist Carl Jung and others. There is no question in my mind that dreams are meaningful and can lead us to useful knowledge about ourselves. However, there are many places where I disagree with Freud, most prominently in his thesis that every dream, when properly understood, is the fulfillment of a wish. For instance, the hundreds of dreams I have collected of the tidal wave type can not in any way, with or without free association, be interpreted as fulfillment of wishes. Rather, they are providing a context for an emotional concern.

Work on dreams after trauma as well as in stressful occurrences, pregnancy, and many other defined situations has led gradually to the following view of dreams, which merely can be sketched briefly here. First of all, dreaming makes connections in the nets of the mind more broadly and loosely than waking does. I believe we have no choice but to consider the mind to be based on the functioning of the human cerebral cortex, made up of billions of somewhat similar units (neurons), with some assistance from subcortical parts of the brain. All that can happen in these nets, awake or asleep, is that patterns of units are activated or deactivated in various ways and connections are made and unmade.

When dreaming, we make connections more broadly and loosely than when awake. Although the connections sometimes may seem far-fetched or bizarre, they often make obvious sense. Four different women, two patients and two friends, have told me something close to this: "I dreamt of Jim—my boyfriend—but he looked very much like my father (or he changed into someone like my father). Upon waking, I realized, 'Yes, of course, Jim is like my father in a lot of ways. It's strange I never noticed that before.'" These dreams simply have put together things in their minds which they have not quite put together in waking. While awake, "father" and "Jim" occupied different channels, or trains of thought. Only in the broadly connected state of dreaming were the two brought together. The connection is meaningful and can be useful.

The connections made in dreaming are not random. They are guided by the dominant emotions of the dreamer. This is where my work in dreams after trauma begins. I believe that, if we want to understand what is going on in dreams, we should not start with a group of random dreams of students, where we don't know much of what is going on. Rather, we should begin when we know clearly what must be going on emotionally in someone's mind.

One such situation occurs in someone who has just been through a traumatic event—a fire or other catastrophe, rape, or attack. This is where we find dreams portraying terror and helplessness: "I was overwhelmed by a tidal wave"; "I was swept away in a whirlwind"; "I was chased off a cliff by a gang"; etc. There clearly is a feeling of fear or terror at those times, and these dreams picture or provide a context for this. We speak of dreams "contextualizing the emotion."

Terror and helplessness are not the only emotions pictured in this way. Any emotion that dominates a person's life is pictured likewise in dreams. I had one patient who was functioning very well except for terrible guilt that she was not a good mother to her children. Over and over, she reported dreams such as this: "I let my son play in the yard and a huge cat grabbed him"; "My children were in the woods and a bear was chasing them"; "I left my children in a hotel room and I couldn't find them." Over all, the more powerful and clear-cut the emotional concern, the more clearly the dreams portray this. These dreams in no way can be considered random or nonsense.

We have developed a scoring system for such contextualing images in dreams and have shown in over 500 dreams scored on a blind basis that these images appear to be more frequent and more intense in traumatic and stressful situations than at other times. Here are some of the clear-cut contextualizing images we have found at times of intense emotion:

**Fear, terror.** "A huge tidal wave is coming at me." "A house is burning and no one can get out." "A gang of evil men, Nazis maybe, are chasing me. I can't get away."

**Helpless, vulnerability.** "I dreamt about children, dolls—dolls and babies all drowning." "He skinned me and threw me in a heap with my sisters. I could feel the pain. I could feel everything." "There was a small wounded animal lying in the road."

**Guilt.** "My father (whom I'm caring for) is swept away in a flood." "I let my children play by themselves and they get run over by a car."

**Grief.** "A large round hill or mountain has split in two pieces, and there are arrangements I have to make to take care of it." "A huge tree has fallen down in front of my house." "I'm in this vast barren empty space. There are ashes strewn all about."

## Connections

Our conclusion based on a great deal of such work is that dreams make connections broadly, but by no means randomly, in the nets of the mind. The connections are guided by the emotional concern of the dreamer. The dreams contextualize or picture the emotional concern. Furthermore,

dreams have their own language for doing this. Dreams obviously do not deal in words or mathematical symbols, but, rather, in pictures—in what we might call picture metaphor. There is a whole continuum in our mental functioning, running from focused waking thought at one end (doing an arithmetic problem, for instance), through looser thought, reverie, daydreaming, and finally dreaming at the other end. As we move from the left-hand end to the right-hand end, we think more in pictures and specifically in picture metaphor.

Thus, dreams contextualize emotional concerns, using the language of picture metaphor. For instance, in our culture, a trip in a car often is a metaphor for the course of lives or relationships. I've heard a large number of dreams something like, "I am in a car going downhill and the brakes don't seem to be working," dreamt when a relationship was in difficulty or seemed to be out of control. I discuss all this in far more detail in my book, *Dreams and Nightmares: The New Theory on the Nature and Functions of Dreaming.*

There is another important question to consider: Does dreaming have a function or use? Is all this broad making of connections guided by emotions in metaphoric form simply something that happens every night and is of no further significance, or does it have a function in our lives and can we make use of dreaming? Here, I must be a bit speculative, but my collaborators and I agree with workers from a number of different directions that dreaming probably does have a function.

Roughly, the most basic function can be called reweaving or interconnecting. Returning to one of the many series of dreams after trauma, we have found that the person first dreams about tidal waves and gangs, then gradually more and more about other related material from his or her life. The dream is making connections and tying things together. It starts with a new piece of distressing information—in an extreme case, trauma—and ties it in, connects it with other images of trauma, other memories related to the same feelings, etc. This process interconnects and cross-connects the material so that next time something similar happens, it will not be quite so frightening since it will be part of a woven pattern in the mind. The dream reweaves a torn net or redistributes excitation, to use two very different images. Over all, we can talk about the dream as calming by cross-connecting.

What dreams appear to do after a traumatic or disturbing event is similar to what a good therapist does. First, a safe place is established. In therapy, this does not mean supplying a nice room with comfortable furniture. The therapist must be someone the patient gradually can learn to trust;

safety comes from a sense of alliance between patient and therapist. The patient is allowed to tell his or her story about the trauma or new event over and over again, making connections to other material, gradually seeing it in a new light. I believe this happens in dreaming as well. The safe place is provided by a bed and the muscular inhibition of REM-sleep, which assures that the sleeper will lie quietly in bed, rather than running around acting out the dream. Once safety is established, the broad connections gradually are made.

Finally, in addition to the basic function of dreaming, which I believe probably helps us even when we do not remember dreams, there are many ways in which dreams can be useful to us when we do remember them. For example, the women who dreamt some version of "Jim turned into my father" generally found this a useful insight, a new way of looking at things that helped in their relationship. Sometimes, the new and broader connections made by dreaming can be helpful in our work and in artistic and scientific discovery.

A number of creative people have made use of dreams in their discoveries. Some of the best known examples are the French chemist Auguste Kekulé, who saw snakes biting their tales in a dream, which led him to the correct ring structure for the benzene molecule. Inventor Elias Howe attributed the discovery of the sewing machine to a dream in which he was captured by cannibals. He noticed as they danced around him that there were holes at the tips of spears, and he realized this was the design feature he needed to solve his problem. Vladimir Horowitz and several other well-known pianists have described playing piano pieces in their dreams and discovering a new fingering they had not tried previously and which turned out to work perfectly. Robert Louis Stevenson said that his book, *The Strange Case of Dr. Jekyll and Mr. Hyde,* came to him in a dream.

In these cases, I am not saying that all the hard work of discovery happened in the dream. Generally, the artist or scientist made one new connection in a dream and then developed the work in the waking state. Stevenson probably saw a respectable doctor turning into a monster—this is, in fact, quite a typical nightmare image—and then his waking writing skills took over from there. In each case, the dreamers were well-versed in their fields and were worrying hard about a particular problem, which thus had become an emotional concern and was pictured in a dream.

I believe that, by its broader connective features, dreaming has obvious uses of this kind and we probably can make a good deal more of our dreams than we do. For instance, many Native American and South American cultures have adopted a methodology for career choice. In puberty, a young man—or, in some cases, young woman—is sent out into the desert to have a dream or a vision. Often, the young person will return with a powerful dream which, with or without help from the elders, leads to a decision about a future life course.

We might tend to dismiss this as superstition having no relevance to our lives. However, I suggest that we can benefit from the techniques of these cultures. I believe they are making good use of the broader connective powers of dreaming. The young person, who clearly has his future role or "career" in mind as an emotional concern, goes out and has a dream that makes connections more broadly than he does in waking life, which pictures something for him based on his concerns, wishes, or fears, and this often turns out to be very useful to him.

I have known a few people who informally have made use of such a technique. In our culture, we generally ask a young person to consider carefully his or her possible choices for a career, make a list of pros and cons, and so on. There is nothing wrong with this, but I have known several cases in which the decision truly came together or felt right only after a dream.

Sometimes, dreams can be extremely useful in our personal lives, scientific or artistic work, or even something as basic as career choice. I certainly am not suggesting substituting the dream for waking thought, but why leave it out entirely? Dreaming is one end of the continuum, a way of making connections more broadly than our focused waking thought, but guided by what is important to us. Why should we not use everything we have and allow ourselves to notice and employ this additional connecting power?

# Unit 6

## Key Points to Consider

❖ What can be done to protect and preserve memory in the aging brain?

❖ Is middle age an anxiety-ridden age? How do men and women differ in their reactions to traumatic events?

❖ What is perimenopause? Why is this concept more acceptable than menopause?

❖ World famous researchers at the Johns Hopkins University Medical School have offered a prescription for long life. What is this prescription?

❖ If stem cells in the hippocampus can regenerate, can other neurons also undergo mitosis? What will this mean for brain disease?

❖ Is the rapid increase in longevity creating a new stage of life? Explain.

❖ How do emotions change in the second half of life? Why or why not?

❖ What characteristics are shared by centenarians? Will a majority of people pass 100 years age in the second millennium? Defend your answer.

 **Links**     **www.dushkin.com/online/**

These sites are annotated on pages 4 and 5.

...ere is a gradual slowing of the rate of mitosis of ...lls of all the organ systems with age. This gradual ...owing of mitosis translates into a slowed rate of ...pair of cells of all organs. By the thirties, signs of ...ging can be seen in skin, skeleton, vision, hearing, ...mell, taste, balance, coordination, heart, blood vessels, ...ngs, liver, kidneys, digestive tract, immune response, ...ndocrine functioning, and ability to reproduce. To ...ome extent, moderate use of any body part (as ...pposed to disuse or misuse) helps it retain its strength, ...tamina, and repairability. However, by middle and late ...dulthood, persons become increasingly aware of the ...ging effects of their organ systems on their total ...hysical fitness. A loss of height occurs as spinal disks ...nd connective tissues diminish and settle. ...Demineralization, especially loss of calcium, causes ...weakening of bones. Muscles atrophy, and the slowing ...of cardiovascular and respiratory responses creates a ...oss of stamina for exercise. All of this may seem cruel, ...but it occurs very gradually and need not adversely ...affect one's enjoyment of life.

Healthful aging, at least in part, seems to be genetically preprogrammed. The females of many species, including humans, outlive the males. The sex hormones of females may protect them from some early aging effects. Males, in particular, experience earlier declines in their cardiovascular system. Diet and exercise can ward off many of the deleterious effects of aging. A reduction in saturated fat intake coupled with regular aerobic exercise contributes to less bone demineralization, less plaque in the arteries, stronger muscles (including heart and lung muscles), and a general increase in stamina and vitality. An adequate intake of complex carbohydrates, fibrous foods, fresh fruits, fresh vegetables, and water also enhances good health.

Cognitive abilities do not appreciably decline with age in healthy adults. Research suggests that the speed with which the brain carries out problems involving abstract (fluid) reasoning may slow, but not cease. Complex problems may simply require more time to solve with age. On the other hand, research suggests that the memory banks of older people may have more crystallized (accumulated and stored) knowledge. One's ken (range of knowledge) and practical skills (common sense) grow with age and experience. Older human beings become more expert at the tasks they frequently do.

The first article in the middle adulthood section of this unit addresses the question of whether exercise, diet and dietary supplements, seminars, audiotapes, and the like can ward off the gradual decline of cognitive processing, especially the decline of abstract reasoning processes. This article reviews many of the potions and practices that the current population of middle-aged adults are using to maintain, restore, or even improve their memories. The authors attempt to sift out the grains of truth from the chaff. Some diets and dietary supplements boost brain power and the authors chart the pros and cons of using them. Seminars and audiotapes only help you pay better attention to what it is you want to remember.

The second article about middle adulthood speaks to the question of stress and anxiety disorders in midlife. Is this an age of anxiety? Do males and females respond differently to severe emotional trauma? Recent brain researchers have been focusing on how stress changes the brain. The limbic system, known to be a regulator of emotions, reacts about eight times more strongly to sad thoughts in women than in men. In contrast, men have twice as much serotonin as women. Serotonin is a neurotransmitter that raises the blood pressure and regulates emotions. How these differences in brain reactivity affect stress reactions is not pinpointed, but it has long been appreciated that stress causes more depression, anxiety attacks, and eating disorders in women than in men; similar traumatic events cause aggression and/or alcohol and drug abuse in men. Have women and men learned to react differently or is biology behind their responses?

The third article discusses the middle years of adulthood in women who are experiencing gradual decreases in estrogen. A sudden cessation of menstruation (the literal meaning of menopause) is rare. Most women experience several perimenopausal (literally, all around and about the end of menstruation) years. During these years their periods are irregular and their level of the hormone estrogen fluctuates erratically. Sharon Begley describes how this affects behavior and reviews traditional and alternative therapies.

Erik Erikson suggested that the most important psychological conflict of late adulthood is achieving a sense of ego integrity. This is fostered by self-respect, self-esteem, love of others, and a sense that one's life has order and meaning. The articles in the subsection on late adulthood reflect Erikson's concern with experiencing ego integrity rather than despair.

The Johns Hopkins School of Medicine has put out a prescription for longevity for older adults entering the new millennium. Surprisingly, it is not all about medical care. Rather, a strong recommendation for a long life is to love others and to cultivate friendships. The experts at Johns Hopkins also recommend stress management exercise, challenging the mind, and pursuing a wholesome lifestyle with diet and health care.

The next article in this late adulthood subsection reports a finding that is really table-turning. For years it has been believed that neurons do not undergo mitosis after birth. In other words, once a neuron dies it was thought to be forever lost. Protecting one's supply of neurons, therefore, was extremely important throughout life. Now scientists have discovered some regeneration of neurons in the hippocampus. What this will mean for treatment of the neurological illnesses of late adulthood is still unknown.

Jack Rosenthal, in "The Age Boom," describes the phenomena of longer life, better health, and greater security in the late years of adulthood. Many elderly people are living life with dignity and spirit. The factors that he weighs most heavily as contributors to their longevity and integrity are family, school, and work.

The fourth and fifth articles late adulthood selections continue with the theme proposed by Erik Erikson: Late adulthood is more positive when humans develop a sense of ego integrity. Laura Carstensen and Susan Turk Charles believe that human development continues uphill into advanced old age where emotional regulation is concerned. Old adults have the potential to turn frowns upside down and smile with life. They can achieve a sense that their lives were what they meant to be and had order and meaning. Relationships with people who recognize their integrity foster positive emotions.

The last article describes several people who are over 100 years old. It is uplifting and reinforces the theme that positive emotions enhance longevity.

# MEMORY

**Forgetfulness is America's latest health obsession. How much is normal? Can we do anything about it? An explosion of new research offers reassuring insights.**

**BY GEOFFREY COWLEY AND ANNE UNDERWOOD**

STAN FIELD KNOWS WHAT AGE can do to a person's memory, and he's not taking any chances with his. He chooses his food carefully and gets plenty of vigorous exercise. He also avoids stress, soda pop and cigarette smoke. But that's just for starters. At breakfast each morning, the 69-year-old chemical engineer downs a plateful of pills in the hope of boosting his brainpower.

He starts with deprenyl and piracetam—drugs that are normally used to treat diseases like Parkinson's but that casual users can get from overseas sources—and moves on to a series of amino acids (glutamine, phenylalarine, tyrosine). Then he takes several multivitamins, some ginkgo biloba (a plant extract), 1,000 units of vitamin E and, for good measure, a stiff shot of cod-liver oil.

Michelle Arnove is less than half Field's age, but no less concerned about her memory. While working round the clock to finish a degree in film studies, the 33-year-old New Yorker had the alarming sensation that she had stopped retaining anything. "I couldn't even remember names," she says. "I thought, 'Oh no, I'm over 30. It's all downhill from here'." Besides loading up on supplements (she favors ginseng, choline and St. John's wort), Arnove signed up for a memory-enhancement course at New York's Mount Sinai Medical Center. And when she got there, she found herself sur-

## Tested Your Memory Lately?

When it comes to our memories we are our harshest critics, focusing not on countless facts recalled every day, but on the forgotten few. This quiz offers a rough guide to how your memory stacks up against the norm. Now, where did you put that pen?

| | |
|---|---|
| 1 point | **Not within the last six months** |
| 2 points | **Once or twice in the last six months** |
| 3 points | **About once a month** |
| 4 points | **About once a week** |
| 5 points | **Daily** |
| 6 points | **More than once a day** |

☐ How often do you fail to recognize places you've been before?

☐ How often do you forget whether you did something, such as lock the door or turn off the lights or the oven?

☐ How often do you forget when something happened—wondering whether it was yesterday or last week?

☐ How often do you forget where you put items like house keys or wallet?

☐ How often do you forget something you were told recently and had to be reminded of it?

☐ How often are you unable to remember a word or name, even though it's "on the tip of your tongue"?

☐ In conversation, how often do you forget what you were just talking about?

☐ **Total points**

**Score: 7–14 = better than average memory; 15–25 = average; 26 or higher = below average**

ADAPTED FROM: "MEMORY," BY DR. BARRY GORDON AND FROM A. SUNDERLAND, ET AL. (1983 AND 1986).

ounded by people who were just as worried as she was.

For millions of Americans, and especially for baby boomers, the demands of the Information Age are colliding with a sense of waning vigor. "When boomers were in their 30s and 40s, they launched the fitness boom," says Cynthia Green, the psychologist who teaches Mount Sinai's memory class. "Now we have the mental-fitness boom. Memory is the boomers' new life-crisis issue." And, of course, a major marketing opportunity. The demand for books and seminars has never been greater, says Jack Lannom, a Baptist minister and longtime memory trainer whose weekly TV show, "Mind Unlimited," goes out to 33 million homes on the Christian Network. Anxious consumers are rushing to buy do-it-yourself programs like Kevin Trudeau's "Mega Memory," a series of audiotapes that sells for $49.97. And supplement makers are touting everything but sawdust as a brain booster.

But before you get out your checkbook, a few questions are in order. Does everyday forgetfulness signal flagging brain function? Is "megamemory" a realistic goal for normal people? And if you could have a perfect memory, would you really want it? Until recently, no one could address those issues with much authority, but our knowledge of memory is exploding. New imaging techniques are revealing how different parts of the brain interact to preserve meaningful experiences. Biologists are decoding the underlying chemical processes—and neuroscientists are discovering how age, stress and other factors can disrupt them. No one is close to finding the secret to flawless recall, but as you'll see, that may be just as well.

To scientists who study the brain, the wonder is that we retain as much as we do. As Harvard psychologist Daniel Schacter observes in his 1996 book, "Searching for Memory," the simple act of meeting a friend for lunch requires a vast store of memory—a compendium of words, sounds and grammatical rules; a record of the friend's appearance and manner; a catalog of restaurants; a mental map to get you to one, and so on.

How do we manage so much information? Brains are different from computers, but the analogy can be helpful. Like the PC on your desk, your mind is equipped with two basic types of memory: "working memory" for juggling information in the present moment, and long-term memory for storing it over extended periods. Contrary to popular wisdom, our brains don't record everything that happens to us and then bury it until a hypnotist or a therapist helps us dredge it up. Most of what we perceive hovers briefly in working memory, a mental play space akin to a computer's RAM (or random-access memory), then simply evaporates. Working memory enables you to perform simple calculations in your head or retain phone numbers long enough to dial them.

## Connections Matter

Our brains aren't designed to retain random bits of information. We remember things by linking them to what we already know. The process is called 'elaborative encoding.'

**Why We Forget** · I'm Carol

**How We Remember** · I'm Joanne

❶ A name is easy to forget when its only point of reference is a face. Lacking links to other memories, it fades within seconds.

❷ As you learn facts about a person, such as her profession, her name gets embedded in a web of thoughts and impressions. If you don't know her, random associations have a similar effect.

❸ As the web of associations grows, so does the number of paths leading back to the name. Well-encoded memories last a lifetime.

DIAGRAM BY CHRISTOPH BLUMRICH—NEWSWEEK

And like RAM, it lets you analyze and invent things without creating a lasting record.

Long-term memory acts more like a hard drive, physically recording past experiences in the brain region known as the cerebral cortex. The cortex, or outer layer of the brain, houses a thicket of 10 billion vinelike nerve cells, which communicate by relaying chemical and electrical impulses. Every time we perceive something—a sight, a sound, an idea—a unique subset of these neurons gets activated. And they don't always return to their original state. Instead, they may strengthen their connections to one another, becoming more densely intertwined. Once that happens, anything that activates the network will bring back the original perception as a memory. "What we think of as memories are ultimately patterns of connection among nerve cells," says Dr. Barry Gordon, head of the memory-disorders clinic at the Johns Hopkins School of Medicine. A newly encoded memory may involve thousands of neurons spanning the entire cortex. If it doesn't get used, it will quickly fade. But if we activate it repeatedly, the pattern of connection gets more and more deeply embedded in our tissue.

We can will things into long-term memory simply by rehearsing them. But the decision to store or discard a piece of information rarely involves any conscious thought. It's usually handled automatically by the hippocampus, a small, two-winged structure nestled deep in the center of the brain. Like the keyboard on your computer, the hippocampus serves as a kind of switching station. As neurons out in the cortex receive sensory information, they relay it to the hippocampus. If the hippocampus responds, the sensory neurons start forming a durable network. But without that act of consent, the experience vanishes forever.

The hippocampal verdict seems to hinge on two questions. First, does the information have any emotional significance? The name of a potential lover is more likely to get a rise out of the hippocampus than that of Warren Harding's Agriculture secretary. Like Saul Steinberg's cartoon map of America (showing the Midwest as a sliver between Manhattan and the West Coast), the brain constructs the world according to its own parochial interests. And it's more attuned to the sensational than the mundane. In a 1994 experiment, researchers at the University of California, Irvine, told volunteers alternate versions of a story, then quizzed them on the details. In one version, a boy and his mom pass a guard on their way to visit his father. In the other version, the boy is hit by a car. You can guess which one had more staying power.

The second question the hippocampus asks is whether the information entering the brain relates to things we already know. Unlike a computer, which stores related facts separately, the brain strives constantly to make associations. If you have already devoted a lot of neural circuitry to American political history, the name of Harding's Agriculture secretary may actually hold some interest. And if the hippocampus marks the name for storage, it will lodge easily among the related bits of information already linked together in the cortex. In short, we use the nets woven by past experience to capture new information. And because our backgrounds vary, we often retain very different aspects of similar experiences.

Sophie Calle, a French artist, illustrated the point nicely by removing Magritte's "The Menaced Assassin" from its usual place at New York's Museum of Modern Art and asking museum staffers to describe the painting. One respondent (the janitor?) remembered only "men in dark suits" and some "dashes of red blood." Another (the conservator?) remembered little about the style or content of the painting but readily described the dimensions of the canvas, the condition of the paint and the quality of the frame. Still another respondent (the curator?) held forth on the painting's film noir atmosphere, describing how each figure in the eerie tableau helps convey a sense of mystery.

By storing only the information we're most likely to use, our brains make the world manageable. As Columbia University neuroscientist Eric Kandel puts it, "You want to keep the junk of everyday life out of the way so you can focus on what matters." Perfect retention may sound like a godsend, but when the hippocampus gets overly permissive, the results can be devastating. Neurologists sometimes encounter people with superhuman memories. These savants can recite colossal strings of facts, words and num-

---

# Alzheimer's: Losing More Than Memory

## Researchers have no good weapons against this devasting disease—but there is hope

CAR KEYS ARE MISPLACED, A NAME resists moving past the tip of the tongue. Often, we respond with humor: "I must be getting Alzheimer's." But the memory loss that age can bring differs greatly from the dementia of Alzheimer's. Slowly, fatally, Alzheimer's erodes memory, personality and self-awareness. As many as 4 million Americans have it—one in 10 people over 65 and half of those over 85.

It has no cure, and few effective treatments. But in the last decade scientists have started to understand the biochemistry behind Alzheimer's. Today at least 17 drugs are in development. "We don't have the penicillin for Alzheimer's yet," says Roger Rosenberg, director of the Alzheimer's Disease Center at the University of Texas Southwestern Medical Center. "But it's coming." And some of what researchers learn about how this illness rots memory might even help those folks who mislaid their keys.

Today's treatments only ease symptoms. One of Alzheimer's main effects is the destruction of brain cells that produce the neurotransmitter acetylcholine, a chemical essential to learning and memory. Neither of the drugs used most widely for Alzheimer's, Cognex and Aricept, slow the death of those cells. Instead, the drugs slow the deterioration by inhibiting the action of acetylcholinesterase, an enzyme that breaks acetylcholine down. "[The drugs] help make the best use of what you have left," says Rudy Tanzi, a neurogeneticist at Harvard. Yet the drugs have limitations: Cognex only works for a few patients and can cause liver problems. Aricept spares the liver, but its benefits are mod-

est. At least three improved acetylcholinesterase inhibitors are on deck; the first could be out by fall.

Future treatments will have to attack the disease more directly. Scientists hope to control the physical changes in the brain that cause the dementia, such as plaques made of a protein called beta amyloid that gum up neurons. Amyloid is found throughout the body but has an abnormal form toxic to neurons in the brain. For reasons no one is sure of, an enzyme can divide a larger protein improperly, creating the dangerous amyloid beta. Some chemicals appear to block the cleaving enzyme; they may someday lead to new usable drugs.

The body's defense against plaques may make matters worse. The rogue form of amyloid beta triggers an immune response, leading to inflammation that cuts off nutrients and oxygen and further damages the Alzheimer's brain. Nonsteroidal anti-inflammatory drugs, such as aspirin and ibuprofen, may protect against Alzheimer's, and a 1997 study suggested the drugs also slowed the disease's progress. Other anti-inflammatories called cyclcooxygenase (COX-2) inhibitors, developed to treat arthritis, are in clinical trials for use in Alzheimer's patients. And a new class of anti-inflammatories that targets the brain, without harming the stomach, liver and kidneys like current NSAIDS, could be only two years away.

The hormone estrogen might also help. Several studies have suggested that post-menopausal women on hormone replacement therapy (HRT) were less likely to get Alzheimer's. Pharmaceutical giant Wyeth-Ayerst is now test-

ing HRT on 8,000 healthy women and will monitor them for Alzheimer's. In women who don't have dementia, the hormone seems to enhance memory, and it may prevent damage to cells in the brain. Alzheimer's experts would love to have a drug that acts like estrogen in the brain, but not in the breasts or uterus, where it may cause cancer. The current danger "is that people will go and self-medicate because of early positive reports," says Zaven Khachaturian, director of the Ronald and Nancy Reagan Research Institute of the Alzheimer's Association.

Other long-shot approaches could have even bigger payoffs. Last week three labs identified the gene responsible for the formation of the abnormal protein tau, the main component of tangled neurons in the Alzheimer's brain. Suppressing "apoptosis," the process by which the body kills its own cells, including neurons damaged by Alzheimer's, might work—if it doesn't spark tumors kept in check by apoptotic machinery. And a company called NeoTherapeutics is touting AIT-082, a chemical it says induces brain cells to reproduce and grow new neurons. Meanwhile, nonprescription remedies like ginkgo biloba or vitamin E might one day be shown to help Alzheimer's, as well as normal memory loss. We may always try to laugh off our fears of the disease, but as research continues, humor need no longer be the best medicine.

KAREN SPRINGEN *and* ADAM ROGERS
*with* THOMAS HAYDEN

bers. But most are incapable of abstract thought. Lacking a filter on their experience, they're powerless to make sense of it.

At the other end of the spectrum stands H.M., a Connecticut factory worker who made medical history in 1953. He was 27 at the time, and suffering from intractable epilepsy. In a desperate bid to stop his seizures, surgeons removed his hippocampus. The operation made his condition manageable without disrupting his existing memories. But H.M. lost the ability to form new ones. To this day, he can't tell you what he had for breakfast, let alone make a new acquaintance. "Nearly 40 years after his surgery," Boston University researchers wrote in 1993, "H.M. does not know his age or the current date [or] where he is living."

It doesn't take brain surgery to disrupt the hippocampus. Alzheimer's disease gradually destroys the organ, and the ability to form new memories (sidebar). Normal aging can cause subtle impairments, too. Autopsy studies suggest that our overall brain mass declines by 5 to 10 percent per decade during our 60s and 70s. And imaging tests show that both the hippocampus and the frontal cortex become less active. As you would expect, young people generally outperform the elderly on tests that gauge encoding and retrieval ability.

Fortunately, the differences are minor. Experts now agree that unless you develop a particular condition, such as Alzheimer's or vascular disease, age alone won't ruin your memory. At worst, it will make you a little slower and less precise. "We continue to encode the general features of our experiences," says Schacter, "but we leave off more details." For example, Schacter has found that young adults are usually better than old folks at remembering the details of a picture. But the oldsters quickly catch up when coached to pay more attention. And not everyone needs coaching. Though *average* scores decline with age, some octogenarians remain sharper and quicker than college kids.

Whatever their age, people vary widely in recall ability. "Bill Clinton will probably always remember more names than you will," says Gordon. "Unless he has to testify." But that's not to say our abilities are completely fixed. Researchers have identified various influences that can keep the brain from working at full capacity. High blood pressure can impair mental function, even if it doesn't cause a stroke. One study found that over a 25-year period, men with hypertension lost twice as much cognitive ability as those with normal blood pressure. Too little sleep (or too many sleeping pills) can disrupt the formation of new memories. So can too much alcohol, or a dysfunctional thyroid gland. Other memory busters include depression, anxiety and a simple lack of stimulation—all of which keep us from paying full attention to our surroundings.

And then there's information overload. "You used to have time to reflect and think,"

## Can Supplements Boost Brain Power?

Enthusiasts have embraced a wide range of herbs, vitamins and hormones as mental elixirs. Unfortunately, few of them have been shown to sharpen recall in healthy people, and some have dangerous side effects.

**Ginkgo Biloba:** The most popular purported memory aid comes from the leaves of an ornamental tree. Ginkgo may help increase oxygen flow to the brain, while acting as an antioxidant. One preliminary study suggests it may help relieve mild dementia.

**Vitamin E:** This antioxidant helps prevent heart disease and boost immune function. Preliminary studies suggest it may also slow the progression of Alzheimer's. But no one has shown it can improve memory in healthy people.

**DHEA:** After the age of 30, the adrenal glands produce less and less of this hormone. Mice given DHEA supplements excel on learning tasks. It's not clear whether people do.

**Aspirin:** Regular use of nonsteroidal anti-inflammatories such as aspirin and ibuprofen may delay the onset of Alzheimer's. These drugs can cause gastrointestinal damage, but new versions may not.

**Estrogen:** Besides lowering the risk of Alzheimer's disease in postmenopausal women, estrogen helps support normal brain function. Studies suggest that estrogen-replacement therapy helps maintain both verbal and visual memory.

**DHA:** This omega-3 fatty acid, abundant in breast milk, is critical for babies' brain development. No one has shown that it enhances cognition later in life, but supplements are popular.

Gordon observes. "Now you're just a conduit for a constant stream of information." It comes at us with terrifying speed—via fax, phone and e-mail, over scores of cable channels, even at the newsstand. And when information bombards us faster than we can assimilate it, we miss out on more than the surplus. As Michelle Arnove (remember her?) discovered, an overwhelmed mind has trouble absorbing anything.

The problem often boils down to stress. Besides leaving us sleepless, distractible and more likely to drink, chronic stress can di-

rectly affect our brain chemistry. Like a strong cup of coffee, a stressful experience can energize our brains in the short run. It triggers the release of adrenaline and other glucocorticoid hormones, which boost circulation and unleash the energy stored in our tissues as glucose. The stress response is nicely tailored to the environments we evolved in—where surprise encounters with hungry predators were more common than looming deadlines and gridlocked calendars. But this fight-or-flight mechanism causes harm if it's turned on all the time. After about 30 minutes, says Stanford neuroscientist Robert Sapolsky, stress hormones start to knock out the molecules that transport glucose into the hippocampus—leaving the brain *low* on energy. And over longer periods, stress hormones can act like so much battery acid, severing connections among neurons and literally shrinking the hippocampus. "This atrophy is reversible if the stress is short-lived," says Bruce McEwen, a neuroscientist at Rockefeller University. "But stress lasting months or years can kill hippocampal neurons."

What, then, are the best ways to protect your memory? Obviously, anyone concerned about staying sharp should make a point of sleeping enough and managing stress. And because the brain is at the mercy of the circulatory system, a heart-healthy lifestyle may have cognitive benefits as well. In a 1997 survey of older adults, researchers in Madrid found an association between high mental-test scores and high intake of fruits, vegetables and fiber. An earlier study, conducted at the University of Southern California, found that people in their 70s were less likely to slip mentally during a three-year period if they stayed physically active. Besides protecting our arteries, exercise may boost the body's production of brain-derived nerve growth factor (BDNF), a molecule that helps keep neurons strong.

What about all those seminars and supplements? Can they help, too? The techniques that memory coaches teach can be powerful, but there's nothing magical about them. They work mainly by inspiring us to pay attention, to repeat what's worth remembering and to link what we're trying to remember to things we already know. To remember a new name, says Green of Mount Sinai, listen intently. Then spell it to yourself and make a mental comment about it. Popping vitamins and herbs is easier, but it's no substitute. Preliminary studies suggest that nutritional supplements such as vitamin E and ginkgo biloba may help preserve brain function (chart). But no one has shown convincingly that over-the-counter remedies improve recall in healthy adults.

Estrogen is a different story. While the hormone may not supercharge your memory, it clearly supports brain function. Barbara Sherwin, codirector of the McGill University Menopause Clinic, revealed estrogen's importance two years ago, by testing verbal memory in young women before and after they underwent treatment for uterine tumors. The women's estrogen levels plummeted after 12 weeks of chemotherapy—as did their scores on tests of reading retention. But when half of the women added estrogen to their treatment regimen, their performance promptly rebounded. Researchers at the National Institute on Aging have since found that estrogen may affect visual as well as verbal memory (though not as strongly). And other studies suggest that women who take estrogen may lower their risk of Alzheimer's disease. The reasons are still unclear, but the hormone seems to fuel the development of hippocampal neurons and boost the production of acetylcholine, a chemical that helps brain cells communicate. Unfortunately estrogen has risks as well as benefits, especially for women predisposed to breast cancer. For now, few experts recommend it as a memory aid.

Estrogen is just one of many compounds that pharmaceutical companies are now eying as potential brain savers. "There are so many drugs under study that I have to believe one or more will make it," says James McGaugh, a neuroscientist at the University of California, Irvine. Most are being developed as treatments for Alzheimer's disease, but researchers foresee a day when people will treat even the minor lapses that come with age. "We want to optimize the opportunity to live a free and independent life," says Columbia's Kandel. "It would be nice to have a little red pill that would take care of it."

Kandel has formed a company called Memory Pharmaceuticals to exploit his seminal findings about memory. You'll recall that the brain stores information by strengthening the connections among stimulated neurons. To lock in a memory, the neurons in question actually sprout new branches, creating more avenues for the exchange of chemical signals. Kandel has identified a pair of genes—CREB1 and CREB2—that help regulate that process. CREB1 initiates the growth process, while CREB2 holds it in check. Together, they act as a kind of thermostat. Kandel hopes that by selectively inhibiting one gene or the other, we may be able to change the setting on that thermostat. Partially disabling CREB2 might help anyone retain things more easily, without becoming an indiscriminate sponge. And a drug that *activated* CREB2 (or hogtied CREB1) might help trauma victims avoid having painful experiences seared so vividly into their brains.

It's a thrilling enterprise, but fraught with possible pitfalls. New treatments create new expectations, and not just for the infirm. "Suppose the drug raises your score on a job test," says McGaugh. "Who gets hired? Does the other guy file suit? Can the employer fire you if you stop taking the drug?" And suppose parents start feeding the drug to their school-age kids. Others would have to take it just to keep up. Those worries may be vastly premature. Our memory systems have evolved over several million years. If a slight modification made them far more efficient, chances are it would have cropped up naturally by now. The fact is, "maximal memory" and "optimal memory" are not synonymous, says Cesare Mondadori, chief of research for nervous-system drugs at Hoechst Marion Roussel. As any savant can tell you, forgetting is as important as remembering. So be careful what you wish for.

*With* KAREN SPRINGEN *and*
T. TRENT GEGAX

# On Your Mind

## Do male and female brains respond differently to severe emotional stress? In a flurry of new research, scientists are finding tantalizing clues.

# The Age of
# Anxiety

**No one knows why depression and other ills strike more women than men. Fortunately, new drugs can help rebuild lives. By Donna Foote and Sam Seibert**

D R. MARK GEORGE ADMITS HIS FIRST IMPULSE WAS TO BACK-BURNER HIS RESEARCH team's startling breakthrough. If that would mean letting other brain investigators luck into the same discovery, so be it. Those guys could have the glory—along with the grief of getting trapped in the ideological cross-fire of the war between the sexes. During the mid-'90s, George recalls, "it was almost taboo to talk about gender differences in the brain." Everyone was afraid of validating old sexual stereotypes and prejudices. George wanted only to keep on quietly doing his job at the National Institute of Mental Health, leading a pioneering effort to map the human brain at work. Through positron emission tomography (PET) scanning, a high-tech way of tracing precise areas of activity within the brain, George and his team were able to witness for the first time the hidden processes of human emotion.

The trouble arose when George began looking at the physiology of sorrow. He asked his experimental volunteers to recall their saddest memories while he tracked the flow of blood inside their brains. The tests included both men and women, although George wasn't looking for discrepancies between them. Neither sex had much difficulty conjuring up suitably sad thoughts, and in both sexes the PET scans displayed a strong increase of circulation to parts of the limbic system, a primitive region deep within the brain. But there was a striking difference: the total area of the brain involved in the reaction was eight times larger in his women subjects than among the men. "I was quite afraid of the way the data might be interpreted in the general press," he says. The last thing he wanted was to be associated with sensational headlines about women's brains' being more "emotional" than men's.

George's boss at the NIMH urged him to publish the discovery promptly. It could be a vital piece in the puzzle of women's susceptibility to depression. The ensuing media reaction wasn't as disruptive as George had feared. Major news organizations, including NEWSWEEK, covered the story, but the press soon moved on and let the scientist get back

From *Newsweek*, Spring/Summer 1999 Special Issue, pp. 68-72. © 1999 by Newsweek, Inc. All rights reserved. Reprinted by permission.

to his lab. He continues his life's work, studying the brain's regulation of emotions. Gender differences are only a side issue for him. In most ways the brains of men and women are very much alike.

Even so, research into important differences has exploded since George's reluctant announcement in 1995. Each new finding inspires a burst of further research as scientists deepen their understanding of men's and women's brains. The explorers' basic equipment is equally new. With the state-of-the-art assistance of tools and techniques like the PET scan and functional magnetic resonance imaging (fMRI), a pathfinding generation of investigators is going where physicians since Hippocrates have barely dreamed of visiting. In some cases the discoveries have no practical value but to let women and men know themselves and each other a little better. In other cases the work has already begun rebuilding lives.

One particularly fruitful area of inquiry has been the study of stress-related ailments. Men traditionally have a higher propensity than women to act out aggressively and to abuse drugs and alcohol. Women, on the other hand, suffer disproportionately from a variety of emotional ailments, such as depression, anxiety attacks and eating disorders. Why? The question is far from academic to people struggling with such crippling problems as chronic depression. For what it's worth, approximately two out of every three depressives are female. At present the World Health Organization ranks depression as the world's fourth most devastating illness, measured in total years of healthy life stolen by death or disability. According to WHO projections, it will have climbed to second place by 2020, exceeded only by heart disease. One recent study says 17.1 percent of all Americans are likely to suffer at least one episode of major depression in their lifetime.

It's scarcely an overstatement to call the situation a public-health crisis. Medical researchers are racing to find solutions, although their progress can sometimes seem infuriatingly slow. "We are such complex and psychologically elegant creatures, it is unlikely there will ever be a 'simple' explanation for any behavioral disorder," says Dr. David Rubinow, clinical director of the NIMH in Bethesda, Md. Gradually scientists are sorting out the subtly interacting variables that lead to depression and other emotional disorders—a tangle of cultural, environmental, biological, genetic and personal factors. "We are learning that biology underlies the emotions," says Dr. Ellen Leibenluft of the NIMH. "Psychological events are *biological* events, with biological underpinnings." Translation: it's *not* all in your head.

Also it's not "just hormones." There's no doubt that estrogen and progesterone occupy pivotal roles in many mood and anxiety dis-

orders—and in the routine metabolic functions of every healthy individual, male or female. Scientists have yet to sort out all the different vital tasks those ubiquitous substances perform, from the regulation of reproductive cycles to the imprinting and evoking of particular emotional responses in the brain. And the puzzle is made more complicated by the fact that different women react quite differently to identical amounts of the same hormone. "Some women's mood states appear to be affected by levels of hormones," says Leibenluft. "But in many women they are not. The question is not 'Do women's moods respond to [estrogen and progesterone]?' The question is 'Which women do the hormones affect, and why?' "

## Did You Know?

About 15 percent of all women suffer from a depressive disorder at some point in their lives; fewer than a third of victims get any form of help. Without treatment the frequency and severity of symptoms tend to increase over the years.

It's a short word and a huge question. Many patients appear to suffer from deficiencies or abnormalities in their neurotransmitters (the chemical messengers by which nerve cells communicate), especially the vasoconstrictor known as serotonin. And in the treatment of most mood and anxiety disorders, some of the most effective drugs belong to the pharmaceutical category of "selective serotonin reuptake inhibitors" (SSRIs), such as Prozac. The precise relationship between hormones, moods and neurotransmitters is at the cutting edge of brain research these days. Scientists at McGill University recently announced a particularly provocative discovery. According to their research, serotonin production is 53 percent higher in men's brains than in women's—one of the biggest gender divergences ever found in human brains. Doctors don't yet know what role serotonin plays in the regulation of emotions. The male's reserves of neurotransmitters may give extra

emotional protection but why should women be shortchanged? It's anybody's guess. These are exciting times for neurophysiologists—and even more so for victims of an array of crippling mood and anxiety disorders.

**CLASSIC DEPRESSION:** Researchers can actually see the shadow of the monster. It's visible on the PET scans of depression sufferers: a chilly blue blob of reduced blood flow on the left prefrontal lobe, along with apparent metabolic abnormalities in the anterior paralimbic regions. Those areas are established centers of emotional response. "It's very exciting," says Dr. Darren Daugherty, a psychiatrist and researcher at Boston's Massachusetts General Hospital. "We've learned which areas aren't working right –and it makes perfect sense that they don't." Neuropharmacologists have even felt the thrill of watching the shadows lift. As SSRI treatment takes effect in the patient's brain, blood flow in the affected areas rises to levels seen in healthy brains.

The transformation can be still more dramatic from the patient's point of view. The symptoms of major depression are devastating, including a prolonged loss of joy in most activities, exaggerated guilt, fatigue, inability to concentrate and recurrent thoughts of death or suicide. "It took everything I had just to get through the day," recalls Linda Cook, 51, a Boston nurse and mother who has battled episodes of severe depression since she was 22. She began taking Prozac 10 years ago. "It was a miracle drug for me," she says. "I just feel so much more like a human being."

Hard questions remain—but answers may be coming. "Nobody has been able to identify a specific genetic or physiological dysfunction that turns depression on and off," says Jerrold Rosenbaum, executive director of the Mood and Anxiety Disorder Institute at the University of Massachusetts Hospital. "That's about 10 years away." As dazzling as the SSRIs can be, talk therapy continues to be an effective treatment for depression. For longtime sufferers like Cook, the growth of medical knowledge has itself been a source of real comfort. She used to think her illness was a personal failure. "I felt I should be able to control it, so I was ashamed," she says. "When I realized this is something I didn't have control over—that it's purely physical—it was a great relief. I could change my attitude toward myself and found that I liked myself a whole lot better."

**ANXIETY DISORDERS:** Fear is healthy. The trick is to keep it from running wild. According to the NIMH, anxiety disorders are the most common of all mental illnesses. The condition's generalized form is characterized by chronic worry and tension, often without apparent provocation, lasting six months or more. Physical symptoms can include headaches, nausea and frequent urination. Another form of anxiety disorder, panic attacks, strikes between 3 million and 6 million Americans annually, two thirds of them women. With no warning the patient suddenly and repeatedly experiences an overwhelming sense of terror. "You try to stand up but you physically can't move," says Louise Ross, 52, a fund-raising consultant who had her first panic attack three years ago. "It's very scary."

SSRIs can help. Meanwhile scientists are searching for the areas of brain circuitry that set off full-blown illness. "We've studied a variety of anxiety disorders," says Dr. Scott Rauch, an associate professor of psychiatry at Harvard Medical School. "There is a common network: the anterior paralimbic system. It seems to be activated across the anxiety disorders and across a variety of intense normal emotional states."

Doctors have made particular progress on the neurological riddles of panic attacks. Dr. Jeremy Coplan, a researcher at Columbia University Medical College, says panic sufferers appear to experience false alarms of smothering, deep in the part of the brain that controls breathing. "When people hyperventilate with panic disorder, they reduce their blood flow to the brain," says Coplan. "The brain interprets this aberrant reduction of blood flow as a sign of suffocation." The sufferer is effectively drowning in fear. Ross has been taking Zoloft, one of the SSRI family, for two years. "It's the answer to my prayers," she says.

**SEASONAL AFFECTIVE DISORDER:** An emotional illness doesn't have to be fully explained before it can be effectively treated. Researchers suspect seasonal affective disorder (SAD) may be set off by the delayed sunrises and short daylight hours of winter. Perhaps the lack of natural light upsets the patient's daily biological rhythms and delays the secretion of melatonin, a hormone linked to the sleep-wake cycle. Researchers say four out of five SAD patients are women in their reproductive years. Women over 55 tend to have about the same incidence as men. The disorder's prevalence among menstruating women would seem to implicate a familiar culprit. "It's got to have *something* to do with the female hormones," says Dr. Alfred Lewy, one of the pioneers of SAD research—but even he is not sure *why* women are more susceptible. The disorder's biological underpinnings remain a mystery.

Sufferers exhibit "atypical" symptoms of depression: overeating, oversleeping, a lack of energy and a loss of concentration. Lewy prescribes light—lots of it. His patients receive daily megadoses of light, preferably first thing every morning, bathing their eyes in the glow of special fluorescent lamps 20 times brighter than standard indoor illumination. Lewy's treatment is usually just what the doctor ordered—most patients start feeling better within a couple of days. The one thing he knows for sure is that SAD is a legitimate illness. "It's not a case of disliking rainy days," he says. "This is a real psychological disorder."

**ANOREXIA AND BULIMIA:** More than nine out of 10 victims of eating disorders are adolescent and young women. Detection is difficult. By the time anorexics see a doctor, they are likely to have become severely ill, often suffering from malnutrition or outright starvation. Sufferers tend to be at least 15 percent below their appropriate body weight—and at the same time to think of themselves as overweight. In severe cases the brain begins to shrink from starvation and become "watery." Some of the changes may be permanent. Bulimia can be even more elusive; sufferers may be at or above normal weight. Yet in extreme cases, bulimia can result in heart failure.

Anorexia and bulimia used to be regarded as medical rarities. Since the 1970s, however, the problem has spread to epidemic levels. Doctors still can't say precisely what triggers the sickness. Apparently it requires a little of everything, from genetics to particular personality traits to pop culture's idealization of thinness. "Eating disorders are multifactorial," says Diana Mickley, who in 1982 established the Wilkins Center for Eating Disorders in Greenwich, Conn. In susceptible individuals, dieting beyond a certain point can apparently set off a cascade of metabolic disruptions, including reduced serotonin levels. Many patients suffer from severe disturbances of the neuroendocrine system, which regulates a wide range of functions, including sex drive and reproductive cycles, appetite and digestion, emotions, memory and the workings of the heart and kidneys.

If a magic bullet exists, no one has found it. Doctors have to treat eating disorders symptom by symptom—with special priority on restoring the patient's weight to normal range. The hope is that a concerted education campaign in the public schools will stop the epidemic.

Beyond the challenge of conquering emotional illnesses, brain investigators are facing vast new territories to chart. "We have entered a whole new era with the new technology," says Dr. Sally Shaywitz, codirector of the Yale Center for the Study of Learning and Attention. She and other scientists at the center have been finding ways in which healthy men and women use their brains differently in such basic tasks as reading. Where men tend to use only the left side of their brains, many women use both—although the choice appears to have little effect on speed or accuracy. "They took two different routes to get the same results," says Shaywitz. She predicts the discovery of many other gender differences in the brain—and many other areas of convergence. There's no telling where such discoveries might ultimately lead. What's important is that the journey will be a fascinating one.

*With* ERIKA CHECK

## ESTROGEN

# Understanding Perimenopause

**It can masquerade as insomnia, moodiness, forgetfulness or depression. But physicians now understand that in the years before menopause, women ride a hormonal roller coaster. The grab bag of symptoms that it brings has a single underlying but treatable cause, so you don't have to take it lying down.**

### By Sharon Begley

FOR A PROFESSIONAL PARTY PLANNER like Bonnie Leopold, irritability is about as welcome as gate crashers. But there it was: Leopold, 48, of Manhattan Beach, Calif., started feeling nonstop grouchy and snappish. She also got hot flashes so often that she didn't dare leave the house without her portable fan. And

## Hormonal Fluctuations

Researchers are beginning to understand more about hormonal ups and downs over a woman's lifetime. A likely journey:

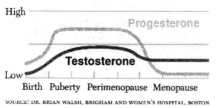

SOURCE: DR. BRIAN WALSH, BRIGHAM AND WOMEN'S HOSPITAL, BOSTON

when she had two menstrual periods in one month, she was convinced she had ovarian cancer. Susan Santacaterina, 46, a Chicago nurse, didn't think she had a fatal disease, but after suffering for months from insomnia and headaches before every period, she had an MRI scan of her brain anyway. Donna Lambert, 47, sums up her situation like this: "I feel like I'm brain-dead." The former day-care director, who lives in Charlottesville,

Va., walks into rooms and wonders why she is there; once able to memorize a two-page grocery list, Lambert now can't go shopping without one.

The three women's disparate symptoms would seem to suggest they've got totally different illnesses. But, in fact, they're all on

> **"There's a lot of variability during perimenopause, and a burgeoning interest in research. We really need to understand midlife."**
>
> **Surveying health:**
> **Sherry Sherman of the National Institute on Aging oversees a national study of women ages 42 to 52**

the same wild hormonal roller-coaster ride, and it's called perimenopause.

If you like the prospect of menopause, you'll love perimenopause. Literally "around

menopause," perimenopause begins when hormone-related changes kick in, as long as 10 years before menopause. Menopause itself begins 12 months after a woman's final period, and in the United States comes at an average age of 52. If you define perimenopause as lasting 10 years, then more than 20 million American women are now going through it. Perimenopause promises many of the same hot flashes, concentration gaps, mood swings, sleep troubles and migraines associated with menopause, as well as irritability and memory loss, with an added sweetener: the symptoms come earlier and last longer. As early as 35 but almost certainly in your 40s, your hormones start to betray you. Estrogens, progesterone and other reproductive hormones no longer work together with the precise timing of a Rolex, but instead act like "a Swiss watch that's gotten rusty," says Dr. Wulf Utian, a reproductive biologist at Case Western Reserve University and executive director of the North American Menopause Society. That is a radically new understanding of perimenopause. Despite claims that its symptoms reflect plunging levels of estrogen, and that women should seek relief through estrogen replacement, perimenopause is marked by hormones riding a roller coaster. Breast surgeon Susan Love, in her "Dr. Susan Love's Hormone Book," calls it "the mirror image of puberty," and that has important implications for treatment.

There is no typical perimenopause, just as there is no typical puberty. But in general perimenopause brings, first and most obviously, wacky menstrual periods: more often, less often, heavier or lighter. It can also worsen PMS, cause night sweats, diminish libido and cause skin, hair and vaginal walls to thin and dry out. Each of these reflects changes in the river of hormones coursing through a woman's body. The better a woman understands these changes, the better care she is likely to get from her doctor, for although perimenopause has been recognized by the American medical establishment since the 1970s, many doctors had not heard of it before the 1990s. It still isn't part of most med-school curricula, and there are still physicians who dismiss a woman's perimenopause symptoms as all in her head. Here's what really happens:

■ Follicle-stimulating hormone (FSH) is secreted by the brain's pituitary gland. True to its name, FSH stimulates eggs to mature. Older ovaries have gotten a little deaf to these signals, so the brain has to pump up the volume: it emits more FSH in order to get some response from the ovaries. "FSH gets cranked up as the pituitary tries to drive the poor ovary to make estrogen," explains Mary Jane Minkin, an OB-GYN at Yale University School of Medicine. FSH also, indirectly, dilates blood vessels that lie just beneath the skin. Dilating a blood vessel can produce a feeling of warmth and may be a cause of hot flashes and night sweats. An FSH level above 30 (in units called milli-international units per milliliter), as measured in a blood test on any of the first six days of a woman's period, is the most reliable indication that she is in perimenopause. But it's not foolproof. If the test is done in a month when the woman has a normal period, her FSH may look normal. That's why the test should be repeated the following menstrual cycle, but at $200 a pop, that gets a little pricey. Minkin tells her patients not to even bother.

■ Progesterone is secreted from empty egg follicles (little sacs within the ovaries that contain one ovum apiece). To become empty, the follicle obviously has to release its ovum; that's ovulation. But if no egg ripens, no ovulation occurs, and no progesterone is released. It's progesterone that both stabilizes the uterine lining and signals when to slough it off. Without progesterone, a perimenopausal woman can therefore miss periods. "Some women are skipping periods all over the place," says Minkin, while others

# Changes Before 'The Change'

*There is no typical perimenopause. Some women experience few or no symptoms.*

*Others are not so lucky; they suffer from a wide range. Some of the most common:*

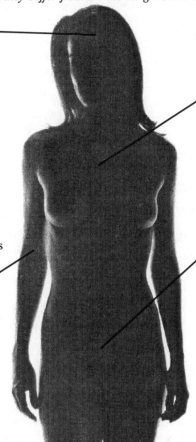

**Memory lapses and loss of concentration** Some women who take estrogen report an improvement in cognitive function.
**Headaches** May be caused by fluctuating hormone levels. Some women begin to suffer migraines.
**Mood swings** Changes in hormone levels may interfere with the production of the body's mood-regulator serotonin. Some women feel anxious or weepy.

**Dry skin** A decrease in the protein collagen—which may be linked to a decline in estrogen—means less elasticity and more wrinkles.
**Bone loss** Declining reproductive hormones translates to less protection for bones. The problem is at its worst after menopause.

**Hot flashes** Many perimenopausal women experience them, mostly around the head and upper body. They usually last several minutes. Nocturnal hot flashes, which are known as night sweats, can lead to insomnia.

**Erratic menstrual cycles** A classic symptom of perimenopause. Cycles vary widely from 18 days to missed periods. Excessive bleeding is common.
**Vaginal dryness** As estrogen levels decline, the vaginal wall thins and becomes less elastic. Intercourse may become painful.
**Urinary incontinence** As the vaginal wall weakens, the bladder loses support and urination is harder to control.

PHOTO ILLUSTRATION BY GEOFF SPEAR

have "screwy bleeding." Progesterone also affects moods: it binds to the same sites in the brain as does a neurochemical, called GABA, that tamps down anxiety (Valium also binds to these GABA sites). The precipitous drop in progesterone after a woman gives birth may trigger postpartum depression; its gradual falloff during the second half of a woman's monthly cycle may usher in the PMS blues. How much progesterone levels dip during perimenopause, and what effect that has, varies from one woman to the next and from one month to the next.

But an otherwise inexplicable weepiness during one's 40s might reflect diminished progesterone.

■ Levels of estrogens rocket up tenfold—as in 1,000 percent—during puberty. They plateau between the ages of 25 and 40 or so. It's downhill from there, as estrogen levels fall by that same tenfold amount, to one tenth their peak, once a woman has passed through menopause. As for what happens between the plateau and the valley—during perimenopause—researchers are scrambling for answers. Despite the drumbeat of stories

## Did You Know?

The body of a seventysomething man makes more than twice as much estrogen as that of a woman the same age. This is because small amounts of testosterone, which the testes produce throughout life, are converted to estrogen.

# What You Can Do

*You don't have to suffer. Both traditional and alternative medicine can help with the hot flashes, night sweats, moodiness and menstrual irregularities of peri- menopause.*

## PRESCRIPTION DRUGS

**Low-dose birth-control pills** Pills such as Alesse combine the hormones estrogen and progestin (synthetic progesterone) to alleviate perimenopausal symptons that result from roller-coastering hormone levels.

**Hormone-replacement therapy** Pills such as Premarin boost estrogen levels. But if your symptoms reflect erratic hormone levels, rather than falling ones, HRT might make them worse.

## VITAMINS AND DIET

**Vitamin B₆** Available in supplements or foods such as chicken, this vitamin helps turn amino acids into the neurotransmitter serotonin, which affects mood. The RDA for women 31 to 50 years old is 1.3 mg.

**Vitamin E** This antioxidant may alleviate hot flashes. The RDA is 8 mg for women 31 to 50.

**Soy** Loaded with plant estrogens, soy may reduce hot flashes. Available in capsules, soy milk, soy flour and tofu (about 2 ounces contain 45 mg)

**Flaxseed** An herb containing omega 3 fatty acids that may reduce heavy menstrual bleeding. Sprinkle 1 to 3 tablespoons of crushed flaxseed on cereal each day or use a few teaspoons a day of flaxseed oil in cooking.

## HERBAL SUPPLEMENTS

**Evening primrose** About 3 grams a day of the oil from this plant might help alleviate breast tenderness and regulate hormone levels.

**Black cohosh root** Available in capsules and tinctures, this root seems to work like estrogen, reducing hot flashes and relieving painful periods.

**Dong quai** A Chinese herb, it is often taken to relieve menstrual cramps. But a recent study found it's no better than placebos. Women typically take 4.5 grams a day in capsules or tinctures.

**Kava** Made from the root of a shrub, kava purportedly helps reduce mood swings, irritability and stress. It is usually taken in 60- to 120- mg capsules.

**Chasteberry** This berry may help with menstrual irregularities and painful breasts, apparently by increasing progesterone levels. Available in capsules or tincture.

**St. John's Wort** The flowering tops of this plant have been called "natural Prozac" because they seem to lift depression and anxiety. The capsules and tinctures should not be taken with prescription antidepressants.

SOURCES: AMERICAN BOTANICAL COUNCIL; NANCY SISKOWIC, R.N., M.S.N.; WYETH-AYHERST; NATIONAL FOOD AND NUTRITIONAL BOARD;

---

about how perimenopause is marked by a relentless fall in estrogen levels, one thing estrogen levels do not do is decline gradually, like a skier down a bunny slope. Most researchers believe instead that estrogen fluctuates wildly during perimenopause. A 1996 study led by researchers at the University of Washington found that all 16 women 40 to 45 whom they studied had overall estrogen levels comparable to the 12 twentysomethings in the group. But during the first few days of their monthly cycle, the older women experienced a rise in estrogen to a level *higher* than in the younger women. So while estrogen levels may decline overall after 40, they decline like a skier on a slope studded with moguls—from towering bump to towering bump. "The best way to think about it," says endocrinologist Richard Santen of the University of Virginia, "is up, down, up, down, stop."

A typical woman might have very low estrogen at the beginning of her menstrual cycle. That could give her hot flashes for two weeks, explains Susan Love. (But you needn't expect the worst: although as many as 70 percent of women in their 40s experience irregular menstrual periods, only 30 percent suffered hot flashes in the three years before menopause, a 1991 study found.) Low estrogen will also goad the pituitary to churn out more FSH. That, in turn, will stimulate the ovaries to produce twice as much estrogen as normal, ushering in the PMS-like symptoms of high estrogen-low progesterone.

What can women do to alleviate the symptoms of perimenopause? Some things are easy calls. It makes sense to avoid alcohol and spicy foods to minimize hot flashes, and to swear off caffeine (especially after midday) to sleep better. Weight-bearing exercise (that includes walking) stimulates the production of new bone, which is a good way to enter menopause itself. But after these no-brainers, the treatment advice depends on what a woman's hormones are up to (or down to).

Say a woman has erratic estrogen levels. The surest sign of such a hormonal roller coaster is weird menstrual cycles, but also mood swings like those of PMS. More doctors are therefore recommending birth-control pills, which even out hormone levels. Alesse, Lo-estrin and Mircette are called low dose, but in fact they contain enough estrogen to suppress ovulation (that's the original point of the pill, after all). This wallop of estrogen "will basically shut down the ovaries," says Dr. Brian Walsh of Brigham and Women's Hospital in Boston, so they no longer secrete estrogen. Hormone levels, now set completely by the medication, settle down. (A woman who smokes or has high blood pressure should not take the pill, however, because it can raise her risk of fatal blood clots. And all women need to consult their doctor about the best way to alleviate the symptoms of perimenopause.)

If a perimenopausal woman is suffering from a dearth of estrogen, she needs different treatment. How can she tell if she's running on empty? Estrogen stimulates production of the brain chemical serotonin, which, among other jobs, regulates sleep and emotion. Less estrogen can bring insomnia and mood swings. In addition, estrogen can twiddle the body's thermostat—the hypothalamus, which sits deep inside the brain. "When estrogen declines," says Walsh, "it causes the temperature center to become unstable." That can trigger hot flashes. Chronically low estrogen can also impair verbal memory. How bad can the memory loss be? Novelist Anna Quindlen, 46, wrote in 1997 about waking up in the middle of the night and "forgetting the names of my children." The reason, new research shows, is that estrogen stimulates neurons to sprout new branches, helps generate new synapses and triggers production of substances that promote neuronal growth—all of which weave brain neurons into networks that learn and remember.

To kick estrogen levels back up, hormone-replacement therapy might seem an obvious choice. Bonnie Leopold, the party planner, swears by the Vivelle estrogen patch on her backside. A two-inch clear oval that resembles a nicotine patch, it slowly releases the form of estrogen called 17 beta-estradiol; she credits it with wiping away her irritability. But many doctors are wary about putting premenopausal women on HRT; such use is not approved by the Food and Drug Administration. An authoritative 16-year study of ome 40,000 nurses found, in June 1997, a 3 percent higher risk for fatal breast cancer among postmenopausal women who took RT for 10 years or more. Other studies ave shown a risk even at five to seven years, says Dr. Nananda Col of New England Medical Center in Boston. That makes starting HRT at, say, 42 a potentially dicey roposition. "It would seem to me that giving estrogen when somebody's got high levels already," says Dr. Gerson Weiss of New rsey Medical School, "is not the best idea."

Women who reject HRT often turn to natural hormone replacement." Supplements like black cohosh (one used by Native Americans) promise to deliver phytoestrogens (from plants) and relieve perimenopausal symptoms. But this market is so underregulated that you can't be sure what's a any of these pills; few have been thoroughly studied. They probably won't cause any harm, but a surer bet is to obtain phytoestrogens from foods like soy (as tofu, soy milk, tempeh, miso) and flaxseed oil. How much do you have to eat? In one study a daily regimen of six tablespoons of soy flour reduced hot flashes, sleep disturbances, depression and loss of libido. You don't have to close your eyes and hold your nose, either. The 1998 book "Estrogen: The Natural Way" contains more than 250 phytoestrogen-packed recipes for, among other delicacies, orange-apricot bars, noodles with creamy sesame sauce and mackerel-and-onion quiche.

Although some women's health activists complain that doctors are "pathologizing" a normal stage of life, there are two sound medical reasons for acknowledging perimenopause. The first is that if a woman doesn't understand that waking up every night at 3 has the same underlying cause as the worst PMS she's ever suffered, and that her insomnia is in turn related to irregular periods and mood swings and an inability to remember where she was in a conversation before the phone rang, she may wind up with a fistful of symptom-by-symptom prescriptions. She'll get sleeping aids, tranquilizers, antidepressants and appointments with thera-

pists, but not treatment for the underlying hormonal swings. Worse, if doctors don't recognize that hormonal upheavals kick in long before menopause, they may dismiss women's perimenopausal complaints as imaginary. "It used to be thought that women didn't really have symptoms until their final period," says Walsh. "But in reality, hot flashes are worst about three or four years before that. If you wait for her final period before you listen to her concerns and treat her, you'll miss most of the misery."

The second reason to recognize perimenopause is to treat it as a wake-up call. You are approaching the next stage of your life, but you've got advance warning. So heed it: give up cigarettes, eat right, exercise, reduce. That way, when you go through menopause itself you will be in the best shape you can. In the meantime, just knowing that your crazy symptoms have a name and a cause might be relief enough.

*With* CLAUDIA KALB *and*
KAREN SPRINGEN

# The Johns Hopkins Prescription for Longevity

As millions of baby boomers slide into middle age, there has never been a better time to be entering the second half of life. During the last century, life expectancy in the United States increased dramatically, from age 47 in 1900 to age 76 today. In the first decade of the 20th century, only about one fifth of Americans lived to celebrate their 65th birthday. On the eve of the 21st century, at least 70% will achieve this milestone. A hundred years ago, centenarians were rare; today there are an estimated 100,000 worldwide. By the year 2050, many experts believe that the average adult will live about 83 years.

Older Americans are also remarkably healthy. According to surveys conducted by the MacArthur Foundation, 89% of those between 65 and 74, 73% of those between 75 and 84, and 40% of those over age 85 report no significant physical or mental disabilities. Even when faced with disability, only a fraction of the elderly require nursing home care.

A healthy middle and old age cannot be taken for granted, however. Nearly half of older Americans suffer from arthritis, about one third have high blood pressure or heart disease, and more than one tenth have diabetes. Cancer, osteoporosis, and chronic obstructive pulmonary disease (chronic bronchitis or emphysema) also are prevalent.

These illnesses—and the disabilities that frequently accompany them—can often be prevented until very late in life. Extensive research (much of it conducted on twins) shows that, with few exceptions, genes account for only about one third of the problems associated with aging. Lifestyle factors, which have a greater impact on health during middle- and late-life than during early adulthood, account for the rest. Experts now know which measures are likely both to increase longevity and to delay the onset of disabling illnesses.

## A POTENT ANTIDOTE FOR AGING

*Health After 50* board members are unanimous in prescribing exercise as the single most important anti-aging measure anyone can follow, regardless of age, disability, or general level of fitness. A sedentary lifestyle accelerates nearly every unwanted aspect of aging. Conversely, physical activity slows the erosion of muscle strength, maintains better cardiovascular and respiratory function, limits the risk of developing diabetes, and increases bone mass, which helps prevent osteoporosis. Exercise also facilitates digestion, promotes efficient bowel function, reduces insomnia, and prevents depression.

Older adults who exercise typically outperform nonexercisers half their age in many sports and usually have fewer risk factors for heart disease (such as high blood pressure, a poor cholesterol profile, or excess weight) than nonexercisers. A recent survey of about 5,000 men and an equal number of women, published in the *Archives of Internal Medicine,* found that the men who exercised vigorously had cholesterol and triglyceride levels 9 to 27% lower than those of the sedentary men. According to the researchers, such a change could reduce the risk of dying of heart disease by up to 25%. The women who reported vigorous exercise also had better cholesterol profiles than their sedentary counterparts.

To be effective, your exercise routine should address the following two major components of fitness:

- **Endurance training** involves any type of total body activity that increases the demand placed on the cardiovascular and respiratory systems. The most popular are walking, jogging, and cycling. The Center for Longevity recommends burning an additional 2,000 to 3,000 calories per week above your normal sedentary baseline—the equivalent of jogging about four miles a day, five days a week.

- **Strength training** uses light weights (between 1 and 12 pounds) to work the major muscle groups. Finding the correct weight is a trial-and-error process. You should be able to complete 10 to 12 repetitions of three sets each. If you cannot do 12 repetitions, the weight is too heavy. Two or three strength training sessions a week are ideal.

But these are only goals. Less rigorous activity is also highly beneficial. One study found that taking a brisk 30-minute walk three times a week can reduce blood pressure an average of 10 mmHg/8.6 mmHg. How much you can and should do depends on your general health, present level of fitness, and degree of disability. To ensure success, begin your routine gradually, and check with your doctor before starting. If you have never exercised before, your doctor may refer you to a physical therapist or other specialist who can offer instruction.

Because older, unconditioned muscles and bones are vulnerable to injury, commitment and constancy are important. Regular use is the best means of protection. Those over 50 should consult a doctor before starting an exercise program.

## OTHER TOP LIFESTYLE CHOICES

Aging experts generally agree that a prescription for mid- and late-life health should also include:

**A healthy diet.** A diet rich in fruits and vegetables cuts the risk of colorectal cancer in half. It also substantially reduces the risk of heart disease and diabetes and decreases common gastrointestinal problems such as diverticulosis (protrusions in the inner lining of the intestine) and constipation. Switching from a high-fat to a low-fat diet often reduces total cholesterol by about 10 mg/dl. It also produces small but significant declines in blood pressure.

Eat at least five servings of fruit and vegetables a day, and two to four low-fat dairy products, primarily for calcium. Because sodium can increase blood pressure, daily sodium intake should not exceed 2,400 mg (the amount in about one teaspoon of salt). People with high blood pressure who are sensitive to the effect of sodium may be advised to consume less. Reduce fat to 30% or less of total calories, making sure that no more than 10% of calories come from saturated fat (abundant in beef and butter). Daily cholesterol intake should not exceed 300 mg.

**Judicious use of supplements.** By age 65, calorie needs have declined by about one third, although most other nutritional needs remain constant. However, among the elderly, getting enough calories, nutrients, and fiber is usually more problematic than getting too much. A sound diet can theoretically provide all the vitamins and minerals you need, but it occasionally falls short. Despite their best efforts, some older adults are deficient in vitamins B6 and B12, folic acid, vitamin D, and calcium. A standard multivitamin can fill in most of these gaps. But older adults, especially women, should generally also take a calcium supplement. When coupled with diet, 500 mg may be sufficient to meet the daily need (1,500 mg). Vitamin E supplements may also be beneficial for limiting the harmful effects of oxygen free-radicals (cellular waste products that have been associated with aging and many age-related illnesses), but this remains controversial.

**Drinking enough water.** Because virtually all chemical processes in the body either take place in water or use it as part of the reaction, adequate hydration is important for optimal organ function. Water also helps maintain body temperature and keeps internal

---

# Exploring the Limits of Aging

Although the average human life expectancy has increased dramatically over the last century, there is no evidence that maximum life expectancy has changed over the millennia. Jeanne Calment, the French women who died in 1997 at the age of 122, is the oldest documented person on record; the previous record holder, Shirechiyo Izumi of Japan, died in 1986 at age 120. However, new research has led to speculation that maximum life expectancy may be expandable. The most intriguing research areas include:

▼ **Telomeres.** The tail, or telomere, of a chromosome, is made up of a short sequence of DNA material repeated thousands of times. Its role is to keep chromosomes structurally stable. Each time a cell divides, its telomeres shorten, suggesting that telomeres may play a role in determining cellular life span. Interestingly, because the telomeres of cancer cells do not shorten, they can run rampant and reproduce indefinitely. Researchers are trying to develop drugs that block the activity of telomerase, the enzyme that shorten telomeres.

▼ **Oxygen free-radicals.** The products of normal chemical reactions, these molecules can damage proteins, cell structures, and DNA. Many of the damaging effects of age are associated with oxygen free-radicals.

▼ **Longevity genes.** Many genes are involved in regulating human aging, and small genetic differences can produce drastic differences in the aging process. Researchers have identified several aging genes in fruit flies and have doubled their average life span through selective breeding. However, human gene manipulation would be far more complicated.

▼ **Glucose cross-linking.** Glucose, a major source of energy, is constantly stored and broken down by the body. Over time, some glucose molecules begin to attach to proteins. As a result, these proteins may bind together (cross-link), which alters their structure and affects their biological role. The process seems to toughen tissues and may cause some of the deterioration associated with aging. Cross-linking increases with age and the onset of diabetes. Diabetes researchers are investigating drugs to boost the body's natural defenses against cross-links.

---

membranes moist so that oxygen and other gases can be exchanged. Older adults are vulnerable to dehydration, especially in warm weather. Drink 64 ounces (about 6 to 8 glasses) of clear fluids daily.

• **Not smoking.** A pack-a-day smoker is four times more likely to develop congestive heart failure than a nonsmoker. Those who smoke half a pack a day are twice as likely to develop the condition. But it's never too late to quit. Five years after they stop, ex-smokers have about the same risk of developing heart disease as someone who has never smoked, regardless of age, number of cigarettes smoked daily, and years spent smoking. In most instances, lung cancer risk returns to normal after 15 years. Quitting also decreases the risk of stroke, some other cancers, chronic bronchitis, and emphysema. It may also improve the cosmetic appearance of the skin and increase circulation.

• **Avoiding excessive sun exposure.** Aging skin and eyes are vulnerable to sun damage because protective pigment diminishes over time, permitting greater penetration of harmful rays. Although a small amount of sunlight is needed to produce vitamin D, too much sun exposure increases the risk of skin cancer. In addition, the sun can cause significant cosmetic damage. Most wrinkles, discoloration, and texture changes are directly related to sunlight.

• **Reducing stress.** Studies show that stress and anxiety impair the immune system and increase susceptibility to illness. Some of the ways to cope with stress are meditation, yoga, and exercise. Find the technique or combination of techniques you prefer, and make a point of setting aside time to practice them.

• **Challenging the mind.** Over time, short-term memory and reaction time decline, and it takes longer to acquire new information. But it's still very possible to learn new skills and maintain old ones. Three key factors predict strong mental function: regular physical activity, strong social support, and belief in your ability. Only about 5% of older adults develop Alzheimer's disease, the most common form of dementia.

• **Avoiding excessive alcohol consumption.** One glass of wine or spirits daily is acceptable and may even provide some cardiovascular benefit. But if you don't drink, don't start. The drawbacks of excessive consumption—the possibility of addiction, liver disease, and even cancer—are too significant and unpredictable to warrant adopting the practice. Furthermore, because age slows alcohol metabolism, the effects of alcohol are more pronounced in older adults. The older you are, the more cautious you should be about drinking, even in small amounts.

• **Cultivating satisfying relationships.** Studies show that positive social interaction, including sexual activity for those who desire it, lowers the level of stress hormones in the blood, helps preserve cognitive function, and prevents depression.

## A CASE FOR PREVENTIVE MEDICATION

Certain drugs can now be used to prevent at least three common medical problems. In postmenopausal women, hormone replacement therapy (HRT), usually a combination of estrogen and some form of progesterone, can reduce the risk of osteoporosis and possibly Alzheimer's disease and heart disease. Although many other hormones, including dehydroepiandrosterone (DHEA), growth hormone, melatonin, and testosterone, are periodically touted in the media, there is not enough evidence to recommend taking any of them for general anti-aging purposes—and they may, in fact, be harmful. However, doctor-supervised use of melatonin may be helpful for certain types of insomnia, and testosterone may restore sex drive in people with abnormally low testosterone levels (which may occur in both men and women).

When lifestyle measures fail to lower blood pressure and total cholesterol, drug therapy should be considered. Diuretics are usually the first choice for high blood pressure, whereas statins are generally chosen for high cholesterol. Most older adults should take low-dose aspirin (one 325-mg adult tablet every other day or one 65mg baby aspirin daily), which can decrease the risk of heart disease and possibly colorectal cancer. Only those with a bleeding ulcer or a history of hemorrhagic stroke, or those taking anticoagulants such as warfarin (Coumadin), should refrain.

# New Nerve Cells for the Adult Brain

*Contrary to dogma, the human brain does produce new nerve cells in adulthood. Can our newfound capacity lead to better treatments for neurological diseases?*

by Gerd Kempermann and Fred H. Gage

Cut your skin, and the wound closes within days. Break a leg, and the fracture will usually mend if the bone is set correctly. Indeed, almost all human tissues can repair themselves to some extent throughout life. Remarkable "stem" cells account for much of this activity. These versatile cells resemble those of a developing embryo in their ability to multiply almost endlessly and to generate not only carbon copies of themselves but also many different kinds of cells. The versions in bone marrow offer a dramatic example. They can give rise to all the cells in the blood: red ones, platelets and a panoply of white types. Other stem cells yield the various constituents of the skin, the liver or the intestinal lining.

The brain of the adult human can sometimes compensate for damage quite well, by making new connections among surviving nerve cells (neurons). But it cannot repair itself, because it lacks the stem cells that would allow for neuronal regeneration. That, anyway, is what most neurobiologists firmly believed until quite recently.

This past November, Peter S. Eriksson of the Sahlgrenska University Hospital in Göteborg, Sweden, one of us (Gage) at the Salk Institute for Biological Studies in La Jolla, Calif.,

BIRTH OF NERVE CELLS, or neurons, in the adult brain has been documented in the human hippocampus, a region important in memory. The steps involved, which occur in the dentate gyrus region of the hippocampus, were originally traced in rodents. First, unspecialized "stem" cells divide at the boundary of the granule cell layer (which contains the globular cell bodies of granule neurons) and the hilus (an adjacent area containing the axons, or signal-emitting projections, of the granule neurons). Then certain of the resulting cells migrate deeper into the granule cell layer. Finally, some of those cells differentiate into granule neurons complete with their characteristic projections.

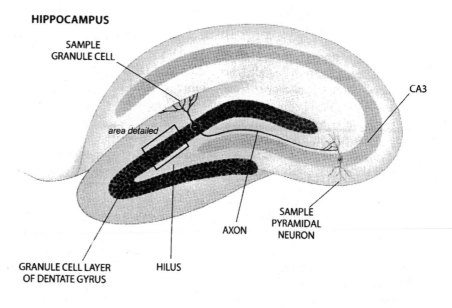

HIPPOCAMPUS

SAMPLE GRANULE CELL

area detailed

CA3

RODENT BRAIN

HUMAN BRAIN

HIPPOCAMPUS

GRANULE CELL LAYER OF DENTATE GYRUS

HILUS

AXON

SAMPLE PYRAMIDAL NEURON

TOMO NARASHIMA

and several colleagues published the startling news that the mature human brain does spawn neurons routinely in at least one site—the hippocampus, an area important to memory and learning. (The hippocampus is not where memories are stored, but it helps to form them after receiving input from other brain regions. People with hippocampal damage have difficulty acquiring knowledge yet can recall information learned before their injury.)

The absolute number of new cells is low relative to the total number in the brain. Nevertheless, considered with recent findings in animals, the November discovery raises some tantalizing prospects for medicine. Current data suggest that stem cells probably make new neurons in another part of the human brain and also reside, albeit dormantly, in additional locations. Hence, the adult brain, which repairs itself so poorly, might actually harbor great potential for neuronal regeneration. If investigators can learn how to induce existing stem cells to produce useful numbers of functional nerve cells in chosen parts of the brain, that advance could make it possible to ease any number of disorders involving neuronal damage and death—among them Alzheimer's disease, Parkinson's disease and disabilities that accompany stroke and trauma.

Although the finding that the mature human brain can generate neurons was surprising, hints had actually appeared for years in studies of other adult mammals. As long ago as 1965, for instance, Joseph Altman and Gopal D. Das of the Massachusetts Institute of Technology had described neuronal production (neurogenesis) in the hippocampus of adult rats—in the precise hippocampal area, known as the dentate gyrus, where it has now been found in human beings.

### Early Hints ... and Doubts

Other studies subsequently confirmed Altman and Das's report, but most researchers did not view the data as evidence of signifi-cant neurogenesis in adult mammals or as an indication that even the human brain might have some regenerative potential. One reason was that the methods then available could not estimate accurately the number of neurons being born nor prove definitively that the new cells were neurons. Further, the concept of brain stem cells had not yet been introduced. Researchers therefore thought that for new nerve cells to appear, fully mature versions would have to replicate—an unbelievably difficult feat. Scientists also underestimated the relevance of the findings to the human brain in part because no one had yet uncovered clear evidence of neurogenesis in monkeys or apes, which are primates and thus are closer to humans genetically and physiologically than are other mammals.

There matters stood until the mid-1980s, when Fernando Nottebohm of the Rockefeller University jarred the field with astonishing results in adult canaries. He discovered that neurogenesis occurred in brain centers responsible for song learning and, moreover, that the process accelerated during the seasons in which the adult birds acquired their songs. Nottebohm and his co-workers also showed that neuron formation in the hippocampus of adult chickadees rose during seasons that placed high demands on the birds' memory system, particularly when the animals had to keep track of increasingly dispersed food storage sites. Nottebohm's dramatic results led to a reawakening of interest in neurogenesis in adult mammals and of course caused investigators to ponder once more whether the mature human brain had any regenerative potential.

Optimism about the possibility of human neurogenesis was short-lived, however. At about the same time, Pasko Rakic and his associates at Yale University pioneered the study of neurogenesis in adult primates. That work, which was well done for its time, failed to find new brain neurons in grown rhesus monkeys.

Logic, too, continued to argue against neuronal birth in the adult human brain. Biologists knew that the extent of neurogenesis had become increasingly restricted throughout evolution, as the brain became more complex. Whereas lizards and other lower animals enjoy massive neuronal regeneration when their brains are damaged, mammals lack that robust response. It seemed reasonable to assume that the addition of neurons to the intricately wired human brain would threaten the orderly flow of signals along established pathways.

Signs that this reasoning might be flawed emerged only a few years ago. First, a team headed by Elizabeth Gould and Bruce S. McEwen of Rockefeller and Eberhard Fuchs of the German Primate Center in Göttingen revealed in 1997 that some neurogenesis occurs in the hippocampus of the primatelike tree shrew. Then, in March 1998, they found the same phenomenon in the marmoset. Marmoset monkeys are evolutionarily more distant from humans than rhesus monkeys are, but they are nonetheless primates.

### Cancer Patients Showed the Way

Clearly, the question of whether humans possess a capacity for neurogenesis in adulthood could be resolved only by studying people directly. Yet such studies seemed impossible, because the methods applied to demonstrate new neuron formation in animals did not appear to be transferable to people.

Those techniques vary but usually take advantage of the fact that before cells divide, they duplicate their chromosomes, which enables each daughter cell to receive a full set. In the animal experiments, investigators typically inject subjects with a traceable material (a "marker") that will become integrated only into the DNA of cells preparing to divide. That marker becomes a part of the DNA in the resulting daughter cells and is then inherited by the daughters' daughters and by future descendants of the original dividing cells.

After a while, some of the marked cells differentiate—that is, they specialize, becoming specific kinds of neurons or glia (the other main class of cells in the brain). Having allowed time for differentiation to occur, workers remove the brain and cut it into thin sections. The sections are stained for the presence of neurons and glia and are viewed under a microscope. Cells that retain the marker (a sign of their derivation from the original dividing cells) and also have the anatomic and chemical characteristics of neurons can be assumed to have differentiated into nerve cells after the marker was introduced into the body. Fully differentiated neurons do not divide and cannot integrate the marker; they therefore show no signs of it.

Living humans obviously cannot be examined in this way. That obstacle seemed insurmountable until Eriksson hit on a solution soon after completing a sabbatical with our group at Salk. A clinician, he one day found himself on call with a cancer specialist. As the two chatted, Eriksson learned that the substance we had been using as our marker for dividing cells in animals—bromodeoxyuridine (BrdU)—was coincidentally being given to some terminally ill patients with cancer of the tongue or larynx. These patients were part of a study that injected the compound to monitor tumor growth.

Eriksson realized that if he could obtain the hippocampus of study participants who eventually died, analyses conducted at Salk could identify the neurons and see whether any of them displayed the DNA marker. The presence of BrdU would mean the affected neurons had formed after that substance was delivered. In other words, the study could prove that neurogenesis had occurred, presumably through stem cell proliferation and differentiation, during the patients' adulthood.

Eriksson obtained the patients' consent to investigate their brains after death. Between early 1996 and February 1998, he raced to the hospital and was given brain tissue from five such patients, who had passed away between the ages of 57 and 72. As hoped, all five brains displayed new neurons—specifically those known as granule cells—in the dentate gyrus. These patients donated their brains to this cause, and we owe this proof of adult human neurogenesis to their generosity. (Coincidentally, at about the time this study was published, Gould's and Rakic's groups both reported that nerve cell production does take place in the hippocampus of adult rhesus monkeys.)

## Do the New Neurons Work?

Of course, the mere demonstration of human neurogenesis is not enough. If the ultimate goal is to stimulate controlled neuronal regeneration in ailing human brains, scientists will want to determine the locations of stem cells capable of evolving into neurons. They will also need to be sure that neurons derived from such cells will be functional and able to send and receive messages appropriately. Fortunately, the discovery that neurogenesis in the rodent hippocampus does, after all, mirror activity in the human brain means that investigators can return to studies in rats and mice to seek clues.

Past work in rodents has revealed that some neurogenesis occurs throughout life not only in the hippocampus but in the brain's olfactory system. Stem cells also reside in such brain regions as the septum (involved in emotion and learning) and the striatum (involved in fine-tuning motor activity) and in the spinal cord. The cells outside the hippocampus and olfactory system do not appear to produce new neurons under normal conditions, though.

If the front part of the animal's brain were transparent, the dentate gyrus portion of the hippocampus would be seen partly as a thin, dark layer, roughly the shape of a sideways V. This V consists of the cell bodies of granule neurons—the globular parts that contain the nucleus. An adjacent layer inside the V is called the hilus. It is composed primarily of the axons, or long signal-carrying projections, through which granule cells relay signals to a hippocampal relay station known as CA3.

The stem cells that give rise to newly born granule cells sit at the boundary of the dentate gyrus and the hilus. These cells divide continuously. Many of the progeny are exactly like their parents, and a good number apparently die soon after being produced. But some migrate deeper into the granule cell layer and assume the appearance of the surrounding granule cells, complete with multiple projections for receiving and sending signals. They also extend their axons along the same tracts used by their already established neighbors.

The stem cells that yield new neurons in the olfactory system line the walls of fluid-filled brain cavities known as lateral ventricles. Arturo Alvarez-Buylla of Rockefeller and his co-workers have demonstrated that certain descendants of these stem cells migrate a good distance into the olfactory bulb, where they take on the characteristic features of neurons in that area.

Given that the new neurons in both brain regions look like their earlier-born counterparts, chances are good that they behave like those neurons. But how might this surmise be proved? Studies analyzing the effects of environment on brain anatomy and learning have been instructive.

In the early 1960s Mark R. Rosenzweig and his colleagues at the University of California at Berkeley removed rodents from their standard, rather spartan laboratory conditions and put them into an enriched environment, where they luxuriated in very large cages and shared the company of many other rodents. They could also explore their surroundings (which were continually changed by the caretakers), take spins in running wheels and play with a variety of toys.

Rosenzweig's group and later that of William T. Greenough of the University of Illinois described amazing consequences of living under such improved conditions. Relative to animals kept in standard cages, those enjoying the high life ended up with slightly heavier brains, greater thickness in certain brain structures, differences in the levels of some neurotransmitters (the molecules that carry stimulatory or inhibitory messages from one neuron to another), more connections between nerve cells and increased branching of neuronal projections. Moreover, they performed better on learning tests; for instance, they were more successful at learning to navigate mazes.

Together the various results implied that the environmental changes had led to improved brain function. Since then, neurobiologists have become convinced that enriching the environment of mature rodents influences brain wiring in ways that enhance brainpower. For years, however, they dismissed the notion that the production of new nerve cells in the adult brain could contribute to such improvements, even though Altman suggested as early as 1964 that such a process should be considered.

New findings have now confirmed that environmental manipulations do affect adult neurogenesis. Applying technology not available in the 1960s, our group demonstrated in 1997 that adult mice given enriched living conditions grew 60 percent more new granule cells in the dentate gyrus than did genetically identical control animals. They also did better on a learning task that involved finding their way out of a pool of water. Enrichment even

TOMO NARASHIMA

**GRANULE CELL DEVELOPMENT** in an embryo is thought to occur through the steps shown in dark gray. A totipotent stem cell, able to give rise to any cell in the body, produces early descendants that include still unspecialized stem cells committed to producing cells of the brain (1). These committed cells later yield "progenitor" cells destined to make only neurons (2) or only glial cells (which promote neuronal survival). Ultimately, neuronal progenitors spawn granule cells in the hippocampus (3) or other kinds of neurons elsewhere in the brain. Steps 2 and 3 now appear to recur throughout life in the human hippocampus.

enhanced neurogenesis and learning performance in very old mice, which have a base rate of neuronal production much lower than that in younger adults.

We do not claim that the new neurons are solely responsible for the behavioral improvements, because changes in wiring configurations and in the chemical microenvironment in the involved brain areas surely play an important part. On the other hand, it would be very surprising if such a dramatic jump in neuron formation, as well as the preservation of adult neurogenesis throughout evolution, served no function.

## Hunt for Controls

If, as we suspect, the neurons born routinely in the brain of the adult human are functional, then an understanding of the controls on their formation could eventually teach neurobiologists how to prompt such neuronal generation where it is needed. Aside from environmental enrichment, various other factors that influence neurogenesis have been identified in animal studies over the past several years.

These results will make the most sense if readers recall that neurogenesis has many steps—from stem cell proliferation, to selected survival of some progeny, to migration and differentiation. It turns out that factors influencing one step along the way may not affect others. An increase in stem cell proliferation can yield a net rise in new neurons if the rates of daughter cell survival and differentiation remain constant, but the neuronal number may not rise if the survival and differentiation rates change in opposite directions. Similarly, neurons will be added if proliferation stays constant but survival and differentiation increase.

Among the regulatory influences that have been uncovered are some that usually seem to discourage neurogenesis. In the past few years, for example, Gould and McEwen have reported that certain everyday inputs into the dentate gyrus may actually keep a lid on nerve cell production. Specifically, neurotransmitters that stimulate granule cells to fire will also inhibit stem cell proliferation in the hippocampus. High levels of glucocorticoid hormones in the blood inhibit adult neurogenesis as well.

Given these findings, it is perhaps no surprise that the team has shown stress to reduce stem cell proliferation in the same region. Stress leads to the release of excitatory neurotransmitters in the brain and to the secretion of glucocorticoid hormones from the adrenals. Understanding inhibition is important for learning how to overcome it. But that aspect of the picture is still far from clear. For instance, the discovery that extreme levels of excitatory transmitters and of certain hormones can constrain neurogenesis does not necessarily mean that lower levels are detrimental; in fact, they may be helpful.

As for factors that promote hippocampal neurogenesis, we and others have been trying to identify which features of an enriched environment have the strongest effect. With her associates, Gould, now at Princeton University, has shown recently that participation in a learn-

ing task, even in the absence of enriched living, enhances the survival of the cells generated by stem cell division, resulting in a net elevation in the number of new neurons.

Meanwhile our group compared neurogenesis in two groups of mice kept in standard cages, one with a running wheel and one without. The mice having unlimited access to the wheels made heavy use of the opportunity and ended up with twice as many new nerve cells as their sedentary counterparts did, a figure comparable to that found in mice placed in an enriched environment. In the runners, a higher rate of stem cell division was involved in the final effect, whereas it played no role in the gains of the enriched-living group. In the latter case (as in Gould's study), stimulating conditions apparently promoted survival of stem cell progeny, so that more of those cells lived to become neurons. This finding highlights once again that the processes regulating neurogenesis in adults are complex and occur on several levels.

Certain molecules are known to influence neurogenesis. We and our co-workers have evaluated epidermal growth factor and fibroblast growth factor, which despite their names have been shown to affect nerve cell development in cell cultures. With H. Georg Kuhn of Salk and Jürgen Winkler of the University of California at San Diego, we delivered these compounds into the lateral ventricles of adult rats, where they evoked striking proliferation by the resident stem cells. Epidermal growth factor favored differentiation of the resulting cells into glia in the olfactory bulb, but fibroblast growth factor promoted neuronal production.

Interestingly, the induction of certain pathological conditions, such as epileptic seizures or stroke, in adult animals can evoke dramatic stem cell division and even neurogenesis. Whether the brain can make use of this response to replace needed neurons is not known. In the case of the seizures, aberrant connections

formed by newborn neurons may be part of the problem. The stem cell division and neurogenesis are more evidence that the brain harbors potential for self-repair. The question is, why does that potential usually go unused?

In the experiments discussed so far, we and others examined regulatory events by holding genes constant: we observed the neurological responses of genetically identical (inbred) animals to different inputs. Another way to uncover controls on neurogenesis is to hold the environment constant and compare genes in strains of animals that differ innately in their rates of neuron production. Presumably, the genes that vary include those affecting the development of new nerve cells. In a similar approach, researchers can compare the genes active in brain regions that display neurogenesis and in brain regions that do not. Genetic studies are under way.

Genes serve as the blueprints for proteins, which in turn carry out the bulk of cellular activities, such as inducing cell division, migration or differentiation. Therefore, if the genes participating in neuronal generation can be identified, investigators should be able to discover their protein products and to tease out the precise contributions of the genes and their proteins to neurogenesis.

## Repairing the Brain

With continued diligence, scientists may eventually be able to trace the molecular cascades that lead from a specific stimulus, be it an environmental cue or some internal event, to particular alterations in genetic activity and, in turn, to rises or falls in neurogenesis. Then they will have much of the information needed to induce neuronal regeneration at will. Such a therapeutic approach could involve administration of key regulatory molecules or other pharmacological agents, delivery of gene therapy to supply helpful molecules, transplantation of stem cells, modulation of environmental or cognitive stimuli, alterations in physical activity, or some combination of these factors.

Compilation of such techniques could take decades. Once collected, though, they might be applied in several ways. They might provide some level of repair, both in brain areas known to manifest some neurogenesis and in sites where stem cells exist but are normally quiescent. Doctors might also be able to stimulate stem cells to migrate into areas where they usually do not go and to mature into the specific kinds of nerve cells required by a given patient. Although the new cells would not regrow whole brain parts or restore lost memories, they could, for example, manufacture valuable amounts of dopamine (the neurotransmitter whose depletion is responsible for the symptoms of Parkinson's disease) or other substances.

Research in related areas of science will contribute to the search for these advanced therapeutic approaches. For instance, several laboratories have learned to culture what are called human embryonic stem cells—highly versatile cells, derived from early embryos, that are capable of giving rise to virtually any cell type in the human body. One day it might be possible to prod these embryonic stem cells into generating offspring that are committed to becoming a selected type of neuron. Such cells might then be transplanted into damaged sites to replenish lost nerve cells [see "Embryonic Stem Cells for Medicine," by Roger A. Pedersen; SCIENTIFIC AMERICAN, April 1999].

Transplants, of course, may be rejected by a recipient's immune system. Scientists are exploring many ways around that problem. One solution could be to harvest stem cells from the brains of the affected patients themselves and to manipulate that material instead of stem cells from a donor. Researchers have already devised relatively noninvasive means of extracting such brain cells from patients.

These medical applications are admittedly goals and are nowhere close to reality at the moment. Indeed, the challenges ahead are huge. Notably, at one point or another analyses of the controls on neurogenesis and of proposed therapies for brain disorders will have to move from rodents to people. To study humans without interfering with their health, researchers will have to make use of extremely clever protocols, such as ones involving the noninvasive imaging techniques known as functional magnetic resonance imaging or positron emission tomography. Further, we will have to develop safeguards ensuring that neurons stimulated to form in the human brain (or transplanted into it) will do just what we want them to do and will not interfere with normal brain function. Nevertheless, the expected benefits of unlocking the brain's regenerative potential justify all the effort that will be required.

## The Authors

GERD KEMPERMANN and FRED H. GAGE have worked together since 1995, when Kempermann began a three-year term as a postdoctoral fellow in Gage's laboratory at the Salk Institute for Biological Studies in La Jolla, Calif. Kempermann, who holds a medical degree from the University of Freiburg in Germany, is now a neurology resident at the University of Regensburg. Gage has been a professor in the Laboratory of Genetics at Salk since 1995 and a professor in the department of neurosciences at the University of California, San Diego, since 1988. He earned his doctorate in neurobiology from John Hopkins University in 1976 and was an associate professor of histology at Lund University in Sweden before moving to California.

## Further Reading

MORE HIPPOCAMPAL NEURONS IN ADULT MICE LIVING IN AN ENRICHED ENVIRONMENT. Gerd Kempermann, H. Georg Kuhn and Fred H. Gage in Nature, Vol. 386, pages 493–495; April 3, 1997.

NEUROGENESIS IN THE ADULT HUMAN HIPPOCAMPUS. Peter S. Eriksson et al. in Nature Medicine, Vol. 4, No. 11, pages 1313–1317; November 1998.

LEARNING ENHANCES ADULT NEUROGENESIS IN THE HIPPOCAMPAL FORMATION. Elizabeth Gould et al. in Nature Neuroscience, Vol. 2, No. 3, pages 260–265; March 1999.

RUNNING INCREASES CELL PROLIFERATION AND NEUROGENESIS IN THE ADULT MOUSE DENTATE GYRUS. Henriette van Praag et al. in Nature Neuroscience, Vol. 2, No. 3, pages 266–270; March 1999.

# The Age Boom

America discovers a new stage of life as many more people live much longer—and better. By Jack Rosenthal

When my father died at 67, leaving my mother alone in Portland, Ore., I thought almost automatically that she should come home with me to New York. Considering her heavy Lithuanian accent and how she shrank from dealing with authority, I thought she'd surely need help getting along. "Are you kidding?" she exclaimed. Managing her affairs became her work and her pride, and it soon occurred to me that this was the first time that she, traditional wife, had ever experienced autonomy. Every few days she would make her rounds to the bank, the doctor, the class in calligraphy. Then, in her personal brand of English, she would make her telephone rounds. She would complain that waiting for her pension check was "like sitting on pins and noodles" or entreat her granddaughter to stop spending money "like a drunken driver." Proudly, stubbornly, she managed on her own for 18 years. And even then, at 83, frustrated by strokes and angry at the very thought of a nursing home, she refused to eat. In days, she made herself die.

Reflecting on those last days, I realize that the striking thing was not her death but those 18 years of later life. For almost all that time, she had the health and the modest income to live on her own terms. She could travel if she chose, or send birthday checks to family members, or buy yet another pair of shoes. A woman who had been swept by the waves of two world wars from continent to continent to continent—who had experienced some of this century's worst aspects—came finally to typify one of its best. I began to understand what people around America are coming to understand: the transformation of old age. We are discovering the emergence of a new stage of life.

The transformation begins with longer life. Increased longevity is one of the striking developments of the century; it has grown more in the last 100 years than in the prior 5,000, since the Bronze Age. But it's easy to misconstrue. What's new is not the number of years people live; it's the number of people who live them. Science hasn't lengthened life, says Dr. Robert Butler, a pioneering authority on aging. It has enabled many more people to reach very old age. And at this moment in history, even to say "many more people" is an understatement. The baby boom generation is about to turn into an age boom.

Still, there's an even larger story rumbling here, and longevity and boomers tell only part of it. The enduring anguish of many elders lays continuing claim on our conscience. But as my mother's last 18 years attest, older adults are not only living longer; generally speaking, they're living better—in reasonably good health and with enough money to escape the anxiety and poverty long associated with aging.

Shakespeare perceived seven ages of man—mewling infant, whining schoolboy, sighing lover, quarrelsome soldier, bearded justice, spectacled wheezer and finally second childhood, "sans teeth, sans eyes, sans taste, sans everything." This special issue of the Magazine examines the emerging new state, a warm autumn that's already altering the climate of life for millions of older adults, for their children, indeed for all society.

## Longer Life

In 1900, life expectancy at birth in America was 49. Today, it is 76, and people who have reached 55 can expect to live into their 80's. Improved nutrition and modern medical miracles sound like obvious explanations. But a noted demographer, Samuel Preston of the University of Pennsylvania, has just published a paper in which he contends that, at least until mid-century, the principal reason was neither. It as what he calls the "germ theory of disease" that generated personal health reforms like washing hands, protecting food from flies, isolating sick children, boiling bottles and milk and ventilating rooms.

*Jack Rosenthal is the editor of The New York Times Magazine.*

Since 1950, he argues likewise, the continuing longevity gains derive less from Big Medicine than from changes in personal behavior, like stopping smoking.

The rapid increase in longevity is now about to be magnified. The baby boom generation born between 1946 and 1964 has always bulged out—population peristalsis—like a pig in a python. Twice as many Americans were born in 1955 as in 1935. Between now and the year 2030, the proportion of people over 65 will almost double. In short, more old people. And there's a parallel fact now starting to reverberate around the world: fewer young people. An aging population inescapably results when younger couples bear fewer children—which is what they are doing almost everywhere.

The fertility news is particularly striking in developed countries. To maintain a stable population size, the necessary replacement rate is 2.1 children per couple. The United States figure is barely 2.0, and it has been below the replacement rate for 30 years. The figure in China is 1.8. Couples in Japan are typically having 1.5 children, in Germany 1.3 and in Italy and Spain, 1.2.

To some people, these are alarming portents of national decline and call for pronatalist policies. That smacks of coarse chauvinism. The challenge is not to dilute the number of older people by promoting more births. It is to improve the quality of life at all ages, and a good place to start is to conquer misconceptions about later life.

## Better Health

"This," Gloria Steinem once said famously, "is what 40 looks like." And this, many older adults now say, is what 60, 70, and even 80 look like. Health and vitality are constantly improving, as a result of more exercise, better medicine and much better prevention. I can't imagine my late father in a sweatsuit, let alone on a Stairmaster, but when I look into the mirrored halls of a health-club gym on upper Broadway I see, among the intent young women in black leotards, white-haired men who are every bit as earnest, climbing, climbing, climbing.

Consider the glow that radiates from the faces on today's cover, or contemplate the standards maintained by people like Bob Cousy, Max Roach, Ruth Bernhard and others who speak out in the following pages.

That people are living healthier lives is evident from the work of Kenneth G. Manton and his colleagues at Duke's Center for Demographic Studies. The National Long-Term Care Survey they started in 1982 shows a steady decline in disability, a 15 percent drop in 12 years. Some of this progress derives from advances in medicine. For instance, estrogen supplements substantially relieve bone weakness in older women—and now seem effective also against other dis-

## I go out and play 18 holes in the morning and then three sets in the afternoon.
## Bob Cousy, 68

Sports Commentator

I still thrive on competition, and when I feel those competitive juices flowing, I've got to find an outlet. Of course, at 68, it's not going to be playing basketball. Basketball's not a sport you grow old with. Sure, I can manage a few from the free-throw line, but being in shape for basketball's something you lose three months after you retire. I stay in shape by doing as little as possible. I play mediocre golf and terrible tennis. My wife calls it my doubleheader days, when I go out and play 18 holes in the morning and then three sets in the afternoon. Now I'm working in broadcasting and schmoozing the corporates. I'm a commentator for the Celtics' away games. I like it because I'm controlling my own destiny. Everything I've done since I graduated from Holy Cross in 1950 has been sports-related, and it's all because I learned to throw a little ball into a hole. A playground director taught me how to play when I was 13. To me it'll always be [a] child's game.

> After 10 weeks of leg-extension exercises, the participants, some as old as 98, typically doubled the strength of the quadriceps, the major thigh muscle. For many, that meant they could walk. Consider what this single change—the ability among other things to go to the bathroom alone—means to the quality and dignity of their lives.

eases. But much of the progress may also derive from advances in perception.

When Clare Friedman, the mother of a New York lawyer, observed her 80th birthday, she said to her son, "You know, Steve, I'm not middle-aged anymore." It's no joke. Manton recalls survey research in which people over 50 are asked when old age begins. Typically, they, too, say "80." Traditionally, spirited older adults have been urged to act their age. But what age is that in this era of 80-year-old marathoners and 90-year-old ice skaters? As Manton says, "We no longer need to accept loss of physical function as an inevitable consequence of aging." To act younger is, in a very real sense, to be younger.

Stirring evidence of that comes from a 1994 research project in which high-resistance strength training was given to 100 frail nursing-home residents in Boston, median age 87 and some as old as 98. Dr. Maria Fiatarone of Tufts University and her fellow researchers found that after 10 weeks of leg-extension exercises, participants typically doubled the strength of the quadriceps, the major thigh muscle. For many, that meant they could walk, or walk without shuffling; the implications for reduced falls are obvious. Consider what this single change—enabling many, for instance, to go to the bathroom alone—means to the quality and dignity of their lives.

Just as old does not necessarily mean feeble, older does not necessarily mean sicker. Harry Moody, executive director of Hunter College's Brookdale Canter on Aging, makes a telling distinction between the "wellderly" and the "illderly." Yes, one of every three people over 65 needs some kind of hospital care in any given year. But only one in 20 needs nursing-home care at any given time. That is, 95 percent of people over 65 continue to live in the community.

## Greater Security

The very words "poor" and "old" glide easily together, just as "poverty" and "age" have kept sad company through history. But suddenly that's changing. In the mid-1960's, when Medicare began, the poverty rate among elders was 29 percent, nearly three times the rate of the rest of the population. Now it is 11 percent, if anything a little below the rate for everyone else. That still leaves five million old people struggling below the poverty line, many of them women. And not many of the other 30 million elders are free of anxiety or free to indulge themselves in luxury. Yet most are, literally, socially secure, able to taste pleasures like travel and education that they may have denied themselves during decades of work. Indeed, many find this to be the time of their lives.

Elderhostel offers a striking illustration. This program, begun in 1975, combines inexpensive travel with courses in an array of subjects and cultures. It started as a summer program with 220 participants at six New Hampshire colleges. Last year, it enrolled 323,000 participants at sites in every state and in 70 foreign countries. Older Americans already exercise formidable electoral force, given how many of them vote. With the age boom bearing down, that influence is growing. As a result, minutemen like the investment banker Peter G. Peterson are sounding alarms about the impending explosion in Social Security and Medicare costs. Others regard such alarms as merely alarmist; either way a result is a spirited public debate, joined by Max Frankel in his column* and by the economist Paul Krugman in his appraisal of the future of Medicare and medical costs.**

Politicians respect the electoral power of the senior vote; why is the economic power of older adults not understood? Television networks and advertisers remain oddly blind to this market, says Vicki Thomas of Thomas & Partners, a Westport, Conn., firm specializing in the "mature market." One reason is probably the youth of copywriters and media buyers. Another is advertisers' desire to identify with imagery that is young, hip, cool. Yet she cites a stream of survey data showing that householders 45 and over buy half

*See page 30, *New York Times Magazine*, March 9, 1997.

**See page 58, *New York Times Magazine*, March 9, 1997.

of all new cars and trucks, that those 55 and over buy almost a third of the total and that people over 50 take 163 million trips a year and a third of all overseas packaged tours.

How much silver there is in this "silver market" is Jerry Della Femina's subject.*** It is also evident from Modern Maturity magazine, published by the American Association of Retired Persons. Its bimonthly circulation is more than 20 million; a full-page ad costs $244,000.

All this spending by older adults may not please everyone. Andrew Hacker, the Queens College political scientist, observes that the longer the parents live, the less they're likely to leave to the children—and the longer the wait. He reports spotting a bumper sticker to that effect, on a passing Winnebago: "I'm Spending My Kids' Inheritance!" Even so, the net effect of generational income transfers remains highly favorable to the next generation. For one thing, every dollar the public spends to support older adults is a dollar that their children won't be called on to spend. For another, older adults sooner or late engage in some pretty sizable income transfers of their own. As Hacker observes, the baby boomers' children may have to wait for their legacies, but their ultimate inheritances will constitute the largest income transfer to any generation ever.

Longer years, better health, comparative security: this new stage of life emerges more clearly every day. What's less clear is how older adults will spend it. The other stages of life are bounded by expectations and institutions. We start life in the institution called family. That's soon augmented for 15 or 20 years by school, tightly organized by age, subject and social webs. Then follows the still-more-structured world of work, for 40 or 50 years. And then—fanfare!—what? What institutions then give shape and meaning to everyday life?

Some people are satisfied, as my mother was, by managing their finances, by tending to family relationships and by prayer, worship and hobbies. Others, more restless, will invent new institutions, just as they did in Cleveland in the 1950's with Golden Age Clubs, or in the 1970's with Elderhostel. For the moment, the institutions that figure most heavily for older adults are precisely those that govern the other stages of life—family, school and work.

FAMILY: The focus on family often arises out of necessity. In a world of divorce and working parents, grandparents are raising 3.4 million children; six million families depend on grandparents for primary child care. And that's only one of the intensified relationships arising among the generations. Children have many more years to relate to their parents as adults, as equals, as friends—a

***See page 70, *New York Times Magazine*, March 9, 1997.

# Sure, someone's probably saying: 'Oh, my God! What's this old bag doing in that suit?'

## Ann Cole

**Age: "Between 59 and Forest Lawn"**
Swimsuit Designer

Everyone has certain features that they hate, and that doesn't change much as you get older—it just gets closer to the ground, as Gypsy Rose Lee once said. So you do just grin and bear it, unless you want to sit indoors and grump about it. I get a lot of women who come in and say, "You wouldn't wear that." And I say, "Why, yes I would." I haven't become more comfortable with my body. I've just taken an attitude that it's easier not to care or worry. Just do it. Sure, someone's probably saying: "Oh, my God! What's this old bag doing in that suit?" I've always been a great advocate of people not listening to their children. There used to be a lot of children who weren't happy unless their mother wore a skirted suit down to her knees. They'd say, "Oh, Mom, you can't wear that." I tried to get people over that in the 60's and 70's, because what do they know? You can't be worried about every bump and lump.

fact demonstrated firsthand by the Kotlowitz-to-Kotlowitz letters. ****

SCHOOL: Increasingly, many elders go back to school, to get the education they've always longed for, or to learn new skills—or for the sheer joy of learning. Nearly half a million people over 50 have gone back to school at the college level, giving a senior cast to junior colleges; adults over age 40 now account for about 15 percent of all college students. The 92d Street Y in New York has sponsored activities for seniors since 1874. Suddenly, it finds, many "New Age Seniors" want to do more than play cards or float in the pool. They are signing up by the score for classes on, for instance, Greece and Rome. At a senior center in Westport, Conn., older adults, far from being averse to technology, flock to computer classes and find satisfaction in managing their finances online and traversing the Internet.

WORK: American attitudes toward retirement have never been simple. The justifications include a humane belief that retirees have earned their rest; or a bottom-line argument that employers need cheaper workers; or a theoretical contention that a healthy economy needs to make room for younger workers. In any case, scholars find a notable trend toward early retirement, arguably in response to pension and Social Security incentives. Two out of three men on Social Security retire before age 65. One explanation is that they are likely to have spent their lives on a boring assembly line or in debilitating service jobs. Others, typically from more fulfilling professional work, retire gradually, continuing to work part time or to find engagement in serious volunteer effort. In Florida, many schools, hospitals and local governments have come to depend on elders who volunteer their skills and time.

FAMILY, SCHOOL, WORK—AND INSTITUTIONS yet to come: these are the framework for the evolving new stage of later life. But even if happy and healthy, it only precedes and does not replace the last of Shakespeare's age of mankind. One need not be 80 or 90 to understand that there comes a time to be tired, or sick, or caught up by the deeply rooted desire to reflect on the meaning of one's life. For many people, there comes a moment when the proud desire for independence turns into frank, mutual acknowledgment of dependence. As the Boston University sociologist Alan Wolfe wrote in The New Republic in 1995, "We owe [our elders] the courage to acknowledge their dependence on us. Only then will we be able, when we are like them, to ask for help."

That time will come, as it always has, for each of us—as children and then as parents. But it will come later. The new challenge is to explore the broad terrain of longer, fuller life with intelligence and respect. One such explorer, a woman named Florida Scott-Maxwell, reported her findings in "The Measure of My Days," a diary she began in her 80's. "Age puzzles me," she wrote, expressing sentiments that my mother personified. "I thought it was a quiet time. My 70's were interesting and fairly serene, but my 80's are passionate. I grow more intense as I age. To my surprise I burst out with hot conviction. . . . I must calm down."

****See page 46, *New York Times Magazine*, March 9, 1997.

# Emotion in the Second Half of Life

## Laura L. Carstensen and Susan Turk Charles[1]

Department of Psychology, Stanford University, Stanford, California

Research on aging has focused primarily on the functional decline people experience as they grow old. Empirical evidence from multiple subdomains of psychology, most notably cognition, perception, and biological psychology, documents reduced efficiency, slowing, and decreased elasticity of basic mental and physical processes with age. Though findings are far more mixed in social aging research, there remains widespread, if tacit, sentiment that the task of gerontological psychology is to assess the ways in which functional declines affect the life of the aging individual.

We assert that the focus on age-related declines in human aging may have steered researchers away from certain questions that, when answered, would paint a more positive picture of old age. Specifically, we argue that changes in the emotion domain challenge models of aging as pervasive loss and point to one central area that is better characterized by continued growth in the second half of life. We posit that old age is marked by greater saliency and improved regulation of emotions, and that emotional well-being, when it does suffer, declines only at the very end of life, when the cognitive and physical disabilities that often precede death in very old age overshadow previously vital areas of functioning (M. M. Baltes, 1998). These ideas are consistent with a curvilinear

pattern of findings that document preserved or improved satisfaction with interpersonal relationships in older age groups (Diener & Suh, 1997), despite increased depressive symptoms and functional difficulties among the oldest old (e.g., Smith & Baltes, 1997).

The research we review here is rooted in socioemotional selectivity theory (Carstensen, 1993, 1995, 1998; Carstensen, Gross, & Fung, 1997; Carstensen, Isaacowitz, & Charles, 1999), a psychological model maintaining that limitations on perceived time lead to motivational shifts that direct attention to emotional goals. The theory posits that the resulting increased attention to emotion results in greater complexity of emotional experience and better regulation of emotions experienced in everyday life. One emotional goal that becomes paramount is interacting with individuals who provide emotionally fulfilling interactions. When people are relieved of concerns for the future, attention to current feeling-states heightens. Appreciation for the fragility and value of human life increases, and long-term relationships with family and friends assume unmatched importance. Because of the inextricable association between age and time left in life, the theory maintains that aging is associated with preferences for and increased investment in emotionally close social relationships, as well as increased focus on other less interpersonal emotional goals. This age-related motivational shift leads to alterations in the dynamic interplay between individuals and their environments, so that optimization of socioemotional experience is prioritized in later life.

---

## SELECTIVE SOCIAL INTERACTION ENHANCES EMOTIONAL ASPECTS OF LIFE

The program of research we have pursued over the years began with consideration of the highly reliable decline in social contact evidenced in later life

and concern for the potential emotional consequences of this reduction. Because human emotions develop within social contexts, and throughout life the most intense emotional experiences, such as anger, sadness, jealousy, and joy, are intimately embedded within them, do fewer social contacts entail emotional costs?

Early theories in psychology and sociology most definitely presumed that reductions in social contact take a toll on emotional life. Although emotional quiescence was in some theories considered the cause and in others the consequence of reduced social contact, for many years no theories contested the idea that emotional experience suffers in old age. Jung (1933) proposed that emotions become progressively generated from internal sources and detached from external events when he wrote that the "very old person . . . has plunged again into the unconscious, and . . . progressively vanishes within it" (p. 131).

Our research on social networks, however, reveals that even though, overall, social networks are smaller in old age, they continue to include comparable numbers of very close relationships throughout later adulthood (Lang & Carstensen, 1994). The reliable age-related decrease in the size of social networks instead appears to result from circumscribed reductions in relatively peripheral relationships. These reductions are not accounted for by poor physical health or declining cognitive status and are not restricted to particular personality styles (Lang & Carstensen, 1994; Lang, Staudinger, & Carstensen, 1998). Moreover, longitudinal analysis suggests that reduction in contact with acquaintances and selective investment in fewer social relationships begins early in adulthood (Carstensen, 1992). It appears that social networks grow smaller across adulthood and are increasingly focused on fewer but emotionally significant social partners.

Socioemotional selectivity theory views the reduction in social contact as a proactive process associated with the

From *Current Directions in Psychological Science,* October 1998, pp. 144-149. © 1998 by Laura L. Carstensen and the American Psychological Society. Reprinted by permission of Blackwell Publishers.

growing desire to have meaningful experiences. We do not regard aging adults as "budding hedonists," directing social interactions solely to those relationships characterized by positive emotions; rather, we argue that the realization that time is limited directs social behavior to experiences that are emotionally meaningful. Moreover, the character of emotional responses changes. Awareness of constraints on time transforms once light-hearted and uniformly positive emotional responses into complex mixtures in which poignancy reigns. Spending time with a close friend, for example, with the awareness that it may be among the last of such occasions inevitably entails sadness along with joy. Our research, along with other findings concerning terminally ill patients, suggests that the prototypical emotional response to approaching endings is not morbid. On the contrary, people facing the end of life often say that life is better than ever before. We understand this evaluation to reflect experiences that are richer, more complex, and emotionally meaningful.

According to the theory, restricting the social world to longtime friends and loved ones in later life is adaptive, reflecting careful allocation of resources to the relationships that engender pleasure and meaning. Such a view helps to reconcile the findings that despite a myriad of well-documented losses and overall reductions in social contact, older people, on average, are even more satisfied with their lives than younger people (Diener & Suh, 1997) and, with the exception of the dementias and other organic brain syndromes, display lower prevalence rates of all psychiatric disorders, including depression (Lawton, Kleban, & Dean, 1993).

## WHEN TIME IS LIMITED, EMOTIONALLY CLOSE SOCIAL PARTNERS ARE PREFERRED

If changes in social networks involve a proactive pruning process, explicit preferences for close over less close social partners should be evident in people faced with limited time. In a series of studies, we found age-related differences in social preferences and also demonstrated the notable malleability of these age differences as a function of perceived time.

In this series of studies, we presented research participants with three prospective social partners, instructed them to imagine that they had 30 min free and wished to spend it with another person, and asked them to choose a social part-

ner from among the three options. Next, the research subjects were presented with experimental conditions in which future time was hypothetically constrained or expanded and were asked once again to indicate their preferred social partners.

The social partners subjects could choose from represented familiar and unfamiliar social partners who were more and less likely to satisfy different social goals: (a) a member of the immediate family, (b) the author of a book the subject just read, and (c) a recent acquaintance with whom the subject seemed to have much in common. Our previous work had shown that all three options promised enjoyable interactions and represented the conceptual categories we intended them to represent. A family member, for example, represents to most people an emotionally close social partner; the author represents a good source of new information; the acquaintance offers prospects in the future. We expected that approaching endings would be associated with preferences for the emotionally meaningful partner.

In our first study using this paradigm, we compared social choices of young and old research participants (Fredrickson & Carstensen, 1990). We hypothesized that older people, but not younger people, would display preferences for the familiar social partner. In a second condition, we imposed a hypothetical time constraint by asking subjects to imagine that they would soon be moving across the country (by themselves) but currently had 30 min free. We then had them choose again from among the same set of social partners. As predicted, older people chose the familiar social partner under both experimental conditions. In the open-ended condition, younger people did not display such a preference. In the time-limited condition, however, younger adults displayed the same degree of preference for the familiar social partner as the older subjects.

Recently, we replicated these findings in Hong Kong (Fung, Carstensen, & Lutz, in press), and even in this very different culture, older people, compared with their younger counterparts, showed a relative preference for familiar social partners. In the Hong Kong study, subjects were asked to imagine an impending emigration as the time-limiting condition. The findings replicated our previous ones. In the emigration condition, younger people also displayed a preference for familiar social partners.

In a third study, instead of limiting time, we presented American subjects with a hypothetical scenario that expanded time. Research subjects in that condition were asked to imagine that they had just received a telephone call

from their physician telling them about a new medical advance that virtually ensured that they would live 20 years longer than they expected in relatively good health (Fung et al., in press). We also included the time-unspecified condition, which replicated previous findings. Older, but not younger, subjects expressed strong preferences for the familiar social partner. However, in the expanded-time condition, the preference observed among older subjects disappeared: Older and younger subjects' choices were indistinguishable. Thus, when the time constraint associated with age is removed, older individuals' preferences for familiar social partners disappear.

In another line of research, we used an experimental approach based on similarity judgments to examine age differences in the emphasis and use of emotion when forming mental representations of possible social partners. In these studies, research participants sorted descriptions of a variety of social partners according to how similarly they would feel interacting with them. A technique called multidimensional scaling was used to identify the dimensions along which these categorizations were based, and we also computed the weights various subgroups placed on particular dimensions.

In three different studies, we found evidence that place in the life cycle is associated with the salience of emotion in mental representations (Carstensen & Fredrickson, 1998; Fredrickson & Carstensen, 1990). Two of these studies examined age differences in the weights placed on the emotion dimension, and a third study compared how the dimensions were weighted by groups of men who were the same age but varied according to their HIV status. In this way, age was disentangled from place in the life cycle. Findings from all three studies suggest that when individuals are closer to end of their lives, whether because of age or health status, emotion is more salient in their mental representations of other people.

In light of findings suggesting increased salience of emotion among people approaching the end of life, we hypothesized that age differences in memory for emotional versus nonemotional material might be evident as well. That is, if emotional information is more salient, it should be processed more deeply than nonemotional information and therefore remembered better subsequently. To test this hypothesis, we employed an incidental memory paradigm and examined age differences in the type of information recalled (Carstensen & Turk-Charles, 1994). Older and younger adults read a two-page narrative that described a social interaction and contained comparable amounts of neutral and emotionally relevant information. Roughly 45 min later, after completing a series of unrelated tasks, participants were asked to recall all that they could about the passage. Responses were transcribed, and the information in them was classified as either emotional or neutral. The proportion of emotional material correctly recalled from the original text was related to age; the proportion of recalled information that was emotional information was greater for older adults than younger adults. The differences in proportions were driven by a decrease in the amount of neutral information recalled by older adults, and not by an increase in their recall of emotional information. We speculate that the increased salience of emotion may have cognitive costs, in this case a focus on emotional information at the expense of nonemotional information, but these ideas are as yet untested (cf. Isaacowitz, Charles, & Carstensen, in press).

Thus, whether one asks people directly about the types of social partners they prefer, examines the ways in which people mentally represent social partners, or measures the proportion of emotional and informational material people remember, those people approaching the end of life appear to place more value on emotion, choosing social partners along affective lines and processing emotionally salient information more deeply.

## THE INTEGRITY OF THE EMOTION SYSTEM IS WELL MAINTAINED IN OLD AGE

Do older adults experience emotions similarly to younger adults, or do age-related biological changes—from facial wrinkles to alterations in the central nervous system—degrade emotional experience? Despite numerous social reasons that could increase the likelihood of negative emotional experiences and biological reasons that might appear to decrease the ability to control them, research findings suggest the opposite.

A biological argument for the reduction of self-reported negative experiences lies in the notion of a reduced capacity to feel emotions. If emotions are not felt as strongly physiologically, they will not be subjectively perceived, and consequently, they will not be reported. However, findings from laboratory studies in which emotions are induced speak against a reduced-capacity argument. In

a study measuring subjective experience, spontaneous facial expression, and psychophysiological responding (Levenson, Carstensen, Friesen, & Ekman, 1991), subjective intensity of emotional experience, outward facial expression, and the specific profiles of physiological activation were indistinguishable among older and younger adults. Interestingly, however, the overall level of physiological arousal was significantly reduced among the elderly. Similar reductions in levels of physiological arousal were observed in a study of married couples we describe later (Levenson, Carstensen, & Gottman, 1994).

## AGE DIFFERENCES IN EMOTIONAL EXPERIENCE ARE POSITIVE

In addition to the findings concerning intact physiological mechanisms and greater emotional salience, there is evidence pointing to greater overall well-being—that is, less negative emotion and equivalent if not greater levels of positive emotions—among older adults compared with younger adults. Survey studies suggest that levels of positive affect are similar across successively older age cohorts, but a reliable reduction in negative affect is observed, and in studies finding reductions in positive affect, a closer analysis of the findings suggests that a circumscribed reduction in surgency (i.e., excitability) may account for this reduction. Excitement and sensation seeking, for example, are relatively reduced in old age. Other positive emotions, such as happiness and joy, are maintained (Lawton et al., 1993; Lawton, Kleban, Rajagopal, & Dean, 1992).

We recently completed a study in which emotions were sampled in everyday life (Carstensen, Pasupathi, & Mayr, 1998). Research participants spanning the ages 18 to 94 years carried electronic pagers and indicated on a response sheet the degree to which they were experiencing each of 19 positive and negative emotions at random times throughout the days and evenings for a week-long period. Findings revealed no age differences in the intensity of positive or negative experience. However, the frequency of negative emotional experience was lower among older than younger adults.

Data collected in this experience-sampling study also allowed us to explore the postulate that emotional experience is more mixed among older than younger people. In day-to-day life, people can experience multiple emotions in response to an event. Socioemotional selectivity theory predicts that

emotional experience becomes more multifaceted with age because awareness of limited time elicits positive emotions and negative emotions, thus changing the very character of the experience. We tested this hypothesis in two ways. First, we computed the simple correlation between positive and negative emotional experience. Although, as expected, the correlation between positive and negative emotions was low, it was positively and significantly associated with age. That is, older adults tended to experience mixed positive and negative emotions more than younger adults. Second, with the use of factor analysis, we computed for each research participant the number of factors that best characterized his or her responses over the course of the study. More factors were required to account for older people's responses, suggesting that their emotional reactions were more complex or differentiated.

Thus, studies that measure subjective emotional experience, either in the laboratory or as they occur in everyday life, speak against an unqualified reduced-capacity argument. Once elicited, positive and negative emotions are experienced subjectively as intensely among the old as the young. Interestingly, the few studies that have measured autonomic nervous system activity have found that the strength of physiological arousal is reduced in the elderly. Whether the reduction is emotion-specific or due to more global age-related degradation of the autonomic nervous system remains unclear. Either way, to the extent that lessened physiological arousal is associated with less subjective discomfort, it may have serendipitously positive consequences. As P. Baltes (1991) argued cogently, deficits in circumscribed domains can sometimes prompt growth in other domains. Reduced physiological arousal associated with negative emotions may represent a case in point, a matter to which we turn in the next section.

## OLDER PEOPLE REGULATE THEIR EMOTIONS BETTER THAN YOUNGER PEOPLE

Socioemotional selectivity theory maintains that an emphasis on emotional goals leads to active efforts on the part of individuals to emphasize and enhance emotional experience. Existing empirical evidence from cross-sectional studies about perceived control over emotions is clear: Compared with younger adults, older adults report greater control over emotions, greater stability of mood, less psychophysiological agitation, and greater faith in their ability to control the internal and external expression of emotions. Remarkably similar age-related patterns have been found across five diverse samples: Catholic nuns; African, European, and Chinese Americans; and Norwegians (Gross et al., 1997).

The consistency of findings across these diverse ethnic, religious, and regional groups reduces concern that the findings reflect stable differences among age groups (viz., cohort effects), as opposed to aging per se. In other words, although cohort effects cannot be ruled out entirely, the reliability of the profile across very different types of samples at least speaks against the alternative that emotional differences are unique to younger and older generations of white Americans.

Findings from three other recent studies also reduce the concern that older people's subjective sense that they have good control over their emotions is limited to their beliefs and fails to reflect age differences in actual control. First, Lawton, Parmelee, Katz, and Nesselroade (1996) examined reported negative affect sampled during the course of a 1-month period in a group of adults. Not only did older adults report relatively low levels of negative affect, but they varied little over time.

Second, in the experience-sampling study described earlier (Carstensen et al., 1998), we examined the probability that negative or positive emotions would occur given their occurrence at the immediately preceding time when subjects reported their emotions. Using the 35 emotion samples collected over a 1-week period for each subject, we examined the duration of positive and negative emotional experience. As did Lawton et al. (1996), we found that the duration of negative emotions was shorter for older than younger adults; interestingly, the natural duration of positive emotional experience was similar for old and young adults (Carstensen et al., 1998). Thus, even when emotions are sampled close to the time they occurred, so that global self-evaluations are avoided, similarly positive profiles of emotional experience are revealed.

Third, we conducted a study involving observations of married couples discussing emotionally charged conflicts in their relationships. Resolution of interpersonal conflict, especially in intimate relationships, provides an opportunity to examine a special case of emotion regulation. Effective resolution of marital conflict requires that spouses deal simultaneously with their own negative emotions and the negative emotions expressed by their partner. In this study, we hypothesized that older couples resolve conflicts better than their middle-aged counter-

parts. Middle-aged and older couples, all of whom had been married many years, were asked to identify a mutually-agreed-upon conflict area and then to discuss the conflict with one another toward its resolution (Carstensen, Gottman, & Levenson, 1995; Carstensen, Graff, Levenson, & Gottman, 1996; Levenson, Carstemen, & Gottman, 1993; Levenson et al., 1994). Discussions were videotaped and psychophysiological responses were measured throughout the interaction. As predicted, compared with middle-aged couples, older couples displayed lesser overall negative affect, expressing less anger, disgust, belligerence, and whining in their discussions. In addition, older couples were more likely to express affection to their spouses during the exchange, interspersing positive expressions with negative ones. The pattern appears to be highly effective in curbing the negative affect typically associated with emotionally charged discussions.

Thus, older adults are notably effective at managing negative emotions. This finding, in combination with findings that positive emotions are maintained in frequency and duration during old age, paints a picture that is quite positive. The findings are in keeping with socioemotional selectivity theory. In the studies reviewed, older individuals limited negative emotional experiences in day-to-day life more effectively than younger individuals. Similarly, older couples engaged in discussions of personally relevant topics in a way that limited their negativity. If, as the theory suggests, people become increasingly aware of endings toward the end of life, aging individuals are increasingly motivated to optimize the emotional climate of their lives. It is not that negative emotions do not occur or that felt emotions are less intense. Rather, negative emotions are better regulated.

## CONCLUSION

The study of emotion in old age is relatively young, yet within a short period of time, empirical findings have suggested a reasonably cohesive profile of emotional experience and emotion regulation in the later years. Efforts on the part of multiple investigative teams have documented the ubiquitousness of emotion in cognitive processing, from mental representations to social preferences; stability in the frequency of positive affect; reductions in negative affect; reduced physiological arousability; and superior regulation of emotion.

Of course, a comprehensive understanding of emotion in later life is only beginning to take shape. Greater em-

phasis on emotional aspects of life probably entails benefits for some areas of functioning and costs to others. The manner in which emotions change and the conditions associated with such change remain elusive. The role of perceived time in emotional experience, suggested in socioemotional selectivity theory, requires further investigation to identify the precise conditions under which emotions grow mixed, are better regulated, and are less negative as people age. Implications of the reduction in the physiological arousal accompanying emotional experience also demand clarification.

The profile of empirical evidence reviewed here provides a far different picture of old age than the literatures on cognitive aging and physical health. Numerous problems are associated with old age. Health insults, loss of economic and political status, and deaths of friends and loved ones are but a few of the problems associated with old age, yet research on emotion and aging suggests that the emotion domain may be well preserved and perhaps selectively optimized (M. M. Baltes & Carstensen, 1996). The inherent paradox of aging refers to the fact that despite loss and physical decline, adults enjoy good mental health and positive life satisfaction well into old age. We suggest that the uniquely human ability to monitor the passage of time, coupled with the inevitable constraints of mortality, heightens the value placed on emotional aspects of life and deepens the complexity of emotional experience as people age.

**Acknowledgments**—We thank Ursula Staudinger for her comments about an earlier draft of this article.

## Note

1. Address correspondence to Laura Carstensen, Department of Psychology, Bldg. 420, Jordan Hall, Stanford University, Stanford, CA 94305; e-mail: llc@ psych. stanford.edu.

## References

Baltes, M. M. (1998). The psychology of the oldest-old: The fourth age. *Current Opinion in Psychiatry, 11,* 411–418.

Baltes, M. M., & Carstensen, L. L. (1996). The process of successful ageing. *Ageing and Society, 16,* 397–422.

Baltes, P. (1991). The many faces of human aging: Toward a psychological culture of old age. *Psychological Medicine, 21,* 837–854.

Carstensen, L. L. (1992). Social and emotional patterns in adulthood: Support for socioemotional selectivity theory. *Psychology and Aging, 7,* 331–338.

Carstensen, L. L. (1993). Motivation for social contact across the life span: A theory of socioemotional selectivity. In J. Jacobs (Ed.), *Nebraska Symposium on Motivation: Vol. 40. Developmental perspectives on motivation* (pp. 209–254). Lincoln: University of Nebraska Press.

Carstensen, L. L. (1995). Evidence for a life-span theory of socioemotional selectivity. *Current Directions in Psychological Science, 4,* 151–156.

Carstensen, L. L. (1998). A life-span approach to social motivation. In J. Heckhausen & C. Dweck (Eds.), *Motivation and self-regulation across the life span* (pp. 341–364). New York: Cambridge University Press.

Carstensen, L. L., & Fredrickson, B. L. (1998). Socioemotional selectivity in healthy older people and younger people living with the Human Immunodeficiency Virus: The centrality of emotion when the future is constrained. *Health Psychology, 17,* 1–10.

Carstensen, L. L. & Gottman, J. M., & Levenson, R. W. (1995). Emotional behavior in long-term marriage. *Psychology and Aging, 10,* 140–149.

Carstensen, L. L., Graff, J., Levenson, R. W., & Gottman, J. M. (1996). Affect in intimate relationships: The developmental course of marriage. In C. Magai & S. H. McFadden (Eds.), *Handbook of emotion, adult development, and aging* (pp. 227–247). San Diego: Academic Press.

Carstensen, L. L., Gross, J., & Fung, H. (1997). The social context of emotion. In K. W. Schaie & M. P. Lawton (Eds.), *Annual review of gerontology and geriatrics: Vol. 17. Focus on emotion and adult development* (pp. 325–352). New York: Springer.

Carstensen, L. L., Isaacowitz, D. M., & Charles, S. T. (1999). Taking time seriously: A life-span theory of social selectivity. *American Psychologist, 54,* 165–181.

Carstensen, L. L. Pasupathi, M., & Mayr, U. (1998). *Emotion experience in the daily lives of older and younger adults.* Manuscript submitted for publication.

Carstensen, L. L., & Turk-Charles, S. (1994). The salience of emotion across the adult life span. *Psychology and Aging, 9,* 259–264.

Diener, E., & Suh, M. E. (1997). Subjective well-being and age: An international analysis. In K. W. Schaie & M. P. Lawton (Eds.), *Annual review of gerontology and geriatrics: Vol. 17. Focus on emotion and adult development* (pp. 304–324). New York: Springer.

Fredrickson, B. F., & Carstensen, L. L. (1990). Choosing social partners: How old age and anticipated endings make us more selective. *Psychology and Aging, 5,* 335–347.

Fung, H. Carstensen, L. L., & Lutz, A. (in press). The influence of time on social preferences: Implications for life-span development. *Psychology and Aging.*

Gross, J. Carstensen, L. L., Pasupathi, M., Tsai, J., Götestam Skorpen, C., & Hsu, A. (1997). Emotion and aging: Experience, expression and control. *Psychology and Aging, 12,* 590–599.

Isaacowitz, D., Charles, S. T., & Carstensen, L. L. (in press). Emotion and cognition. In F. I. M. Craik & T. A. Salthouse (Eds.), *Handbook of aging and cognition* (2nd ed.) Mahwah, NJ: Erlbaum.

Jung, C. G. (1933). The stages of life. In *Modern man in search of a soul* (pp. 109–131). London: Kegan, Paul, Trench & Trubner.

Lang, F., Staudinger, U., & Carstensen, L. L. (1998). Socioemotional selectivity in late life: How personality and social context do (and do not) make a difference. *Journal of Gerontology: Psychological Sciences, 53,* P21–P30.

Lang, F. R., & Carstensen, L. L. (1994). Close emotional relationships in late life: Further support for proactive aging in the social domain. *Psychology and Aging, 9,* 315–324.

Lawton, M. P., Kleban, M. H. & Dean, J. (1993). Affect and age: Cross-sectional comparisons of structure and prevalence. *Psychology and Aging, 8,* 165–175.

Lawton, M. P., Kleban, M. H., Rajagopal, D., & Dean, J. (1992). The dimensions of affective experience in three age groups. *Psychology and Aging, 7,* 171–184.

Lawton, M. P., Parmelee, P. A., Katz, I., & Nesselroade, J. (1996). Affective states in normal and depressed older people. *Journal of Gerontology: Psychological Sciences, 51,* P309–P316.

Levenson, R. W., Carstensen, L. L., Friesen, W. V., & Ekman, P. (1991). Emotion, physiology, and expression in old age. *Psychology and Aging, 6,* 28–35.

Levenson, R. W., Carstensen, L. L., & Gottman, J. M. (1993). Long-term marriage: Age, gender and satisfaction. *Psychology and Aging, 8,* 301–313.

Levenson, R. W., Carstensen, L. L., & Gottman, J. M. (1994). Marital interaction in old and middle-aged long-term marriages: Physiology, affect and their interrelations. *Journal of Personality and Social Psychology, 67,* 56–68.

Smith, J., & Baltes, P. B. (1997). Profiles of psychological functioning in the old and oldest old. *Psychology and Aging, 12,* 458–472.

# The Centenarians Are Coming!!

**The remarkable achievement of centenarians isn't just the fact that they've made it to 100; it's that they've made living beyond 100 seem a worthwhile goal.**

*By Cynthia G. Wagner*

Jeanne Calment was 13 years old when a Dutch painter named Vincent van Gogh came to her home town, Arles, in the south of France in 1888. A century later, she could still remember him: "Very ugly, ungracious, impolite, crazy. I forgive him. They called him 'the Nut.' "

Both van Gogh and Calment have become world famous—van Gogh, for painting pictures that people pay millions of dollars for, and Calment, for becoming the world's oldest person.

Jeanne Calment was born in 1875, before the Eiffel Tower was built. She was both van Gogh's contemporary and, a century later, ours. When she died in 1997 at age 122, she had broken all human longevity records. But her record may not last long. Centenarians—people living to age 100 and beyond—are on the rise.

## Counting the Superold

Centenarians as a group are not easy to count. For one thing, it is difficult to verify cases of exceptional longevity; sloppy historians and ambiguous records may inadvertently add years to an individual's life because he or she was given the same name as an older relative who had died. People allegedly living to 150 years and beyond in the Russian Caucasus were discredited when many were found to be using birth certificates of aunts and uncles with the same names, according to preeminent centenarian researcher Thomas Perls, director of the New England Centenarian Study at Harvard Medical School.

Until recent years, there haven't been enough centenarians to count separately from other senior citizens. Now, global record keepers such as the United Nations Population Division are raising the bar: "Elderly" now means "85 and older," rather than merely "65 and older," reflecting the swelling ranks of people nearing the century mark. Today, a 65-year-old must live 57 more years to catch up with Jeanne Calment.

The U.N.'s 1998 World Population Revision, released last October,

COURTESY OF NATIONAL CENTENARIAN
AWARENESS PROJECT

**Athlete Ben Levinson, age 103,** practices a shot put at the 1998 Nike World Masters Games. Studies show that persons of extraordinary age tend to experience a slower aging process than others and that, if they make it past their 90s, most enjoy good health until the very end of life.

included for the first time the numbers of octogenarians (people aged

80–89), nonagenarians (90–99), and centenarians (100 and older). (Yet to make it into the statisticians' books are *decacentenarians*—persons in their 110s—and *dodecacentenarians*—those in their 120s, like Jeanne Calment.)

"In 1998, around 135,000 persons in the world are estimated to be aged 100 or over," the Population Division reported. "The number of centenarians is projected to increase 16-fold by 2050 to reach 2.2 million persons."

## Research on Centenarians

The rapid growth in the number of centenarians has been a neglected phenomenon, but researchers are now showing interest, according to Michel Allard, Victor Lèbre, and Jean-Marie Robine, co-authors of the case study *Jeanne Calment: From Van Gogh's Time to Ours*. Allard is a physician and gerontologist, Lèbre was Calment's physician and friend, and Robine is a demographer.

France began studying centenarianism seriously in 1989 when the IPSEN Foundation, a nonprofit organization specializing in longevity research, began a major epidemiological study, the authors report.

"Madame Jeanne Calment was one of a small group of centenarians," Allard, Lèbre, and Robine write. "For example, in 1953, there were scarcely 200 centenarians in her native France; in 1988, the number exceeded 3,000. At the time, nothing, or almost nothing, was known about them. However, they foreshadow the emergence of a new stratum of the population, illustrating a more and more probable, almost certain future, both individual and collective. Today, the number is over 6,000."

The U.S. Census Bureau estimates nearly 66,000 Americans now over age 100, compared with about 3,500 in 1900. Entertainer George Burns died in 1996 shortly after turning 100; the Delany sisters became best-selling authors (*Having Our Say*) well after entering their second cen-

tury of life; legendary theater director George Abbott worked into his 90s and, at age 106 in 1994, advised on the revival of his hit musical *Damn Yankees;* he died at 107.

Centenarians' personal stories were collected for *Centenarians: The Bonus Years*, a 1995 book by Lynn Pe-

---

**Always keep a smile** I attribute my long life to that. I believe I will die laughing. That's part of my program.

*—Jeanne Calment*

---

ters Adler, founder of the Arizona Centenarian Program and the National Centenarian Awareness Project. While the book celebrates the achievement of long life, Adler notes that the centenarians are not just "our living links to the past," but also pioneers and role models for future centenarians: "Hopefully, the models of centenarians here will give assurance that such longevity is becoming more possible and often desirable, as well as raise thought-provoking issues to be addressed for and by future centenarians."

## Decreasing Mortality Rates

Mortality rates have fallen almost everywhere in the world during the twentieth century, according to Joseph Chamie, director of the U.N. Population Division's Department of Economic and Social Affairs. Improved public health, nutrition, and medical breakthroughs such as the development of antibiotics and vaccines are all part of the twentieth century's reduction of mortality. One observer credits plumbers more than doctors for humans' increased survival rates, as improved sanitation has reduced the incidence of infectious diseases.

Economic progress, in general, helps people live longer, as evidenced by the higher mortality rates in less-developed regions: Major exceptions to the global success story

include Africa, where HIV/AIDS is taking a devastating toll, and eastern Europe, where declining economic conditions since the breakup of the Soviet Union have thwarted attempts to improve life expectancy and death rates.

Genetics may help explain why certain individuals live longer than others. The Calment family clearly lived well in Arles, with four generations proving resilient against food shortages, plagues, and other privations between 1700 and 1900. The researchers conclude, "Two factors are evident: a greater longevity and a vigor in this family."

Gender also is a factor, as women tend to outlive men in general. The United Nations reports that there are nearly two women to every man above the age of 80; among centenarians, the ratio is four to one. The good news for men is that those who survive into their 100s tend to retain better mental function than their female peers, according to Harvard's Thomas Perls.

## Lifestyles of the Superold

There does not seem to be a single, one-lifestyle-fits-all formula for centenarianism, but people who live a long time tend to make life worth living. Strict diets and fitness regimens may make you healthier and thus improve your chances for living longer, but such programs are not for everyone. The current "world's oldest person," Sarah Clark Knauss (118) of Allentown, Pennsylvania, reportedly feasts on chocolates, pretzels, and potato chips and shuns vegetables. Her advice for longevity is not to worry about your age.

I don't want to achieve immortality through my work. **I want to achieve it through not dying.**

*—Woody Allen*

Jeanne Calment smoked in moderation, but finally quit of her own accord when she was 117 (offering hope that it is never too late for anyone to quit smoking). She drank port (vintage only, please) and enjoyed chocolates. She married and outlived her husband; she also outlived her one child.

On the other hand, American centenarians Sadie and Bessie Delany never married. Bessie (who died at 104 in 1995) was quoted, "When people ask me how we've lived past 100, I say, 'Honey, we never married; we never had husbands to worry us to death.' " Indeed, a low level of "worry," or stress, is a strong marker in successful agers, as is a facility for coping with stress when it does come about. As *Centenarians* author Lynn Adler observes, "People who reach 100 are not quitters."

Centenarians also exercise their minds: The Delany sisters, black women in post-slavery America, both attended college, as did their eight brothers and sisters; Bessie became a dentist and Sadie (who died this year at age 109) became a high-school teacher in an era when most women stayed home.

Education and the desire to keep on learning throughout life are two factors associated with longevity in general. Education is an important sociodemographic factor because it increases individuals' chances for a higher economic and health status.

Now, researchers at the Charles A. Dana Foundation in New York and at the Harvard Medical School are working with centenarians to learn what the impacts of brain health are on aging. Brain autopsies of centenarians have revealed a remarkable lack of the physical ravages of Alzheimer's disease and dementia, according to Margery Silver of Harvard's New England Centenarian Study. "It has been common thinking that dementia is inevitable with old age. That isn't so," she says.

Harvard researcher Thomas Perls postulates that this puzzling good brain health among centenarians may be a "survival of the fittest" phenomenon; since Alzheimer's claims the lives of its victims in their 80s and early 90s, those who reach their late 90s are likely to hang on to their superior mental faculties for years to come.

## Life-Span vs. Life Expectancy

Perls points out that life-span and life expectancy are two very different things. Average life expectancy refers to how long individuals are expected to survive given the circumstances of their birth—and this number has soared in the twentieth century from an average of about 45 years to 63 for men and nearly 68 for women worldwide, according to U.N. figures. Life expectancy remains low in less-developed countries—51 years for men, 53 for women—but is higher in more-developed countries—71 for men, 78 for women.

Life-span, on the other hand, refers to the maximum potential age of human beings; that is, the age they may reach if their lives are not taken by disease or misadventure.

While life expectancy has clearly increased, life-span has not. The maximum life-span remains about 120 years.

As science learns more about the aging process, researchers hope to develop techniques to slow or even reverse the effects of aging. Already, observation of centenarians has shown them to have slower rates of biological aging.

Perls notes the association of late motherhood with longer lives: "As we reviewed the pedigrees of a number of our centenarian subjects living in the suburban Boston area, we came across a substantial number of women who had children in their 40s," he wrote in *Scientific American* (January 1995). "There was even one that had a child at the age of 53 years. This struck us as unusual given that maternal age greater than 40 is a relatively rare event. . . . However, a history of older maternal age among our centenarian subjects made sense to us since aging relatively slowly is a likely necessary characteristic of achieving extreme old age and women who do so should be able to bear children at an older age."

Perls concluded that "it is not the act of having a child in your 40s that promotes long life, but rather it is an indicator that the woman's reproductive system is aging slowly. A slow rate of aging would therefore bode well for the woman's subsequent ability to achieve very old age."

So slowing down the aging process would seem to be a key in extending the human life-span—the potential outer limits of human aging. A new branch of health science has emerged around the concept of anti-aging, finding the genetic keys to slowing or reversing the aging

If I'd known I was going to live this long, **I'd have taken better care of myself.**

*—Eubie Blake (on his 100th birthday)*

Trend Analysis

# The Increase of the Elderly in the Population

The surge in centenarians is part of the global increase in elderly people (85 and up). To clarify the implications of this trend, the staff of the World Future Society has identified a number of the causes of the trend and possible effects that the trend will have. The information is organized according to the six-sector format used in the World Trends & Forecasts section.

## Demography

**Causes:** Women bear fewer children, allowing more resources for those they do have. Higher levels of education lead to better self-care and use of medical services.

**Effects:** Declining percentage of children in population. Fewer elderly will have working family members to help them with their disabilities and living problems. Increase in percentage of disabled in the population. Elderly may face backlash from younger people forced to pay for their upkeep. Elderly may break up into new categories—octogenarians, nonagenarians, centenarians, superold (over 110).

## Economics:
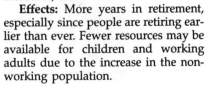
**Causes:** Rising living standards—more abundant food, shelter, public-health measures, etc.

**Effects:** More years in retirement, especially since people are retiring earlier than ever. Fewer resources may be available for children and working adults due to the increase in the non-working population.

## Environment

**Causes:** Careful treatment of sewage and other sanitary measures. Protection of soil, water, and other resources. Reduction of air pollution.

**Effects:** Need for more resources of almost every kind to meet needs of swelling elderly population. Special pressures on areas favored by elderly—e.g., Florida, Arizona.

## Government

**Causes:** Social Security ensures basic support for needy; tax-advantaged retirement programs also help elderly meet their needs. Government funding of medical research allows steady flow of new medical knowledge and treatments. Laws protect people against physical abuse or injury from employers, environment, criminals, etc.

**Effects:** Increasing burden on Social Security and government programs to assist elderly and disabled. Elderly grow as political constituency demanding benefits. People may agitate against laws requiring that they spend down their individual retirement accounts. Government finances strain under burden of supporting retirees paying few taxes.

## Society
**Causes:** Communications media and educational system influence people to safeguard their health.

**Effects:** Families have more elderly to care for. Parents' resources may be diverted from their children to aging relatives. Elderly may become increasingly prominent in TV, other media. More products, programs, and institutions will be designed specifically for the elderly.

## Technology
**Causes:** New drugs and medical devices preserve lives. Communications and transportation improvements make resources more available.

**Effects:** Elderly will push innovation by providing a growing market for drugs and technologies to overcome their disabilities. Techno-furnishings—high-tech chairs, beds, tables, sinks, toilets, etc.—may become popular as elderly seek solutions to their living problems. If researchers gain understanding of senescence (aging process), a means might be found to extend human lives for centuries.

## Implications

You don't expect to live to 100? Neither did most centenarians, but it happened. If you live to be 90 or 100, will you outlive your retirement savings? People now are retiring earlier than ever, often involuntarily. Should you think about a second or third career?

You may find yourself caring for old-old relatives when you yourself are old. New technologies and home care may enable you to continue to live in your home, but you may be asked to share it with a great grandson or daughter.

There is likely to be a growing market for services used by the elderly—medical, home care, etc. Products designed for disabled elderly people—drugs, prosthetics, etc.—should be in growing demand. These trends may suggest career and investment opportunities. Should you think about targeting the elderly as prospects for your products or services?

And watch for events featuring octogenarians, nonagenarians, and centenarians: Olympics for nonagenarians? Caribbean cruises limited to people over 80? Movies, books, computer games for the very old?

*—Edward Cornish with the staff of the World Future Society*

# Are You Ready to Be a Centenarian?

This five-part "centenarian strategy" for planning a successful long life is offered by David Mahoney, chairman of The Charles A. Dana Foundation, a brain-research think tank:

**1. Diversify your career.** Plan to do more than one thing, including devoting more time to avocations such as art, philanthropy, or political activism. "Being 'double-minded or triple-minded' about your career allows for a balanced life and provides the means to shift gears when necessary," says Mahoney.

**2. Plan for your own financial independence.** "Take advantage of your opportunity to wind up a millionaire," Mahoney advises. Members of the post-baby-boom generations are especially warned against relying on social safety nets. Reduce your debt, avoid taxes by using IRAs and other retirement plans, and invest for long-term capital growth.

**3. Invest in your family.** The companionship of a spouse and children enriches life and ensures an emotional support system.

**4. Pace yourself.** Age slowly by living slowly and deliberately. "Taking the long view of success means measuring it in personal satisfaction, not getting to the top of some heap as fast as possible," says Mahoney.

**5. Plan for the shock that's sure to come.** Successful aging means being a futurist (taking a long-term view) and being flexible: rolling with the punches. By anticipating that setbacks will inevitably occur—career disruptions, deaths in the family, etc.—the strategic centenarian can find new directions more easily.

In addition, would-be centenarians might follow the "DARE" regimen—Diet, Attitude, Renewal, and Exercise—devised by physician Walter Bortz, former president of the American Geriatrics Society and a clinical associate professor at Stanford University Medical School.

Diet and exercise are linked because exercise boosts metabolism; if you don't exercise, you must be very careful about what you eat, says Bortz. Renewal has to do with resilience—the ability to pick oneself up after a fall, since age brings about inevitable losses.

Attitude is a crucial and sometimes overlooked aspect of longevity. "Believe in 100," says Bortz. "If you want to do something, such as stop smoking, you must believe you can. You need to set the goal first and have a plan. And remain optimistic."

Sources: David Mahoney, The Charles A. Dana Foundation, 745 Fifth Avenue, Suite 700, New York, New York 10151. Telephone 1–212–223–4040; Web site www.dana.org.

Walter M. Bortz II, Stanford University Medical School, Stanford, California 94305. Telephone 1–415–723–2300; Web site www.stanford.edu.

## World and U.S. Centenarians
## 1998 and 2050

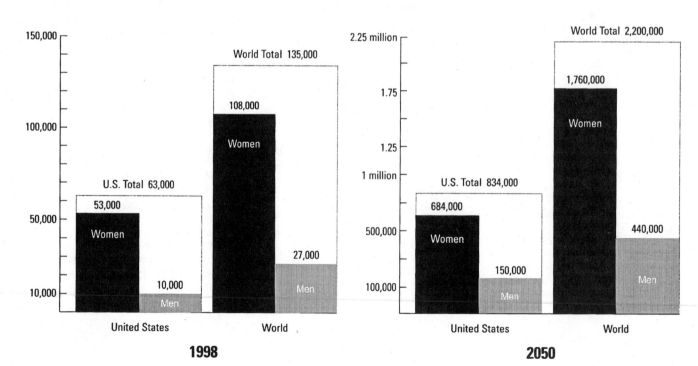

# Emerging Issues in an Aging Society

Many businesses will benefit from the growing number of elderly in the population. There will likely be increasing demand for golfing, cruises, drugs and health services of all kinds, eyeglasses, hearing aids, and telemetry bracelets for absent-minded elderly who wander off and need to be located.

Many products will be redesigned to better fit with elderly needs: There will be more easy-grip doorknobs, phones with bigger buttons, larger-sized type in books and magazines, bigger traffic signs, and longer "yellow" lights.

## Reversal of Trend Toward Early Retirement?

One growing issue is the rapid reduction in the retirement age. In 1890, about 68% of Americans over 65 continued to work. This dropped to 56% in 1920, then 41% in 1950. By 1970, only 25% of people over 65 worked, and that number was cut to 12.2% in 1980. In 1993, only 10.9% of Americans over 65 were still on the job.

Social Security, pensions, and personal savings have encouraged people to retire early. When the early retirement trend is combined with the trend toward greater longevity, the result is a growing challenge to government and private retirement programs. A likely result is that the trend toward early retirement will reverse, and more people over 65 will remain in the work force.

## Intergenerational Issues May Heat Up

The extension of the life-span is raising a number of important issues:

- Women in their 60s are now able to have babies thanks to advancing science. Older parents may be less able to care for children and are more likely than younger parents to die or become incapacitated.
- Elderly retired people are consuming an increasing share of government funds. Must working adults with young children support older people who are still capable of working but choose not to?
- Euthanasia and assisted suicide are increasingly tolerated. How should society respond?
- "Deadbeat kids"—children who evade supporting their elderly parents—may join "deadbeat dads" as a focus of social opprobrium. Children may become angry as their idle parents fritter away the children's hoped-for inheritance.
- Scarcity of resources will lead to more rationing of services and hard choices: Should a heart transplant be given to a wealthy 85-year-old or a 40-year-old with five children to support?
- Conflicts will intensify between the needs of the elderly and the needs of the workplace. Caregivers will feel torn. Results may include absenteeism, interrupted workdays, decreased productivity.
- Workers may express growing anger about taxes they must pay to support retirees. A proposal in Singapore would give a worker two votes against one for a retiree.

*___Graham T.T. Molitor*

Graham T.T. Molitor is vice president of the World Future Society and president of Public Policy Forecasting, 9208 Wooden Bridge Road, Potomac, Maryland 20854. Telephone 1–301–762–5174.

COURTESY OF NATIONAL CENTENARIAN AWARENESS PROJECT

**Centenarian advocate Lynn Peters Adler** (center), chats with 103-year-old Merle McEathron (right) and 102-year-old Lenore Schaeffer, the world's oldest competitive ballroom dancer.

process. While some researchers, such as Harvard's Thomas Perls and colleagues, focus on understanding the genetic makeup of centenarians, others are looking for genetic fixes for the rest of us, such as the work on telomeres by researchers at the University of Texas Southwestern Medical Center and elsewhere. Telomeres are the protective caps on the ends of chromosomes that normally shorten with cell division; researchers believe that resupplying cells with the enzyme telomerase will rebuild the telomeres and rejuvenate older cells—thus extending the human life-span indefinitely.

## Rethinking Old Age

Aging itself is not a disease; it is the aging *process* that leads to death. Among centenarians—the survivors of the ravages of the aging process—death tends to come quickly, with shorter periods of disability. A study in 1995 by James Lubitz of the Health Care Financing Administra-

The idea is to die young as late as possible.

*—Ashley Montague*

# Resources on Centenarians and Longevity

**Books:**

- *Jeanne Calment: From Van Gogh's Time to Ours* by Michel Allard, Victor Lèbre, and Jean-Marie Robine. W.H. Freeman, 41 Madison Avenue, New York, New York 10010. 1998. 136 pages. $22.95. (Save 30% by ordering from **www.wfs.org/specials.htm.**)
- *Centenarians: The Bonus Years* by Lynn Peters Adler. Foreword by Walter M. Bortz II. Health Press, P.O. Drawer 1388, Santa Fe, New Mexico 87504. 1995. 348 pages. Illustrated. $25. (Save 30% by ordering from **www.wfs.org/specials.htm.**)
- *The Longevity Strategy: How to Live to 100 Using the Brain-Body Connection* by David Mahoney and Richard Restak. The Dana Press/John Wiley & Sons, Inc. 1998. 250 pages. Paperback. Available from the Futurist Bookstore for $14.95 ($13.50 for Society members), cat. no. B–2157.
- *Reversing Human Aging* by Michael Fossel. Quill. 1996. 307 pages. Paperback. Available from the Futurist Bookstore for $16 ($14.50 for Society members), cat. no. B–1999.
- *Stopping the Clock* by Ronald Klatz and Robert Goldman. Keats Publishing. 1996. 369 pages. Available from the Futurist Bookstore for $22.95 ($20.95 for Society members), cat. no. B–2002.
- *Cheating Death* by Marvin Cetron and Owen Davies. St. Martin's Press. 1998. 224 pages. Available from the Futurist Bookstore for $21.95 ($19.95 for Society members), cat. no. B–2119.
- *Life without Disease* by William B. Schwartz. University of California Press. 1998. 178 pages. Available from the Futurist Bookstore for $22 ($19.95 for Society members), cat. no. B–2171.
- *Age Right* by Karlis Ullis with Greg Ptacek. Simon & Schuster. 1999. 319 pages. Available from the Futurist Bookstore for $23 ($21.50 for Society members), cat. no. B–2252.

**Journal:**

- *Journal of Anti-Aging Medicine* edited by Michael Fossel. Mary Ann Liebert, Inc., Publishers, 2 Madison Avenue, Larchmont, New York 10538. Telephone 1–914–834–3100; Web site www.liebertpub.com.

**Articles:**

- "Reversing Human Aging: It's Time to Consider the Consequences" by Michael Fossel, THE FUTURIST (July–August 1997).
- "Extended Life-Spans: Are You Ready to Live to 120 or More?" by Marvin Cetron and Owen Davies, THE FUTURIST (April 1998).
- "The Conquest of Disease: It's Almost within Sight" by William B. Schwartz, THE FUTURIST (January 1999).

**Organizations:**

- The New England Centenarian Study, Harvard Division on Aging, 643 Huntington Avenue, Boston, Massachusetts 02115. Web site www.med.harvard.edu.
- National Centenarian Awareness Project, Attention Lynn Peters Adler, 3135 East Marshall Avenue, Phoenix, Arizona 85016. Web site www.adlercentenarians.com.
- American Medical Association, Web site www.ama-assn.org.
- American Academy of Anti-Aging Medicine, 1510 West Montana Street, Chicago, Illinois 60614. Web site www.liilongevity.com.

tion showed that death is far less costly among the very old: The last two years of life for those who died at 70 averaged $22,600 in medical expenses, compared with just $8,300 for centenarians.

"The research implies, happily, that as the oldest old become more numerous, they may not become a massive drain on the economy," Perls says. "Counter to prevalent theories of aging, many people in their late 90s or 100s lead active, healthy lives. If they represent a survival of the fittest cohort, the time may have come to abandon our past perceptions of our oldest citizens."

And aging baby boomers have been a driving force in a society-wide health and fitness trend for the past few decades that may pay off. Says Perls, "People used to say, Who would want to be 100?' Now they're realizing it's an opportunity."

## Centenarians as Time Travelers?

Just as Jeanne Calment connected us to the nineteenth century, future centenarians will connect us to the twenty-second. Madame Calment's biographers offer this scenario:

"Let's now imagine that a little girl is born in 1999: If she reaches the same age as Madame Calment, she will live to the year 2122. By then, living conditions, hygiene, medicine (preventative and curative), lifestyles, behavior, and genetics (why not?) will have progressed and she will easily live 10% longer—not just 122 years, but 135—which will take her to the year 2135. What a prospect! She might be your child or grandchild, but we know neither who nor where, only that she will see a third of the twenty-second century."

**About the Author**
Cynthia G. Wagner is managing editor of THE FUTURIST

# AE Article Review Form

We encourage you to photocopy and use this page as a tool to assess how the articles in **Annual Editions** expand on the information in your textbook. By reflecting on the articles you will gain enhanced text information. You can also access this useful form on a product's book support Web site at **http://www.dushkin.com/online/.**

NAME: _____     DATE: _____

TITLE AND NUMBER OF ARTICLE:
_____

BRIEFLY STATE THE MAIN IDEA OF THIS ARTICLE:
_____

LIST THREE IMPORTANT FACTS THAT THE AUTHOR USES TO SUPPORT THE MAIN IDEA:




_____

WHAT INFORMATION OR IDEAS DISCUSSED IN THIS ARTICLE ARE ALSO DISCUSSED IN YOUR TEXTBOOK OR OTHER READINGS THAT YOU HAVE DONE? LIST THE TEXTBOOK CHAPTERS AND PAGE NUMBERS:




_____

LIST ANY EXAMPLES OF BIAS OR FAULTY REASONING THAT YOU FOUND IN THE ARTICLE:




_____

LIST ANY NEW TERMS/CONCEPTS THAT WERE DISCUSSED IN THE ARTICLE, AND WRITE A SHORT DEFINITION:

ANNUAL EDITIONS revisions depend on two major opinion sources: one is our Advisory Board, listed in the front of this volume, which works with us in scanning the thousands of articles published in the public press each year; the other is you—the person actually using the book. Please help us and the users of the next edition by completing the prepaid article rating form on this page and returning it to us. Thank you for your help!

## ANNUAL EDITIONS: Human Development 00/01

**ARTICLE RATING FORM**

Here is an opportunity for you to have direct input into the next revision of this volume. We would like you to rate each of the 41 articles listed below, using the following scale:

**1. Excellent: should definitely be retained**
**2. Above average: should probably be retained**
**3. Below average: should probably be deleted**
**4. Poor: should definitely be deleted**

Your ratings will play a vital part in the next revision.
So please mail this prepaid form to us just as soon as you complete it.
Thanks for your help!

**We Want Your Advice**

**RATING**

**ARTICLE**

1. Designer Babies
2. Nature's Clones
3. The Role of Lifestyle in Preventing Low Birth Weight
4. A State of the Art Pregnancy
5. Fetal Psychology
6. Drug-Exposed Infants
7. Sperm under Siege
8. Temperament and the Reactions to Unfamiliarity
9. Baby Talk
10. The Cultural Context of Infant Caregiving
11. The Language Explosion
12. Defining the Trait That Makes Us Human
13. Highlights of the Quality 2000 Initiative: Not by Chance
14. The Genetics of Cognitive Abilities and Disabilities
15. Basing Teaching on Piaget's Constructivism
16. The First Seven . . . and the Eighth: A Conversation with Howard Gardner
17. Bell, Book, and Scandal
18. The Death of Child Nature: Education in the Postmodern World
19. In Search of . . . Brain-Based Education
20. Caution—Praise Can Be Dangerous

**RATING**

**ARTICLE**

21. Father Love and Child Development: History and Current Evidence
22. The Parent Trap
23. Kids Who Don't Fit In
24. The Effects of Poverty on Children
25. Effects of Maltreatment and Ways to Promote Children's Resiliency
26. Tomorrow's Child
27. Growing Up Goes On and On and On
28. Why the Young Kill
29. The Secret Life of Teens
30. Brain Sex and the Language of Love
31. The Infertility Challenge
32. The Science of a Good Marriage
33. The Nature and Uses of Dreaming
34. Memory
35. The Age of Anxiety
36. Understanding Perimenopause
37. The Johns Hopkins Prescription for Longevity
38. New Nerve Cells for the Adult Brain
39. The Age Boom
40. Emotion in the Second Half of Life
41. The Centenarians Are Coming!!

(Continued on next page)

## BUSINESS REPLY MAIL
FIRST-CLASS MAIL  PERMIT NO. 84  GUILFORD CT

POSTAGE WILL BE PAID BY ADDRESSEE

**Dushkin/McGraw-Hill**
**Sluice Dock**
**Guilford, CT 06437-9989**

NO POSTAGE
NECESSARY
IF MAILED
IN THE
UNITED STATE

## ABOUT YOU

Name                                                                Date

Are you a teacher? ☐   A student? ☐
Your school's name

Department

Address                                          City                        State      Zip

School telephone #

## YOUR COMMENTS ARE IMPORTANT TO US !

Please fill in the following information:
For which course did you use this book?

Did you use a text with this *ANNUAL EDITION*?  ☐ yes  ☐ no
What was the title of the text?

What are your general reactions to the *Annual Editions* concept?

Have you read any particular articles recently that you think should be included in the next edition?

Are there any articles you feel should be replaced in the next edition? Why?

Are there any World Wide Web sites you feel should be included in the next edition? Please annotate.

May we contact you for editorial input?  ☐ yes  ☐ no
May we quote your comments?  ☐ yes  ☐ no